GitHub Foundations Certification Guide

Essential skills, real-world labs, and exam strategies for GitHub beginners

Ayodeji Ayodele

‹packt›

GitHub Foundations Certification Guide

Portfolio Director: Kunal Chaudhary

Relationship Lead: Rithika Shetty

Project Manager: Ashwin Dinesh Kharwa

Content Engineer: Sushma Reddy

Technical Editor: Rohit Singh

Copy Editor: Safis Editing

Indexer: Rekha Nair

Proofreader: Sushma Reddy

Production Designer: Ajay Patule

Growth Lead: Vinishka Kalra

First published: August 2025

Production reference: 2030925

Published by Packt Publishing Ltd.
Grosvenor House
11 St Paul's Square
Birmingham
B3 1RB, UK.

ISBN 978-1-83620-605-7

www.packtpub.com

To my family, Adeola, Luke, and Jude. You are my rock!

– Ayodeji Ayodele

Forewords

In today's technology landscape, where innovation cycles are accelerating and software is at the heart of every industry, the ability to collaborate effectively and deliver secure, scalable code has never been more essential. Platforms such as GitHub do more than merely enabling this evolution; they lead it. As the world's leading platform for developer collaboration, GitHub has become synonymous with modern software development, DevOps maturity, and open source excellence.

It is within this context that Ayodeji's work on the GitHub Foundations Certification emerges as both timely and valuable. This book is not just a study guide; it is a gateway into the core practices that define today's high-performing engineering teams. For developers, team leads, and IT professionals at any stage of their career, the GitHub Foundations Certification, and by extension this book, provides a structured pathway to mastering the core capabilities of GitHub. The chapters are well structured, with hands-on labs, and build incrementally on the knowledge required to learn the version control, collaboration, automation, and security capabilities of the platform.

What sets this work apart is Ayodeji's unique ability to distill complex concepts into accessible insights while grounding them in real-world relevance. His experience in the field, combined with a deep understanding of developer workflows, gives this book an authority that extends beyond exam preparation. You will gain the skills needed to pass the certification and also come away with a deeper appreciation of how GitHub can transform the way individuals and teams build software.

As someone who works closely with enterprise leaders and software practitioners alike, I have seen firsthand how foundational knowledge of GitHub can unlock efficiencies across the entire software life cycle. It fosters collaboration, enables faster innovation, and embeds security and compliance by design. In short, it turns good teams into great ones.

Ayodeji's contribution here will help nurture that transformation across countless careers and organizations. Whether you're a student just starting out, an educator shaping future engineers, or a professional looking to formalize your skills, this book will serve as a reliable companion on your journey. It mirrors the advice and enablement we provide to our developer communities and enterprise customers.

I commend Ayodeji for this important work and encourage you, the reader, to approach it not just as a manual for certification but as a step toward mastering the tools and practices that will define the future of software.

Irshad Burtally

Senior Director, Customer Success Architecture,

GitHub

The GitHub Foundations Certification marks an important milestone not just for individuals looking to validate their skills but for anyone seeking to build a deeper understanding of the tools that power modern software development and collaboration. As GitHub becomes increasingly central to how the world builds software, this certification offers a clear, accessible path for learners at all levels to demonstrate foundational knowledge and confidence in using GitHub effectively.

This book was created to help you prepare for that journey.

Rooted in the real-world expertise of GitHub's own Ayodeji Ayodele, who works within our Customer Success team, this guide combines the same best practices we use to onboard our enterprise customers with curated learning pathways designed for public learners. You'll gain practical insight into workflows, terminology, collaboration strategies, and the core concepts behind repositories, version control, and project automation—essentials for anyone using GitHub in today's workplace.

But we also recognize that technology is constantly evolving. That's why this book doesn't just help you prepare for the certification—it also points you to where you can find the most up-to-date information, ensuring you stay current well beyond the exam.

This book also complements the content and hands-on labs available through GitHub Learn and aligns with training developed in collaboration with Microsoft Worldwide Learning and other trusted third-party providers. Whether you prefer instructor-led training, on-demand videos, or interactive labs, the GitHub Foundations Certification journey meets you where you are, making learning accessible, engaging, and relevant.

We're also at a unique moment in the evolution of learning itself. The rise of generative AI is transforming how we write, build, and think. GitHub Copilot is just one example of how AI is enabling both developers and non-developers to accelerate their work—and with it comes a growing need for individuals to understand the foundational tools that support this new wave of innovation.

This book is your guide to mastering the fundamentals, validating your skills, and joining a global community of learners and builders. Whether you're just getting started or looking to formalize your knowledge, the GitHub Foundations Certification—and the journey you will take through these pages—will help you take that next step with clarity and confidence.

Let's get started!

Ali Condah

Senior Director, Certification & Enablement,

GitHub

Contributors

About the author

Ayodeji Ayodele, also known as **"Ayo,"** is a seasoned architect, software engineer, and DevOps coach with over 20 years of experience across industries including finance, tech, FMCG, and the public sector. Currently a senior customer success architect at GitHub, he helps enterprise clients unlock the full potential of modern software delivery. Ayo is passionate about building innovative, user-centric solutions and has worked with teams across Asia, Oceania, and Africa to champion Agile and DevOps practices. When he's not immersed in technology, Ayo enjoys football, music, and exploring new places around the world.

I want to especially thank my loving wife and sons for their patience, and the people who are close to me and have guided me all these years. To my great colleagues and amazing hubbers helping the world build software, Merci!

About the reviewers

Massimo Bonanni, a Microsoft Technical Trainer, excels in tech and community leadership. A six-time Microsoft MVP, Intel Black Belt, and Software Innovator, he drives Azure skill enhancement. He has delivered over 200 conference sessions in a decade. Massimo has founded Italian tech communities. He is also a dog lover, reader, and LEGO enthusiast.

My deep gratitude to the editorial team. To my wife, Floriana, and to my family: your unwavering support is invaluable. Thanks to the vibrant tech community: your enthusiasm fuels my work.

Jerome Hardaway is a software engineer, instructor, and technical author with a background in the United States Air Force. He is the founder and executive director of Vets Who Code, a non-profit that helps military veterans transition into tech careers. With over a decade of experience, Jerome has contributed to developer education at LinkedIn Learning, Frontend Masters, and GitHub, and has been featured by major tech organizations. He has authored and reviewed several publications focusing on developer tools, career growth, and open source. Jerome is passionate about using technology to create economic empowerment and increase access to opportunity.

I want to thank the Vets Who Code community for their inspiration, and my wife, Shatara, for her love and patience. My deep gratitude to Natalia, whose thoughtful critiques and notes sharpen my thinking and make all my work better. I'm also thankful for my family's support, and to Ayumi for her constant insight and empathy. I'm honored to have played a part in bringing this book to life.

Join us on Discord!

Read this book alongside other users, developers, experts, and the author himself.

Ask questions, provide solutions to other readers, chat with the authors via Ask Me Anything sessions, and much more. Scan the QR or visit the link to join the community.

https://packt.link/deep-engineering

Table of Contents

Part 1: Git and GitHub Essentials   15

Chapter 1: Introduction to Version Control with Git   17

Chapter 6: Pull Requests and Code Reviews   149

Part 3: Leveraging GitHub for Career Advancement   237

Chapter 10: Building and Showcasing Your GitHub Presence   239

Chapter 11: Contributing to Open Source Projects   255

Part 4: Advanced GitHub and Exam Preparation 311

Chapter 14: Project Management with GitHub Projects 313

Preface

Hello! Welcome to *GitHub Foundations Certification Guide*. GitHub is the most advanced AI-powered collaborative developer platform; hundreds of millions of developers across the world build software on it. This book is a guide to the GitHub Foundations Certification, one of the five exams available as of the time of writing. It is the entry-level exam, and arguably the easiest of the five (although this is subjective!).

GitHub Certifications help you to reinforce your knowledge, establish your skills, and prove your proficiency in using the platform.

This book serves as a comprehensive guide to preparing for the GitHub Foundations Certification exam, detailing the critical components, expectations, and strategies necessary for success. It outlines the significance of the GitHub Foundations Certification, which validates expertise in Git and GitHub, and highlights the competitive edge it provides in the job market. The certification validates skills in navigating the platform, collaborating securely, and contributing effectively to software and open source projects.

I will provide information on the exam structure, preparation strategies, and domains to focus on to increase your chances of acing the exam. In addition, I will dive deeper into the world of Git and GitHub, highlighting the various features and products. You will learn the basics of Git repositories, source control management on GitHub, GitHub issues, pull requests, projects, GitHub Actions, Copilot, Discussions, and many other features that have made the world love it so much.

There are two relevant takeaways from Insight's report in January 2025 (`https://interviewprep.org/are-software-developers-in-demand-opportunities-and-growth/`):

- **Digital transformation**: The ongoing digital transformation across various industries, such as healthcare, finance, and retail, is driving the demand for skilled developers. Companies are enhancing their digital presence and operational efficiency, which requires continuous development and optimization of software solutions.

- **Emerging technologies**: The integration of emerging technologies such as **artificial intelligence (AI)**, machine learning, and blockchain is creating new opportunities for developers. Businesses need developers proficient in both traditional programming languages and cutting-edge innovations.

Excellence in teamwork and practical experience with collaborative tools and version control systems would be sought after. Proficiency on GitHub will set you apart!

Who this book is for

This book is for software developers and engineers looking to master Git and GitHub for efficient code management, project collaboration, and streamlined workflows. Infrastructure engineers and system administrators will benefit from learning how to manage scripts and track infrastructure changes.

Educators and trainers can use this guide to teach software development and prepare students for industry certifications. Aspiring developers and tech professionals will find it a valuable resource for building essential GitHub skills and advancing their software development careers.

It is aimed at entry-level developers, seasoned software engineers, platform engineers, and project managers, providing a pathway to exciting career opportunities.

What this book covers

Sprint 0, Preparing for the Certification, helps you get ready for the certification journey, outlining the necessary preparations and mindset.

Chapter 1, Introduction to Version Control with Git, introduces the concept of version control, its importance in software development, and the basics of Git. You will learn why Git is the industry standard for version control and how it can significantly improve coding efficiency and collaboration.

Chapter 2, Navigating the GitHub Interface, explores the GitHub platform, helping you understand its interface and learn how to navigate through its various features. This chapter is crucial for utilizing GitHub effectively for project management and collaboration.

Chapter 3, Repository Creation and Management, discusses creating and managing GitHub repositories, including best practices for naming, initializing, and licensing.

Chapter 4, Basic Git Commands and Workflows, guides you through intermediate Git commands, flags, and workflows, including setting up repositories, making changes, collaborating with others, and troubleshooting common issues. You will learn how to use Git for everyday development tasks, ensuring a smooth and efficient workflow.

Chapter 5, Branching and Merging Strategies, examines the branching model, as well as branching and merging strategies in Git and GitHub, highlighting structured branching for team collaboration and techniques to enhance productivity and code quality.

Chapter 6, Pull Requests and Code Reviews, explains the concept of pull requests and code reviews on GitHub for maintaining code quality and fostering collaboration in software development. It highlights best practices for maintaining code quality through peer reviews.

Chapter 7, Issues, Projects, Labels, and Milestones, provides a basic guide to GitHub's project management tools, focusing on issues, labels, and milestones, and includes practical exercises to enhance understanding and application. It also teaches you how to use these features to track progress and organize work within a team.

Chapter 8, GitHub Actions and Automation, provides an introductory guide to GitHub Actions, covering its role in **continuous integration and continuous delivery (CI/CD)**, the concept of pipeline as code, key components and terminologies, practical lab exercises, and best practices for creating and managing workflows.

Chapter 9, Engaging with the Community through GitHub Discussions, teaches you about GitHub Discussions, a platform feature that fosters community engagement. This chapter covers how to start discussions, respond to queries, and build a community around projects.

Chapter 10, Building and Showcasing Your GitHub Presence, explores how to build and showcase a professional GitHub presence, including creating a standout profile, effectively showcasing projects and contributions, and utilizing GitHub Pages for personal branding.

Chapter 11, Contributing to Open Source Projects, discusses how to contribute to open source projects on GitHub, covering topics such as navigating the open source landscape, identifying suitable projects, understanding open source licensing, and the benefits of contributing to the open source community.

Chapter 12, Enhancing Development with GitHub Copilot, explores the transformative impact of generative AI on software development, focusing on GitHub Copilot's capabilities, setup, usage, and best practices to enhance development workflows and elevate coding experiences.

Chapter 13, Funding Your Projects with GitHub Sponsors, teaches you how to set up and manage GitHub Sponsors to secure financial support for open source projects, including creating an appealing sponsorship profile, engaging with sponsors, and leveraging sponsorship tiers for sustained project growth.

Chapter 14, Project Management with GitHub Projects, is a guide on using GitHub Projects for effective project management, covering setup, customization, key features, and automation to enhance team collaboration and workflow efficiency.

Chapter 15, Security Practices and User Management, provides an in-depth exploration of GitHub's security practices and user management, covering topics such as two-factor authentication, branch protection rules, security configurations, managing access and permissions, and best practices for repository security.

Chapter 16, Mock Exams and Study Strategies, includes deeper preparation tips, mock exam questions, study strategies, and tips for mastering Git and GitHub features.

To get the most out of this book

You will need to have a basic knowledge of writing/editing code or scripts in one language, as well as the following tools.

Software/hardware covered in the book	Operating system requirements
Visual Studio Code 1.99.3	Windows, macOS, or Linux
Command Prompt, PowerShell, or Terminal	
GitHub.com account	

Obtaining a GitHub.com account is free. You can sign up at www.github.com.

If you are using the digital version of this book, we advise you to type the code yourself or access the code from the book's GitHub repository (a link is available in the next section). Doing so will help you avoid any potential errors related to the copying and pasting of code.

Download the example code files

The code bundle for the book is hosted on GitHub at https://github.com/PacktPublishing/GitHub-Foundations-Certification-Guide. We also have other code bundles from our rich catalog of books and videos available at https://github.com/PacktPublishing. Check them out!

Download the color images

We also provide a PDF file that has color images of the screenshots/diagrams used in this book. You can download it here: https://packt.link/gbp/9781836206057.

Conventions used

There are a number of text conventions used throughout this book.

CodeInText: Indicates code words in text, database table names, folder names, filenames, file extensions, pathnames, dummy URLs, user input, and Twitter/X handles. For example: "This will initialize a new repository and create a new .git directory containing all the necessary files for version control."

A block of code is set as follows:

```
public class HelloWorld {
    // This program prints "Hello, World!" to the console
    public static void main(String[] args) {
        System.out.println("Hello, World!");
    }
}
```

Any command-line input or output is written as follows:

```
git config --global user.name "Your Name"
```

Bold: Indicates a new term, an important word, or words that you see on the screen. For instance, words in menus or dialog boxes appear in the text like this. For example: "Select the **Commit directly to the main branch** option and click on **Commit changes**."

> Warnings or important notes appear like this.

> Tips and tricks appear like this.

Get in touch

Feedback from our readers is always welcome.

General feedback: If you have questions about any aspect of this book or have any general feedback, please email us at customercare@packt.com and mention the book's title in the subject of your message.

Errata: Although we have taken every care to ensure the accuracy of our content, mistakes do happen. If you have found a mistake in this book, we would be grateful if you reported this to us. Please visit http://www.packt.com/submit-errata, click **Submit Errata**, and fill in the form.

Piracy: If you come across any illegal copies of our works in any form on the internet, we would be grateful if you would provide us with the location address or website name. Please contact us at copyright@packt.com with a link to the material.

If you are interested in becoming an author: If there is a topic that you have expertise in and you are interested in either writing or contributing to a book, please visit http://authors.packt.com/.

Share your thoughts

Once you've read *GitHub Foundations Certification Guide*, we'd love to hear your thoughts! Scan the QR code below to go straight to the Amazon review page for this book and share your feedback.

https://packt.link/r/1836206054

Your review is important to us and the tech community and will help us make sure we're delivering excellent quality content.

Sprint 0
Preparing for the Certification

Welcome to the GitHub Foundations certification journey! Before you dive in, it's important to gain a solid understanding of what the certification exam entails. In this chapter, we'll break down the key components, expectations, and strategies to help you succeed.

Up until early 2024, developers and software engineers didn't have a way to show proficiency in GitHub. In the past, people would use measures such as the number of repositories on your GitHub profile (which may include forked repos), the greenness of your contribution graph, your open source contributions, and sometimes your achievement badges to judge your proficiency. Many of these metrics would not be reliable for someone with fewer repositories in the public space or who has not contributed to many high-profile open source projects.

From January 2024 and beyond, GitHub published the general availability of five certifications, the GitHub Foundations certification being one of them:

- GitHub Foundations certification
- GitHub Actions certification
- GitHub Advanced Security certification
- GitHub Administration certification
- GitHub Copilot certification

Earning a GitHub certification will help you showcase your expertise on GitHub, giving you a competitive edge as a professional.

This book focuses on everything you need to know to pass the GitHub Foundations certification exam. In this chapter, we'll take a closer look at what the exam involves and how to prepare for it with confidence:

- What is the GitHub Foundations certification?
- Preparation strategies
- Exam-day test center requirements
- Exam-day online requirements

What is the GitHub Foundations certification?

The GitHub Foundations certification is a prestigious credential that validates your expertise in Git and GitHub. It is the Level 100 certification designed to introduce you to the basic concepts of Git and GitHub (yes, they are two different things: Git is not GitHub; this book will help you learn the difference), its products, and features.

GitHub is home to over 150 million developers; it is the home of software developers. Some part of the software you are using right now is likely built on GitHub.

Target audience

This certification is designed for entry-level developers, platform engineers, IT operations and support engineers, project managers, or program managers. It's also a great option for experienced professionals looking to formalize their GitHub skills or fill in foundational gaps.

The certification demonstrates your ability to navigate the platform, collaborate securely, and contribute effectively to software projects and open source projects.

When you pass this exam, you will earn a badge that looks like the following figure:

Figure 0.1: GitHub Foundations certification badge

Exam structure

Now, let's look at the structure of the exam. We will cover the main areas to expect questions from and the different forms the questions can take. You will be timed in the exam.

The exam covers a range of topics related to Git and GitHub. You'll encounter questions on version control, Git commands, collaboration workflows, and more. Make sure to review the official certification guide for a detailed breakdown of the content. This is available at examregistration.github.com. The content covers seven objective domains, providing a structured outline that highlights specific topics and skills that the exam will cover.

The following are the objective domains; we will cover them all in this book.

Your combined performance across all 7 domains must total at least 72% to pass (as at the time of writing this book; this may vary slightly). These are shown in the **Skills measured** section at the preceding link.

Domain	Exam Percentage
Domain 1: Introduction to Git and GitHub	18%
Domain 2: Working with GitHub Repositories	10%
Domain 3: Collaboration Features	28%
Domain 4: Modern Development	11%
Domain 5: Project Management	9%
Domain 6: Privacy, Security, and Administration	15%
Domain 7: Benefits of the GitHub Community	9%

Table 0.1: Objective domains of the certification exam

The following shows a breakdown of each domain.

Domain 1: Introduction to Git and GitHub

Git and GitHub basics
Describe version control
Define distributed version control
Describe Git
Describe GitHub
Explain the difference between Git and GitHub
Describe a GitHub repository
Describe a commit

Describe branching
Define a remote in Git terminology
Describe the GitHub flow
Describe Git flow

GitHub entities
Describe the different GitHub accounts (personal, organization, and enterprise)
Describe GitHub's products for personal accounts (free and Pro)
Describe GitHub's products for organization accounts (free for organizations and teams)
Describe the different deployment options for GitHub Enterprise
Describe the features in the user profile (metadata, achievements, profile README, repositories, pinned repositories, stars, etc.)

GitHub Markdown
Identify the text formatting toolbar on issue and pull request comments
Describe Markdown
Identify the basic formatting syntax (headings, links, task lists, comments, etc.)
Explain where to find and use slash commands

GitHub Desktop
Explain the difference between GitHub Desktop and `github.com`
Describe the available features with GitHub Desktop

GitHub Mobile
Describe the available features with GitHub Mobile
Explain how to manage notifications through the GitHub Mobile app

Domain 2: Working with GitHub Repositories

Understanding GitHub repositories
Describe the components of a good README and the recommended repository files (`LICENSE`, `CONTRIBUTING`, and `CODEOWNERS`)
Explain basic repository navigation
Explain how to create a new repository
Describe repository templates

Describe the different features of maintaining a repository
Describe how to clone a repository
Describe how to create a new branch
Explain how to add files to a repository
Identify how to view repository insights
Explain how to save a repository with stars
Identify keyboard shortcuts
Explain feature previews
Using the command palette

Domain 3: Collaboration Features

Issues
Describe how to link a PR to an issue
Describe how to create an issue
Describe the difference between an issue, discussion, and pull request
Explain how to create a branch from an issue
Identify how to assign issues
Describe how to search and filter issues
Describe how to pin an issue
Explain basic issue management
Explain the difference between issue templates and issue forms
Explain how to use keywords in issues

Pull requests
Describe a pull request
Explain how to create a new pull request
Describe the base and compare branches in a pull request
Explain the relationship of commits in a pull request
Describe draft pull requests
Describe the purpose of the pull request tabs (conversation, commits, checks, and files changed)
Identify how to link activity within a pull request
Explain the different pull request statuses

Recognize how to comment on a posted link to a line or lines of code from a file
Describe code review with a `CODEOWNERS` file
Explain the different options for providing a code review on a pull request (comment, approve, request changes, and suggested changes)

Discussions
Describe the difference between discussions and issues
Explain the options available with discussions (announcements, ideas, polls, Q&A, and show and tell)
Identify how to mark a comment as an answer to a discussion
Explain how to convert a discussion to an issue
Recognize how to pin a discussion

Notifications
Describe how to manage notification subscriptions
Explain how to subscribe to notification threads
Describe how to find threads where you are @-mentioned
Identify the notification filtering options
Explain the different notification configuration options

Gists, wikis, and GitHub Pages
Explain how to create a GitHub gist
Describe how to fork and clone a gist
Explain GitHub wiki pages
Describe how to create, edit, and delete wiki pages
Explain the visibility of wiki pages
Describe GitHub Pages

Domain 4: Modern Development

GitHub Actions
Describe GitHub Actions (basic understanding)
Explain where you can use GitHub Actions within GitHub (general event types)
Explain where you can find existing GitHub Actions

GitHub Copilot
Describe GitHub Copilot
Describe the different plans for GitHub Copilot
Explain how to get started using GitHub Copilot

GitHub Codespaces
Describe GitHub Codespaces
Identify how to start a GitHub codespace
Describe the codespace life cycle
Describe the different customizations you can personalize with GitHub Codespaces
Recognize how to add and configure dev containers
Explain how to add an `Open in GitHub Codespaces` badge to a README file
Explain how to use the `github.dev` editor
Explain the differences between the `github.dev` editor and a GitHub codespace

Domain 5: Project Management

Manage your work with GitHub Projects
Describe GitHub Projects
Explain the layout options for projects
Describe the configuration options for projects
Explain what can be accomplished with project views
Explain the use of labels
Explain the use of milestones
Describe how to use and create template repos
Explain how to create, edit, and delete saved replies
Describe the benefits of using a saved reply
Recognize how to add assignees to issues and pull requests
Explain how to use project workflows
Describe how to convert checklist items to sub-issues

Domain 6: Privacy, Security, and Administration

Authentication and security
Explain how to secure your account with 2FA
Describe the different access permissions
Explain **Enterprise Managed Users (EMUs)**

GitHub administration
Explain how to enable and disable features
Recognize repository permission levels
Identify the options for repository visibility
Explain repository privacy setting options (branch protections, codeowners, and required reviewers)
Describe the main features and options in the **Security** tab
Define repository insights
Explain how to manage collaborators
Explain how to manage organization settings
Describe members, teams, and roles in a GitHub organization

GitHub Secure Development
Describe the Dependency Graph
Explain what Dependabot is
Describe Dependabot security updates
Explain Dependabot version updates
Define code scanning
Define secret scanning
Explain push protection

Domain 7: Benefits of the GitHub Community

Describe the benefits of the open source community
Describe open source
Describe how GitHub advances open source projects
Identify how to follow people (receive notifications and discover projects in their community)
Explain how to follow organizations (receive notifications about their activity)
Describe the GitHub Marketplace and its purpose

Describe how to apply the benefits of open source
Describe Innersource
Identify the differences between Innersource and open source
Describe forking and contributing to open source projects
Describe the components of a discoverable repository

Question types

The exam has **75 questions** in all (as at the time of writing this book) and you have **2 hours** to answer them. Expect a mix of multiple-choice questions, scenario-based challenges, and practical tasks. A few questions may require you to analyze short code snippets (a few lines of code or command line).

Other questions may want to test your detailed understanding by providing multiple similar answers, though only one of them is correct. You will also come across questions where you are required to select more than one answer. These questions will provide checkboxes next to each answer rather than the single-select boxes. However, the question will explicitly specify exactly how many answers it expects you to select, such as **(Select two)** or **(Please select three)**. To get full marks on such a question, you should select exactly that number of answers. Stay sharp and practice different question formats.

Time limit

The certification exam is time-bound (**2 hours**). Allocate your time wisely across the sections. Remember that efficient time management is key to success.

For example, take a look at the percentage breakdown of the objective domains in *Table 1. Two domains, Introduction to Git and GitHub and Collaboration Features*, collectively carry 46% of your score. It would be wise to spend the best of your time on these questions. In addition, a higher score has been earmarked to Privacy, Security and Administration. Be sure to read about the security features on GitHub, particularly GitHub Advanced Security.

Preparation strategies

In this section, we will explore various strategies that will help you pass the exam.

Study resources

Explore a variety of study materials, including official documentation, online courses, and practice exams. Familiarize yourself with Git concepts, branching strategies, and GitHub workflows. Read this book!

The following are some recommended study resources:

- This book! Be sure to read it from cover to cover. It has numerous helpful guides, practical exercises, and mock questions to prepare you for the exam.
- I have curated a list of online resources on a GitHub gist (`https://gist.github.com/ayode jiayodele/524ccd4865c968bad12fcbbfd07c8834`). These include official training courses, hands-on labs, YouTube videos, and other learning materials to supplement your learning.

Hands-on practice

Set up a GitHub repository and practice real-world scenarios. Create branches, merge pull requests, and resolve conflicts. The more hands-on experience you gain, the better prepared you'll be. You will find some lab exercises at `https://github.com/PacktPublishing/GitHub-Foundations-Certification-Guide`.

Mock exams

Take advantage of mock exams and practice questions available in *Chapter 15, Mock Exams and Study Strategies*. These simulate the actual test environment and help you gauge your readiness. Identify areas where you need improvement and focus your efforts accordingly.

In addition, there are practice questions at the end of each chapter to quickly test your knowledge and establish what you have learned.

Exam registration

You will need to schedule your exam **in advance** once you are prepared and ready. To register for the exam, visit the certification details page (`https://examregistration.github.com/certification/GHF`). The registration page will ask you to log in with your GitHub account. If you are new to GitHub or you don't have a GitHub account, follow the instructions on how to create a free GitHub account in *Chapter 2, Navigating the GitHub Interface.*

Figure 0.2: The exam registration landing page

After signing in, the registration will take you through a scheduling process. Here, you can choose whether you want to take the exam at the **test center** nearest to you or **online** supervised by a proctor. Available test centers and their locations will depend on your country and city. Both test center and online exams are managed and scheduled by the same body (PSI Exams).

As of the time of writing this book, the exam cost is $49 (US dollars).

GitHub offers discounts and partner benefits on the exam cost in a number of ways. I will advise you to explore what options are available to you. For example, your employer may be a partner, a GitHub Enterprise customer, or a Microsoft Enterprise Agreement customer, and these offer discount vouchers that range as high as 100% (Yay! Free!). Secondly, if you are a student, you may be able to get this for free. For more information about how GitHub supports students and many student freebies, visit `https://education.github.com`.

Exam-day test center requirements

Once registered, you will receive email confirmation of your exam appointment. Be sure to review your exam name, date, start time, and location and confirm they are correct. The email will also have directions to the exam location.

Identity requirements

A government-issued form of identification will be required, usually an international passport, driver's license, or similar.

Exam accommodations

You may request exam accommodations such as special equipment for those with low vision or who are hard of hearing, breaks for medical reasons, or extra time for testing because the exam is not in your native language. There are other forms of accommodations that can be considered as well. Please read the handbook for more details and ensure you request this many weeks before the exam day; it **must be made before you schedule** the exam.

For more information, please read the *Candidate handbook* section of this chapter.

Finally, I would suggest arriving at least 30–40 minutes before your exam time. If you have any documentation to show, take both physical and electronic copies with you.

Exam-day online requirements

If you choose to take the exam online, there are some requirements you need to meet.

System requirements

- **Supported operating systems**: 64-bit Windows 10, Windows 11, macOS 11(Big Sur), macOS 12(Monterey), and macOS 13 (Ventura)
- **Screen resolution**: 1,366 x 768 or higher
- **Internet bandwidth**: Minimum 300 kbps download/upload speed
- **Camera and microphone**: Must be turned on throughout the exam

To be sure your system will be compatible with the online exam, you can perform a system check. This check involves a series of instructions to follow that may include downloading the testing software to your computer, performing sound tests of your microphone, validating access to your webcam, and so on.

For more information, please read the *Candidate handbook* section of this chapter.

Workspace requirements

There is a minimum level of tidiness required at your desk and immediate surroundings. No one else can be in the same room as you during the exam. Therefore, if you choose a home or office space to sit for the exam, you must make sure it is empty of people and rid of clutter. For more information, please read the *Candidate handbook* section of this chapter.

Identity requirements

You will be required to present a government-issued form of identification before you can check in for the exam, both physically at a testing center or online. For more information, please read the *Candidate handbook* section of this chapter.

Top tips

Here are some tips I would recommend:

- Perform system checks before and on the exam day.
- Be ready at least 20–30 minutes before your exam time.
- Choose a private location free of distractions.
- Ensure you have a great internet connection. Have a backup in case one fails.
- Make sure your mobile phone is reachable. Proctors may want to call you during the exam if they can't reach you through the in-app chat.
- Use a reliable computer with a webcam.

Candidate handbook

The candidate handbook (`https://www.pearsonvue.com/content/dam/VUE/vue/en/documents/tech-specs/online-proctored/onvue-technical-requirements.pdf`) offers a comprehensive guide on preparing for the exam, exam registration, exam scoring, and reports. Get familiar with the handbook before the exam day.

Conclusion

Understanding the certification exam is the first step toward achieving your GitHub Foundations certification. Stay committed, study diligently, and soon you'll be well prepared to ace the exam!

Useful links

- GitHub Foundations certification exam registration: `https://examregistration.github.com/certification/GHF`

- Certification study guide: `https://assets.ctfassets.net/wfutmusr1t3h/1kmMx7AwI4q H8yIZgOmQlP/79e6ff1dfdee589d84a24dd763b1eef7/github-foundations-exam-study-guide__1_.pdf`

- GitHub Education—GitHub Foundation certification preparation resources: `https://education.github.com/experiences/foundations_certificate`

- Candidate handbook: `https://www.pearsonvue.com/content/dam/VUE/vue/en/documents/tech-specs/online-proctored/onvue-technical-requirements.pdf`

- Additional learning resources: `https://gist.github.com/ayodejiayodele/524ccd486 5c968bad12fcbbfd07c8834`

Part 1

Git and GitHub Essentials

This part covers the basics and building blocks of mastering the Git version control system, as well as providing a general understanding of what GitHub is, the functions of its products, and basic repository creation. Upon completion, you will have built a solid foundation in Git and GitHub, essential for any software development and version control tasks.

This part of the book includes the following chapters:

- *Chapter 1, Introduction to Version Control with Git*
- *Chapter 2, Navigating the GitHub Interface*
- *Chapter 3, Repository Creation and Management*
- *Chapter 4, Basic Git Commands and Workflows*

Part I

1

Introduction to Version Control with Git

This chapter introduces you to the concept of version control, its importance in software development, and the basics of Git. You will learn why Git is the industry standard for version control and how it can significantly improve coding efficiency and collaboration.

This chapter covers the following topics:

- Version control basics
- Overview of Git
- Lab 1: Setting up Git
- Some common challenges

Getting the most out of this book — get to know your free benefits

Unlock exclusive **free** benefits that come with your purchase, thoughtfully crafted to supercharge your learning journey and help you learn without limits.

Here's a quick overview of what you get with this book:

Next-gen reader

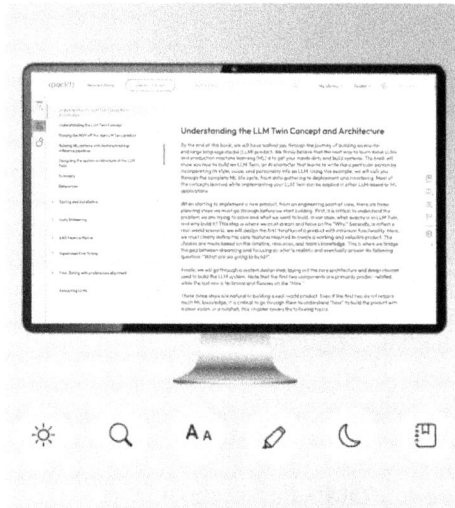

Figure 1.1: Illustration of the next-gen Packt Reader's features

Our web-based reader, designed to help you learn effectively, comes with the following features:

⊙ Multi-device progress sync: Learn from any device with seamless progress sync.

🖺 Highlighting and notetaking: Turn your reading into lasting knowledge.

🔖 Bookmarking: Revisit your most important learnings anytime.

☀ Dark mode: Focus with minimal eye strain by switching to dark or sepia mode.

Interactive AI assistant (beta)

Figure 1.2: Illustration of Packt's AI assistant

Our interactive AI assistant has been trained on the content of this book, to maximize your learning experience. It comes with the following features:

✦ Summarize it: Summarize key sections or an entire chapter.

✦ AI code explainers: In the next-gen Packt Reader, click the Explain button above each code block for AI-powered code explanations.

Note: The AI assistant is part of next-gen Packt Reader and is still in beta.

DRM-free PDF or ePub version

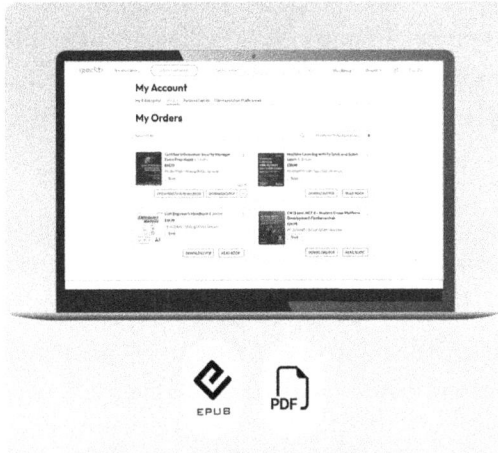

Learn without limits with the following perks included with your purchase:

- Learn from anywhere with a DRM-free PDF copy of this book.
- Use your favorite e-reader to learn using a DRM-free ePub version of this book.

Figure 1.3: Free PDF and ePub

Unlock this book's exclusive benefits now

UNLOCK NOW

Scan this QR code or go to packtpub.com/unlock, then search for this book by name. Ensure it's the correct edition.

Note: Keep your purchase invoice ready before you start.

Version control basics

Concept analogy: version control as a recipe book

Imagine you've perfected a lasagna recipe over weeks of experimentation. Each tweak you make—extra cheese, less salt, a new baking time—is tracked in a notebook. Later, you decide which version was the best and share that one with friends. That's essentially what Git does for your code: it tracks every change, lets you revisit earlier versions, and helps you collaborate without confusion.

Version control is a fundamental practice that significantly impacts the efficiency, reliability, and collaboration within software projects. Here are three key aspects highlighting its importance:

- **Tracking changes and history**: **Version Control Systems (VCSs)** allow developers to track changes made to their codebase over time. Each modification, addition, or deletion is recorded as a commit, preserving a detailed history.

- **Effective collaboration**: In collaborative environments, version control enables seamless teamwork:

  - **Branching and merging**: Developers can work on separate branches, experimenting with new features or bug fixes. Merging these branches ensures a cohesive codebase.

  - **Conflict resolution**: When multiple contributors modify the same file, a VCS helps resolve conflicts systematically.

- **Maintaining code quality**: Version control promotes best practices and quality assurance:

  - **Code refactoring**: Developers can refactor code confidently, knowing they can revert if necessary.

  - **Continuous Integration (CI)**: CI pipelines rely on version control to automate testing, ensuring code quality.

So, how are these aspects beneficial? Let us discuss the benefits.

Benefits of version control

Here are a few benefits of using version control:

- **Granular history**: Developers can review the evolution of a project, pinpointing when specific features were added, or bugs were introduced.

- **Accountability**: Commits are associated with authors, promoting accountability and transparency.

- **Rollbacks and reverts**: If a mistake occurs, reverting to a previous state is straightforward.

- **Parallel development**: Teams can work simultaneously without interfering with each other's changes.

- **Code reviews**: VCS facilitates code reviews by providing a clear diff (*difference*) between versions.

- **Stability**: A well-maintained version-controlled repository ensures stability and reliability.

- **Traceability**: Issues and bug fixes are linked to specific commits, aiding debugging.

What if you don't use version control? Let us look at some challenges one may encounter without it.

Challenges without version control

When you don't use version control, here are a few challenges that you might face:

- Manually managing different versions of files can lead to confusion, lost changes, and accidental overwrites.
- Coordinating changes becomes cumbersome, leading to conflicts and delays.
- Code quality suffers due to a lack of systematic tracking and collaboration.

In summary, version control is indispensable for modern software development, offering benefits such as historical tracking, collaboration support, and code quality maintenance. Without it, teams face challenges related to coordination, accountability, and code stability. In the next section, we will explore some examples of version control systems.

Examples of version control systems

Here, we'll introduce various version control systems and compare their features. We'll focus on Git as the industry standard and explain why it's widely adopted. Several VCS options exist beyond Git, each with its own features and use cases. Here are a few notable ones:

- **Subversion (SVN):** Subversion, often abbreviated as SVN, is a centralized VCS. In this model, users access a master repository via clients, and their local machines hold only working copies of the project tree. Changes made in a working copy must be committed to the master repository before propagating to other users. While SVN has been widely used, Git's distributed nature has largely overshadowed it.
- **Mercurial:** Mercurial is another distributed VCS, similar to Git. It offers an alternative to Git's complexity while maintaining a decentralized approach. Mercurial emphasizes simplicity and ease of use, making it a viable choice for smaller projects or teams.
- **Team Foundation Version Control (TFVC):** This is a centralized version control system provided by Microsoft. TFVC supports two types of workspaces: server workspaces, where the server maintains the version history, and local workspaces, where the version history is maintained on the developer's machine. Developers can check out code, make changes, and check in their changes to the server, where they are integrated with the rest of the codebase.

In the next section, we will discuss why Git has soared so high in popularity and adoption.

Git's dominance and popularity: why it stands out

Git has become the industry standard for version control due to several factors:

- **Decentralization**: Git's distributed model allows developers to work offline, commit changes locally, and synchronize with remote repositories later. This flexibility enhances collaboration and resilience.

- **Performance**: Git's speed and efficiency in handling large repositories and complex histories make it a preferred choice for both small and large-scale projects.

- **Community and ecosystem**: Git's vast community, extensive documentation, and rich ecosystem of tools (such as GitHub, GitLab, and Bitbucket) contribute to its widespread adoption.

> *"Git is a free and open source distributed version control system designed to handle everything from small to very large projects with speed and efficiency."*
> - https://git-scm.com/

In summary, while other VCS options such as Subversion and Mercurial still have their merits, Git's dominance and popularity stem from its decentralized architecture, performance, and robust community support. Up next, let's explore Git and its fundamentals.

Overview of Git

Let's now dive into Git! We'll cover the basics: what Git is, how it works, and its core components (commits, branches, and repositories). This section sets the foundation for the rest of the chapter.

Git's distributed nature

Git (*/git/* pronounced like *get*) is a distributed VCS designed to manage source code and track changes in software projects in a decentralized manner. Each developer has a complete copy of the entire **repository**, including its history. Git allows collaboration, offline work, and efficient handling of large projects.

In Git, a **commit** represents a snapshot of the project at a specific point in time. Developers create commits to record changes (additions, modifications, or deletions) to files. Each commit has a unique hash, author information, timestamp, and a reference to its parent commit(s).

Branching and merging

This is the most outstanding feature that separates it from many other VCS tools. Git encourages branching. Developers create **branches** to work on specific features or fixes independently. Branches allow parallel development without affecting the main codebase. Merging then combines changes (commits) from one branch into another (e.g., merging a feature branch into the main branch). Git's merge algorithms handle conflicts and ensure a consistent history. For more information about Git's differentiator, you can learn more at `https://www.git-scm.com/about`.

A repository contains one or more branches. The first one is usually named `main` or `master`, and a branch will contain a copy of the code along with the history of the commits made to that branch.

Understanding the Git concept

Let's now walk through three real-world Git scenarios to understand how commits, branches, and timelines work together in practice. Each example builds on how Git tracks changes and enables collaboration.

When a new Git repository (repo) is created, it comes with the first branch (`main` or `master`). This branch is called the default branch. This is *Scenario 1*.

Scenario 1: Committing changes on the main branch

Every change you make to the code is recorded as a commit that remains forever in the history of the branch's timeline. You can revert to any specific previous commit on the timeline and the code in that branch will take that previous form. So, see this as restoring a backup.

The following diagram shows a Git graph of a repo (**My repository**), showcasing multiple commits with their timestamps:

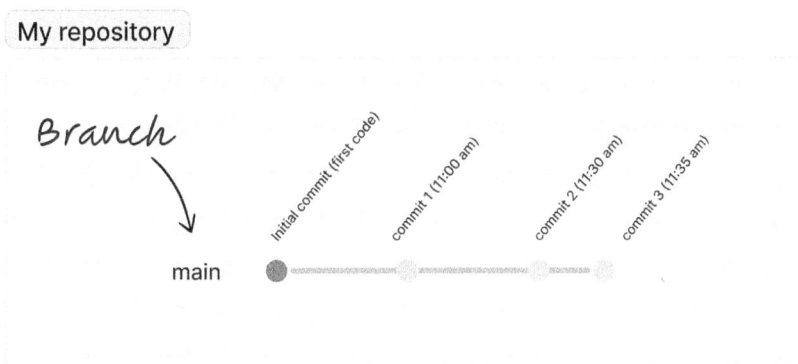

Figure 1.4: A diagram of a Git graph showing a timeline of commits (changes) in the main branch of the repository

Scenario 2: Creating a feature branch

Say I want to make some major changes to the code without affecting the last commit I made (**commit 3**). If I would like to develop an entirely new feature for a mobile app, I would create a copy of the branch at its latest timestamp and begin my fresh work from there. All additional commits I make would be in my new feature branch. The following diagram illustrates how a new branch continues with the history from its source branch:

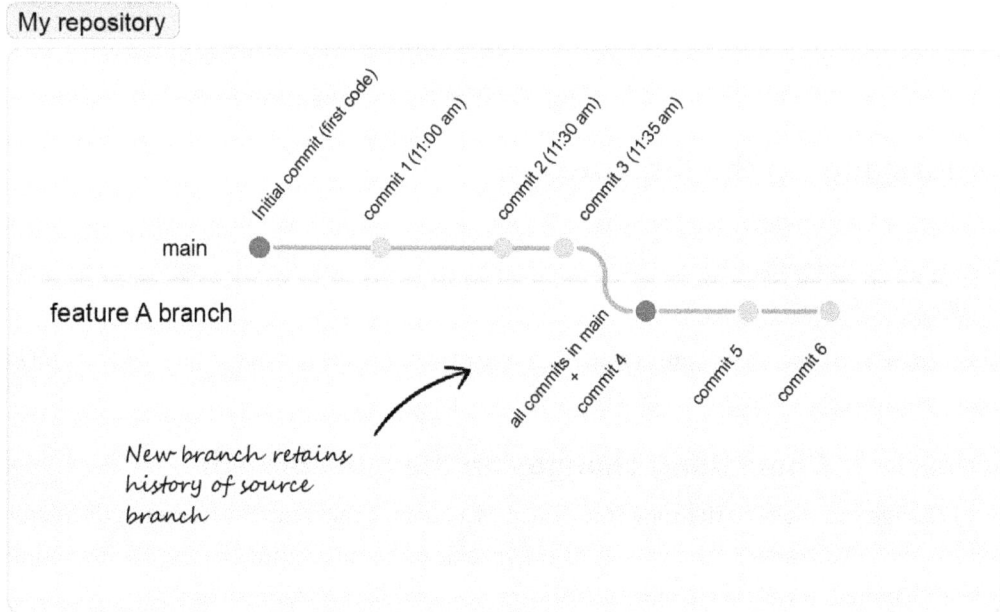

Figure 1.5: A new branch (feature A) is created from main to begin another body of changes

This way, I can test my feature changes in a controlled environment and add more commits without impacting the working code in the main branch. I can choose to roll out my mobile app with the test features to select people who will test it with me, while everyone else will be using the code in the main branch in production.

Scenario 3: Fixing a bug while developing a feature

While you are still in the process of developing a new feature in the feature A branch, you received some not-so-great news about a bug identified in production that needs to be fixed. You can fix the bug in the main branch while keeping your new development work intact (*you could create another fix branch from the commit 3 node as well, but this is just an example*). This can be seen in the following diagram:

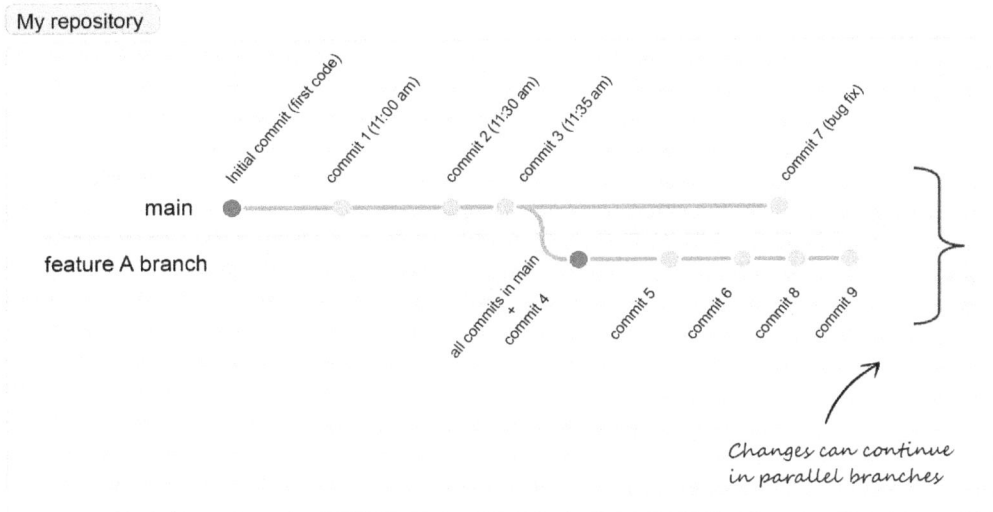

Figure 1.6: Parallel changes – fixing bugs while developing new features

In the preceding diagram, you can see how you can make multiple commits across the timeline. Commit numbers were only used for brevity; timestamps tell the positions of the commits across the timeline. In addition, every commit is assigned a unique identifier called the **commit SHA** (or **hash**). This is a 40-character hexadecimal value that represents the commit's content and metadata. It is derived from the commit's content (code changes) and other information (author, timestamp). Often, you'll see a shorter version (usually the *first seven characters*) of the full SHA.

Example of a full commit SHA

42e2e5af9d49de268cd1fda3587788da4ace418a

42e2e5a is the shorthand for the same commit.

Merging

Now you're done with the development of the new feature(s) and you would like to make this available for full production use. You can merge the feature branch back to the main branch. With this, all code from inception, including the bug fixes and feature changes, will become one whole coherent codebase in the main branch.

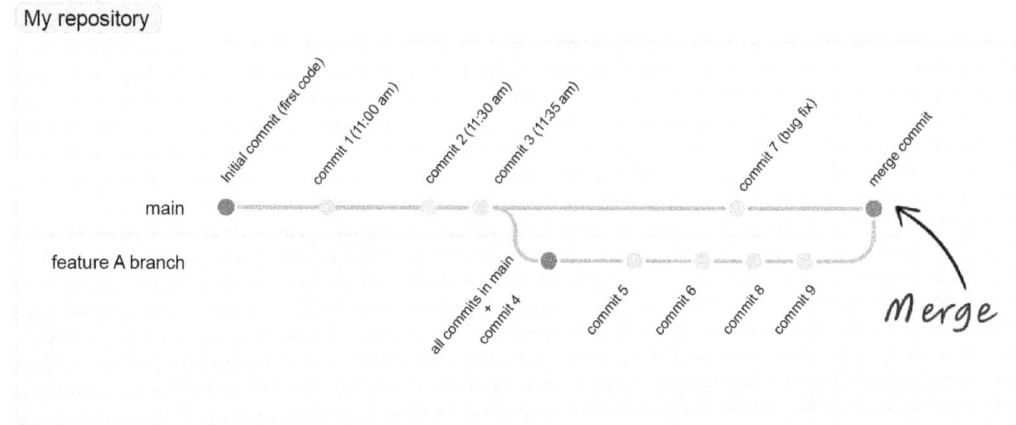

Figure 1.7: Changes can be consolidated by merging branches

When you merge a branch with another branch, a merge commit is created, marking the snapshot of the amalgamation.

Cloning

If two or more developers need to make parallel changes to **My repository**, the repo will have to be stored in a central place (server) while the developers interact independently with the server from their local machine. The way Git ensures this is done without creating overreliance on the server is another unique feature that sets Git apart. Git does this by cloning the repo from the remote server.

When you *clone* a Git repository, you're creating a local copy of an entire project (including all its files, history, and branches) from a remote server (such as GitHub, BitBucket, or GitLab). This allows you to work on the code locally, make changes, and contribute back to the project.

The difference between Git and GitHub

Git is the local technology on your machine for creating and interacting with repositories, while GitHub is the remote server where Git repos can be stored centrally to aid collaboration between two or more people on the codebase.

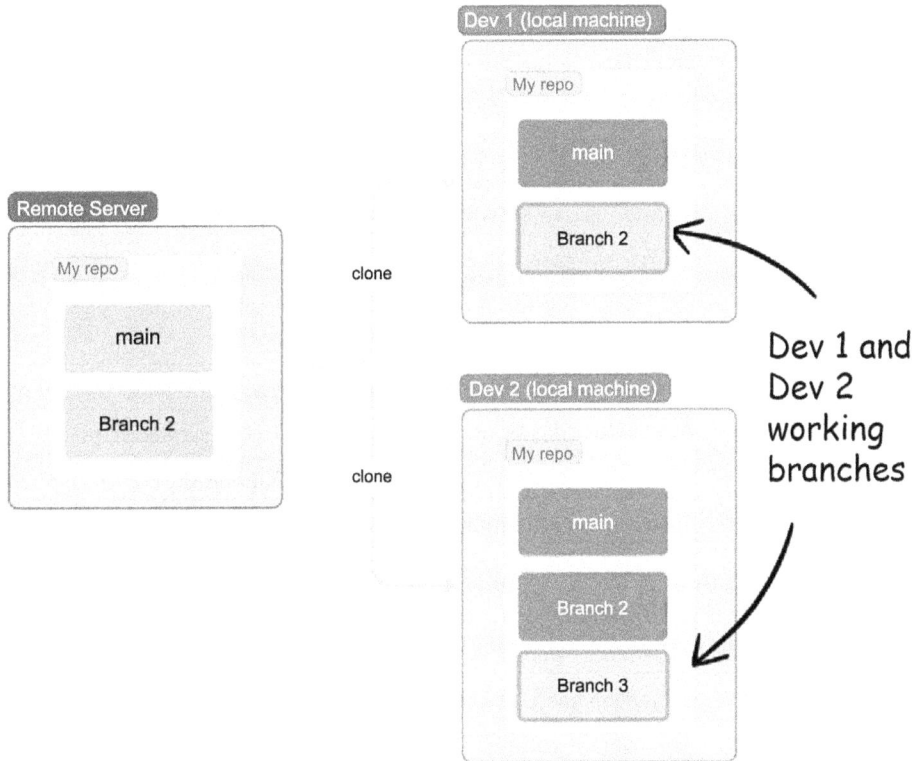

Figure 1.8: Two developers working on different variations of a repo cloned from the remote server

In the preceding diagram, **Dev 1** and **Dev 2** each cloned a copy of the repo from the central location (remote), which is the *origin* where the codebase is stored. In addition to this, **Dev 1** started working on the code in **Branch 2** as their working branch, whereas, **Dev 2** has created a new branch (from either **main** or **Branch 2**) called **Branch 3** as their working branch.

Git jargon and commands

Before diving into the world of Git, it's important to familiarize yourself with the terminology and commands used in this version control system. In the following section, we'll introduce you to some common Git jargon and commands that you'll encounter as you work with repositories, branches, and commits. Understanding these terms and commands will help you navigate Git with confidence and ease.

As it is with every command in the **Command Line Interface (CLI)**, every Git command starts with the word or verb `git`, then a space and the command. Here is a list of 15 commonly used Git commands and their functions:

	Git Command	Function
1	`git init`	Initializes a new Git repository
2	`git clone`	Creates a copy of a remote repository on the local machine
3	`git status`	Displays the status of the working directory, including any changes made
4	`git add`	Adds changes to the staging area, in preparation for a commit
5	`git commit`	Records changes to the repository, creating a new commit
6	`git branch`	Lists all branches in the repository and shows the current branch
7	`git checkout`	Switches between branches or restores files in the working directory
8	`git merge`	Merges changes from one branch into another
9	`git pull`	Fetches changes from a remote repository and merges them into the current branch
10	`git push`	Pushes changes to a remote repository
11	`git log`	Shows the commit history of the current branch
12	`git diff`	Shows the differences between the working directory and the most recent commit
13	`git remote`	Manages remote repositories
14	`git fetch`	Fetches changes from a remote repository but does not merge them
15	`git stash`	Temporarily saves changes in the working directory that are not ready to be committed

Table 1.1: List of 15 commonly used Git commands

Beyond your source files, Git repositories may also contain some additional files called configuration files. Let's examine these in detail.

Git configuration files

Remember that a commit is a snapshot of the project at a timestamp? A repository may contain multiple files – source code, configuration files, test suites, libraries, and documentation. In addition, a repository contains Git configuration files that help Git understand how to interpret your repository and the files in it. Many of these configuration files, though present in the directory (folder) the repo is stored in, are hidden from view.

The following table is a list of some examples of Git configuration files and their purposes:

Git Configuration File	Purpose
.gitignore	Specifies intentionally untracked files to ignore
.gitattributes	Defines attributes per path
.gitmodules	Defines the mapping between the project's submodules and their URLs
Config	Contains repository-specific configuration options
HEAD	Points to the currently checked-out branch
Description	Contains a short description of the repository

Table 1.2: List of Git configuration files present in a repo

Now, let's get practical! In the next section, we will go through a lab exercise in our first venture into using Git.

Certification tip

Expect **a lot** of questions on Git commands and using configuration files. For example, you may be asked about scenarios where you need to use the .gitignore file or a use case where a file is not to be tracked in the repo.

.gitignore

For more information about .gitignore, please refer to *Chapter 3, Repository Creation and Management*.

Lab 1: Setting up Git

In this section, you will learn how to install Git, configure your user information (name and email), and set up your first repository. We'll guide you through the initial setup process.

The steps in this lab exercise require a computer. Your computer can be Windows, Linux, or macOS. You will be running these steps in the terminal/CLI. You will not be able to do this on a phone or tablet.

> **Video guides**
>
> If you prefer to follow a step-by-step video guide as you take this lab exercise, visit *Chapter 1, Lab 1: Setting Up Git* video from the book's video playlist link here (`https://www.youtube.com/playlist?list=PLuX8xLieCtTP3-AsobdFLmaqAcbBxJ39w`).

Installing Git

Launch your terminal in macOS or Linux, or Command Prompt or PowerShell in Windows:

1. First, check if Git is already installed on your system by opening a terminal or command prompt and typing the following:

    ```
    git --version
    ```

    If Git is installed, you will see the installed version number.

2. If Git is not installed, you can download it from the official website (`https://git-scm.com/downloads`) and follow the installation instructions for your operating system.

Configuring user identity

Every commit in a Git repo is registered against the "committer" and timestamped for record-keeping purposes.

Before you can commit changes to any Git repo, the Git system needs to save your display name as well as your email address on the system you are using. This is only needed the first time you install Git.

Follow these steps to register your user identity for the first time:

1. After installing Git, you need to configure your user identity by setting your name and email address.

2. In the terminal or command prompt, type the following:

    ```
    git config --global user.name "Your Name"
    ```

    This command sets the name that will be associated with your Git commits globally on your system. This means that every time you make a commit, Git will use Your Name as the author name.

3. Then type the following:

```
git config --global user.email your_email@example.com
```

This sets the email address that will be associated with your Git commits globally on your system. This means that every time you make a commit, Git will use this email address as the author email.

Creating a local repository

Before you create a local repository, I would recommend you set aside a separate directory designated as a parent directory for storing your local Git repos. Every Git repo resides in a separate directory. You may, for example, want to create the following structure:

Figure 1.9: A sample directory structure with a parent directory for storing local repos

Let's get started, with the following steps:

1. Skip this step if you already have a desired location. Otherwise, type the following:

```
mkdir all_my_repos && cd all_my_repos
mkdir app1 && cd app1
```

2. To create a new local repository, navigate to the desired location on your computer using the terminal or command prompt. If you are new to the CLI, you can read this article (https://opensource.com/article/21/8/linux-change-directories) on how to navigate to a directory in the terminal. Type the following:

```
git init
```

This will initialize a new repository and create a new .git directory containing all the necessary files for version control.

Your repo has now been initialized. Any changes you make to that directory – for example, creating a file, modifying a file, adding a file, deleting a file, and so on – will be tracked.

3. Check the status of Git by typing the following:

```
git status
```

You should get the following result:

```
On branch main
No commits yet
```

This indicates that your working branch is *main* and no changes or commits have been detected yet in this repo.

Creating your first application source code

We will now create a simple file with basic code or script to simulate what it is like to write code.

Follow these steps:

1. In your initialized directory, create a new file *(you can also move an existing file into it)* by typing the following:

```
echo "alert("Hello world")" >> my_new_file.js
```

2. Now check the status of your repo again by typing git status. You should get the following result:

```
Here, a new file has been detected but it has not been tracked for
versioning yet.
```

3. To include the new file in version control so that subsequent changes to it will be tracked, type the following:

```
git add "my_new_file.js"
```

Where <file> is the filename of the new file you added. Then type git status again. You should get the following result:

```
On branch main
No commits yet
Changes to be committed:
  (use "git rm --cached <file>..." to unstage)
new file:    "my_new_file.js"
```

The change in this file has now been recognized and the change detected is that it is a *new file* added. It is now in the staging area, meaning that it is ready for a commit.

4. To commit the changes in your staging area (you can stage multiple files and commit all at once), you will use the git commit command followed by the -m flag and then your message in quotes. Type the following:

```
git commit -m "Adds my first source code file"
```

Congratulations! You have completed your first version control exercise. Your source code is in safe hands.

In the next section, we will examine some challenges of Git and common pitfalls to avoid.

Some common challenges

Git is quite versatile, but there are certain file extensions and scenarios that can cause issues or require special handling:

*   **Binary files**: Git treats files with non-ASCII characters or very long lines as binary. If a file contains UTF-16 encoding or other non-ASCII content, Git may consider it binary. To explicitly define how Git interprets files, use a .gitattributes file.

*   **Unsupported protocols**: Git supports various protocols (HTTP, SSH, etc.) for remote repositories. However, some older versions of Git Extensions had issues with SSH. Ensure you're using a recent version and the correct protocol.

- **SHA-1 hash issues**: Sometimes Git may struggle with specific files due to their content. If you encounter problems, try locating the unique SHA-1 hash for the file using `git hash-object -w filename`.

- **Large files and large repos**: Git is designed to handle source code and small text files efficiently, but it can struggle with large binary files or very large repositories. Here are some common issues:

  - **Performance**: Large files can slow down operations such as cloning, fetching, and pushing.

  - **Storage**: Large files increase the size of the repository, which can be problematic for storage and bandwidth.

  - **History**: Every version of a file is stored in the repository's history, so large files can quickly bloat the repository size.

To manage large files, you can use tools such as Git **Large File Storage** (**LFS**), which stores large files outside the main repository and replaces them with lightweight references. This helps keep the repository size manageable and improves performance.

Remember, Git's flexibility allows you to adapt to different scenarios, but understanding these nuances can help you work more effectively!

Summary

In this chapter, we delved into the essentials of Git and how it differs from GitHub, providing a comprehensive introduction to version control and its significance in software development. We began by outlining the key aspects of version control, such as tracking changes, effective collaboration, and maintaining code quality.

We also discussed the benefits of version control, including granular history, accountability, rollbacks, parallel development, code reviews, stability, and traceability. We highlighted the challenges faced without version control, emphasizing the potential for confusion, lost changes, and decreased code quality.

Next, we introduced various version control systems, focusing on Git as the industry standard, and explaining Git's decentralized nature, performance, and the strong community and ecosystem that support it. Afterward, we looked at an overview of Git's core components, such as commits, branches, and repositories, and described how Git's branching and merging capabilities facilitate parallel development and conflict resolution.

Throughout the chapter were practical examples and diagrams to illustrate key concepts, such as creating new branches, fixing bugs, and merging changes. We also covered essential Git commands and their functions, helping you become familiar with the terminology and commands used in Git.

Let's have a quick test of your knowledge.

Test your knowledge

1. Git and GitHub can be used interchangeably

    a. True

    b. False

2. Which of the following is not a version control system?

    a. Git

    b. GitHub

    c. SVN

    d. TFVC

3. You made some changes to Python code in your repository. You need to ensure that these changes have been added to version control. Which two commands do you need to run to ensure your changes have been recorded?

    a. `git --version` and `git record`

    b. `git status` and `git add`

    c. `git status` and `git commit`

    d. `git add` and `git commit`

Useful links

- Branching and Merging: `https://git-scm.com/about/branching-and-merging#branching-and-merging`
- How to open and close directories in the Linux terminal: `https://opensource.com/article/21/8/linux-change-directories`

Unlock this book's exclusive benefits now

Scan this QR code or go to packtpub.com/unlock, then search this book by name.

Note: Keep your purchase invoice ready before you start.

2

Navigating the GitHub Interface

Welcome to *Chapter 2, Navigating the GitHub Interface*. Get ready to dive into the world of GitHub and discover its many features. In *Chapter 1*, we only discussed Git, which is the universal system that most VCS platforms use, including GitHub. We will now discuss GitHub proper. In this chapter, you will learn how to navigate the platform's interface – an essential skill tested in the GitHub Foundations certification exam. We'll explore GitHub's offerings, its core features, and the account types you'll need to know about for both personal and team collaboration. Let's get started!

We will cover the following main topics:

- GitHub overview and offerings
- GitHub account types
- Lab 2.1: Familiarity with the GitHub interface
- Introduction to GitHub product features
- Other GitHub tools and features

Technical requirements

You will need a GitHub account for the lab exercises in this chapter. You can get a GitHub account for free. To create one, use the documentation on GitHub (`https://docs.github.com/en/get-started/start-your-journey/creating-an-account-on-github`) or follow the *Chapter 2, Lab 2: Signing up for a Github account* video, from the book's video playlist link (`https://www.youtube.com/playlist?list=PLuX8xLieCtTP3-AsobdFLmaqAcbBxJ39w`).

GitHub overview and offerings

GitHub is a powerful platform that has revolutionized the way developers work. Over 100 million developers are on GitHub, by far the largest developer ecosystem I know of. It has made it easier for developers to collaborate, share code, and manage projects. With its intuitive interface and robust features, GitHub has become an essential tool for developers of all skill levels. In this chapter, we will explore the many features of GitHub and how you can use them to improve your workflow.

What is GitHub?

GitHub is a hosting platform for developers to store and manage Git repositories (source code) and collaborate on software development and software releases, providing them with multiple interfaces and capabilities to work together. It is the library/bookshelf that can help you store many cookbooks for different recipes, not just lasagna. GitHub only supports the Git version control system; you cannot store an SVN repository, for example. GitHub is widely known to be an open source platform, but also provides significant support for private use for individuals and enterprise-grade use for businesses.

GitHub is available to be deployed as a cloud service on `GitHub.com` (**Software-as-a-Service (SaaS)**) managed by GitHub or as a self-hosted server (on-premises or cloud).

Differences between Git and GitHub

In comparison to Git, GitHub adds far greater advantages:

- **Redundancy eliminates a single point of failure**: Since Git is locally installed on the machine, your Git repo is only as safe and secure as your laptop or desktop. Damage to it will mean you may lose all your source code. GitHub mitigates **single points of failure (SPOFs)** associated with Git by providing a distributed, web-based platform for hosting Git repositories. Unlike Git, which operates locally and relies on individual installations, GitHub centralizes repository hosting, user management, and collaboration features. By hosting repositories on GitHub, developers benefit from redundancy, robust infrastructure, and built-in user management, reducing the risk of SPOFs that could disrupt code sharing and version control.

- **Collaboration and real-time edits**: GitHub is a platform that hosts code repositories both in the cloud and on-premises (on-prem). It makes it easier for multiple developers to work on the same project simultaneously, seeing each other's edits in real time. This collaborative environment fosters teamwork and efficient development.

- **Project organization and management**: In addition to version control, GitHub includes features for project organization and management. You can create issues, track tasks, manage milestones, and collaborate with team members. It provides a holistic solution for both code hosting and project management.

These are core differences. Now let us look at the other general differences to provide additional context.

Additional context

Here are some contextual differences between Git and GitHub:

Aspect	Git	GitHub
Definition	Software for version control	Web-based Git repository hosting service
Tool Type	Command-line tool	**Graphical user interface (GUI)**
Installation	Local (installed on your system)	Hosted on the web
Maintained By	Linux Foundation	GitHub (Microsoft)
Focus	Version control and code sharing	Centralized source code hosting
Purpose	Manage source code history	Host Git repositories, collaborate on building and releasing software *(testing, CI/CD, security are all natively embedded)*
Release Year	2005	2008
User Management	No built-in feature	Built-in user management
Licensing	Open source	Free-tier and pay-for-use tiers
Tool Integration	Minimal external tool configuration	Active marketplace for tool integration
Desktop Interface	Git GUI (for Git)	GitHub Desktop (for GitHub)
Similar Technologies	CVS, Azure DevOps Server, Subversion	GitLab, Bitbucket, AWS Code Commit, etc.
Brand/Logo	git	GitHub

Table 2.1: Differences between Git and GitHub

Remember that Git is the underlying version control technology, while GitHub provides a platform for hosting Git repositories and adds additional features.

Beyond just developers

While we generally refer to users of GitHub as developers, we broadly mean all writers of code, that is, anyone who writes code, scripts, or configurations, or who writes other software assets as code – documentation, design, tests, infrastructure, architecture, and so on. The social collaborative features of GitHub have aided this expansion, bringing all software professionals and practitioners into one inclusive ecosystem.

In fact, since the advent of **Generative AI** and **GitHub Copilot**, there has been an exponential growth in the number of other professions writing code on GitHub.

In the next section, we will examine the core functionalities of GitHub.

Core functionalities

GitHub operates in about five groups of core functionalities:

Collaboration

GitHub focuses on collaboration at its core. It provides a series of product features, such as repos, issues, pull requests, merge queues, projects, and discussions, to foster teamwork among contributors by reducing approval times, aiding pair programming, reducing friction when combining work, introducing code reviews conducted by your peers or automation bots, and tracking and managing work related to feature development and bugs.

Productivity

GitHub is feature-rich in user-friendly tools. It encourages automation, reduces onboarding and setup time, and introduces efficiency into how you build and release software. Tools and features such as CI/CD with **GitHub Actions**, **Codespaces**, and **Copilot** help developers to be more productive and efficient. GitHub prides itself on the principle of **Everything as Code (EaC)** – a DevOps practice of managing all stages of the software development lifecycle –planning, building, delivery, and so on – by defining and storing them using code and version control systems. These may include infrastructure, database schema, test suites, and pipelines stored alongside the application source code itself. Essentially, it extends the application development approach to other components of IT, ensuring best practices are consistently followed with minimal manual effort. By treating all components of a system as code, EaC enables repeatability and scalability and reduces the risk of human error. Examples include **Infrastructure as Code (IaC)**, **Configuration as Code**, **GitOps**, and **Kubernetes**, which allow teams to define and control various aspects of software deployment and management using code-based configurations. This principle aids automation and increases productivity levels.

Security

Throughout the **software development lifecycle (SDLC)** on GitHub, you will find at different stages various security features embedded natively into your work. This includes while developing in your IDE or on GitHub.com UI, during code merges and code reviews, in deployment runs, in storage for packages and artifacts, as well as various means to protect your code at rest, your business's vital intellectual property, and user identities.

Scale

GitHub is home to developers. You will find *millions* of apps by individuals, apps for mini school projects, small to large-scale software by start-up businesses, and even enterprise-grade globally used software by long-established companies, all on GitHub. This means your software product(s) can grow with you without the concern of moving to another platform. Backed by Microsoft, GitHub (cloud) expands to the scale your codebase requires.

AI and automation

Finally, but most importantly, GitHub is powered by AI. GitHub Copilot, powered by OpenAI, Claude and other models, is by far the front-runner of code assistant tools (`https://stackoverflow.blog/2024/05/29/developers-get-by-with-a-little-help-from-ai-stack-overflow-knows-code-assistant-pulse-survey-results/`) that leverage the capabilities of **Generative AI (GenAI)** in software development. GitHub enhances the core pillars mentioned above with AI. For example, you can learn to write code or write code faster with better quality, enhance pull requests and issues, automate security checks, and fix vulnerabilities faster than you naturally would without the help of AI.

Understanding the open source concept

The **open source concept** refers to a type of software development model where the source code is made available to the public. This means anyone is allowed to view, modify, and distribute the code (sometimes with a defined caveat). This approach promotes community-driven development, accepting suggestions for improvement and aiding collaboration and transparency. Open source software is often developed in a collaborative manner, extending borders beyond your locality, with contributions from developers around the world.

For a deep dive into open source and how you might contribute to open source projects, please read *Chapter 11, Contributing to Open Source Projects*.

GitHub is the largest code hosting and collaboration platform and is widely regarded as the most popular platform for open source development. There are millions of public repositories on GitHub. These are repositories where you can access their source code, even without a GitHub account. However, you will need a GitHub account if you want to contribute to them. Non-public repositories can be either private or internal. Therefore, there are three repo types on GitHub:

Repo Type	Description
Public	These are accessible to anyone on the internet, allowing anyone to view, clone, and contribute to the code.
Internal	Available only to members of an organization, these repos are used for projects that need to be shared within a company but not with the public.
Private	These are restricted to the owner, and specific users or teams who are granted access, ensuring that only authorized individuals can access and contribute to the code.

Table 2.2: List of GitHub repo types

The following diagram illustrates the repository types and how restrictions tighten as you go to the right.

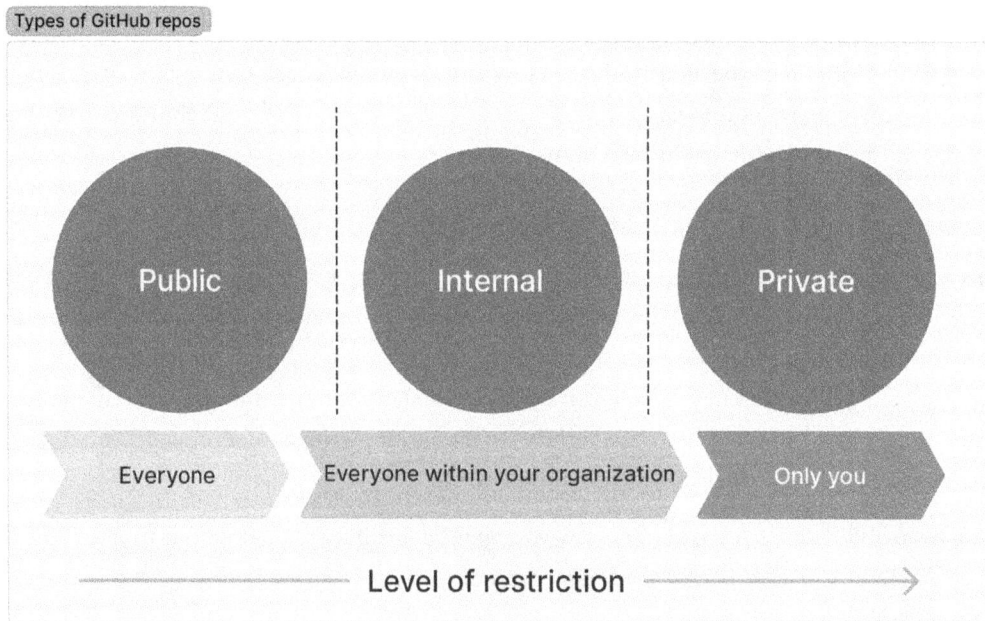

Figure 2.1: GitHub repo types and their access levels

Available plans and offerings

GitHub has different plans to suit the various needs of individuals, start-ups, and established businesses. Now let us examine available plans and prices.

> **Note**
>
> Features and prices offered in these plans were accurate at the time of writing this book. Expect some changes in what is now obtainable.

GitHub Free

GitHub's Free plan is designed to cater to individuals and organizations looking for a no-cost option to manage their code repositories. With the Free plan, the number of collaborators and the number of public repositories that users can work with are unlimited, plus, it includes a full feature set. Additionally, users can manage unlimited private repositories with a limited feature set. This plan is particularly suitable for open source projects or individual developers starting out, as it provides essential version control features and collaborative tools without any charge.

The Free plan also includes some valuable features for private repositories, such as 500 MB of GitHub Packages storage and 2,000 minutes per month of GitHub Actions, which can be used for **continuous integration/continuous deployment (CI/CD)** purposes. For public repositories, these features are available without any limits. Moreover, the plan offers community support, automatic security vulnerability updates, and deployment protection rules for public repositories. It's a robust platform for developers to share their work with the community, contribute to other projects, and collaborate on code development.

GitHub Pro

GitHub Pro is a step up from the free GitHub plan, designed for developers who need more advanced tools and insights for their private repositories. With GitHub Pro, users get 3,000 GitHub Actions minutes per month, 2 GB of GitHub Packages storage, and 180 GitHub Codespaces core hours per month. Additionally, they receive 20 GB of GitHub Codespaces storage and GitHub Support via email. This plan is ideal for individuals who want to maximize their coding experience with enhanced security, better insights, and more flexibility.

The Pro plan also includes advanced features such as required pull request reviewers, protected branches, and code owners for better management of code reviews and collaborations. Users can also benefit from auto-linked references, GitHub Pages, and wikis for comprehensive documentation and insights. These features make GitHub Pro a powerful tool for developers looking to streamline their workflow and collaborate more effectively on private projects.

GitHub Team

The **GitHub Team** plan is tailored for organizations and teams that require advanced collaboration features. Priced at $4 USD per user/month (as of the time of writing this chapter), this plan includes everything from the Free plan, plus additional tools and insights for private repositories. Users get 3,000 GitHub Actions minutes per month and 2 GB of GitHub Packages storage. It's ideal for growing teams that need more than the basics, offering sophisticated security and administrative features to manage member access and protect data across multiple projects.

Moreover, the Team plan provides access to features such as GitHub Codespaces, team review requests, code owners, protected branches, multi-reviewers, and draft pull requests. These features enhance the code review process and project management, making it easier for teams to collaborate efficiently. Organization owners can also choose to enable or disable GitHub Codespaces for their private repositories and pay for the usage of members and collaborators, giving them flexibility and control over their development environment.

GitHub Enterprise

GitHub Enterprise is designed for businesses that need to support their entire software development lifecycle. It is the most comprehensive of all plans offered by GitHub. It includes all the features of the Free and Team plans, plus additional features such as SAML and **Single Sign-On (SSO)** authentication, Enterprise-Managed Users which enables bringing in your own identity provider, internal repositories, and free tier of usage-based products such as GitHub Actions and Codespaces. In addition to these, businesses get a single place to manage their billing, configure settings, enforce policies, and audit access centrally. It also offers the option to add GitHub Advanced Security and GitHub Premium Support, which are paid offerings.

GitHub Enterprise Cloud is a deployment option within GitHub Enterprise that adds advanced features to GitHub.com for large businesses and teams. It includes SAML authentication, additional GitHub Actions minutes, restricted email notifications to verified domains, privately published GitHub Pages sites, managed user accounts, and repository rulesets. An enterprise account in GitHub Enterprise Cloud gives administrators a central point for managing multiple organizations, providing a seamless experience with compliance reports and advanced management options.

Comparatively, **GitHub Enterprise Server** is the self-hosted version that allows organizations to run their own GitHub instance, either on-premises or on a public cloud service. This option gives organizations greater control, scalability, customization capabilities, and dedicated support. It caters to enterprises seeking enhanced security, compliance, and the flexibility to tailor GitHub to their specific needs. GitHub Enterprise Server administrators can create accounts for users and authenticate using the built-in system or an external identity provider. Administrators can also enable GitHub Connect to benefit from features that rely on GitHub.com, such as Dependabot alerts and actions hosted on GitHub.com.

> **Certification tip**
>
> You may be asked to select the odd one out of a list of GitHub plans – for example, one incorrect option might be introduced to the list of options.

GitHub account types

GitHub offers three types of accounts: *Individual (User)*, *Organization*, and *Enterprise*. Each account type serves different needs, from individual developers to large enterprises, offering a range of tools and features to support collaboration, security, and management of software development projects.

Individual

An individual or user account on GitHub is a personal account that represents a single user. It's your identity on GitHub, with a unique username and profile. This account type can own resources such as repositories, packages, and projects. Actions taken on GitHub, such as creating issues or reviewing pull requests, are attributed to your individual account. Individual accounts can use either *GitHub Free* or *GitHub Pro*. With GitHub Free, you can own an unlimited number of public and private repositories, but private repositories have a limited feature set. Upgrading to GitHub Pro provides a full feature set for private repositories.

They are ideal for developers who want to host and manage their own repositories, collaborate on open source projects, or contribute to other developers' projects. Repositories owned by individual accounts are sometimes called **user-scoped repos**:

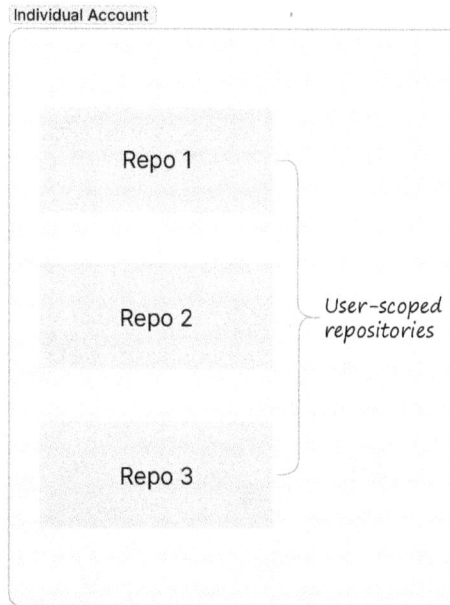

Figure 2.2: An individual account can own multiple user-scoped repositories

One more important thing: an Individual account can also use *GitHub Enterprise Cloud*, albeit with an additional layer of enterprise security using SAML Single Sign-On authentication. Here, the GitHub individual account (personal) is linked with an external **Identity Provider** (**IdP**), thereby making it two conjoined identities for authentication.

Organization

Organization accounts are designed for businesses and teams. They provide a shared space for collaboration, allowing multiple developers to work on the same repositories and manage access to code and project management features. It's a container for shared work, giving the work a unique name and brand. Organization accounts can own resources such as repositories and packages, but *you cannot sign into an organization directly*. Instead, you collaborate on shared projects by joining the same organization account with your individual account. Organization accounts offer sophisticated security and administrative features to manage access to the organization's resources. Organization accounts are available in both free and paid plans, with the latter offering additional features and support for larger teams.

Enterprise

Enterprise accounts are designed for large businesses and organizations. They provide an enterprise account experience, advanced security and compliance features, and additional administrative tools for managing large teams and complex projects. Enterprise accounts are available *only as a paid plan* and include all the features of the Free and Team plans, with pricing based on the number of users and the level of support required. With enterprise accounts, you have a single place to manage billing and settings, enforce policies, and audit access across multiple organizations:

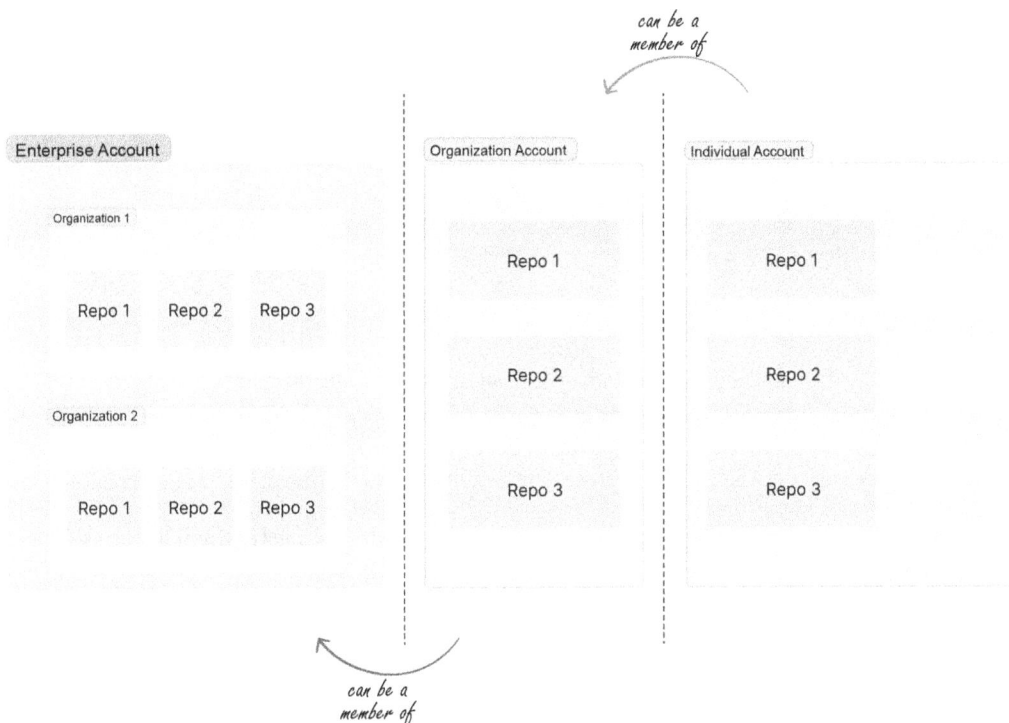

Figure 2.3: Relationships between individual, organization, and enterprise accounts

In the preceding diagram, the group on the far right shows an individual account with multiple repositories (user-scoped). These repositories belong to your identity. The group in the middle is an organization containing multiple repositories. Although these are organization-owned repositories, you will need an individual account to contribute to them. On the far left is an Enterprise account containing multiple organizations, which in turn contain multiple repositories (organization-scoped):

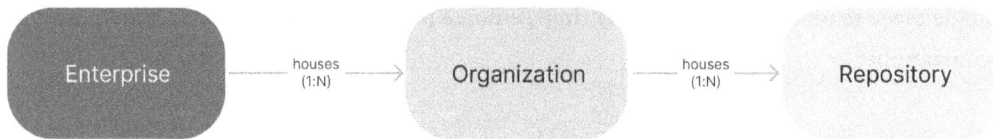

Figure 2.4: An Enterprise account contains multiple orgs, which in turn contain multiple repos

An Enterprise account cannot own a repository; only an individual or organization can:

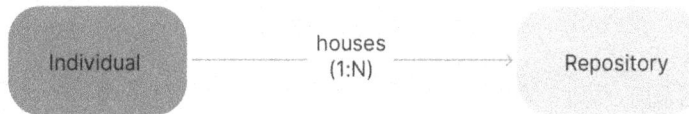

Figure 2.5: An Individual account can house multiple repos

Each organization can be independently managed while still inheriting all enterprise-defined rules, policies, and behaviors. An organization can be a member of an enterprise or stand on its own.

Let's get hands-on a little bit! Up next, we will delve into a lab exercise that will help us get used to the GitHub interface.

Lab 2.1: Familiarity with the GitHub interface

In this lab, we will walk through the basics of the GitHub interface and get exposed to the terminologies used and the menus. By the end of this lab, you will be able to find your way around GitHub.

Exploring open source repos

> **Note**
>
> You do not need a GitHub account for this.

Let us explore some open source repos in the following steps:

1. Visit `https://github.com/explore`. This is where you can explore the latest about GitHub, such as developer and open source news, the latest videos, trending developers, trending repos, and popular topics.

2. Click on **Trending**. This will show you a list of the current most popular open source repos. You can filter by spoken language, programming/scripting language, and period:

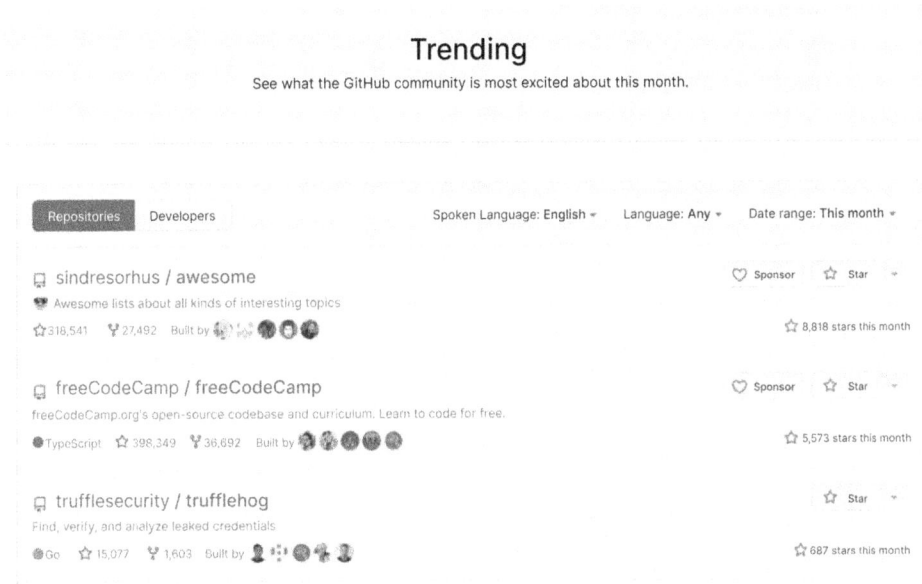

Figure 2.6: Example of trending repositories on GitHub

On each row of records, you will find important information about each repo:

-   **The repository name**: This is usually in the format {owner}/{repo_name}, where owner is the owner of the repo, that is, either individual or organization; and repo_ name is the name of the repository.

-   **Stars**: The number of stars a repository has is the number of people (developers) that have bookmarked the repo. A repo earns a star every time someone stars that repo (adds it to their bookmarks).

-   **Language**: This is the language the source code in the repo is mostly written in. This is derived from the language with most lines of code across all the files in the repo. Remember, a repo can have multiple languages co-existing in different files in it. This may be a programming, scripting, markup, or markdown language.

- **Built by:** This is a list of the top contributors to the repo's contents. This is usually represented by their avatars. Clicking on the avatar will take you to the profile page of the contributor.

Here's a close-up of a repo showing the vital stats:

Figure 2.7: Summarized info of a repo showing vital stats

3. Visit `https://github.com/freeCodeCamp/freeCodeCamp`. This will take you to the freeCodeCamp repository, one of the most widely used open source repos. Scroll down to read the **README** section. Then, explore the source code by browsing through the directories you see there.

> **Note**
>
> The **README** section is the landing page of a GitHub repo where you can find an overview of what the repo contains. It is crucial documentation you provide to help visitors and contributors understand the repo.

4. Visit `https://github.com/torvalds/linux`. This will take you to the primary open source repository containing the source code for the Linux kernel, maintained by Linus Torvalds and the Linux community. Explore the source code by browsing through the directories you see there.

The preceding *steps 3* and *4* are examples of open source repos, millions of which exist on GitHub. Notice how the word **Public** is written next to the repository name at the top left? This indicates that the repo is public. You are free to view the source code, suggest changes, or outrightly contribute to it as the license permits. More information is available about open source licenses in *Chapter 11, Contributing to Open Source Projects.*

You will also realize that you have been browsing all these repositories and source code without an account or without signing in. Next, let us sign in with a GitHub individual account and see the difference.

Exploring the interface

You will need a GitHub account for this exercise:

1. Visit github.com and sign in by clicking on **Sign in** at the top right. This will take you to the GitHub **Dashboard** page, a landing page to help you stay organized and get quick access to what is important to you.

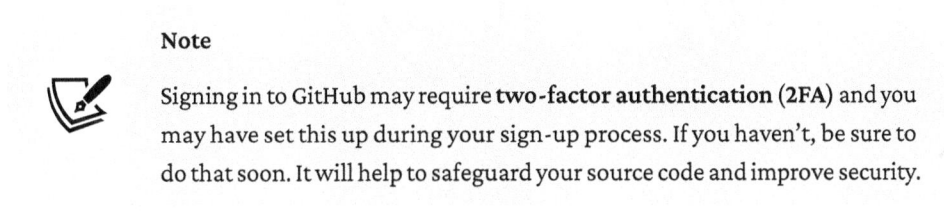

> **Note**
>
> Signing in to GitHub may require **two-factor authentication (2FA)** and you may have set this up during your sign-up process. If you haven't, be sure to do that soon. It will help to safeguard your source code and improve security.

The following screenshot is a sample of what your dashboard may look like:

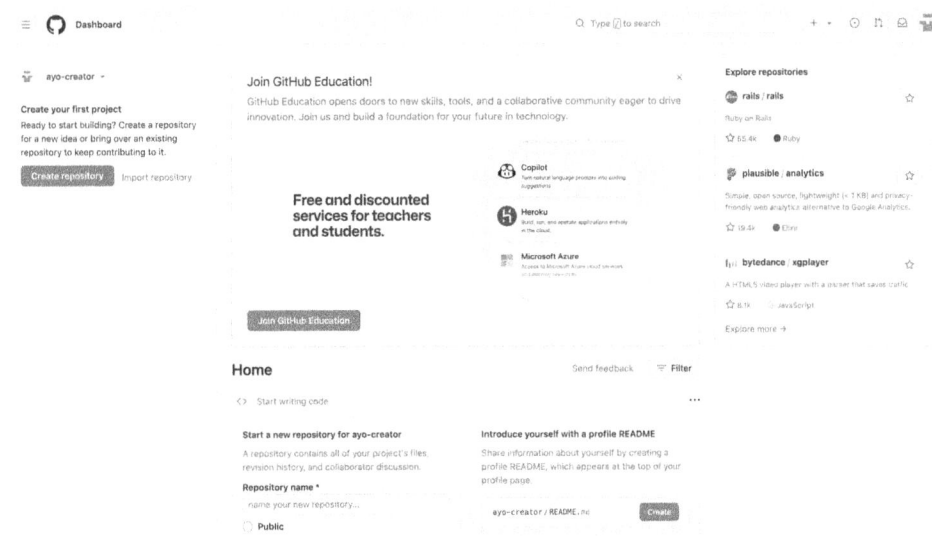

Figure 2.8: The GitHub dashboard, your default landing page

2. In the top-left corner, click on the hamburger menu to see the options available. This will display a quick shortcut to various GitHub features. As you continue to use GitHub, the list in this menu may expand to show additional shortcuts to repos, teams, and more:

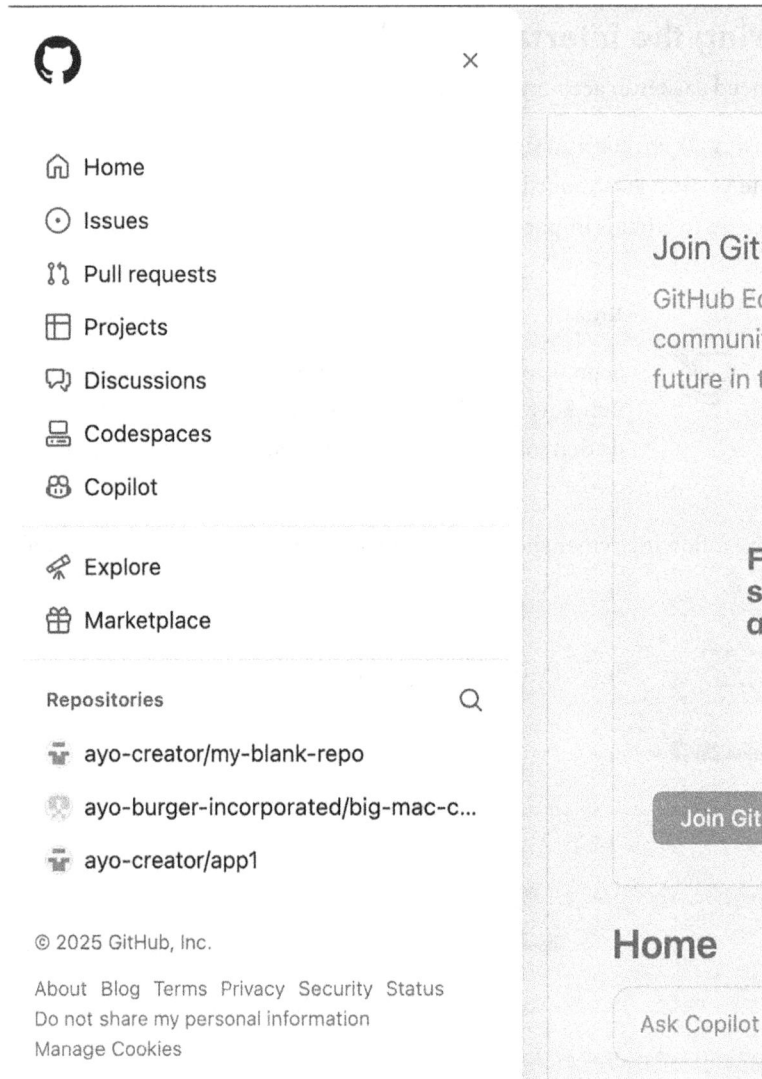

Figure 2.9: Contents of the GitHub hamburger menu

3. Also, in the top-right corner is a set of useful shortcuts and tools. Hover over each of them to see what they are:

Note

The icons you see may depend on what GitHub plan you have subscribed to or what features are enabled to be accessible to your GitHub account.

Figure 2.10: Some of the icons available in the top-right toolbox

Let's examine each one:

1. **Search box**: this allows you to search for anything across repos, organizations, and your enterprise.

2. **Copilot:** this launches the Copilot conversational chat. The all-new GenAI feature that answers questions from generic GitHub topics to writing actual coding tasks.

3. **Create new...:** you can create new items from here.

4. **Issues**: This takes you to all the issues across all repositories.

5. **Pull requests**: This takes you to all pull requests across all repositories.

6. **Notifications**: You can view/manage all your assigned issues and read notifications.

7. **Profile avatar**: You can manage your profile, configure settings, and view shortcuts to account-related menu items.

Now that you are more familiar with the GitHub interface, let us create our first repo.

Creating your first user-scoped repository

In this exercise, we will create a user-scoped repo, that is, a repository owned by an individual:

1. Ensure you are signed in to GitHub. At the top right, click on **+**, then select **New repository**:

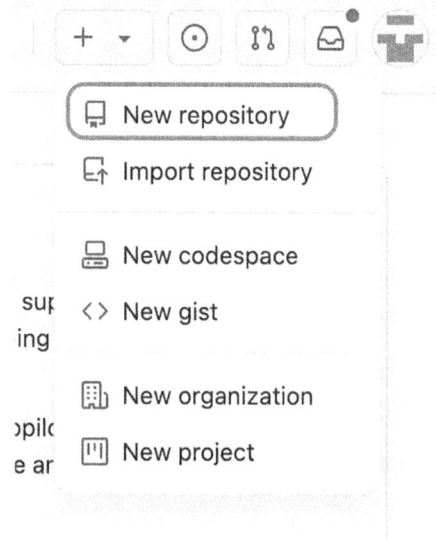

Figure 2.11: Drop-down menu when you click on New... (+)

2. Type a name for the repository – let's use my-first-repo. GitHub will also suggest a random name that you can choose to use.

> **Note**
>
> On the left of the repository name is a dropdown showing the owner of the repo, which defaults to your GitHub username (we also call this your **GitHub handle**).

The repository name is unique to the owner; you cannot create another user-scoped repository with the same name to be owned by this individual account.

3. Optionally, type a meaningful description for the repo.

4. Select **Private**. This will ensure your repository is only accessible to you.

5. Under **Initialize this repository with**, select **Add a README file**.

6. Click on **Create repository** to create your repository using the information you have supplied.

You have now created a new repository. This will now be displayed under the **Code** tab listing with your README.md as the only file content. In addition, you will see the content of the README. md (showing your repo name and description you supplied) displayed on the page.

The extension (.md) of the README file is **markdown**, which is a file format common for writing documentation in repositories. We will learn more about markdown in the next chapter.

Great job! You have created your first repository. Let's now create an organization repository.

Creating your first org-scoped repository

To create a repository owned by an organization, we must first have an organization to create it in:

1. At the top right, click on +, then select **New organization**. If you're prompted to select a plan, select the **Free** plan and continue to create a free organization.
2. Type a name for the organization. Like your GitHub username, *organization names are unique across GitHub*. Therefore, you cannot create another organization with the same name, whether within this GitHub personal account or otherwise. No one else can either.
3. Provide a contact email address.
4. Under **This organization belongs to**, select **My personal account**.
5. Complete the verification challenge under **Verify your account**, select **I hereby accept the Terms of Service...** after you have read the terms, and click **Next**. Optionally, you may select the **Get GitHub Copilot Business in this organization** add-on at a cost (*more about GitHub Copilot in later chapters*).
6. The next page you see presents you with the option to invite other people to join your new organization. You can skip this step for now by clicking on **Skip this step**.

Awesome! You have managed to create your first globally unique organization. Now let's create a repository inside this.

1. At the top right, click on +, then select **New repository**.
2. Under **Owner**, now select your newly created organization.
3. Type a name for the repository – let's use my-first-repo again. You are allowed to use the same repository name since it belongs to a different *owner*.
4. Repeat *steps 3-6* of the user-scoped repository creation we did previously.

Done! You have successfully created an organization-scoped repo.

Let's compare these two repositories side by side:

1. Duplicate your current browser tab so that you have the landing page of your new organization-scoped repo displayed on both.

2. On one of the two tabs, click on your profile avatar in the top right-hand corner and select **Your repositories**. This will list all the repositories under your personal account.

3. Select **my-first-repo**. This should take you to the landing page of your user-scoped repo.

Notice the URL of the two browser tabs. This should look like this:

*   **Org-scoped**: `https://github.com/{org-name}/my-first-repo`
*   **User-scoped**: `https://github.com/{username}/my-first-repo`

You now see how it is possible to use the same repository name as long as there are different owners. It is good practice to take note of the URL when you're collaborating on code to be sure you're working in the right context and repo.

Let's move on to the exciting part where we talk about all the various product features that make GitHub a great platform.

Introduction to GitHub product features

Here, we will discuss GitHub products, the main top-level features you will be interacting with throughout a software development lifecycle.

Repos

Repositories, or **repos** for short, are the fundamental building blocks of GitHub. They are used to store and manage source code, documentation, and other project-related files. Repos can be **public** or **private** and can be owned by an individual or an organization. In an organization, there is a third repository visibility called **internal**. Public repositories are visible to anyone on the internet, private repos are visible only to the owners and anyone else given explicit access to them, while internal repos are visible to anyone within an organization. In addition to files, you will also find that many other GitHub product features are accessible in a repository, which means they host both Git-tracked content and other project-level tools and integrations.

Issues and pull requests

Issues are used to track bugs, feature requests, and other project-related tasks. Pull requests, on the other hand, are used to propose changes to a codebase. They allow developers to review, discuss, and merge code changes.

Projects

Projects are used to organize and track work on GitHub. They provide a visual way to manage tasks, issues, and pull requests.

Discussions

Discussions provide a space for developers to have conversations, ask questions, and share ideas. They are a way to foster community and collaboration on GitHub.

Actions

Actions are used to automate software development workflows. They allow developers to build, test, and deploy code directly from GitHub.

Copilot

Copilot is an AI-powered coding assistant that integrates directly into code editors and the GitHub platform, where it helps developers by suggesting code snippets, entire functions, and even complex algorithms in real time based on natural language comments and the context of the code being written, thereby accelerating development, reducing repetitive tasks, and enhancing productivity across a wide range of programming languages and frameworks.

Advanced security

Advanced security provides tools to help developers secure their code. It includes features such as code scanning, secret scanning, and dependency review.

Packages

Packages provide a way to publish and manage software packages on GitHub. They support multiple package managers and can be used with public or private repos.

Codespaces

Codespaces is a cloud-based development environment that allows developers to code from any device with pre-configured, secure environments native to GitHub. It provides instant access to a fully configured development environment, reducing setup time and ensuring consistency across different machines. Developers can customize their Codespaces with specific tools, languages, and configurations, making it easier to collaborate and maintain a consistent workflow.

Certification tip

You may be presented with a scenario and be asked to choose which GitHub product you need to use. For example, a customer raised a bug about your application, and you would like to analyze the bug to triage it. Where will you find the current bugs already submitted against your repo?

Important

There is a stark difference between a Git repository and a GitHub repository. A GitHub repository will contain a Git repo, issues, pull requests, discussions, linked projects, Actions workflow runs, build packages, as well as other artifacts scoped to a GitHub repository but not stored in Git.

The following screenshot shows the horizontal menu of GitHub product features available to a repository. Clicking each one will take you to the related items scoped to that GitHub repository. **Note** that some items may be missing in your own horizontal menu (e.g. **Discussions**) compared to the following screenshot. This may be due to some features that are turned off by default in the **General** settings of the GitHub repository or due to the level of permissions you have:

<> Code   ⊙ Issues 319   ⌁ Pull requests   ⊡ Discussions   ▷ Actions   ⊞ Projects 7   ⊘ Security 2   ⋌ Insights

Figure 2.12: A cross-section of GitHub products featured as horizontal tabs in a GitHub repo

Let's look at some other GitHub tools – products that complement the core features above.

Other GitHub tools and features

Now that we have a solid understanding of the GitHub interface and its various features, let's delve sideways and look at other GitHub tools that complement how you work on GitHub in your software development lifecycle.

GitHub Desktop

GitHub Desktop is a thick client (a **thick client** is a type of software that runs on a user's computer or device) that simplifies the process of managing Git repositories on your local machine. It provides a user-friendly interface for performing common Git operations such as cloning repositories, creating branches, making commits, and handling pull requests. This way, you do not have to remember Git commands and syntaxes, as most of the tasks can be performed by clicking buttons. GitHub Desktop seamlessly integrates with GitHub.com, allowing users to synchronize their local changes with remote repositories, review code changes, and collaborate with other developers more effectively. Additionally, it offers visual diff tools to compare changes and resolve merge conflicts, making it easier for users to understand the modifications in their codebase.

GitHub Mobile

GitHub Mobile is an app designed to bring the core functionalities of GitHub to mobile devices, enabling developers to manage their projects on the go. It allows users to triage notifications, review and merge pull requests, and browse repositories all from their smartphones or tablets. GitHub Mobile provides a seamless experience for collaborating with team members, enabling code discussions, and keeping up with project activities without the need for a desktop environment. The app offers a responsive and intuitive interface, ensuring that developers can maintain productivity and stay connected with their projects anytime, anywhere.

GitHub CLI

GitHub CLI (gh) is a powerful command-line tool designed to seamlessly integrate GitHub features into your terminal. It allows developers to manage repositories, issues, pull requests, releases, and more without leaving the command line. This integration streamlines workflows by providing a consistent and efficient interface for interacting with GitHub.

With GitHub CLI, you can clone repositories, create and manage pull requests, view and comment on issues, and even manage workflows and actions, all with simple commands. The tool is designed to work alongside Git, enhancing its capabilities by adding GitHub-specific functionality. This makes it easier to perform common tasks such as creating pull requests or checking the status of issues directly from the terminal. You begin every command with gh followed by the function you want to perform – for example, `gh pr create`.

Installation and usage of GitHub CLI are straightforward, with support for macOS, Linux, and Windows. The tool is highly customizable, allowing users to configure aliases and shortcuts for frequently used commands. Overall, GitHub CLI is an essential productivity tool for developers who prefer to work in the terminal and want to streamline their GitHub workflows.

GitHub Marketplace

The **GitHub Marketplace** is a platform where developers can discover, purchase, and integrate various tools and applications to enhance their workflows on GitHub. It offers a wide range of tools, including those for continuous integration, project management, code review, generative AI development, and product extensions that help enhance existing functionalities.

Here are some key features of the GitHub Marketplace:

- **Variety of tools**: You can find both free and paid tools that cater to different aspects of the development process
- **Seamless integration**: Tools available on the marketplace can be easily integrated into your GitHub projects without the need for multiple accounts or payment methods
- **Categories**: The tools are categorized to help you find exactly what you need, such as testing, documentation, feature management, performance optimization, and Generative AI

If you're a developer looking to streamline your workflow or add new functionalities to your projects, the GitHub Marketplace is a great place to explore!

> **Certification tip**
>
> You will likely come across 2-3 questions about GitHub Desktop and the GitHub Marketplace. Be sure to get familiar with their purpose and their general interfaces.

Summary

In this chapter, we navigated the GitHub interface, exploring its features and functionalities. We started by understanding the technical requirements, such as needing a GitHub account, which can be created for free. GitHub is a powerful platform that has revolutionized the way developers work, making it easier to collaborate, share code, and manage projects. With over 100 million developers, it is the largest developer ecosystem.

GitHub is a hosting platform for Git repositories, providing multiple interfaces and capabilities for collaboration. It supports both cloud-based and self-hosted deployments. Unlike Git, which operates locally, GitHub centralizes repository hosting, user management, and collaboration features, reducing the risk of single points of failure.

We also explored the differences between Git and GitHub, highlighting GitHub's advantages in redundancy, collaboration, project management, and tool integration. GitHub's core functionalities include collaboration, productivity, security, scale, and AI. GitHub Copilot, powered by OpenAI, enhances these functionalities by providing code assistance and automation.

GitHub offers various plans and account types to cater to different needs, from individual developers to large enterprises. The plans include GitHub Free, GitHub Pro, GitHub Team, and GitHub Enterprise, each offering different features and support levels.

We finally looked at the various GitHub products, features, and tools that add more functionality to Git and aid collaboration while building software.

In *Chapter 3*, we will dive deeper into the creation and management of repositories. We will look at the various ways in which to interact with Git repos, some good practices for enabling collaboration securely, and take a quick peek at the **GitHub Flavored Markdown** style.

Before we move on to *Chapter 3*, let's do a quick test of your knowledge.

Test your knowledge

1. A Git repository contains which of the following? (Select one):

    a. Issues

    b. Pull requests

    c. .gitignore

    d. Projects

2. Which of the following can own a repository on GitHub? (Select two):

    a. Individual

    b. Enterprise

    c. Organization

    d. Team

3. You have just joined an online fashion store company as a web developer and your new manager has asked you to run `gh issue create -t "New Employee" -a "@onboarding-bot"` to begin your onboarding process. On which of the following tools/products will you run this?

    a. GitHub Desktop

    b. Git

    c. GitHub CLI

    d. GitHub Projects

Useful links

- Creating an account on GitHub: `https://docs.github.com/en/get-started/start-your-journey/creating-an-account-on-github`

- GitHub Features: `https://github.com/features`

- GitHub CLI Reference Manual: `https://cli.github.com/manual/gh`

- Developers get by with a little help from AI: Stack Overflow Knows code assistant pulse survey results: `https://stackoverflow.blog/2024/05/29/developers-get-by-with-a-little-help-from-ai-stack-overflow-knows-code-assistant-pulse-survey-results/`

3

Repository Creation and Management

Chapter 3 covers essential topics such as creating a new repository, understanding repository settings, managing collaboration and permissions, cloning repos using VS Code, and making the first commit by adding a README.md file. Additionally, it introduces the Markdown language and its GitHub-specific variant, **GitHub Flavored Markdown (GFM)**, explaining how to format text, create lists, add emphasis, blockquotes, code, links, and images. Then, we will talk about security and access control, webhooks and GitHub Apps, and using GitHub insights to monitor repository activity and health.

We will cover the following main topics:

- Creating a new repository
- Lab 3.1 – Creating a blank repository
- The markdown language and the GitHub markdown
- Lab 3.2 – Enriching README Files with Markdown Syntax
- Repository settings and management
- Collaboration and permissions

Technical requirements

Before you begin, you will need the following for the lab exercises:

- A GitHub account (we created this in *Chapter 2*)

- A working computer

- An **Integrated Development Environment** (**IDE**) that is Git-compatible and that you are comfortable with. There are some popular IDEs that can be freely installed on your computer. You can consider installing **Visual Studio Code** (**VS Code**), a very commonly used lightweight editor. We will be using VS Code as the preferred option throughout this book. To install VS Code, visit `https://code.visualstudio.com`, download the one compatible with your computer and install it.

Creating a new repository

This section will guide you through the process of creating a new repository on GitHub, emphasizing the importance of initial setup for long-term project success.

A **git repository**, often referred to as a **repo**, is a central location where all the files for a particular project are stored. It tracks all changes made to these files, allowing multiple people to collaborate on the project. It serves as a centralized hub where all project files, including code, documentation, and other resources, are stored. Repositories enable version control, allowing you to track changes, revert to previous states, and collaborate with others seamlessly. Understanding the structure and purpose of a repository is essential for effective project management and collaboration.

When creating a new repo, there are some good practices to consider. Let us discuss them one by one.

Repository naming conventions

Choosing the right name for your repository is crucial for clarity and discoverability. Here are some best practices for naming your repositories:

- **Be descriptive:** Use a name that clearly describes the project's purpose or functionality.

- **Keep it short:** Aim for a concise name that is easy to remember and type.

- **Use hyphens:** Separate words with hyphens (e.g., my-awesome-project) for readability.

- **Avoid special characters:** Stick to alphanumeric characters and hyphens to avoid issues with URLs and command-line tools.

- **Consistency**: Follow a consistent naming convention across all your repositories to maintain organization.

Initializing with README and .gitignore

Initializing your repository with a README and .gitignore file is a good practice that sets the stage for a well-organized project:

- README: The README file is the first thing visitors see when they visit your repository. It should provide an overview of your project, including its purpose, how to install and use it, and any other relevant information. A well-written README helps others understand and contribute to your project.

- .gitignore: The .gitignore file specifies which files and directories Git should ignore. This is useful for excluding files that are not relevant to the project, such as temporary files, build artifacts, and sensitive information. By keeping your repository clean, you ensure that only necessary files are tracked and shared.

Choosing a license

Choosing a license for your repository is an important decision that determines how others can use, modify, and distribute your project. Here are some common licenses and their implications:

- **MIT license**: A permissive license that allows others to use, modify, and distribute your project with minimal restrictions.

- **GNU General Public License (GPL)**: A copyleft license that ensures the software and any modifications to it remain free and open for everyone, meaning your work must be released under the same license.

- **Apache License 2.0**: A permissive license that includes a patent grant, providing additional protection for contributors.

- **Creative Commons Licenses**: Suitable for non-software projects, these licenses offer various levels of permissions and restrictions. Selecting the right license ensures that your project is used in a way that aligns with your intentions and legal requirements.

These practices are highly recommended for the long-term sustainability and maintainability of your source code.

> **Certification tip**
>
> You may be asked to identify which license allows modification and redistribution without disclosure. That would be the MIT license.

Let us go straight into practical and generate content in a new GitHub repository.

Lab 3.1 – Creating a blank repository

In this lab, we are going to create a repository without initializing a README or any content. You can follow along in the lab video *Chapter 3 Lab 3.1: Creating a Blank Repo* in the playlist https://www.youtube.com/playlist?list=PLuX8xLieCtTP3-AsobdFLmaqAcbBxJ39w.

Create a new GitHub repo

Let's create a new GitHub repo:

1. Ensure you are logged into your GitHub account.

2. Click the + icon in the top-right corner and select **New repository**.

3. Use my-blank-repo as the name for your repository in the **Repository name** field.

4. Add a brief **Description** of your project (optional but recommended).

5. Next, you are faced with two options in the field **Public** or **Private**. In this case, select **Private** (visible only to you and your collaborators).

6. This is important: Ensure you do *not* initialize your repository with a README file. That is, **Add a README file** must be *deselected*.

7. For the **Add .gitignore** field, select **None**. This is also important.

8.   For the **License** field, select **None**:

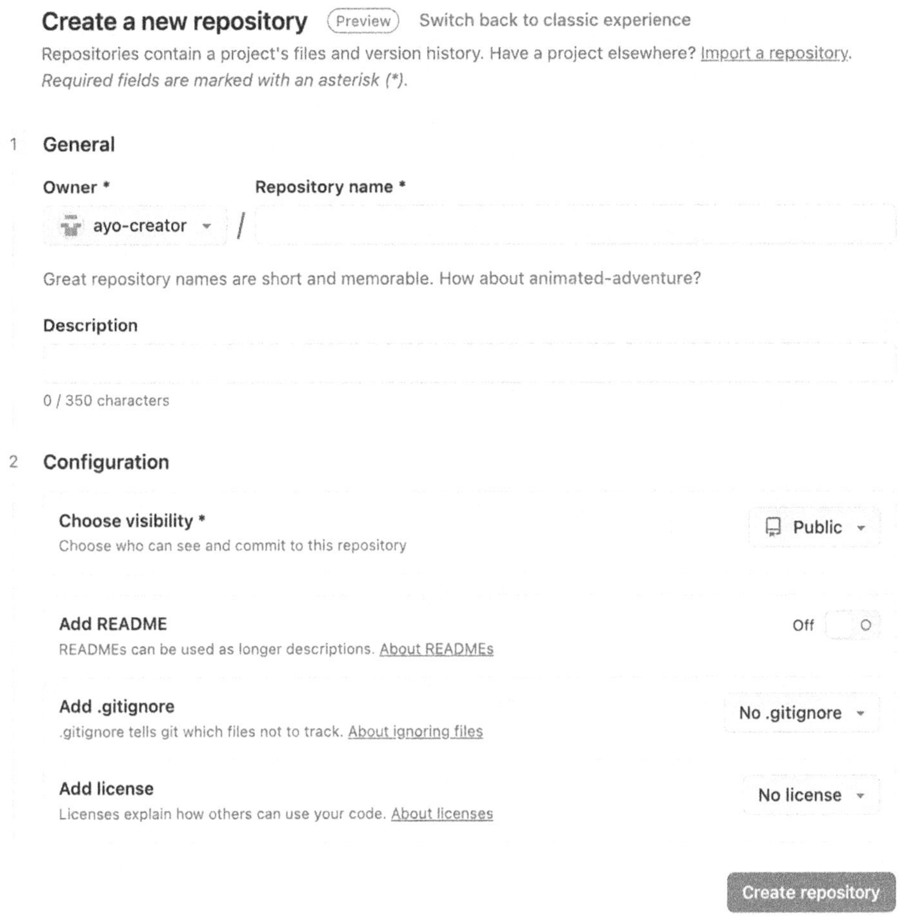

Create a new repository (Preview)   Switch back to classic experience

Repositories contain a project's files and version history. Have a project elsewhere? Import a repository.
Required fields are marked with an asterisk (*).

1   **General**

Owner *   **Repository name ***

ayo-creator ▾   /

Great repository names are short and memorable. How about animated-adventure?

Description

0 / 350 characters

2   **Configuration**

Choose visibility *   🖵 Public ▾
Choose who can see and commit to this repository

Add README   Off   ○
READMEs can be used as longer descriptions. About READMEs

Add .gitignore   No .gitignore ▾
.gitignore tells git which files not to track. About ignoring files

Add license   No license ▾
Licenses explain how others can use your code. About licenses

Create repository

Figure 3.1: Repository creation form, leaving README, .gitignore and License options blank

9. Click the **Create repository** button to finalize the process.

    Your newly created repository would look like the following figure:

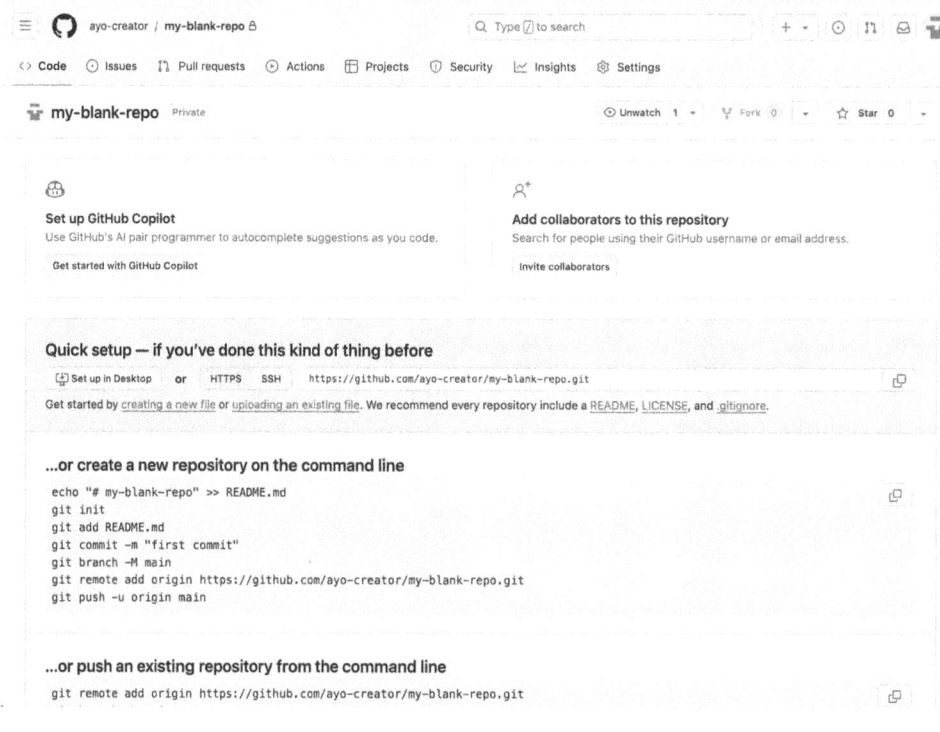

Figure 3.2: A blank repo will show quick setup instructions

🔍 **Quick tip:** Need to see a high-resolution version of this image? Open this book in the next-gen Packt Reader or view it in the PDF/ePub copy.

📖 **The next-gen Packt Reader** and a **free PDF/ePub copy** of this book are included with your purchase. Scan the QR code OR visit `packtpub.com/unlock`, then use the search bar to find this book by name. Double-check the edition shown to make sure you get the right one.

If you haven't initialized any files in a repo, you will be presented with quick setup instructions on how to create a local Git repo (Git repo stored locally on your computer) or push an existing one. Leave this page open on your browser as we will come back to it. Within the **Quick setup — if you've done this kind of thing before** box, copy the HTTPS URL so that you have it handy on your clipboard for future use.

Let us now connect with an IDE.

Sign in to GitHub on VS Code and Clone Git Repository

Cloning a Git repository means creating a local copy of a remote repository (e.g. from GitHub). See *Figure 1.4* in *Chapter 1* for a diagram that explains cloning.

Let us clone this blank repo we just created on GitHub (remote) to our local machine. You can follow along this lab exercise with the corresponding video – *Chapter 3 Lab 3.1: Creating a Blank Repo*:

1. Launch VS Code from your computer.

2. Select **Clone Git repository…**

   This will pop up the search bar/command palette at the top-center of your window asking for the URL to the repo you would like to clone.

3. You can paste the URL copied in *step 9* in the previous subsection and press *Enter*. This would launch an authentication screen on your browser. Alternatively, click on **Clone from GitHub.**

4. The difference between these two options is that the latter will automatically integrate your IDE (VS Code) to your GitHub account such that you can directly see a list of all your repos from VS Code. This has the benefit of you not needing to remember the URL or avoid typo errors since you are just selecting from a list:

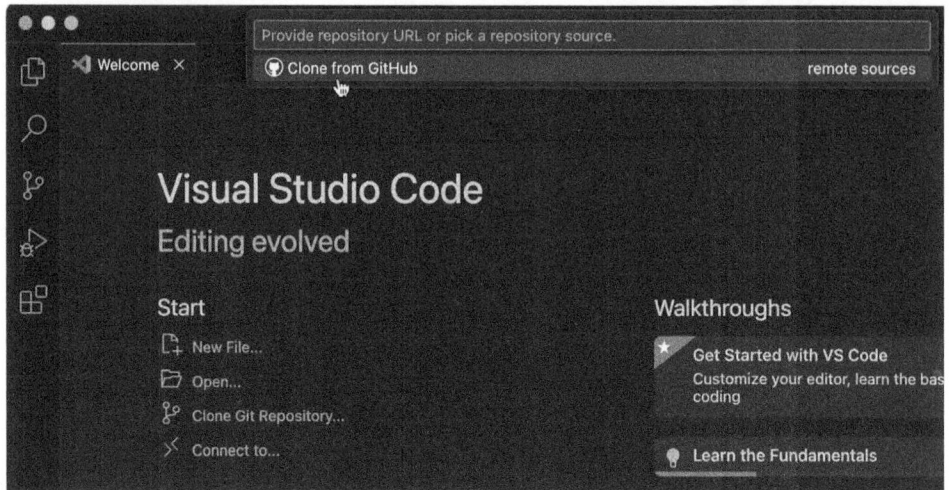

Figure 3.3: Cloning from GitHub helps to pick from listed GitHub repos

5. This will ask if you want to allow the GitHub extension to sign in to GitHub. Select **Allow**. A new browser window will launch for you to authorize the extension.

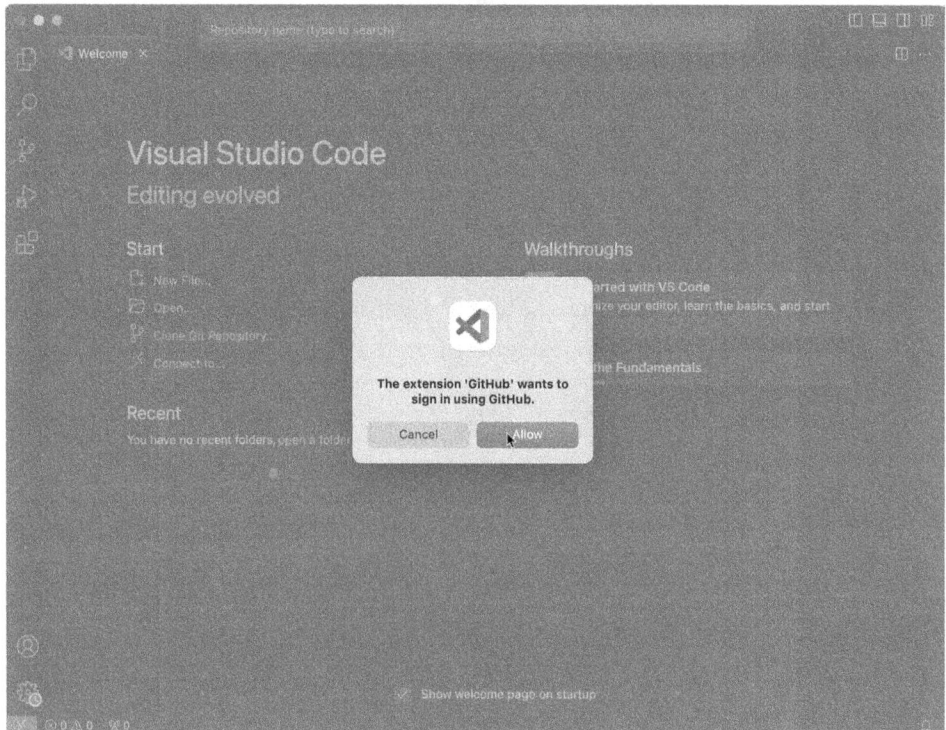

Figure 3.4: Allow GitHub authentication to launch

6. For VS Code extension to integrate seamlessly with your GitHub account, it will need some of your profile information and repository metadata, which you must give consent to by authorizing it. Select **Authorize Visual-Studio-Code**:

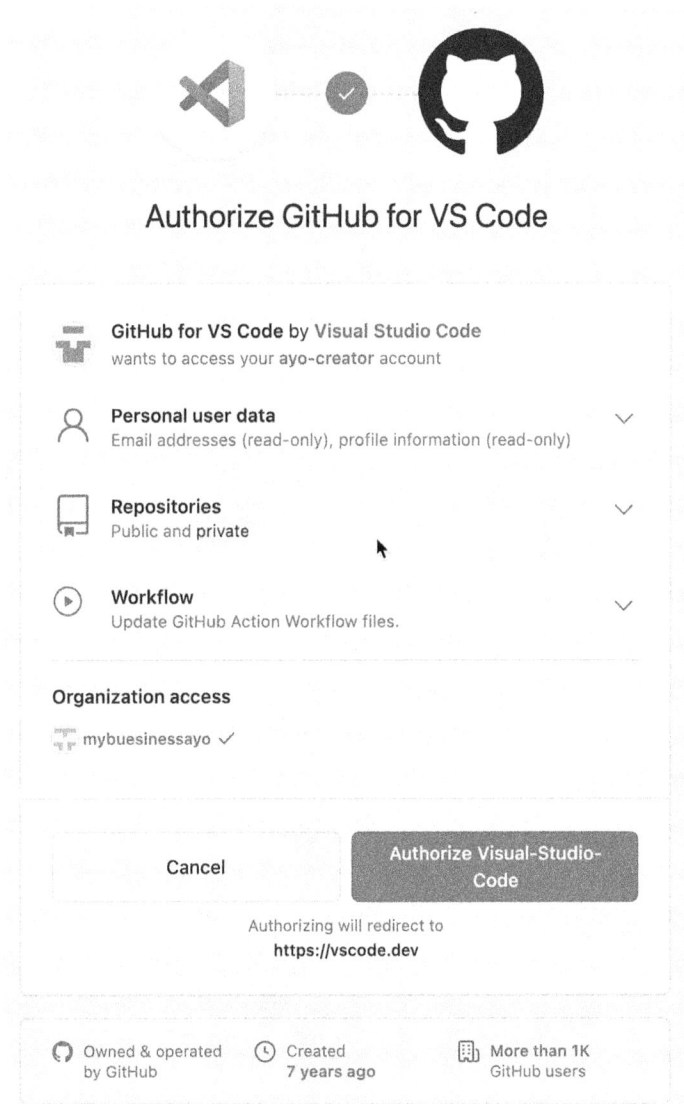

Figure 3.5: Authorize the GitHub app to access basic user info and repo details

7. If the authorization was successful, it will ask you to return to VS Code. Click **Open Visual Studio Code**:

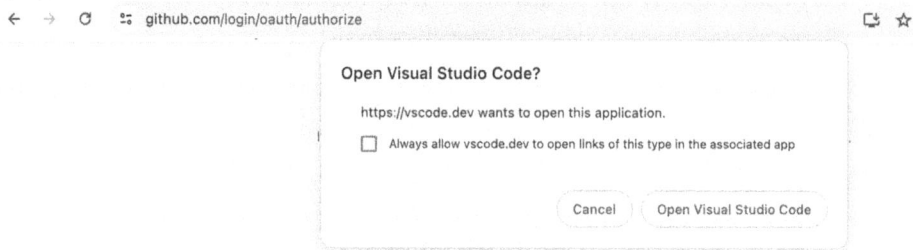

Figure 3.6: Open VS Code once authorization is successful

You will now be able to see a list of all the repos you have on GitHub displayed in VS Code.

Select **my-blank-repo** from the list:

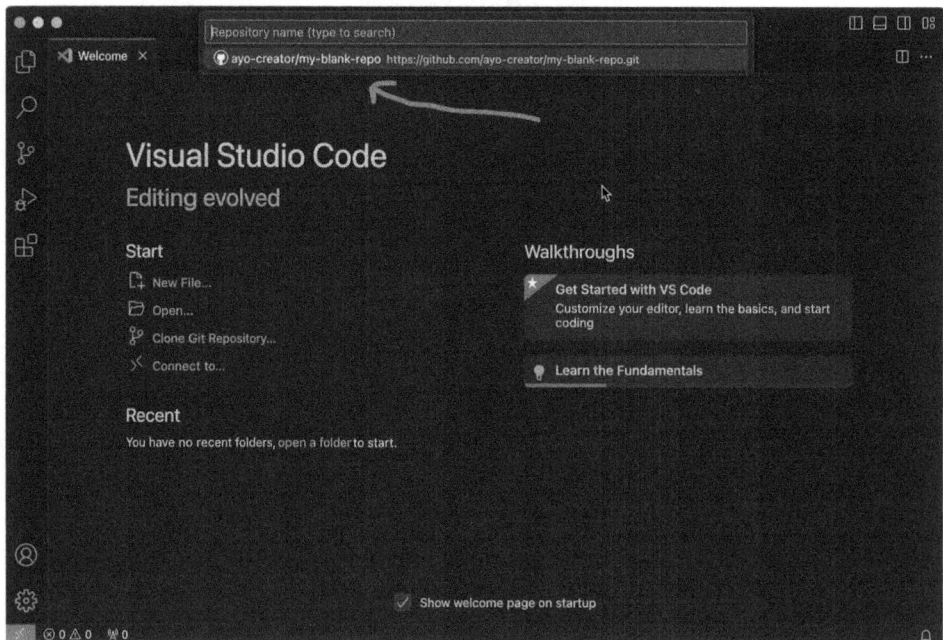

Figure 3.7: GitHub is integrated to VS Code and access to repository list is seamless going forward

8. Navigate to your desired location to store the cloned repo locally and click on **Select as repository destination**. VS Code will then download the files from the remote Git repo on GitHub to the destination you selected locally in a corresponding folder named after the repo.

9. Once the download is completed, VS Code will prompt you to open the cloned repo. Select **Open** or **Open in New Window**.

You are now ready to work! If you are new to the VS Code interface, you can learn more about the interface at `https://code.visualstudio.com/docs/getstarted/userinterface`.

Commit changes into Git

Now let us make some changes and commit the changes to Git:

1. As this is an empty repo, let us start by adding a `README` file. Create a new file by clicking on the **New File...** icon on the primary side bar on the left:

Figure 3.8: The New File... icon

2. Type `README.md` as the name of the file.

3. In the new file in the code editor, type some text as a description of the repo. A few lines should be fine. Save the file by pressing *Cmd + S* or *Ctrl + S*.

4. Click on the **Source Control** icon from the activity bar on the left. Then, from the primary side bar, click the + icon next to the file (**README.md**).

5. This will stage the file, ready for a Git commit:

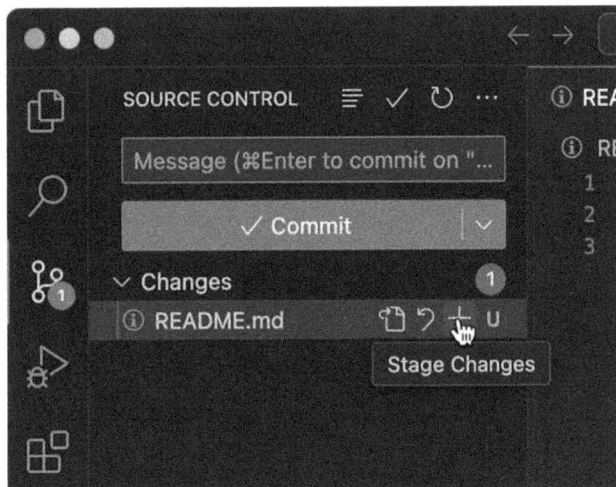

Figure 3.9: Stage changes to git

6. Type the commit message into the text box above it and select **Commit**.

7. Then, publish your changes by selecting **Publish Branch** or synchronizing changes by clicking on the refresh icon in the bottom-left corner of the status bar:

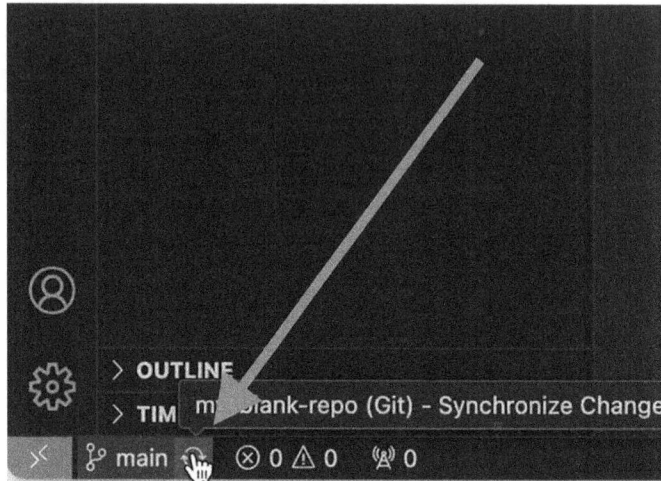

Figure 3.10: The synchronize icon helps to keep the remote repo and local repo in sync

8. Go back to the browser tab of the repo that you left open earlier. Refresh the page. You will see the changes you made to your local repo reflect in the GitHub repo:

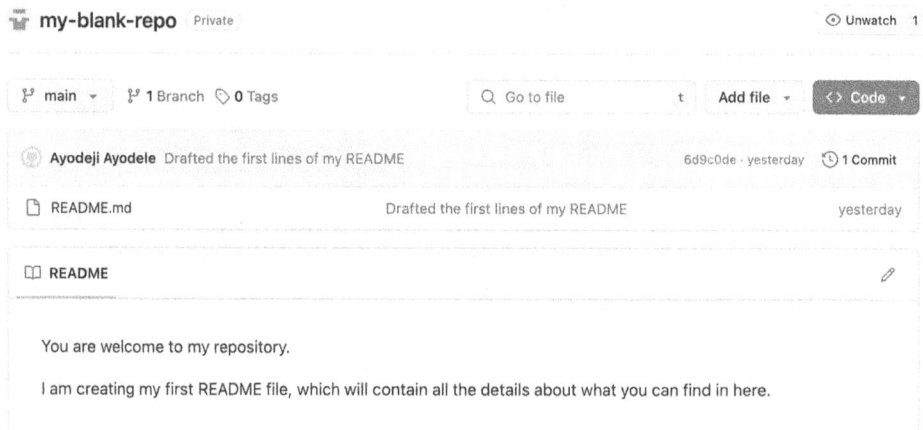

Figure 3.11: GitHub repo reflecting new changes

Great job! So far, you have been able to:

1. Create a GitHub repository,

2. Clone that repository to a local machine,

3. Make changes to it by adding a `README` file,

4. Commit the changes to the repo, and

5. Synchronize the changes in the local repo with the remote repo

Now let us talk more about the `README` file. The `README` file is usually saved with the file extension `.md`, which is for markdown files. This means the file is saved as `README.md`. Markdown files are written in a special format known as the **Markdown** language.

In the next section, we will discuss the universal Markdown language, its syntax, and the specific variance for GitHub named the **GitHub Flavored Markdown (GFM)**.

The markdown language and the GitHub markdown

Markdown is a simple and easy-to-read markup language designed to format plain text and is widely used for writing software documentation, `README` files, and blog posts because of its simplicity and readability. It allows you to create well-structured documents using plain text syntax that is easy to read and write. By learning Markdown, you can create clean and professional-looking documents without needing to learn complex formatting languages.

GFM

GFM is an extension of the standard Markdown language, tailored specifically for use on GitHub. GFM includes additional features that enhance the functionality and presentation of Markdown documents on GitHub. These features include support for tables, task lists, strikethrough text, and automatic linking of URLs. Understanding GFM allows you to take full advantage of GitHub's capabilities for creating rich and interactive documentation.

Formatting text

Let us cover the basics of formatting text using Markdown, including headings, lists, emphasis, and more.

Formatting text in Markdown is straightforward and intuitive. Here are some common formatting options:

Headings

Use # for headings. The number of # symbols indicates the heading level (e.g., # is Heading 1, ## is Heading 2). See the following example:

```
# This is my biggest heading
## This is my next biggest heading
### This is my not-too-big heading
#### Well, quite a heading
```

The resulting view would be as follows:

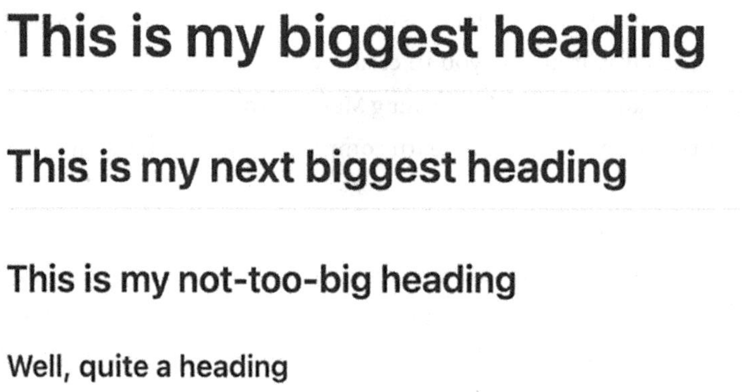

This is my biggest heading

This is my next biggest heading

This is my not-too-big heading

Well, quite a heading

Figure 3.12: View of the headings

Lists

Create unordered lists with - or *, and ordered lists with numbers (e.g., 1., 2.). Here's an example:

```
Here is a numbered list of fruits:
1. Orange
2. Apple
3. Grapes


and, here is an unordered list of veggies:
- Broccoli
- Spinach
```

The resulting view would be as follows:

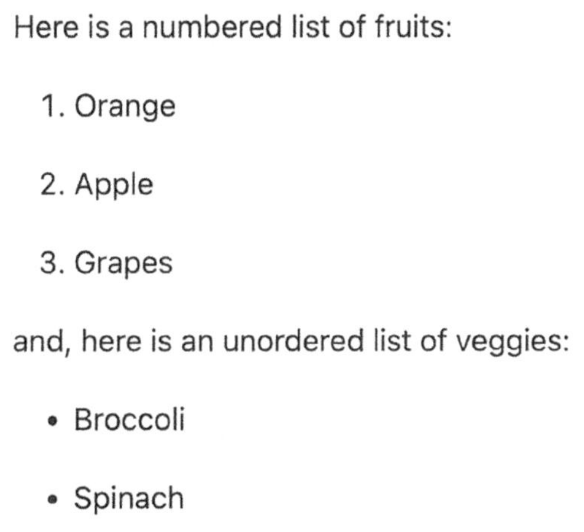

Here is a numbered list of fruits:

1. Orange

2. Apple

3. Grapes

and, here is an unordered list of veggies:

- Broccoli

- Spinach

Figure 3.13: View of the lists

Emphasis and blockquotes

For emphasis, use * or _ for italic text (e.g., *italic*), and ** or __ for bold text (e.g., **bold**).

For blockquotes, use > to create blockquotes (e.g., > This is a blockquote). Let's use them in an example:

```
We have to be **strong** and help those that are _not as strong_.


> The best way to find yourself is to lose yourself in the service of
others.
```

The resulting view would be as follows:

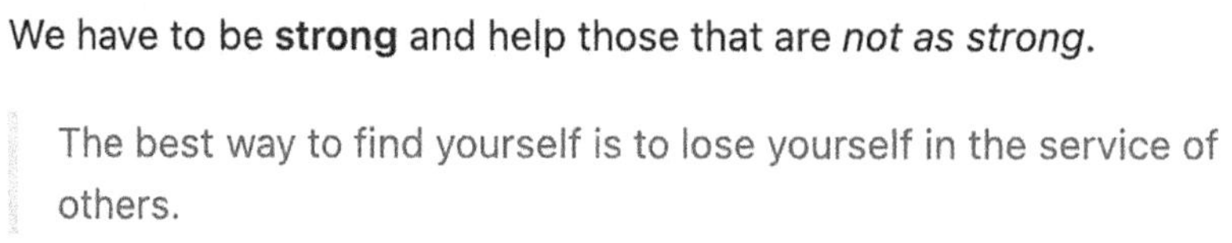

> We have to be **strong** and help those that are *not as strong*.
>
>> The best way to find yourself is to lose yourself in the service of others.

Figure 3.14: View of the emphasis and blockquotes

Code

Use backticks (`` ` ``) for inline code (e.g., `` `code` ``) and triple backticks for code blocks (e.g., ```` ``` ````):

```
Compiled languages can be transformed into machine code. Languages such as
`C, C++ and Java` are great examples.


```

```
public class HelloWorld {
    // This program prints "Hello, World!" to the console
    public static void main(String[] args) {
        System.out.println("Hello, World!");
    }
}
```

```java
// This example shows syntax highlighting, which uses color and style of
source code to make it easier to read.
public class HelloWorld {
    // This program prints "Hello, World!" to the console
    public static void main(String[] args) {
        System.out.println("Hello, World!");
    }
}
```

> ♀ **Quick tip**: Enhance your coding experience with the **AI Code Explainer** and **Quick Copy** features. Open this book in the next-gen Packt Reader. Click the **Copy** button (**1**) to quickly copy code into your coding environment, or click the **Explain** button (**2**) to get the AI assistant to explain a block of code to you.

```
                                                      Copy      Explain
function calculate(a, b) {
    return {sum: a + b};                               1          2
};
```

> 🔒 **The next-gen Packt Reader** is included for free with the purchase of this book. Scan the QR code OR go to packtpub.com/unlock, then use the search bar to find this book by name. Double-check the edition shown to make sure you get the right one.

The resulting view would be as follows:

Compiled languages can be transformed into machine code. Languages such as C, C++ and Java are great examples.

```
public class HelloWorld {
    // This program prints "Hello, World!" to the console
    public static void main(String[] args) {
        System.out.println("Hello, World!");
    }
}
```

```
// This example shows syntax highlighting, which uses color and style of source code to make it easier to read.
public class HelloWorld {
    // This program prints "Hello, World!" to the console
    public static void main(String[] args) {
        System.out.println("Hello, World!");
    }
}
```

Figure 3.15: View of the code

Creating links and images

Let's talk about how to add links and images to your Markdown files, enhancing the interactivity and visual appeal of your documents. Adding links and images in Markdown is simple and enhances the usability of your documents:

- **Links**: Use `[text](link)` to create a hyperlink (e.g., `[GitHub](https://www.github.com)`). This can also be a relative URL pointing to a location within the files in the repo, e.g., `docs/setup-instructions.md`.

- **Section links**: Use `#heading-text-without-spaces` to link directly to a section in the same file. You can usually get this by hovering over the section heading and copy the link address, e.g., `#Chapter-1`.

- **Images**: Use `![alt text](image-link)` to embed an image. (e.g., `![GitHub Octocat]`
`(https://myoctocat.com/assets/images/base-octocat.svg)`). By incorporating links and images, you can provide additional context and visual elements to your documentation, making it more engaging and informative.

Tables

What about how to create tables, useful for organizing data? Markdown supports the creation of tables, which are essential for organizing information and displaying code. Use pipes | and hyphens - to create tables. For example:

```
| Header 1 | Header 2 |
|----------|----------|
| Row 1    | Data 1   |
| Row 2    | Data 2   |
```

The first line indicates the column headers while the second is more of an underline indicating the beginning of the data rows. Tables help in organizing data neatly.

Advanced markdown features

Markdown includes several advanced features that enhance the functionality and interactivity of your documents:

- **Task lists**: Use `- [ ]` for unchecked tasks and `- [x]` for checked tasks:

    ```
    - [ ] Task 1
    - [x] Task 2
    ```

- **Mentions**: Use @username to mention a GitHub user, which notifies them of the mention.

- **Emojis**: Use :emoji_name: to add emojis (e.g., :smile: for 😊). GitHub supports a wide range of emojis that can be used to add a touch of fun to your documents. These advanced features make your Markdown documents more interactive and engaging, fostering better collaboration and communication.

Visit https://docs.github.com/en/get-started/writing-on-github/getting-started-with-writing-and-formatting-on-github/basic-writing-and-formatting-syntax to learn more about the GFM and syntax.

> **Certification tip**
>
> You will encounter several questions about markdown, Spend some time to practise the following lab, and try out various output formats.

Let us try these out shortly in a lab exercise!

Lab 3.2 – Enriching README Files with Markdown Syntax

In this lab exercise, we will modify the README.md file that we created in *Lab 3.1* in this chapter. We will also showcase how to make changes to files in a repo without the IDE or CLI (Terminal or Command Prompt). Remember, every change is a commit and this change is no exception:

1. Open up the **my-blank-repo** repo on GitHub (you may still have this open already from the previous lab exercise).

2. On the right-hand of the home page (**README**), click on the pencil icon to edit the file. This will take you to the edit mode of the markdown file:

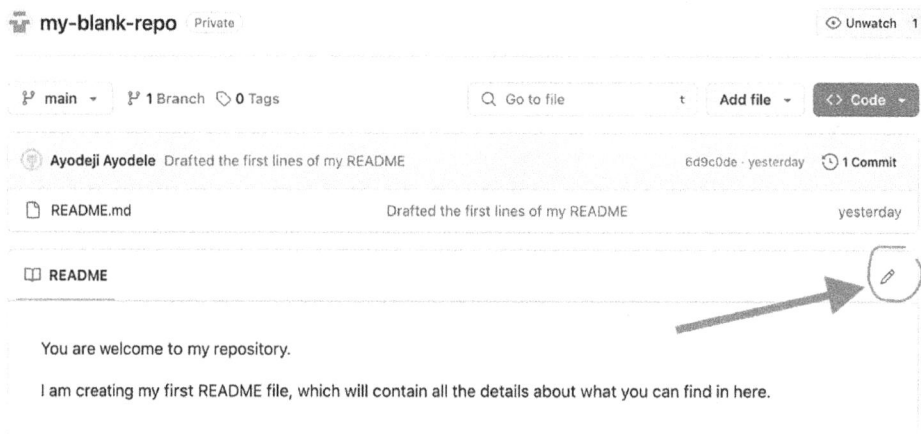

Figure 3.16: You can edit the README.md directly from the home page

3. Copy the following text, and append or replace the existing content:

```
# The Blank Repo
Welcome to the blank repo.

## A Tale of Markdown


In a **blank repo**, so pristine and clear,
No code to run, no bugs to fear.
Just a canvas, waiting to be filled,
With dreams and code, and skills instilled.
```

Links to Dreams

[Visit GitHub](https://github.com) to start your quest,
Where coders gather, and ideas manifest.
A hyperlink to worlds unknown,
Where every coder finds their own.

Images of Hope

![GitHub Logo](https://github.githubassets.com/images/modules/logos_
page/GitHub-Mark.png)
An image speaks a thousand lines,
In Markdown, it perfectly aligns.

Codeblocks of Creation

```python
def hello_world():
    print(&quot;Hello, World!&quot;)
```

In codeblocks, our dreams take flight,
With every line, we chase the light.

Tables of Structure

Feature	Status
Ideas	Pending
Code	In Progress
Success	Achieved

In tables, we find our way,
Organizing thoughts, come what may.

The End

```
So here's to the repo, blank and pure,
A place where dreams and code endure.
With Markdown styles, we pave the way,
For a brighter, coded day.
```

4. Select the green button, **Commit changes...**, on the top-right side of the page.

5. Modify the commit message to: **Enrich my README with markdown**.

    Optionally, you can add more text into the larger box.

6. Select the option **Commit directly to the main branch** and click on **Commit changes**:

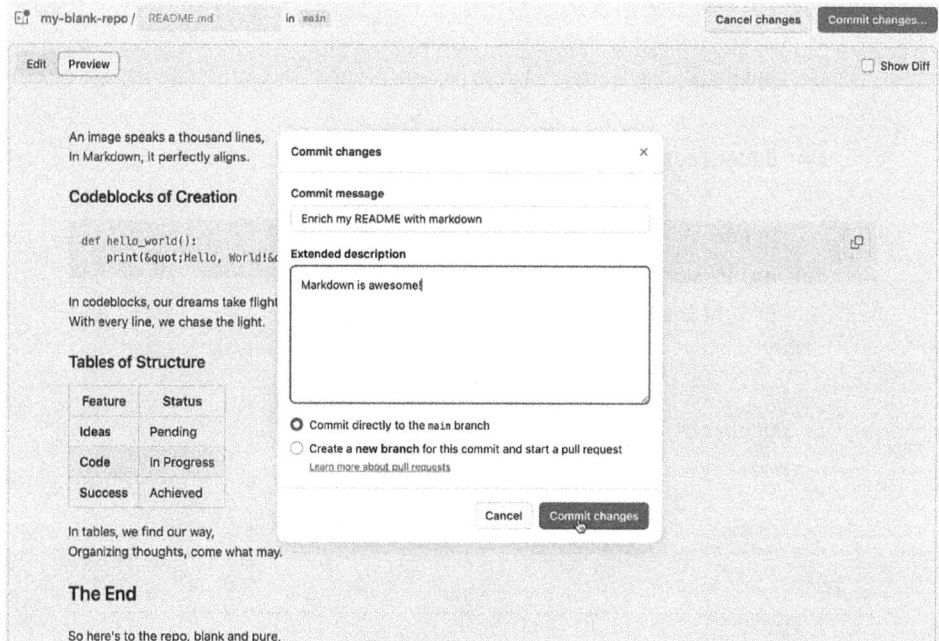

Figure 3.17: Commit changes made to the repository with a commit message

Perfect! You have just learned Markdown 101. Congratulations! 🎉

Your **my-blank-repo** should look like the following image, better styled and beautiful:

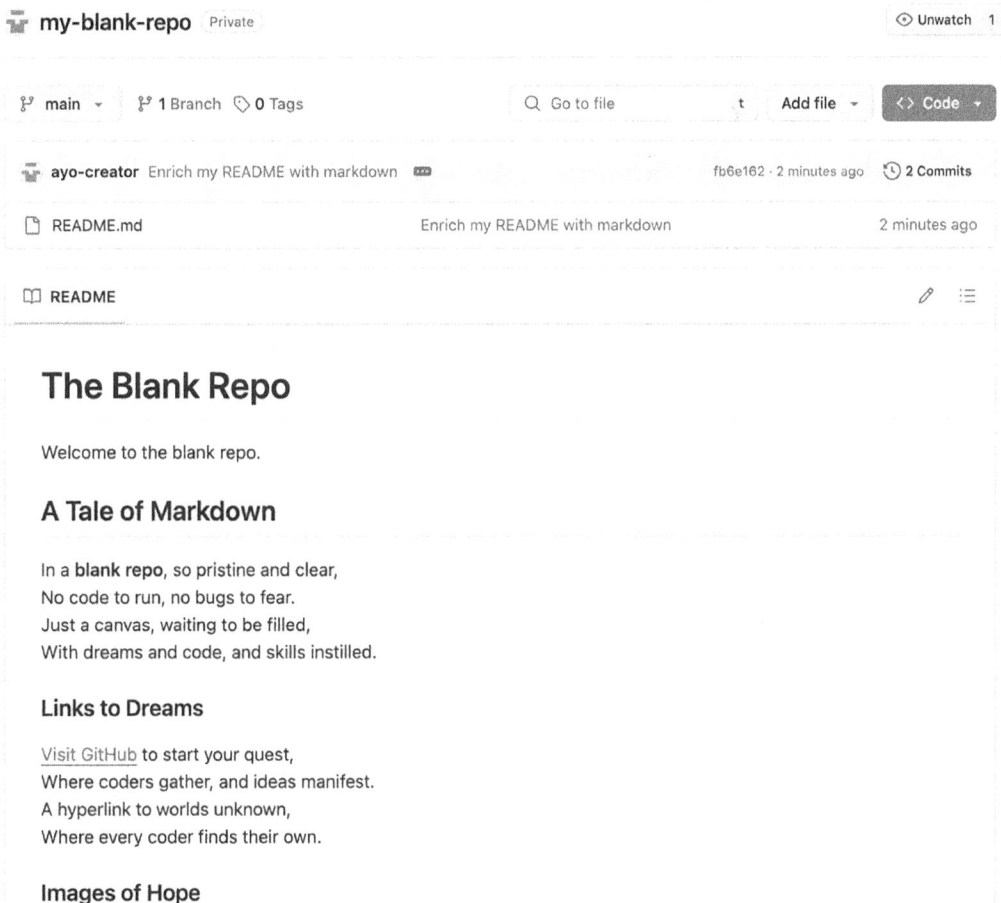

Figure 3.18: Final view of the README markdown on the repo landing page

We've dealt well with the basics of creating a repo, making changes to files and formatting documents with markdown. In the next section, we will talk about some fundamentals of repository management on GitHub.

Repository settings and management

This section provides an overview of the repository settings page on GitHub, highlighting the various options available for managing your repository.

The repository settings page on GitHub is where you can configure various aspects of your repository. To access the settings, navigate to your repository and click on the **Settings** tab. Here, you can manage general settings, branches, webhooks, integrations, and more. Understanding these settings is crucial for maintaining a well-organized and secure repository. Key areas include repository details, access control, and advanced settings.

Some things to consider when managing a repo include:

Branch management

This section covers how to create, delete, and manage branches within a repository, enabling effective version control and collaboration.

Branches are an essential feature of GitHub that allow you to work on different versions of a project simultaneously. Here's how to manage branches:

- **Creating a branch**: To create a new branch, go to the repository's main page, click the **branch** dropdown (*main is currently selected in the image below*), type a new branch name, and press *Enter*:

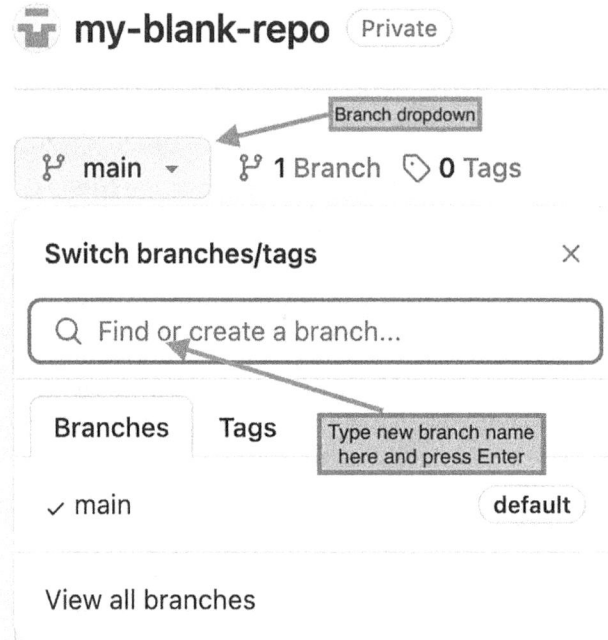

Figure 3.19: Creating a new branch using the search box

- **Switching branches**: Use the branch dropdown to switch between branches.
- **Deleting a branch**: To delete a branch, click on **Branches** next to the branch dropdown, find the branch you want to delete, and click the delete icon 🗑 next to it.
- **Merging branches**: To merge changes from one branch to another, create a pull request and merge it after review. Effective branch management allows multiple collaborators to work on different features or fixes without interfering with each other's work.

Managing issues and pull requests

Up next are issues and **pull requests (PRs)**, vital tools for smooth collaboration on GitHub:

- **Issues**: Use issues to track bugs, enhancements, and other tasks. Create a new issue by clicking the **Issues** tab and then **New issue**. Assign labels, milestones, and assignees to organize and prioritize issues.
- **PRs**: PRs are used to propose changes to the repository. Create a PR by clicking the **Pull requests** tab and then **New pull request**. Review and discuss the changes before merging them into the main branch.
- **Best practices**: Clearly describe issues and PRs, use labels and milestones for organization, and conduct thorough code reviews to maintain code quality. Managing issues and PRs effectively ensures that your project stays on track and that contributions are reviewed and integrated smoothly.

> **Certification tip**
>
> Branch protection and collaborator access are common topics on the exam. Be sure you understand the difference between pushing directly vs. pull requests under a protected branch.

Security and access control

Now, we will explain how to set up security policies and manage access permissions to protect your repository and control who can contribute.

Managing who can access and contribute to your GitHub repository is essential for maintaining code integrity and project security. Here's how to set up access permissions and implement key security measures:

Access permissions

To manage access:

1. Navigate to your repository on GitHub.

2. Click **Settings | Collaborators** under the **Access** section.

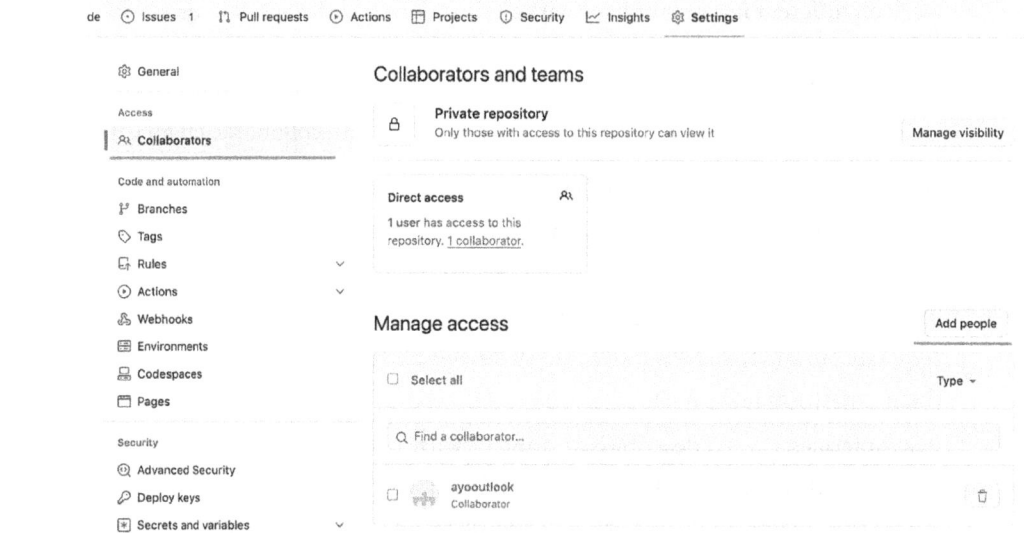

Figure 3.20: Add collaborators to the repository from the settings page

3. Click **Add people** to invite collaborators.

4. Type the GitHub handle and click on **Add <name>** to add them.

Newly added collaborators will receive an invitation by email. They will be able to collaborate on the repo once they accept the invitation.

> **Note**
>
> For personal repositories, you can invite collaborators directly. For more granular control, consider using an organization repository.

Security policies

There are two ways you might implement security policies:

- **Branch protection rules:** Prevent unauthorized changes by enforcing rules on key branches.

    a. Go to **Settings | Branches**.

    b. Click **Add branch ruleset** to configure protections like required reviews, status checks, or commit signing.

- **SECURITY.md:** Add a SECURITY.md file to your repository to guide users on how to report vulnerabilities responsibly. This file helps streamline the disclosure process and ensures timely responses from maintainers.

Automated security tools

There are also automatic security tools that you can set up to continually ensure the security of your code. Let's consider one of them.

Dependabot alerts: Enable Dependabot to automatically scan your dependencies for known vulnerabilities and suggest updates. To enable Dependabot, go to **Settings | Advanced Security**, and enable **Dependabot alerts** and **Dependable security updates**.

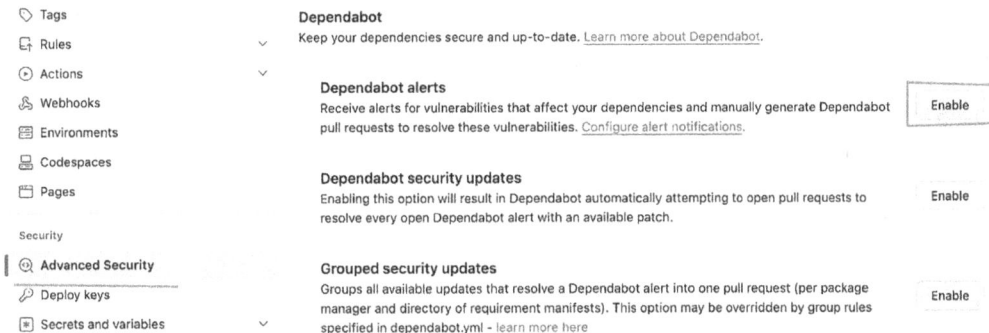

Figure 3.21: Enable Dependabot alerts from the repository settings

By combining access controls with proactive security practices, you can protect your repository from unauthorized changes and ensure a secure collaboration environment.

Webhooks and GitHub apps

This section covers what are webhooks and GitHub Apps that help integrate your repository with other tools and services to enhance functionality and automation.

Webhooks and integrations allow you to extend the functionality of your GitHub repository:

- **Webhooks**: Webhooks are automated messages sent from your repository to a specified URL when certain events occur (e.g., push, pull request). To set up a webhook, go to **Settings | Webhooks** and click **Add webhook**. Enter the payload URL and configure the events you want to trigger the webhook.

- **GitHub Apps:** GitHub Apps are integrations built on the GitHub platform that automate workflows, enhance development processes, and provide additional functionality directly within repositories. They can perform tasks like managing issues, automating code reviews, deploying code, or integrating with external services. GitHub Apps use fine-grained permissions and can act on behalf of a user or independently, making them ideal for both individual developers and organizations looking to streamline their DevOps pipelines. Navigate to **Settings | GitHub Apps** to see which GitHub Apps are currently installed in the repository. You can visit the GitHub Marketplace to search for integrations that suit your workflow and then install in your organization or repository. Using webhooks and GitHub App integrations, you can automate tasks, streamline workflows, and enhance collaboration.

Repository insights

This section explains how to use GitHub insights to monitor repository activity and health, providing valuable information for project management.

GitHub provides various insights and analytics tools to help you monitor the activity and health of your repository. All these options appear under the **Insights** tab of your horizontal menu:

- **Pulse**: The **Pulse** page gives an overview of recent activity, including commits, pull requests, and issues.

- **Code frequency**: The **Code frequency** section provides detailed analytics on code frequency, displaying code additions and deletions over a period of time Access it by clicking **Insights | Code frequency**.

- **Traffic**: The **Traffic** page shows data on repository views and clones, helping you understand how people are interacting with your project.

- **Contributors**: The **Contributors** page lists all contributors and their contributions, giving you insight into who is actively working on the project. By regularly reviewing these insights, you can make informed decisions about project management and identify areas for improvement.

Note

To use repository insights features, you need to make the repository public or at least a GitHub Pro subscription.

We have now discussed a few things that can help you configure and manage your repository as a unit. This can set you up before you can now invite team members to collaborate on its contents. There are a few more important things you should know if you want to scale such as managing multiple repositories at the organization level and the enterprise level. For now, we will look at what's next to learn at the repo level, collaboration.

Collaboration and permissions

This section will explore how to effectively collaborate with others on GitHub, including managing permissions and fostering a collaborative environment. These include practices for managing collaborators and teams, forking and pull requests, code reviews, managing conflicts in code, and collaborating on projects.

Collaborators and teams

Adding collaborators and managing team access are essential for effective collaboration on GitHub:

- **Adding collaborators**: We briefly discussed how to invite collaborators to a repository earlier in this chapter under the *Security and access control* section. There are additional ways you can unlock collaboration at the organization level. For example, GitHub has additional roles out of the box that allow you to separate the level of access people have. This will be discussed more in detail in later chapters.

- **Outside collaborators**: If you're working within a GitHub organization, you can grant repository access to individuals who are **not members of the organization** by adding them as outside collaborators. You can then choose the level of access to grant for each outside collaborator. Adding an outside collaborator to a private repository will use a paid license, unless you are on a free plan.

- **Managing teams**: If you are part of an organization, you can create teams to manage access more efficiently. Go to your organization's page, click **Teams**, and create a new team. Add members to the team and assign repository access levels. By organizing collaborators and teams, you can streamline collaboration and ensure that everyone has the appropriate level of access.

Forking and PRs

Forking and PRs are fundamental to open-source collaboration on GitHub. It enables contributors to propose changes and improvements:

- **Forking a repository**: Forking creates a personal copy of someone else's repository. To fork a repository, go to the repository page and click the **Fork** button. This creates a copy under your GitHub account, where you can make changes without affecting the original repository.

- **Creating PRs**: Once you've made changes in your forked repository, you can propose these changes to the original repository by creating a PR. Navigate to the **Pull requests** tab in the original repository and click **New pull request**. Select the branches to compare and describe your changes. Submit the PR for review. Forking and PRs enable you to contribute to projects while maintaining the integrity of the original codebase.

> **Certification tip**
>
> Spend some time in understanding the concept of forking a repo and in what scenarios do you need one. For example, you want to contribute changes to an open source repository. What will be the first step before you start making your code changes?

Code reviews

Code reviews are a critical part of the development process, helping to maintain code quality and share knowledge. Let's discuss some good practices for conducting code reviews, ensuring high-quality contributions and fostering a collaborative development process:

- **Reviewing code**: When a PR is submitted, reviewers should thoroughly examine the changes. Look for code quality, adherence to coding standards, and potential bugs. Use inline comments to provide feedback and suggest improvements.

- **Best practices**: Be constructive and respectful in your feedback. Focus on the code, not the person. Encourage open discussion and collaboration to resolve issues.

- **Approving and merging**: Once the code meets the required standards, approve the pull request and merge it into the main branch. Use GitHub's merge options to choose the appropriate merge strategy (e.g., *merge commit, squash and merge, rebase and merge*). We will dive deeper into branching and merging strategies in *Chapter 5*. Effective code reviews ensure that only high-quality code is integrated into the project, fostering a culture of continuous improvement.

Managing conflicts

You need strategies for resolving **merge conflicts**, which occur when changes from different branches conflict with each other. Merge conflicts can arise when changes from different branches overlap. Here's how to manage and resolve conflicts:

- **Identifying conflicts**: GitHub will notify you of conflicts when you attempt to merge branches. Conflicts must be resolved before the merge can proceed.

- **Resolving conflicts locally**: To resolve conflicts, clone the repository and switch to the branch with conflicts. Open the conflicting files and manually merge the changes. Look for conflict markers (e.g., <<<<<<<, =======, >>>>>>>) and decide which changes to keep.

- **Committing the resolution**: After resolving the conflicts, remove the conflict markers, save the files, and commit the changes. Push the resolved branch back to GitHub.

- **Using conflict resolution tools**: Many IDEs and Git tools offer conflict resolution features that simplify the process. By effectively managing conflicts, you can ensure a smooth and collaborative development process.

Project boards

You can use GitHub project boards for project management, helping teams organize tasks and track progress. GitHub project boards are a powerful tool for managing tasks and tracking progress:

- **Creating a project board**: Navigate to the repository's **Projects** tab and click **New project**. Choose a template (e.g., **Kanban, automated**) or create a custom board.

- **Adding and managing cards**: Create cards for tasks, issues, or pull requests. Drag and drop cards between columns to reflect their status (e.g., **To Do, In Progress, Done**).

- **Automation**: Use automation to move cards based on certain triggers (e.g., when a PR is merged, move the card to **Done**).

- **Collaboration**: Assign cards to team members, add labels, and set due dates to keep everyone on track. Project boards provide a visual overview of your project's progress, making it easier to manage tasks and collaborate effectively.

We have now considered a fair bit about creating and managing GitHub repositories. Wow, that was a brain workout! But don't worry, the best is yet to come. Let's recap what we've conquered so far.

Summary

In this chapter, we delve into the intricacies of GitHub, focusing on repository creation and management. We start by guiding you through the process of creating a new GitHub repository, emphasizing the importance of initial setup for long-term project success. We cover best practices for naming repositories, initializing with a README and .gitignore file, and choosing an appropriate license.

Next, we move on to practical exercises, where we create a blank repository, clone it to our local machine using VS Code, and make our first commit by adding a README.md file. We also explain how to synchronize changes between the local and remote repositories.

In the latter part of the chapter, we introduce the Markdown language and its GitHub-specific variant, GFM. We cover the basics of formatting text, creating lists, adding emphasis, blockquotes, code, links, and images. By mastering these skills, we can create well-structured and professional-looking documentation for our projects.

Overall, this chapter equips you with the knowledge and practical skills needed to effectively manage repositories on GitHub and create comprehensive documentation using Markdown. In *Chapter 4*, we will learn the git commands a bit more so that you can feel confident managing your changes through git and collaborating on source code with others integrating your changes with a remote codebase.

Test your knowledge

1. A developer on your team created a log file temporarily in their local repo. This log file is still important for local development, but they don't want to commit it to the repo. What can they do to keep the file saved without adding it to version control?

    a. Add //DO NOT COMMIT comment at the top of the file to warn other developers

    b. Cut and paste the file into another directory

    c. Add the log file's name to .gitignore

2. Which of the following markdown statements will produce this output: The **Universe** is vast, *reach for the stars.*

    a. The ```` ```Universe``` ```` is vast, *reach for the stars.*

    b. The [Universe] is vast, |reach for the stars.|

    c. The **Universe** is vast, _reach for the stars._

Useful links

- Download VS Code: `https://code.visualstudio.com`
- VS Code Interface: `https://code.visualstudio.com/docs/getstarted/userinterface`
- Basic writing and formatting syntax: `https://docs.github.com/en/get-started/writing-on-github/getting-started-with-writing-and-formatting-on-github/basic-writing-and-formatting-syntax`
- Creating and managing repositories: `https://docs.github.com/en/repositories/creating-and-managing-repositories`
- Best practices for repositories: `https://docs.github.com/en/repositories/creating-and-managing-repositories/best-practices-for-repositories`

4

Basic Git Commands and Workflows

We are beginning to get deeper into layers of Git and GitHub. So far, we have dealt with the basic concept of Git and experimented with a few Git commands in *Lab 1: setting up Git* in *Chapter 1*.

In this chapter, we will go deeper by learning about some intermediate Git commands and flags. A **flag** is an extra option or parameter appended to a command to modify its behavior, supply more context/data, or influence its output. Flags are typically preceded by a hyphen (-) or double hyphen (--). For example, in the following diagram, looking at the git --version command, --version is a flag that tells the git command to display the version number of Git installed:

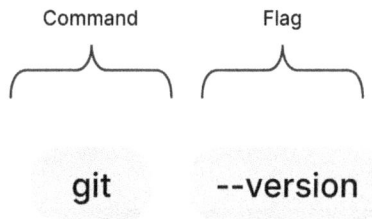

Figure 4.1: The behavior of a command can be modified with a flag

What else are we going to explore? We will be covering the following topics:

- Common Git commands
- Lab 4.1: Linking a remote repo and pushing changes
- Git workflows
- Troubleshooting common issues

Let's get started!

Technical requirements

For the labs in this chapter, you will need the following:

- A working computer with Git installed
- The my-blank-repo created in *Chapter 3* in *Lab 3.1* and updated in *Lab 3.2*

Common Git commands

So far in this book, we have discussed the following Git commands. Let's discuss them in more detail.

Setting up a repository

Here are some commands to use when setting up a repo.

Creating a new repository with git init

The git init command initializes a new Git repository. This command sets up all the necessary files and directories that Git uses to track changes in your project. Until you do this, the directory is regarded as an ordinary folder with no version control.

- **Steps:**
    1. Open your terminal or command prompt.
    2. Navigate to the directory where you want to create the repository.
    3. Run the git init command.
    4. Git will create a new .git directory in your project folder, indicating that the repository has been initialized.
- **Usage:**

```
git init
```

- **Example:**

```
mkdir myapp
cd myapp
git init
```

Configuring repository settings using git config

When setting up a new repository or after installing Git on your computer for the first time, you can use `git config` to configure repository or global options. These options include setting the user information (e.g., email and name) for signing commits, the default text editor, aliases for commands, colorizing Git outputs, line endings, and so on.

- **Usage:**

```
git config
```

- **Example:**

```
git config --global user.email "your_email@example.com"
```

Making changes and committing

After the repo setup, here are some commands you will use when making changes to your source code.

Editing files and checking the status with git status

After making changes to your files, you can use the `git status` command to see which files have been modified, which are staged for commit, and which are untracked. It displays the state of the working directory and the staging area.

- **Steps:**

    1. Edit your files as needed.
    2. Run the `git status` command.
    3. Git will display the status of your working directory, showing modified, staged, and untracked files.

- **Usage:**

```
git status
```

Staging changes with git add

The git add command stages changes, marking them for inclusion in the next commit. You can stage individual files or all changes at once. It adds changes in the working directory to the staging area.

- **Steps:**

    1. To stage a specific file, run git add <file_name>.

    2. To stage all changes, run git add.

    3. Replace <file_name> with the name of the file you want to stage.

- **Usage:**

    ```
    git add <file_or_directory>
    ```

- **Example:**

    ```
    git add README.md
    ```

Committing changes with git commit

The git commit command records the staged changes in the repository's history. Each commit should have a meaningful message describing the changes.

- **Steps:**

    1. Run the git commit -m "Your commit message" command.

    2. Replace "Your commit message" with a brief description of the changes.

- **Usage:**

    ```
    git commit -m "commit message"
    ```

- **Example:**

    ```
    git commit -m "Add initial project files"
    ```

Now let us consider a few more Git commands that are essential for managing your source files and collaborating with others.

Some more common commands

We will discuss some other common Git commands in an easy-to-understand way.

Picture this! You are in an art exhibition and, before you, you see four distinct stalls, as depicted in the pictures that follow.

Fetching changes from a remote repo

At this first stall is Mr. Fetch, a messenger with a bag full of newspapers. Mr. Fetch is at a newsstand, collecting the latest newspapers and stuffing them into his bag. He doesn't read them, just collects them:

Figure 4.2: Mr. Fetch at the newsstand

Fetch always checks for the latest changes but does nothing with them besides collecting the newspapers:

- **Description:** git fetch retrieves updates from a remote repository without merging them into a local branch. It's a quick way to check whether there have been newer commits in the remote repo in comparison to your local copy.
- **Usage:**

```
git fetch
```

Cloning an existing repository with git clone

At the second stall is Ms. Clone, a photocopy machine operator. She's at the copy shop, making an exact copy of a book. She hands the copy to a customer who looks exactly like her:

Figure 4.3: Ms. Clone at the copy shop

Clone saves a replica of the remote Git repo on the local machine:

- **Description:** The git clone command copies an existing Git repository into a new directory on your local machine. This is useful for working on projects that are hosted on remote servers such as GitHub.

  In a sense, git clone is the inverse of git init, in that git init helps you initialize a local directory to become a *brand-new Git repo*, whereas git clone helps you to copy an *existing Git repo* from a remote server to your local machine.

- **Steps:**

  1. Open your terminal or command prompt.

2. Run the `git clone <repository_url>` command.

3. Replace `<repository_url>` with the URL of the repository you want to clone.

    Git will create a new directory with the name of the repository and copy all the files and history into this directory.

- **Usage:**

```
git clone <repository_url>
```

- **Example:**

```
git clone https://github.com/user/repo.git
```

Downloading changes from others with git pull

Alright, this is getting more interesting. Let's look at the third stall. Here, you will find Mr. Pull, a fisherman, fishing at a pond with a fishing rod. He catches a fish and adds it to his basket, which already has some fish:

Figure 4.4: Mr. Pull at the fishing pond

Pull integrates new changes fetched from upstream into the local repo:

- **Description**: The `git pull` command fetches and integrates changes from the remote repository to the local repository.

- **Usage**:

```
git pull <remote> <branch>
```

- **Example**:

```
git pull origin main
```

Pushing changes with git push

At the last stall, you will find Ms. Push, a delivery person with a cart full of packages. She is at a delivery station, loading packages onto a truck. She waves goodbye as the truck drives off:

Figure 4.5: Ms. Push at the delivery station

Push will send all the changes you committed to the remote server:

- **Description:** The git push command uploads your local commits to a remote repository. This is essential for sharing your changes with others.

- **Steps:**

    1. Run the git push origin <branch_name> command.

    2. Replace <branch_name> with the name of the branch you want to push (e.g., main).

- **Usage:**

```
git push <remote> <branch_name>
```

- **Example:**

```
git push origin main
```

Now let us look at a few more commands quickly.

Linking a local Git repo to a remote repo with git remote add

When you create or initialize a new Git repo locally and you want to be able to share this with other developers to collaborate on, you need to connect it to a corresponding repo on a remote server so that others can have access to clone it. You also want to back up your source code outside your local machine. You cannot carry out upstream-related actions such as git push or git fetch without a remote repo connected.

- **Description:** The git remote add command adds a remote repository URL to your local repository, allowing you to push and pull changes.

- **Steps:**

    1. Run the git remote add origin <remote_repository_url> command.

    2. Replace <remote_repository_url> with the URL of your remote repository.

    3. The name origin is a common convention for the main remote repository.

Creating new branches with git branch

Creating branches allows you to work on different features or fixes in isolation from the main codebase. With the git branch command, you can list, create, or delete branches.

- **Steps:**

    1. Run the git branch <branch_name> command.

2.   Replace <branch_name> with the name of the new branch.

- **Usage:** List, create, and delete branches.

```
git branch
git branch <branch_name>
git branch -d <branch_name>
```

- **Example:**

```
git branch feature-branch
```

Switching between branches with git checkout

Switching branches allows you to move between different lines of development. The git checkout command switches branches or restores working tree files.

- **Steps:**

  1.   Run the git checkout <branch_name> command.

  2.   Replace <branch_name> with the name of the branch you want to switch to.

- **Usage:**

```
git checkout <branch_name>
```

- **Example:**

```
git checkout main
```

Merging changes between branches with git merge

Merges changes from one branch into another.

- **Usage:**

```
git merge <branch_name>
```

- **Example:**

```
git merge feature-branch
```

Certification tip

You will encounter many questions on Git and activities on a Git repo. You may be given a Git command on a single line and given a list of options to choose from that best says what the command will do. Some other questions may give you the inverse, where you are given the output or objective, and then given a list of options to choose from which is the command that produced such output – for example: You have been asked to delete a branch named "uat-test." Which of the following commands would you run to achieve this?

We have now examined quite a few common commands. Now let's get hands-on, putting some of the things we have learned into practice.

Lab 4.1: Linking a remote repo and pushing changes

In this lab, we will examine connecting a local repository to an empty remote repo. We will then push our changes across to the remote repo to make it available to other developers to collaborate on.

For the following steps, you will need the local app1 repository created in *Lab 1* in *Chapter 1*.

Linking a local repo to a remote repo

First, let's create a new blank GitHub repo by repeating the steps in *Lab 3.1: Creating a blank repository*:

1. Click the + icon in the top-right corner and select **New repository**.
2. Use app1 as the name for your repository in the **Repository name** field.
3. Add a brief description of your project in the **Description** field (optional but recommended).
4. Then, select **Private** (visible only to you and your collaborators).
5. **IMPORTANT**: Ensure you do *not* initialize your repository with a README file – **Add a README file** must be *deselected*. This is only required when you need to link an existing local Git repo that already contains files.
6. In the **Add .gitignore** field, select **None**. This is also important.

7. In the **Choose a License** field, select **None**.

> **Note**
>
> We ensure that the Git repo is *completely empty* because we already have a local repo that is not empty, and pushing a local repo to a newly linked remote repo that is not empty will cause conflicts as the repo contents and commit history are not aligned.

8. Click the **Create repository** button to finalize the process. Copy the HTTPS URL within the **Quick setup** box. You will need it in later steps.

Now let's go to VS Code and link the local repo:

1. Launch VS Code and select **Open...** from the options in the new window (you can also use the **File** menu and select **Open Folder...**).

2. Navigate to the all_my_repos/app1 directory you created back in *Chapter 1*. You should see the single file you created:

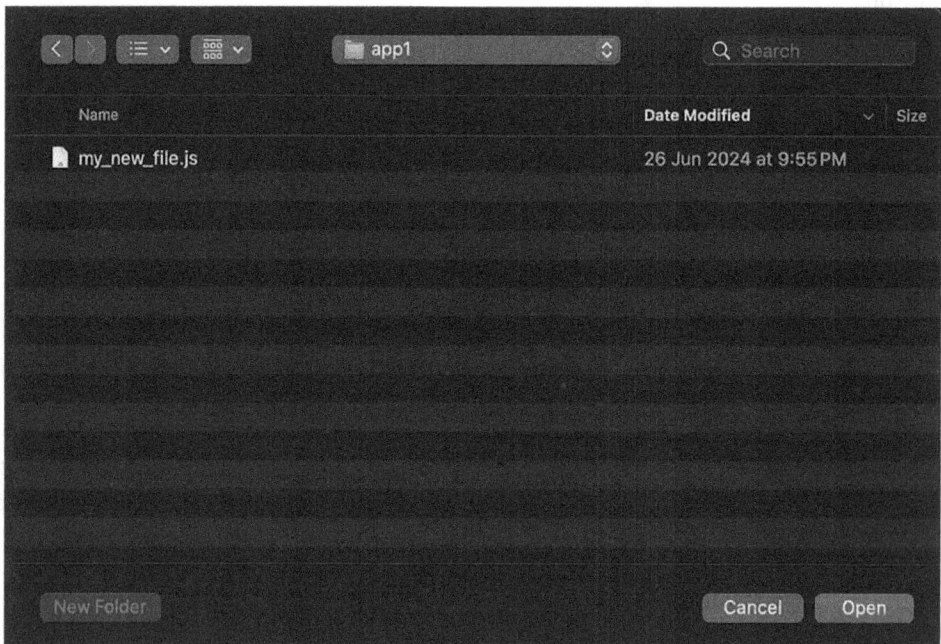

Figure 4.6: Navigate to your repo directory

3. Don't select the file. Then select **Open**. This will open the directory structure of app1 in your IDE.

4. From the **Terminal** menu, select **New Terminal**. This will divide your IDE screen and open the Terminal CLI interface at the bottom. This Terminal embedded within your IDE is for ease of use. It is virtually the same as the Terminal or Command Prompt CLI you would have launched directly from your operating system:

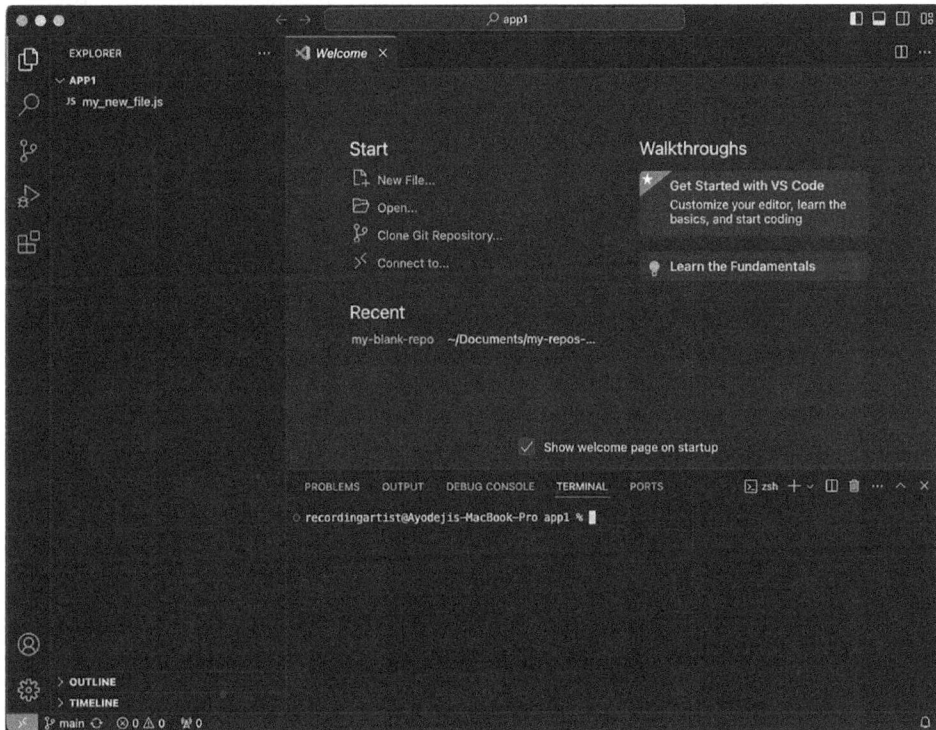

Figure 4.7: VS Code after the Git repo directory has been opened

5. Run the following command:

```
git remote add origin <remote_repository_url>
```

Replace <remote_repository_url> with the URL you copied in *step 8* earlier.

Your local repo is now linked to the remote repo and you can subsequently synchronize changes between them.

6. Run the following command:

```
git push --set-upstream origin main
```

This will upload all your file changes – additions, modifications, or deletions (along with the commit history) – to the remote repo (origin) in the main branch (*you can adjust the remote and branch names if they're different in yours*). The --set-upstream origin main flag is only required if no upstream branch has been linked with the local Git repo branch you are on, therefore, you only need to do this the first time. Subsequently, just git push is enough. Alternatively, you can synchronize changes by clicking on the refresh icon in the bottom-left corner of the status bar. This will perform both a Git push and a Git pull operation.

7. Go back to the GitHub repository page on the browser and *refresh the page*. All the changes you made locally are now present in the remote repo, safely backed up.

Congratulations! You now have a copy of your repo available on a remote server and can now share your repository with other developers to collaborate on.

Before you start collaborating on your source code, it is good to consider which Git workflow is best for you and your team (collaborators). In the next section, we will examine some popular Git workflows.

Git workflows

Git workflows refer to the overall process, sequence, and practices that a team adopts, when using Git, to streamline the development process and improve collaboration. Workflows sometimes encompass the entire development process, including how branches are used, and they define how and when code is integrated, tested, and deployed.

Some common Git workflows include the following:

- **Git Flow**: This is a structured workflow where separate branches are to be used for features, releases, and hotfixes. In this process, you and your collaborators will create a new branch for a new feature or bug fix and continue working in it until it is completed. This means there will be no merge into the default or main branch for a long time. These are called **long-lived branches**.

Git Flow is one of the earliest established branching flows. However, it is rarely used as there are some newer workflows that are considered superior and better practice.

- **GitHub Flow:** The GitHub Flow (yes, named after GitHub) is a much simpler workflow that uses a single main branch with short-lived feature branches. In this process, collaborators will create a separate branch only to work on a set of related changes, and then merge. This makes it lightweight, and it makes continuous deployment easier to implement.

  The GitHub Flow was created by Scott Chacon, one of the cofounders of GitHub.

- **Trunk-based development:** Here, your collaborators work on short-lived branches and merge changes into the main branch frequently, often multiple times a day, deleting these branches as soon as they are merged into the trunk. It facilitates continuous integration, ensuring that collaborators continually re-integrate their work back to the main source code, leaving only one version for reference and subsequent deployments or consumption.

  Remember that all changes to history are merged into the trunk, you can always revert to any point in time commit from the history, thereby making keeping long-lived branches irrelevant and unnecessary.

Choosing the right Git workflow for your team can enhance collaboration, set expectations, and aid efficient software delivery to the end user. Which workflow benefits you will depend on your needs. The latter two are considered to be more modern and best practice.

While collaborating on your Git repo, you may encounter some issues that may impact the stability and functioning of your repo. We will consider some common issues and how to troubleshoot them in the next section.

Troubleshooting common issues

Developing problem-solving skills for Git is crucial for maintaining a smooth workflow. This section will help you identify and resolve common issues that may arise during development.

Common issues and solutions

Here are some common issues and how you might solve them.

Merge conflicts

These occur when changes from different branches conflict with each other.

- **Identification**: Git will notify you of conflicts during a merge.
- **Resolution**:

  a. Open the conflicting files and manually resolve the conflicts.

  b. Use `git add` to stage the resolved files.

  c. Complete the merge with `git commit`.

Detached HEAD state

This happens when HEAD points to a commit instead of a branch.

- **Identification**: Git will indicate that you are in a detached HEAD state.
- **Resolution**:

  a. Create a new branch from the detached HEAD state with `git checkout -b <new-branch-name>`.

  b. Switch back to the main branch with `git checkout main`.

Reverting changes

There might be situations when you need to revert or undo the changes you made to the repo. Here are some ways to revert changes:

- Using `git revert`:
  - **Description**: Creates a new commit that undoes the changes from a previous commit.
  - **Usage**:
    ```
    git revert <commit-hash>
    ```
- Using `git reset`:
  - **Description**: Moves the current branch to a specified commit.
  - **Usage**:
    ```
    git reset --hard <commit-hash>
    ```

Resolving issues with remote repositories

As you often synchronize your local repo with the remote repo, there are bound to be connectivity issues at times during your interaction. Here are some common ones.

- **Authentication problems:**

  - Ensure you have the correct credentials.

  - Use SSH keys for authentication.

- **Connectivity problems:**

  - Check your internet connection.

  - Verify the remote repository URL with `git remote -v`.

Best practices for troubleshooting

Let us look at some best practices:

- **Keeping commits small and frequent**: Make small, incremental changes and commit them frequently to minimize conflicts.

- **Writing clear and descriptive commit messages**: Use meaningful commit messages to describe the changes made.

- **Regularly pulling updates from the remote repository**: Frequently pull updates to stay in sync with the remote repository and avoid conflicts.

Great job! You have now mastered basic to intermediate knowledge of Git commands and workflows. Many of the commands here were treated in brief. Be sure to dive deeper into each of these commands by reading the additional useful links at the end of this chapter and experiment a lot with them on your own.

Let us summarize what we have learned.

Summary

We began by delving deeper into the layers of Git and GitHub. Initially, we dealt with the basic concept of Git and experimented with a few Git commands from *Lab 1* in *Chapter 1*. Then, we went deeper by learning about some intermediate Git commands and flags. A flag is an extra option or parameter appended to a command to modify its behavior, supply more context/data, or influence its output. For example, in the `git --version` command, the `--version` flag told the Git command to display the version number of Git installed.

We learned about and mastered several Git commands, such as setting up a repository with `git init`, configuring repository settings using `git config`, editing files and checking the status with `git status`, staging changes with `git add`, and committing changes with `git commit`. We also discussed other common Git commands in an easy-to-understand way, such as fetching changes from a remote repo with `git fetch`, cloning an existing repository with `git clone`, downloading changes from others with `git pull`, and pushing changes with `git push`.

Additionally, we examined linking a local Git repo to a remote repo with `git remote add`, creating new branches with `git branch`, switching between branches with `git checkout`, and merging changes between branches with `git merge`.

Finally, we considered some popular Git workflows, such as Git Flow, GitHub Flow, and trunk-based development, and discussed troubleshooting common issues such as merge conflicts.

Test your knowledge

1. When setting up a new repo, which of the following Git commands do you need to run to make the directory Git-aware?

    a. `git merge`
    b. `mkdir`
    c. `git init`
    d. `git rebase`

2. Which of the following branching models does not support short-lived branches?

    a. GitHub Flow
    b. Git Flow
    c. Trunk-based development

3. You made some changes in your local branch and want to upload them to GitHub. Which command should you use?

    a. `git pull`
    b. `git push`
    c. `git clone`
    d. `git init`

4. You want to see a list of all the branches in your Git repository. Which command should you use?

   a. `git status`
   b. `git branch`
   c. `git log`
   d. `git checkout`

Useful links

- Git Reference: `https://git-scm.com/docs`
- GitHub flow: `https://docs.github.com/en/get-started/using-github/github-flow`
- Common Git Problems and Their Fixes: `https://www.geeksforgeeks.org/common-git-problems-and-their-fixes/`

Unlock this book's exclusive benefits now

Scan this QR code or go to `packtpub.com/unlock`, then search this book by name.

Note: Keep your purchase invoice ready before you start.

Part 2

Collaborative Development on GitHub

This part delves into advanced collaboration techniques on GitHub, enabling you to work effectively with teams and contribute to projects. Upon completion, you will have a comprehensive understanding of branching and merging strategies, pull requests, code reviews, and project management tools on GitHub. This knowledge is essential for any collaborative software development tasks.

This part of the book includes the following chapters:

- *Chapter 5, Branching and Merging Strategies*
- *Chapter 6, Pull Requests and Code Reviews*
- *Chapter 7, Issues, Projects, Labels, and Milestones*
- *Chapter 8, GitHub Actions and Automation*
- *Chapter 9, Engaging with the Community through GitHub Discussions*

5

Branching and Merging Strategies

In the next few chapters, we will be focusing on collaborative development on GitHub. You will learn advanced collaboration techniques, enabling you to work effectively with teams and contribute to projects on GitHub.

In this chapter, we will delve into the branching model in Git and on GitHub, exploring various strategies for creating, managing, and merging branches. This chapter emphasizes the importance of a well-structured branching strategy for team collaboration. We will cover the following topics:

- Understanding branches in Git
- Merging and conflict resolution
- Branch management techniques

Let's get right into it!

Understanding branches in Git

Let's look at what branches are in Git and their purposes.

Introduction to branches

Branches are a fundamental concept in Git, allowing developers to diverge from the main codebase and work on features, bug fixes, or experiments in isolation.

Branches enable parallel development by creating a separate *line of development work*. They help in managing different versions of a project and facilitate collaboration among team members. Usually, a branch is created from the default branch in a repo, which means it carries all the history of its parent branch from which it was cloned. Therefore, a newly cloned branch and its parent branch will have identical *heads*.

> **Note**
>
> A **head** is the tip of a branch denoted by a named reference to the latest commit.

In Git, there is a subtle difference between a branch head and **HEAD**.

> **Note**
>
> HEAD is a special pointer that refers to the current branch or commit that you are working on.

In other words, all branches have heads but there can only be one HEAD, which is the tip of the current working branch.

Now, there are a few benefits that branching brings to collaboration. Let's look at a few.

Benefits of using branches

Using branches in version control offers several significant benefits, especially in collaborative development environments. Here are some key advantages:

- **Parallel development and enhanced collaboration**: It allows multiple developers to work on different features simultaneously without interfering with each other's work. Multiple branches enable parallel development, thereby increasing productivity and accelerating the development process.

- **Isolation of work and safe experimentation**: Branches allow developers to work on different features and bug fixes, or to experiment on an idea in isolation without affecting the main codebase. This isolation helps prevent conflicts and ensures that incomplete or unstable code does not disrupt the main project. If the work done is no longer required, the branch can be deleted without any impact.

- **Simplified code reviews**: Branches facilitate code reviews by allowing developers to submit pull requests (we will talk more about pull requests in the next chapter, *Chapter 6, Pull Requests and Code Reviews*) for specific branches. Reviewers can focus on the changes in the branch, making the review process more manageable and thorough.

- **Rollback capability**: If a feature or change introduced in a branch causes issues, it can be easily rolled back by reverting the branch or discarding it altogether. This rollback capability ensures that the main codebase remains stable and reliable.

By leveraging these benefits, teams can improve their development processes, enhance code quality, and collaborate more effectively.

Creating branches

Creating branches is a straightforward process in Git. You can create branches directly by running `git` commands in the CLI, through the GitHub interface, or from your preferred IDE.

Using the git command

The basic command to create a branch is `git branch <branch-name>`. To create and switch to a new branch simultaneously, use `git checkout -b <branch-name>`.

Using the GitHub website

From the GitHub.com interface on the web browser, you can create a branch using the following steps:

1. **Navigate to your repository**: Go to the repository where you want to create a new branch.
2. **Use the branch dropdown**: Click on the branch drop-down menu, which is usually labeled with the current branch name (e.g., **main** or **master**).

3. **Create a new branch**: In the dropdown, type the name of your new branch in the text box. You will see an option to create a new branch from the current branch. Click on the option that says **Create branch <branch-name> from <current-branch>**.

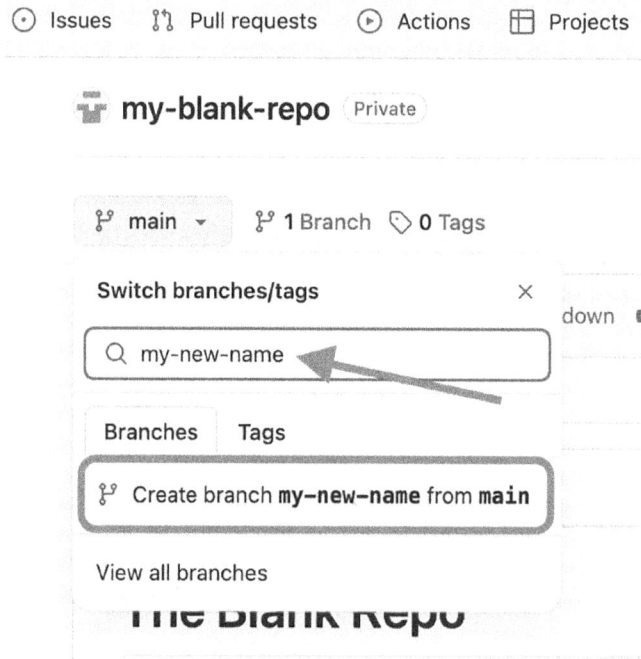

Figure 5.1: Creating a new branch on the GitHub UI

Using the IDE

From the IDE, taking VS Code for instance, you can do this in one of two ways.

Using the VS Code interface

1. **Open VS Code**: Launch Visual Studio Code and open your project repository.
2. **Open the Source Control view**: Click on the **Source Control** icon in the activity bar on the side of the window (it looks like a branch icon in the bottom-left corner).

3. **Open the branch menu:** In the **Source Control** view, click on the branch name at the bottom of the window (next to the checkmark icon). This will open the branch menu.

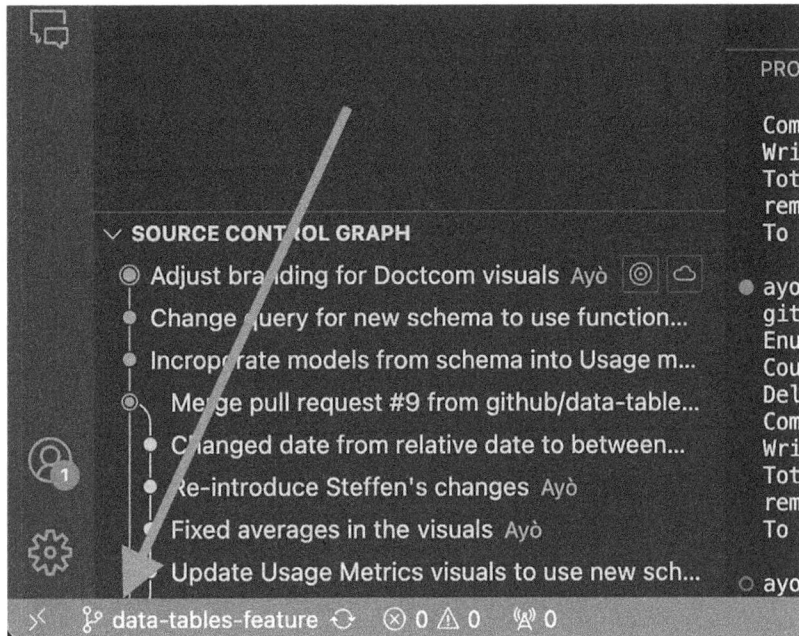

Figure 5.2: Clicking on the branch name to launch the branch-related menu

4. **Create a new branch:** Select **Create new branch...** from the drop-down menu:

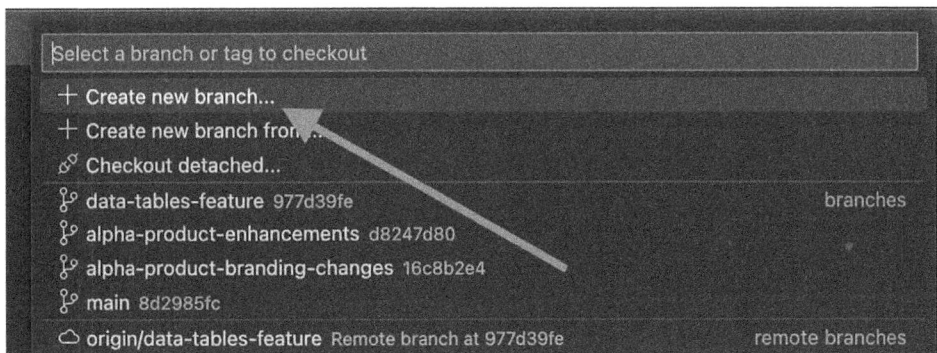

Figure 5.3: Selecting to create a new branch

5. **Name your branch:** Enter the name of your new branch and press *Enter*. VS Code will create the new branch and switch to it automatically.

Using the Command Palette

1. **Open the Command Palette**: Press *Ctrl + Shift + P* (or *Cmd + Shift + P* on macOS) to open the Command Palette.

2. **Use the Git: Create Branch command**: Type `Git: Create Branch` and select it from the list of commands:

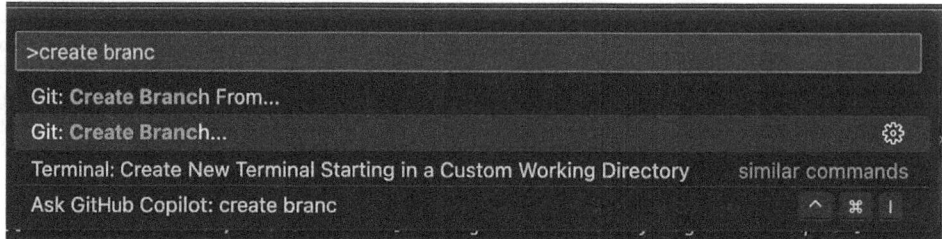

```
>create branc
Git: Create Branch From...
Git: Create Branch...                                                              ⚙
Terminal: Create New Terminal Starting in a Custom Working Directory    similar commands
Ask GitHub Copilot: create branc                                              ^  ⌘  I
```

Figure 5.4: Creating a new branch using the Command Palette

3. **Name your branch**: Enter the name of your new branch and press *Enter*. VS Code will create the new branch and switch to it automatically.

What is the best way to name your branch? We will look at some factors influencing nomenclature in the next section.

Naming conventions and best practices

It's important to follow consistent naming conventions for branches to avoid confusion. Using a consistent naming convention for repository branches offers several benefits, particularly in collaborative environments. Here are some key advantages:

- **Clarity and readability**: Clear and descriptive branch names make it easier for team members to immediately understand the purpose of each branch. This reduces confusion and improves communication within the team.

- **Organization**: Consistent naming helps keep the repository organized. It allows developers to quickly locate and identify branches related to specific features, bug fixes, or releases.

- **Efficiency**: When branch names follow a predictable pattern, it becomes easier to automate workflows and integrate with CI/CD pipelines. Scripts and tools can be configured to recognize and handle branches based on their names.

- **Collaboration**: Standardized branch names facilitate better collaboration by ensuring that all team members follow the same conventions. This consistency helps in managing pull requests, code reviews, and merges more effectively.

- **Tracking and management:** Naming conventions aid in tracking the progress of different tasks and managing the life cycle of branches. It becomes simpler to identify which branches are active, which are ready for review, and which can be deleted.

Let us consider some good practices for naming branches:

- **Use prefixes:** Use prefixes to categorize branches by their purpose. Common prefixes include the following:

    - `feature/` for new features (e.g., `feature/login-page`)
    - `bugfix/` for bug fixes (e.g., `bugfix/fix-login-error`)
    - `hotfix/` for urgent fixes (e.g., `hotfix/security-patch`)
    - `release/` for release preparation (e.g., `release/v1.0.0`)

- **Use descriptive names:** Choose descriptive names that clearly indicate the branch's purpose. Avoid using generic names such as `dev` or `test`.
- **Use hyphens or slashes:** Separate words with hyphens or slashes to improve readability (e.g., `feature/user-authentication`).
- **Avoid special characters:** Stick to alphanumeric characters and hyphens. Avoid using special characters or spaces in branch names.
- **Keep it short and simple:** While being descriptive, try to keep branch names concise. Long branch names can be cumbersome to work with.
- **Include issue or ticket numbers:** If your project uses an issue tracker, include the issue or ticket number in the branch name to link the branch to a specific task (e.g., `feature/1234-add-user-login`).
- **Use a consistent case:** Decide on a case convention (e.g., all lowercase) and stick to it for consistency.

Here are some examples of naming conventions:

- `feature/add-user-authentication`
- `bugfix/fix-login-error`
- `hotfix/security-patch`
- `release/v1.0.0`
- `chore/update-dependencies`
- `test/integration-tests`

By following these best practices, you can ensure that your repository remains organized, your workflows are efficient, and your team can collaborate effectively.

After creating your branch, you want to switch to that new branch to begin work.

Switching between branches

Switching between branches allows developers to move their working directory to a different branch. The `git checkout <branch-name>` command is used to switch to an existing branch. With *Git 2.23* and later, `git switch <branch-name>` can also be used.

When you switch to a different branch in Git, several things happen to ensure your working directory reflects the state of the branch you're switching to. Here's a breakdown of the process.

Updating the working directory

Git updates the files in your working directory to match the state of the branch you're switching to. This means the following:

- **File changes**: Any files that are different between the current branch and the target branch will be updated. This includes adding new files, modifying existing files, and deleting files that are not present in the target branch. If you open the repo's directory in Finder (macOS) or Explorer (Windows) before and after switching between two branches that are different, you will notice the change in the content despite opening the same path:

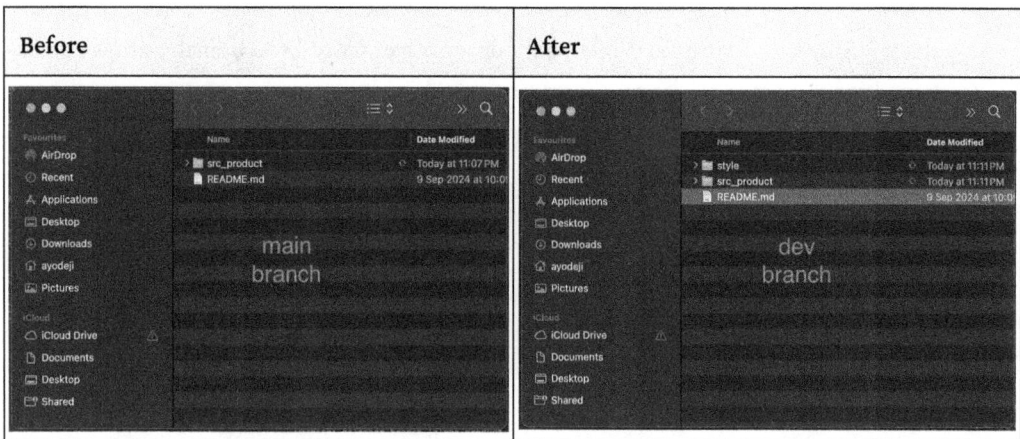

Figure 5.5: Switching between branches changes the physical contents of the directory to match

- **Staging area:** The staging area (index) is also updated to reflect the state of the target branch.

Preserving uncommitted changes

If you have uncommitted changes in your working directory, Git will handle them in one of two ways:

- **Clean working directory**: If your working directory is clean (no uncommitted changes), Git will switch branches without any issues.

- **Uncommitted changes**: If you have uncommitted changes, Git will attempt to apply them to the new branch. If the changes can be applied cleanly, Git will switch branches. If there are conflicts, Git will prevent the switch and prompt you to either commit, stash (this is explained in the later section), or discard your changes.

Updating the branch pointer

Git updates the HEAD pointer to point to the new branch. The HEAD pointer indicates the current branch you are working on. When you switch branches, the HEAD pointer is updated to reference the latest commit on the target branch.

Stashing changes (optional)

If you have uncommitted changes that you want to keep but need to switch branches, you can use the `git stash` command to temporarily save your changes. After switching branches, you can apply the stashed changes using `git stash apply`.

Here are some example commands:

- Switching branches:

```
git checkout <branch-name>
```

or

```
git switch <branch-name>
```

(`git switch` only works in Git version 2.23 and later.)

- Stashing changes:

```
git stash
git checkout <branch-name>
git stash apply
```

💡 **Quick tip**: Enhance your coding experience with the **AI Code Explainer** and **Quick Copy** features. Open this book in the next-gen Packt Reader. Click the **Copy** button (1) to quickly copy code into your coding environment, or click the **Explain** button (2) to get the AI assistant to explain a block of code to you.

```
                                                            Copy        Explain
function calculate(a, b) {
  return {sum: a + b};                                       1            2
};
```

📱 **The next-gen Packt Reader** is included for free with the purchase of this book. Scan the QR code OR go to packtpub.com/unlock, then use the search bar to find this book by name. Double-check the edition shown to make sure you get the right one.

Switching branches in Git updates your working directory to reflect the state of the target branch, preserves uncommitted changes if possible, and updates the HEAD pointer. This allows you to seamlessly move between different lines of development while maintaining the integrity of your work.

Developers often switch branches to review code, test features, or work on different tasks. Understanding when and why to switch branches is crucial for efficient workflow management.

When you are done with your development in the current working branch, you want to reintegrate the changes you made to the main codebase in the default or source branch, preferably after rigorous testing to be sure your new code will not introduce breaking changes to the main codebase. The process of reintegrating your changes to the main codebase or trunk is called a **merge**.

In the next section, we will examine different merge types, how to perform them, and how to manage conflicts that may arise in the process.

Merging and conflict resolution

A merge is the process of combining the changes from one branch into another. This is a fundamental operation in version control that allows you to integrate different lines of development.

Types of merges

Understanding the different types of merges is essential for managing how changes are integrated into the main codebase.

Merge commit

This is the default merge strategy in Git. It creates a new commit that combines the histories of the merged branches. This method preserves the complete history of changes but can result in a more cluttered commit history. Combining the history is in two forms:

- **Fast-forward merge**: If the target branch has not diverged from the source branch, Git simply moves the pointer of the target branch forward to the latest commit of the source branch. This is a straightforward merge with no new commits created.
- **Three-way merge**: If the branches have diverged, Git performs a three-way merge. It uses the common ancestor of the two branches and the latest commits from both branches to create a new merge commit that combines the changes.

Squash merge

This is a merge strategy that combines all the commits from a feature branch into a single commit before merging it into the `main` branch. This means that instead of seeing all the multiple commits you made in your working branch, there will be *only one commit in the target branch* after the merge. It simplifies the commit history, making it easier to follow, but loses the granular history of individual commits. The following figure is a visual representation.

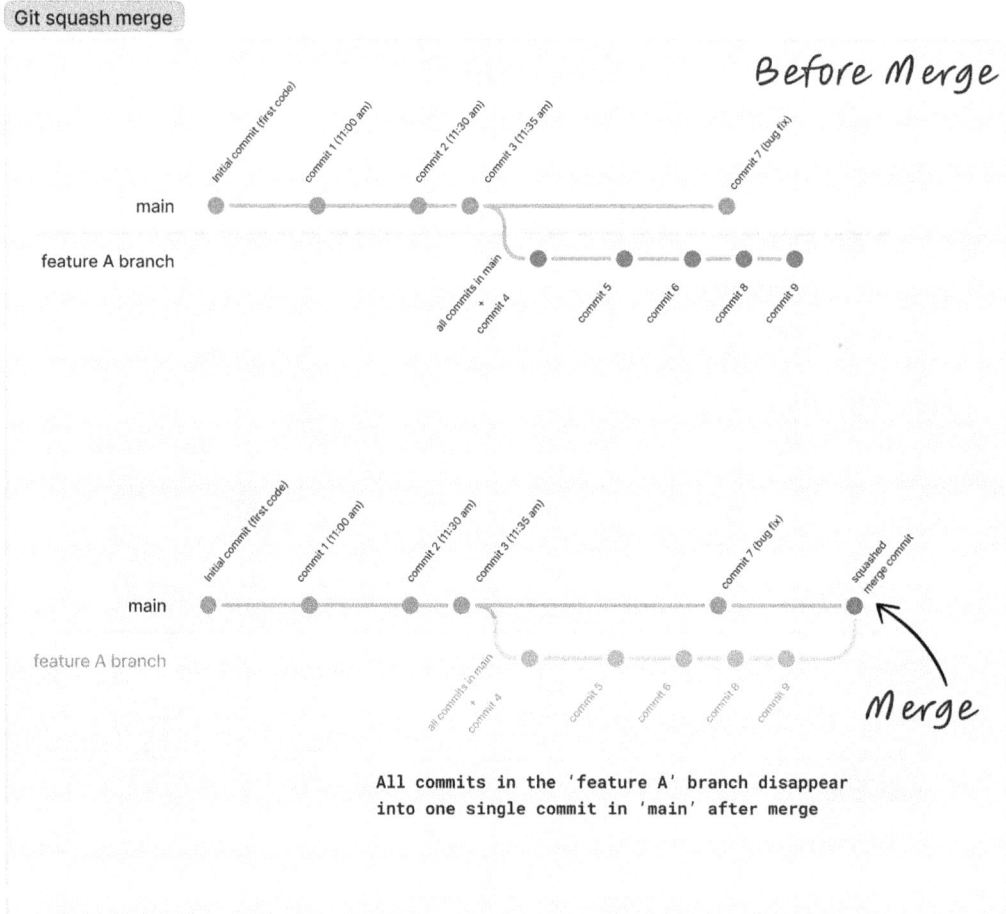

Figure 5.6: Only the merge commit is visible in the history of the target branch after the merge

When performing a squash merge in Git, the commit message typically combines the commit messages of all the individual commits being squashed into a single, consolidated message. This helps provide context and a summary of the changes introduced by the feature or branch being merged. Now, what will the commit message be?

Default commit message

By default, Git generates a commit message for a squash merge that includes the following:

- **Title**: A summary of the merge, usually indicating the branch being merged
- **List of squashed commits**: A list of the commit messages from all the commits that were squashed together

Let's look at an example.

Suppose you have a `feature/new-feature` branch with the following three separate commits:

- `Add initial implementation of new feature`
- `Refactor code for new feature`
- `Fix bug in new feature`

When you perform a squash merge, the default commit message might look like this, but in one single commit:

```
Merge branch 'feature/new-feature'

* Add initial implementation of new feature
* Refactor code for new feature
* Fix bug in new feature
```

Customizing the commit message

You can also customize the commit message during a squash merge to provide a more concise or detailed summary. When you initiate the squash merge, Git opens your default text editor, allowing you to edit the commit message before finalizing the merge.

Rebasing and merging

Rebasing replays the commits from the source branch onto the base/target branch, creating a linear history. This method keeps the commit history clean but can be more complex and risky, especially if conflicts arise during the rebase process. The following figure is a visual representation.

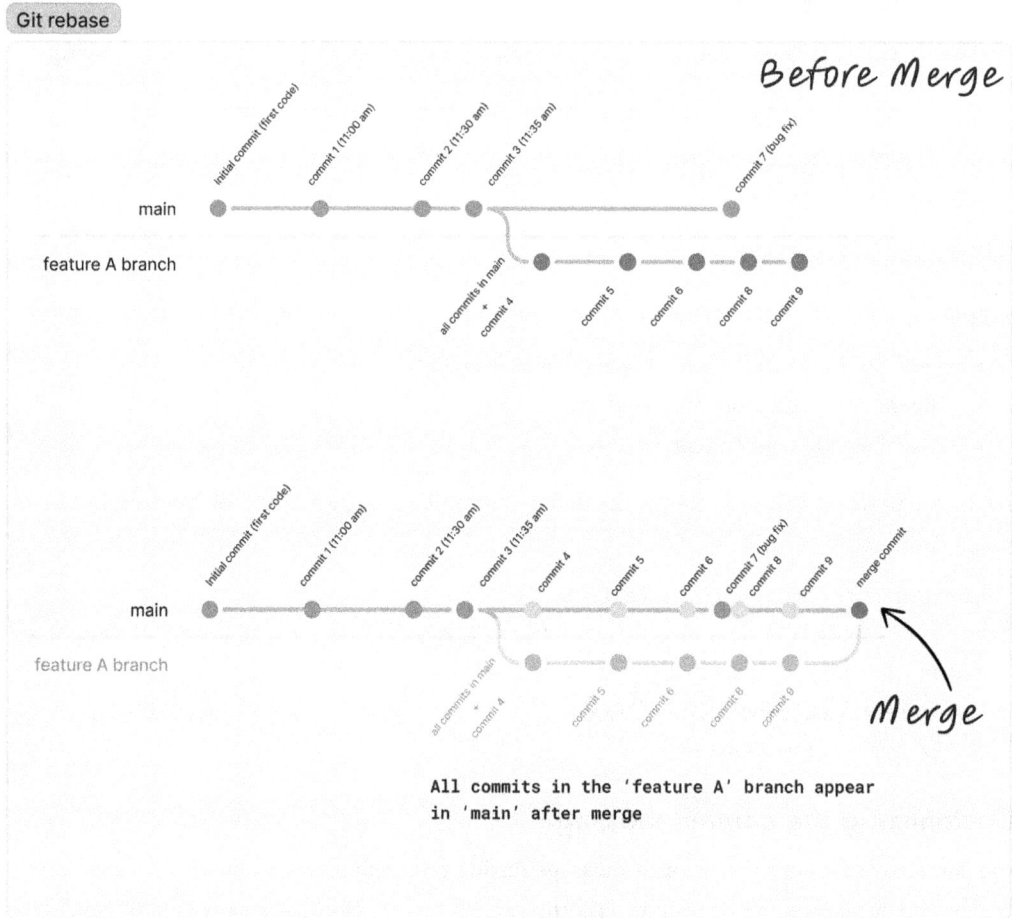

Figure 5.7: Commits from the source branch are replayed in the exact timelines onto the target branch

🔍 **Quick tip**: Need to see a high-resolution version of this image? Open this book in the next-gen Packt Reader or view it in the PDF/ePub copy.

📖 **The next-gen Packt Reader** and a **free PDF/ePub copy** of this book are included with your purchase. Scan the QR code OR visit `packtpub.com/unlock`, then use the search bar to find this book by name. Double-check the edition shown to make sure you get the right one.

Key differences between squash merge and rebase merge

Here's a table summarizing the key differences between rebase merge and squash merge:

Feature	Rebase Merge	Squash Merge
Purpose	Replay commits from one branch onto another	Combine all feature branch commits into one
Commit history	Preserves individual commits (rewritten)	Creates a single new commit
Branch history	Appears linear and clean	Simplified, but loses granular commit detail
Use case	When maintaining a detailed commit history is useful	When wanting a clean, summarized commit
Original commits	Rewritten (new SHAs)	Replaced with a new commit
Conflict resolution	May need to resolve multiple times (per commit)	Conflicts resolved once during squash
Final merge commit	No merge commit; commits appear as if written linearly	Single new commit added to target branch
Command example	`git rebase main`	`git merge --squash feature`

Table 5.1: Differences between rebase merge and squash merge

Performing merges

Executing merges correctly ensures that changes are integrated smoothly. This section will explain.

Commands for merging branches

The basic command for merging is `git merge <branch-name>`, which merges the specified branch into the current branch. For squashing commits before merging, use `git merge --squash <branch-name>`. To rebase, use `git rebase <branch-name>`.

Performing a regular merge

Here's how you can perform a regular merge:

1. Switch to the target branch: `git checkout main`.

2. Merge: `git merge feature/new-feature`.

Performing a squash merge

Here's how you can perform a squash merge:

1. Switch to the target branch: `git checkout main`.

2. Squash and merge: `git merge --squash feature/new-feature`.

3. Commit the squashed changes: `git commit`.

During the `git commit` step, Git will open the commit message editor with the default message, which you can then edit as needed.

Performing a rebase

You can perform a rebase in four easy steps:

1. Switch to your feature branch: `git checkout feature/new-feature`.

2. Rebase onto the target branch: `git rebase main`.

3. Resolve any conflicts if they arise during rebasing.

4. Fast-forward or force-push your changes to update your remote branch (if necessary):

    *   Fast-forward push (if no conflicts):

        ```
        git push origin feature/new-feature
        ```

    *   Force-push (if conflicts were resolved):

        ```
        git push origin feature/new-feature --force
        ```

You may be given a scenario in the exam where you are required to merge, given certain conditions (e.g., you don't want to retain the history of every commit in a change), and then asked to choose which merge type you need to achieve it.

There are some good practices to consistently ensure a clean merge.

Best practices for clean merges

Always ensure that your working directory is clean (i.e., no uncommitted changes) before starting a merge. Regularly pull the latest changes from the main branch to minimize conflicts. Use meaningful commit messages to document the purpose of the merge.

Sometimes, changes in the source and target branches overlap, leading to conflicts. It is not uncommon for another developer to have introduced changes and reintegrated since the time you created your working branch. To move forward and complete the merge, you need to resolve the conflict. Let us consider conflict resolution during a merge.

Conflict resolution

Merge conflicts occur when changes in different branches overlap. Here are a few recommendations for resolving conflicts:

- **Identifying merge conflicts**: Git will notify you of conflicts during a merge or rebase. Conflicted files will be marked, and you can use git status to see which files need attention.

- **Strategies to resolve conflicts**: Open the conflicted files and look for conflict markers (<<<<<<<, =======, >>>>>>>). Manually edit the files to resolve the conflicts, then stage the resolved files with git add <file>. Finally, complete the merge with git commit or the rebase with git rebase --continue.

- **Tools and commands for conflict resolution**: Git provides several tools to assist with conflict resolution. Use git mergetool to launch a merge tool that can help visualize and resolve conflicts. Popular merge tools include KDiff3, Meld, and Beyond Compare.

Note

git mergetool is a Git command that allows you to use an external merge tool to resolve merge conflicts. When you encounter conflicts during a merge, git mergetool helps you visualize the differences between conflicting files and provides a user-friendly interface to resolve these conflicts.

`git mergetool` launches a graphical or text-based merge tool that displays the conflicting changes side by side. You can configure Git to use your preferred merge tool. Some merge tools offer automated conflict resolution features, such as accepting all changes from one side or the other, which can speed up the resolution process.

To use `git mergetool`, you must first configure your preferred merge tool.

You can set your preferred merge tool in your Git configuration. To do this, use the following `git config --global merge.tool <merge-tool-name>` command, where `merge-tool-name` is the name of the merge tool. For example, to set Meld as your merge tool, you can use the following command:

```
git config --global merge.tool meld
```

When you encounter a merge conflict, Git will notify you and mark the conflicted files. Then, you start the merge tool by running `git mergetool`.

The merge tool will open, displaying the conflicting changes. You can then manually resolve the conflicts using the tool's interface. Once you have resolved the conflicts, save the changes and close the tool.

After resolving all conflicts, you need to stage the resolved files and complete the merge:

```
git add <resolved-file>
git commit
```

Some additional commands that are useful during a merge and that can help resolve conflicts include the following:

- `git reset`: Used to undo changes by moving the HEAD and branch pointer to a previous commit. It can be used to unstage changes (`--soft`), remove changes from the working directory (`--hard`), or both.
- `git revert`: Creates a new commit that undoes the changes from a previous commit, preserving the history.

Up next, we will explore how to manage branches effectively on GitHub.

Branch management techniques

Effective branch management is crucial for maintaining a clean and organized repository. This section will cover how we can manage branches both on Git and GitHub. They are not interchangeable but are mutually beneficial.

Managing branches in Git

Managing branches on Git is mostly operational:

- **Listing branches**: To view all branches in your repository, use the `git branch` command for local branches and `git branch -r` for remote branches. The `git branch -a` command lists both local and remote branches.

- **Deleting branches**: Once a branch is no longer needed, it can be deleted to keep the repository tidy. Use `git branch -d <branch-name>` to delete a local branch that has been merged, or `git branch -D <branch-name>` (note the uppercase) to force-delete a branch. For remote branches, use `git push origin --delete <branch-name>`.

Now let's see how you can manage branches on GitHub. GitHub offers a more robust set of features.

Branch protection rules on GitHub

Branch protection rules help ensure that the code in important branches remains stable and secure. Protecting branches prevents direct pushes and accidental deletions, enforces code reviews, and ensures that all changes meet the required standards before being merged. This is particularly important for branches such as `main` or `master`.

On GitHub, you can set up branch protection rules by navigating to the repository **Settings** tab under **Branches**. Options include requiring pull request reviews, enforcing status checks, and restricting who can push to the branch:

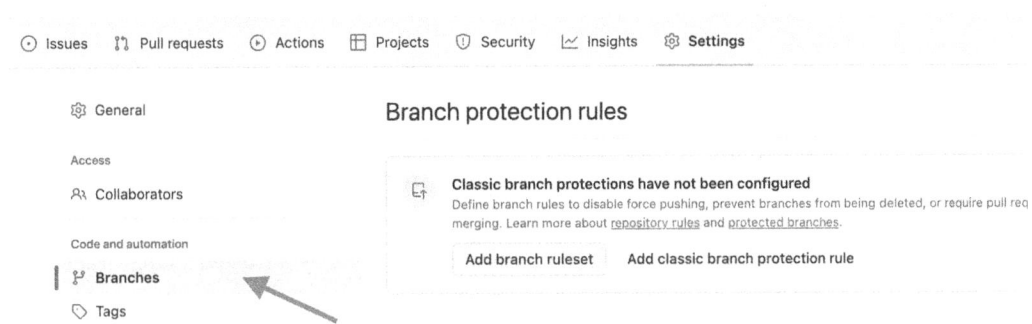

Figure 5.8: Branch protection rules on GitHub

Select **Add branch ruleset** to reveal the configuration screen.

Here are some key rulesets supported.

Require a pull request before merging

This rule mandates that one or more team members review the code changes before they can be merged into the protected branch. You can specify the number of required reviewers and whether they must be code owners.

Benefit: It ensures that at least one other team member reviews the code before it is merged, promoting code quality and collaboration.

Require status checks to pass

This rule requires that all specified status checks pass before a pull request can be merged. Status checks can include automated tests, code quality checks, and CI/CD pipeline results.

Benefit: It mandates that all required status checks (such as CI/CD pipelines) pass before merging, ensuring that the code meets predefined quality standards.

Require conversation resolution before merging

This rule ensures that all comments and discussions on a pull request are resolved before it can be merged. All conversations marked as unresolved must be addressed.

Benefit: It ensures that all comments and discussions on a pull request are addressed, fostering thorough code reviews and communication.

Require signed commits

This rule requires that commits are signed with a GPG or S/MIME key. Only commits with verified signatures are allowed.

> **Note**
>
> Signing a commit with a **GNU Privacy Guard (GPG)** or **Secure/Multipurpose Internet Mail Extensions (S/MIME)** key is a way to verify the authenticity and integrity of the commit. It ensures that the commit was made by a trusted source and has not been tampered with.

Benefits:

- **Security**: It ensures that commits are made by trusted contributors and have not been tampered with
- **Accountability**: It provides a clear record of who made each change, which is especially useful in collaborative projects
- **Trust**: It builds trust in the codebase by verifying the identity of committers

Require linear history

This rule enforces a linear commit history, avoiding merge commits. Only rebase and squash merges are allowed.

Benefit: It enforces a linear commit history, avoiding merge commits and making the project history cleaner and easier to follow.

Require merge queue

This rule manages the order of merges to ensure that all required checks are rerun in the correct sequence. Pull requests are added to a queue and merged in order.

> Note
>
> A merge queue is another great feature GitHub offers for seamless integrations of code at scale. We will talk more about this in the next chapter, *Chapter 6, Pull Requests and Code Reviews*.

Benefit: It manages the order of merges to ensure that all required checks are rerun in the correct sequence, maintaining the stability of the main branch.

Require deployments to succeed

This rule ensures that the code has been successfully deployed in a staging environment before it is merged. Deployment status checks must pass. This is beneficial to CI/CD processes.

Benefit: It ensures that the code has been successfully deployed in a staging environment before it is merged, reducing the risk of deployment issues.

Lock branch

This rule prevents any changes to the branch, ensuring that it remains stable and unchanged until explicitly unlocked. Only administrators can unlock the branch. For instance, you might want to lock a release branch once it is in production so that you will always have a working version of that release version to come back to in the future without disrupting the main branch.

Benefit: It prevents any changes to the branch, ensuring that it remains stable and unchanged until explicitly unlocked.

Do not allow bypassing the above settings

This rule ensures that the branch protection rules that have been configured are strictly enforced, even for administrators. No one can bypass the rules.

Benefit: It ensures that the branch protection rules are strictly enforced, even for administrators, maintaining the integrity of the branch.

Restrict who can push to matching branches

This rule limits the users who can push to the branch. You can specify individual users or teams who have push access.

Benefit: It limits the users who can push to the branch, reducing the risk of unauthorized changes.

Other rules include restricting creations, deletions, or updates of branches:

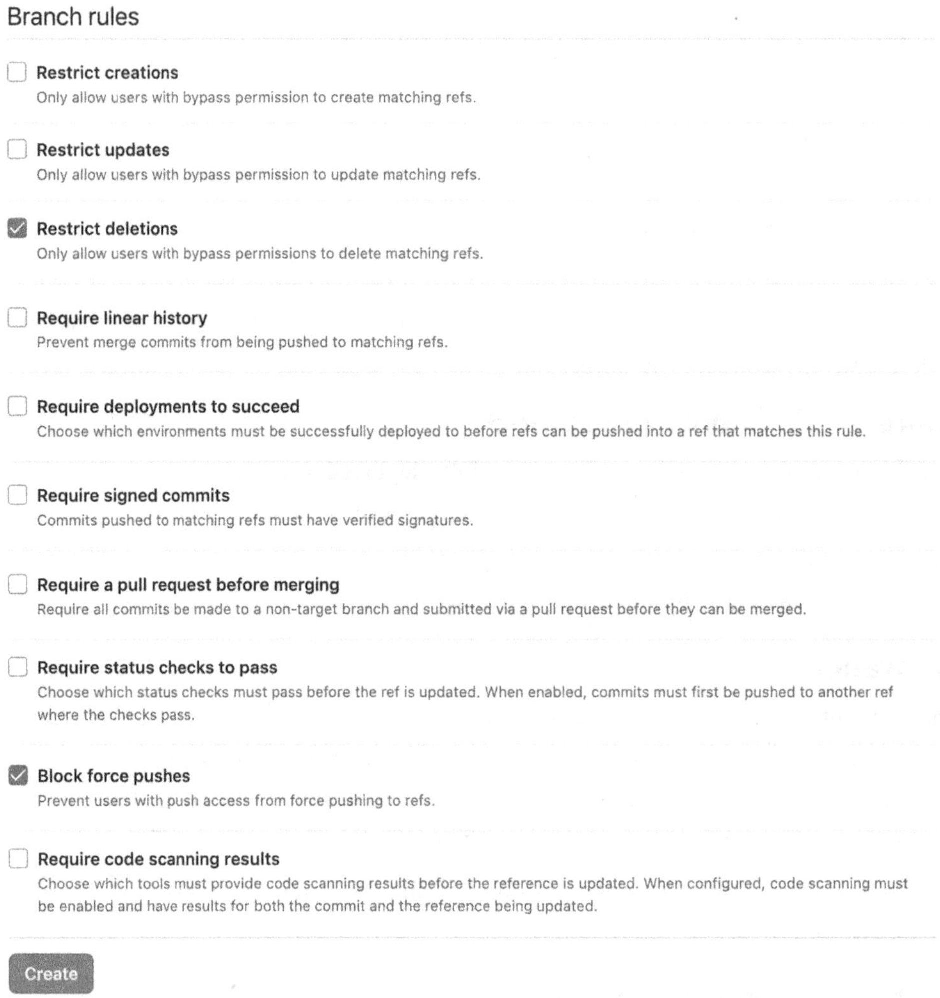

Branch rules

☐ **Restrict creations**
Only allow users with bypass permission to create matching refs.

☐ **Restrict updates**
Only allow users with bypass permission to update matching refs.

☑ **Restrict deletions**
Only allow users with bypass permissions to delete matching refs.

☐ **Require linear history**
Prevent merge commits from being pushed to matching refs.

☐ **Require deployments to succeed**
Choose which environments must be successfully deployed to before refs can be pushed into a ref that matches this rule.

☐ **Require signed commits**
Commits pushed to matching refs must have verified signatures.

☐ **Require a pull request before merging**
Require all commits be made to a non-target branch and submitted via a pull request before they can be merged.

☐ **Require status checks to pass**
Choose which status checks must pass before the ref is updated. When enabled, commits must first be pushed to another ref where the checks pass.

☑ **Block force pushes**
Prevent users with push access from force pushing to refs.

☐ **Require code scanning results**
Choose which tools must provide code scanning results before the reference is updated. When configured, code scanning must be enabled and have results for both the commit and the reference being updated.

Create

Figure 5.9: Cross-section of available branch protection rules

All these rules can be configured to *target* specific branches or all branches.

Targeting branches

You can decide which branches you want to make a ruleset for. Branch targeting determines which branches will be protected by the ruleset. These branches can be explicitly named or dynamically inferred through some targeting criteria:

Target branches

Branch targeting determines which branches will be protected by this ruleset. Use inclusion patterns to expand the list of branches under this ruleset. Use exclusion patterns to exclude branches.

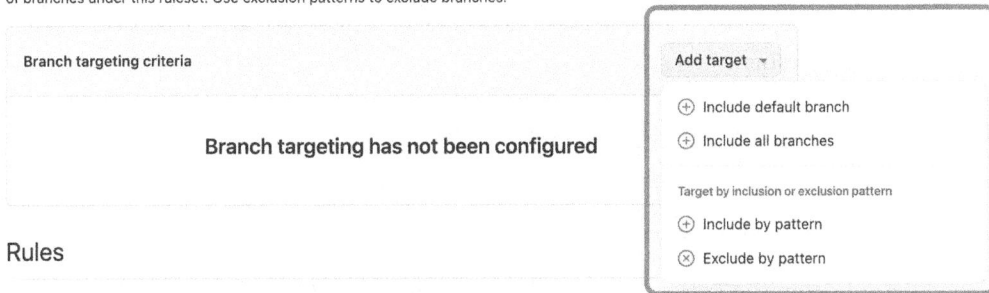

Branch targeting criteria	Add target ▾
Branch targeting has not been configured	⊕ Include default branch
	⊕ Include all branches
	Target by inclusion or exclusion pattern
	⊕ Include by pattern
	⊗ Exclude by pattern

Rules

Figure 5.10: Branches can be targeted explicitly or dynamically

On GitHub, you can dynamically target branches in a branch ruleset using patterns with the fnmatch syntax. This allows you to apply rules to branches that match specific naming patterns, making it easier to manage rules across multiple branches without having to specify each one individually.

There are two options for dynamically targeting branches:

- **Include by pattern**: Branches that match the pattern specified will be targeted
- **Exclude by pattern**: Branches that match the pattern will not be targeted

About the patterns, let's go a little deeper into understanding the fnmatch syntax.

Using the fnmatch syntax

The fnmatch syntax supports wildcards and patterns to match branch names. Here are some common patterns you can use:

- Wildcard (*):
  - Matches any string of characters except for the directory separator (/)
  - Example: feature/* matches feature/branch1, feature/branch2, etc.
- Double asterisk (**):
  - Matches any string of characters, including directory separators.
  - Example: release/** matches release/v1.0, release/v1.0/patch1, etc.

- Question mark (?):

  - Matches any single character

  - Example: `bugfix/?` matches `bugfix/a`, `bugfix/b`, etc.

> **Certification tip**
>
> A question might list different `fnmatch` wildcard and pattern combinations in its answers, and you may be asked to choose which `fnmatch` syntax best interprets the question.

Steps to configure dynamic branch targeting

Follow these steps from within the **Add branch ruleset** configuration screen:

1. Define the branch name pattern:

   a. Within the **Target branches** section and on the **Branch targeting criteria** box, click on the **Add target** dropdown (see *Figure 5.10*).

   b. Select **Include by pattern** or **Exclude by pattern**.

   c. In the **Branch naming pattern** field, enter your pattern using the `fnmatch` syntax.

   The following example targets all branches starting with `feature/`, enter `feature/*`.

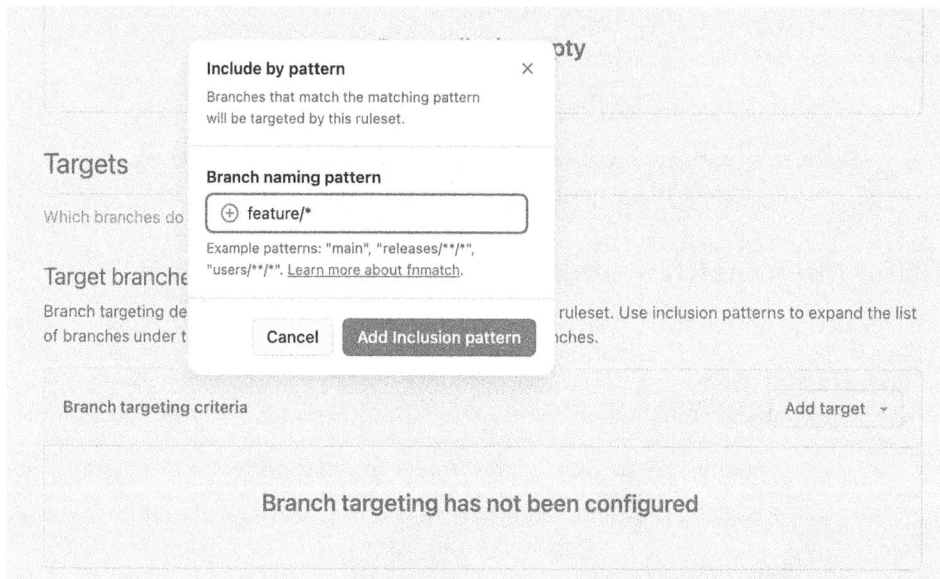

Figure 5.11: Dynamically targeting branches by the fnmatch pattern

2. Configure the protection rules:

    a. Set the desired protection rules (e.g., require pull request reviews, status checks, etc.).

    b. Save the changes.

Here are some example patterns:

- `main`: Targets the `main` branch specifically
- `release/*`: Targets all branches that start with `release/`
- `hotfix/**`: Targets all branches that start with `hotfix/` and include any subdirectories
- `*`: Targets all branches in the repository

Here are some benefits:

- **Scalability**: Easily apply rules to multiple branches without manually specifying each one
- **Consistency**: Ensure consistent rules across branches that follow a naming convention
- **Flexibility**: Adapt to different branch naming schemes and project structures

Configuring the default branch

We might have mentioned this before but in case we didn't, here it is. A default branch is the primary branch of a repository. It is the branch that GitHub displays when someone visits the repository, and it is the initial branch that Git checks out locally when someone clones the repository. Typically, this is where the production codebase resides.

Historically, default branches in Git repos have been named `master` or `main`. However, nothing stops you from changing this.

To configure or change the default branch for a repository, follow these steps:

1. **Navigate to the repository Settings tab**:

    a. Go to your repository on GitHub.

    b. Click on the **Settings** tab.

2. **Access the branch settings**:

    a. In the left sidebar, click on **Branches**.

3. **Change the default branch:**

    a. Under the **Default branch** section, you will see the current default branch name.

    b. Click the drop-down menu next to the default branch name and select the branch you want to set as the new default.

    c. Click **Update**.

4. **Confirm the change:**

    a. Read the warning message that appears, as changing the default branch can affect open pull requests and local clones.

    b. If you understand the implications, click **I understand, update the default branch**.

You can also set the default branch name for all new repositories you create:

1. **Go to your account settings:**

    a. In the upper-right corner of any GitHub page, click your profile photo, then click **Settings.**

2. **Access the repository settings:**

    a. In the **Code, planning, and automation** section of the sidebar, click **Repositories**.

3. **Change the default branch name:**

    a. Under the **Repository default branch** section, enter the desired default branch name in the text field and click **Update**.

This will apply to any new repositories you create. Alternatively, if you wish to change it for just one existing repository, follow these steps:

1. Click **Settings** from the horizontal menu on the repository you wish to modify.

2. Go to **General** from the left-hand navigation.

3. Under the **Default branch** section, click the pencil icon ✏ to edit.

4. Enter the new name and click **Rename branch**.

Benefits of setting a default branch

Here are some benefits of setting the default branch:

- **Consistency**: Ensures a consistent starting point for all collaborators
- **Clarity**: Makes it clear where the main development happens

- **Automation:** Many CI/CD tools and workflows are configured to work with the default branch

Collaborative branch management

Collaboration is a key aspect of modern software development. Let's briefly explain a few tips for improving collaborative management:

- **Strategies for team collaboration:** Effective collaboration involves clear communication and well-defined workflows. Teams often use feature branches for new features, bugfix branches for bug fixes, and release branches for preparing production releases.
- **Pull requests and code reviews: Pull requests (PRs)** are a GitHub feature that facilitates code reviews and discussions before merging changes into the main branch. This process helps maintain code quality and encourages knowledge sharing among team members. In the next chapter, *Chapter 6, Pull Requests and Code Reviews*, we will discuss this in detail.

Perfect! This marks the end of our chapter. Let's summarize the amazing things we discussed.

Summary

In this chapter, we focused on collaborative development on GitHub, exploring advanced techniques to work effectively with teams. We delved into the branching model in Git and on GitHub, emphasizing the importance of a well-structured branching strategy for team collaboration.

We started by understanding branches in Git, which allow us to diverge from the main codebase to work on features, bug fixes, or experiments in isolation. Branches enable parallel development, helping us manage different versions of a project and collaborate efficiently. We discussed the benefits of using branches, such as enhanced collaboration, isolation of work, simplified code reviews, and rollback capability.

Next, we covered the process of creating branches using the git command, the GitHub website, and IDEs such as VS Code. We also highlighted the importance of consistent naming conventions for branches to avoid confusion and improve collaboration.

Switching between branches is another crucial aspect we explored. We explained how to update the working directory, preserve uncommitted changes, and update the branch pointer. We also discussed the process of stashing changes if needed.

In addition, we examined merging and conflict resolution. We described different types of merges, such as merge commits, squash merges, and rebase merges. We provided best practices for clean merges and strategies for resolving conflicts that may arise during the merge process.

Finally, we looked at various ways to manage and configure branches, including administering on Git, as well as protecting branches on GitHub using feature-rich protection rulesets.

By following these strategies and best practices, we can improve our development processes, enhance code quality, and collaborate more effectively on GitHub. Up next, we will cover how to get your code peer-reviewed through a now well-established concept we call **pull requests**. Strap your seat belt for another exciting chapter.

Test your knowledge

1. What is the primary benefit of using branches in Git for collaborative development?

    a. It allows developers to work on different features simultaneously without interfering with each other's work

    b. It simplifies the commit history by combining all commits into a single commit

    c. It ensures that the main codebase remains stable and reliable by preventing any changes

    d. It automatically resolves conflicts between different branches

2. Which command is used to create and switch to a new branch simultaneously in Git?

    a. `git branch <branch-name>`

    b. `git checkout <branch-name>`

    c. `git checkout -b <branch-name>`

    d. `git switch <branch-name>`

3. What is a squash merge in Git?

    a. A merge strategy that combines the histories of the merged branches without creating a new commit

    b. A merge strategy that combines all the commits from a feature branch into a single commit before merging it into the `main` branch

    c. A merge strategy that replays the commits from the source branch onto the base/target branch, creating a linear history

    d. A merge strategy that automatically resolves conflicts between different branches

Useful links

- Git head and HEAD: `https://git-scm.com/docs/gitglossary#def_head`

- Managing a branch protection rule: `https://docs.github.com/en/repositories/configuring-branches-and-merges-in-your-repository/managing-protected-branches/managing-a-branch-protection-rule`

- Using the fnmatch syntax: `https://docs.github.com/en/repositories/configuring-branches-and-merges-in-your-repository/managing-rulesets/creating-rulesets-for-a-repository#using-fnmatch-syntax`

- Changing the default branch: `https://docs.github.com/en/repositories/configuring-branches-and-merges-in-your-repository/managing-branches-in-your-repository/changing-the-default-branch`

6

Pull Requests and Code Reviews

Welcome to the more exciting part of GitHub – pull requests. 🚀

In the world of collaborative software development, the **pull request** (**PR**) process stands as a cornerstone for maintaining code quality and fostering teamwork. This chapter delves into the intricacies of pull requests and code reviews on GitHub, providing you with the tools and knowledge necessary to navigate this essential workflow effectively.

As we explore the process, you'll learn how to conduct effective code reviews that not only enhance the quality of the code but also promote a culture of constructive feedback within your team. By mastering these skills, you will gain the confidence to integrate changes safely, ensuring that your projects remain robust and maintainable.

Get ready to dive into the world of pull requests and code reviews, where collaboration meets quality assurance and every line of code counts!

We will cover the following main topics:

- What is a pull request?
- The pull request lifecycle
- Lab 6.1: Conducting a code review with a pull request
- Conducting effective code reviews
- Integrating changes with confidence

Technical requirements

For the labs in this chapter, you will need the following:

- A working computer with Git installed
- The my-blank-repo created in *Lab 3.1* in *Chapter 3* and last updated in *Lab 4.1* in *Chapter 4*
- You will also need a second GitHub individual account that will be used as a reviewer of code

What is a pull request?

The concept of the pull request was popularized by GitHub. You could say GitHub invented this idea, launching this feature way back in February 2008 (https://github.blog/news-insights/the-library/oh-yeah-there-s-pull-requests-now/). It was designed to facilitate the process of merging code changes. A pull request is a request to merge code changes from one branch into another, typically from a feature branch into the main branch. It facilitates code review and discussion, ensuring that all changes are vetted before becoming part of the project. A **pull request** allows developers to notify other team members maintaining the repo that their work is ready to be reviewed and can be merged after a successful review.

A PR is more than just a request to merge code; it represents a dialogue between developers, where ideas are exchanged, improvements are suggested, and code is refined. Understanding the pull request lifecycle is crucial, as it encompasses everything from the initial creation of a PR to the final integration of changes into the main codebase.

> **Importance in collaborative development**
>
> In a team environment, pull requests promote transparency and collaboration. They enable team members to review each other's work, share knowledge, and maintain high code quality, ultimately leading to more robust and maintainable software.
>
> Pull requests are now a household feature, common to most modern version control systems, particularly Git-based platforms.

But before them, what were teams using? Let's discuss this in the next section.

How was code managed before pull requests existed?

Before pull requests, code management relied on various practices and tools for collaboration and version control. Here are four key methods that were used:

Version control systems (VCSs):

- **Concurrent Versions System (CVS)**: An early VCS that allowed multiple developers to work simultaneously but lacked modern features such as branching
- **Subversion (SVN)**: More popular than CVS, SVN improved branching and merging but still required manual code reviews

Manual code reviews:

- **Email and patch files**: Developers sent code changes as patch files via email, leading to potential miscommunication
- **In-person reviews**: Teams discussed code changes in meetings, which fostered collaboration but was time-consuming

Branching and merging:

- **Local branches**: Developers created local branches for features, merging changes manually, often resulting in conflicts
- **Centralized repositories**: Teams pushed changes to a single server, complicating conflict management

Documentation and change logs:

- **Change logs**: Maintained to document changes, requiring discipline for consistency
- **Commit messages**: Used but often lacked clarity, relying on memory for context

In the next section, we will look at the lifecycle of a pull request.

The pull request lifecycle

Now let us go through a typical review process for a developer who has just finished making some changes in their development branch. On GitHub, you create a pull request.

Creating a pull request

Creating a pull request is a straightforward process, but following best practices can enhance clarity and effectiveness. Here's a step-by-step guide on initiating a pull request:

1. **Complete your changes**: Ensure your feature or bug fix is ready in a *separate branch*.
2. **Push your branch**: Push your changes to the remote repository on GitHub.
3. **Open a pull request**: Navigate to the repository on GitHub, click on the **Pull requests** tab, and select **New pull request**.

4.   **Select branches**: Choose the base branch (usually the main branch) and compare it with your feature branch.

5.   **Fill in details**: Provide a clear title and a detailed description of the changes made, including any relevant context or issue references.

Before we talk about the code review process itself, let's discuss the concept of a diff.

What is a diff?

A **diff** (short for "difference") is a tool or format used to show the changes between two versions of a file or codebase. In the context of version control systems such as Git, a diff highlights what has been added, removed, or modified between commits, branches, or even individual files.

Key points about diffs:

- **Comparison**: Diffs allow you to compare different versions of files, making it easier to see what changes have been made over time

- **Format**: Typically, a diff will display lines that have been added with a + sign and lines that have been removed with a - sign

- **Usage**: Diffs are commonly used in code reviews, pull requests, and when merging changes to ensure that the modifications are clear and understandable

- **Example**: If you modified a line in a code file, a diff might show the following:

Figure 6.1: Visual representation of a diff

This visual representation and color coding help developers quickly identify changes and understand the evolution of the codebase.

> **Certification tip**
>
> You may be given a visual representation of a diff and choose from the options what the final line of code will be.

Now let us talk about some good practices to consider when raising a PR.

Good practices for writing clear descriptions

I would recommend the following good practices when creating a pull request:

- **Be concise but informative**: Summarize what the changes do and why they are necessary.

- **Use bullet points**: Highlight key changes or features for easy readability.

- **Reference issues**: Link to any related issues or discussions to provide context. To reference issues on GitHub, use the hashtag (#) followed by the issue number. This will automatically link the issue once the PR is created/updated. We will try this out in the lab exercise in this chapter.

Review process overview

The review process is crucial for maintaining code quality and fostering collaboration among team members, particularly when maintaining a large codebase. The roles involved in the review process are typically as follows:

- **Author**: The developer who created the pull request and is responsible for addressing feedback

- **Reviewers**: Team members who assess the code changes, provide feedback, and approve or request modifications

- **Maintainers**: Often project leads or senior developers who oversee the merging process and ensure adherence to project standards

In terms of timeline and expectations, three things should be considered:

- **Initial review**: Reviewers should aim to provide feedback within a reasonable timeframe, typically within a few days

- **Iterative feedback**: Authors may need to make several revisions based on reviewer comments, fostering an iterative dialogue

> **Note**
>
> One great thing about GitHub's pull request is that it tracks everything visually in a single timeline – the commits, the comments/reviews, and all other work related to the PR.

- **Final approval**: Once all feedback is addressed and the code meets the project's standards, the pull request can be approved and merged

Understanding the pull request lifecycle is essential for effective collaboration in software development. By mastering the creation and review of pull requests, developers can contribute to a culture of quality and teamwork, ensuring that every change enhances the project.

Before we go into the lab, the following diagram illustrates the flow of a typical code review process. This will help you visualize what steps each person takes.

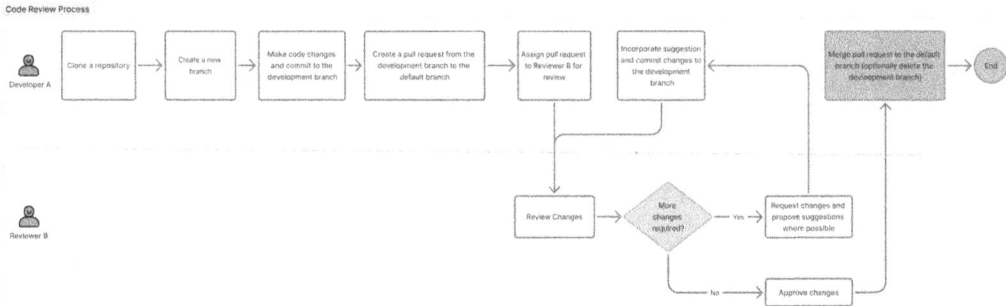

Figure 6.2: Flow diagram of the code review process between Developer A and Reviewer B

🔍 **Quick tip:** Need to see a high-resolution version of this image? Open this book in the next-gen Packt Reader or view it in the PDF/ePub copy.

📖 **The next-gen Packt Reader** and a **free PDF/ePub copy** of this book are included with your purchase. Scan the QR code OR visit `packtpub.com/unlock`, then use the search bar to find this book by name. Double-check the edition shown to make sure you get the right one.

In the preceding flow diagram, the yellow box is a critical decision point at which **Reviewer B** determines whether the code changes have satisfied the requirements for a merge. If not, the loop cycle around the yellow decision box continues until no more changes are required. Once the review is complete and the change is approved, it can then the merged to the trunk branch (green box) to mark the end of the pull request and review cycle.

Let us now see this in practice in the following lab exercise.

Lab 6.1: Conducting a code review with a pull request

Grab a coffee or tea! This lab exercise may take you some time. Let's go! 🫖

In this lab, we will make some code changes, submit them for review by creating a pull request, and go through the review process to have it approved before merging it into the main/production branch.

Step 1: Create a new GitHub user for review

1. **Sign up for GitHub**: Before we go on, we need at least two GitHub individual accounts. If you don't have a second account to use, go to GitHub and create an additional individual account. You can watch the *Chapter 2, Lab 2: Signing up for a GitHub account* video. This will be your reviewer account. Creating a GitHub account is free.

2. **Verify your email**: Follow the instructions in the verification email to activate your account.

Here's your GitHub launch code, @ayooutlook!

Continue signing up for GitHub by entering the code below:

87577753

Open GitHub

Once completed, you can start using all of GitHub's features to explore, build, and share projects.

Not able to enter the code? Paste the following link into your browser: https://github.com/users/ayooutlook/emails/196249568/confirm_verification/87 577753?via_launch_code_email=true

Figure 6.3: Verify new GitHub account email to complete registration

For this lab, let us call your first GitHub account **Developer A,** and we will call the newly created account **Reviewer B.**

Step 2: Invite a collaborator

1. **As Developer A, navigate to your repository:**

    a. Click on your profile icon in the top-right corner.

    b. Select **Your repositories** from the drop-down menu.

    c. Click on the repository you want to add a collaborator to.

2. **Go to Settings:**

    a. In your repository, look for the **Settings** tab (usually found on the right side of the menu):

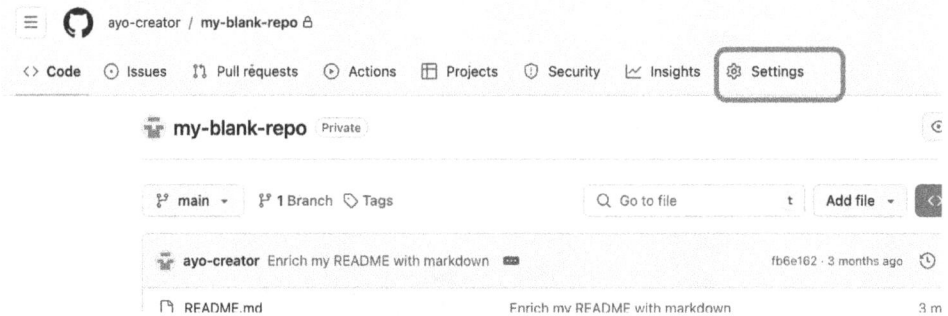

Figure 6.4: Settings tab on the repository menu

3. **Select Collaborators:**

    a. In the left sidebar, click on **Collaborators** (if you are using an Org-scoped repo, the menu you see here will display as **Collaborators and teams**):

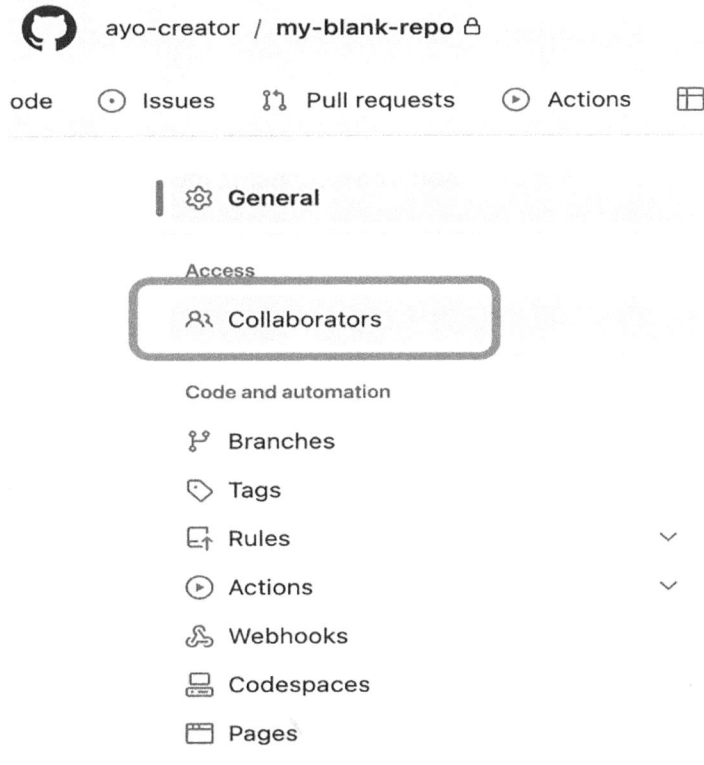

Figure 6.5: Collaborators menu in Settings

4. **Invite a collaborator**:

    a. Click on the **Add people** button.

    b. In the search box, type the GitHub handle (username) of Reviewer B:

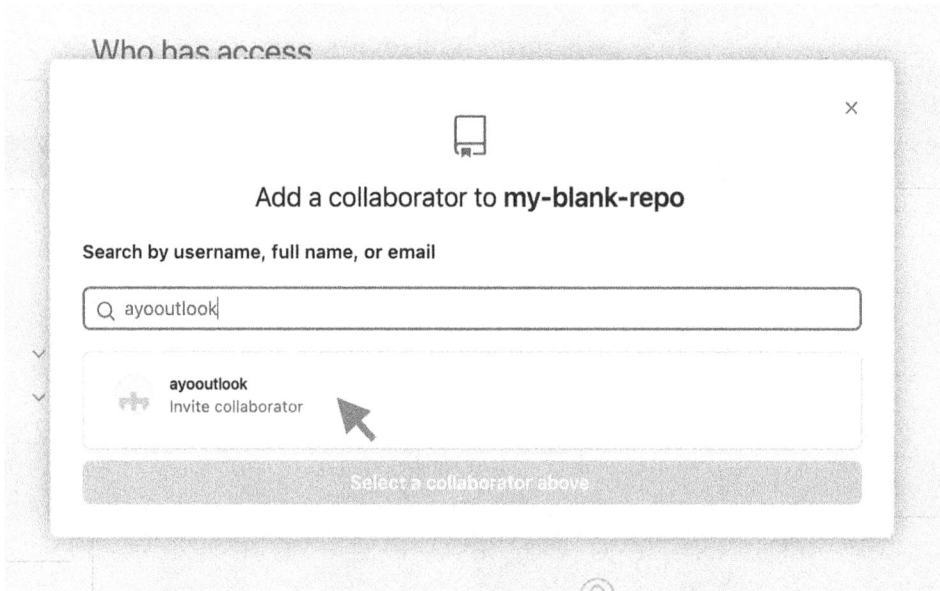

Figure 6.6: Select collaborator from the search result

5. **Send invitation**:

    a. Click on **Add \<username\>** (where **\<username\>** represents the handle of Reviewer B. This will send an invitation to Reviewer B.

    b. Reviewer B will receive an email notification and must accept the invitation to gain access.

c.   In the email sent to Reviewer B, click the **View invitation** button in the email:

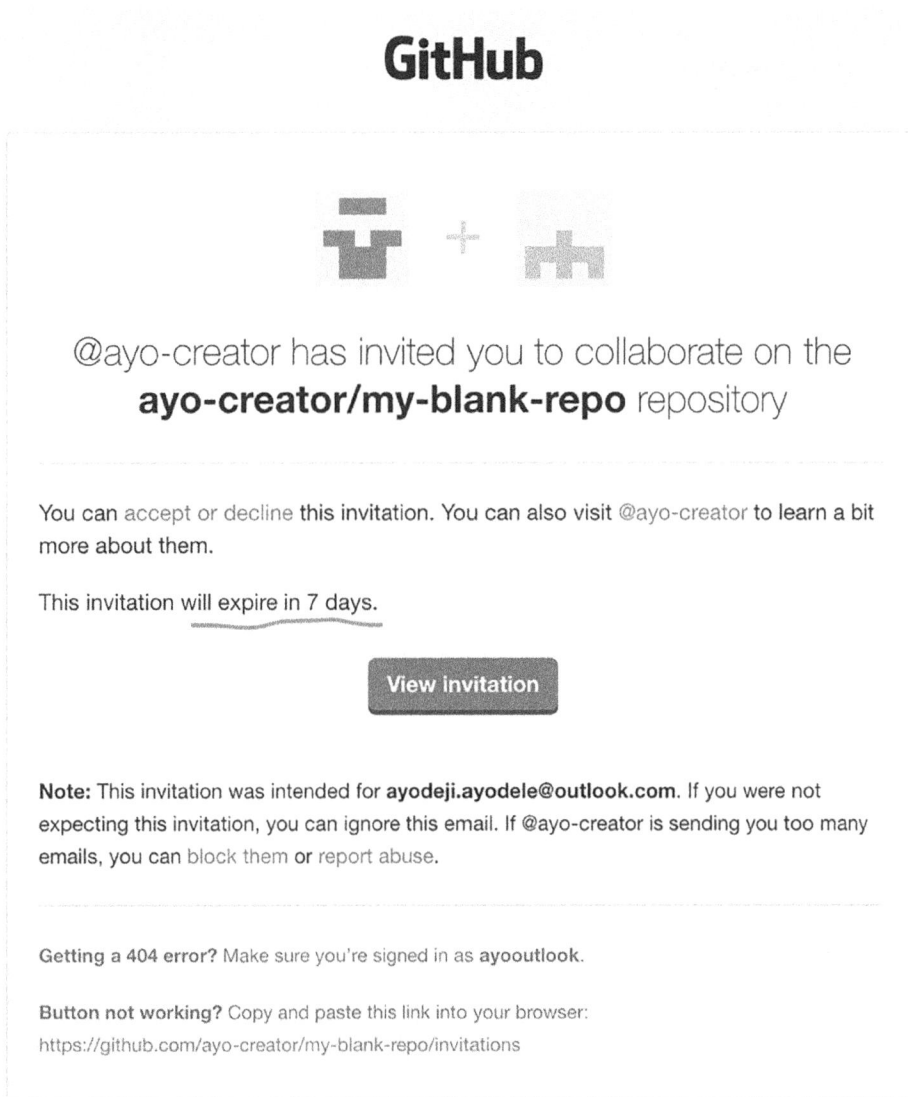

GitHub

@ayo-creator has invited you to collaborate on the
ayo-creator/my-blank-repo repository

You can accept or decline this invitation. You can also visit @ayo-creator to learn a bit more about them.

This invitation will expire in 7 days.

View invitation

Note: This invitation was intended for **ayodeji.ayodele@outlook.com**. If you were not expecting this invitation, you can ignore this email. If @ayo-creator is sending you too many emails, you can block them or report abuse.

Getting a 404 error? Make sure you're signed in as **ayooutlook**.

Button not working? Copy and paste this link into your browser:
https://github.com/ayo-creator/my-blank-repo/invitations

Figure 6.7: Sample invitation email

6. **Accept invitation:**

   a. Log in to the ensuing web page launched from the previous step as Reviewer B and click on **Accept invitation:**

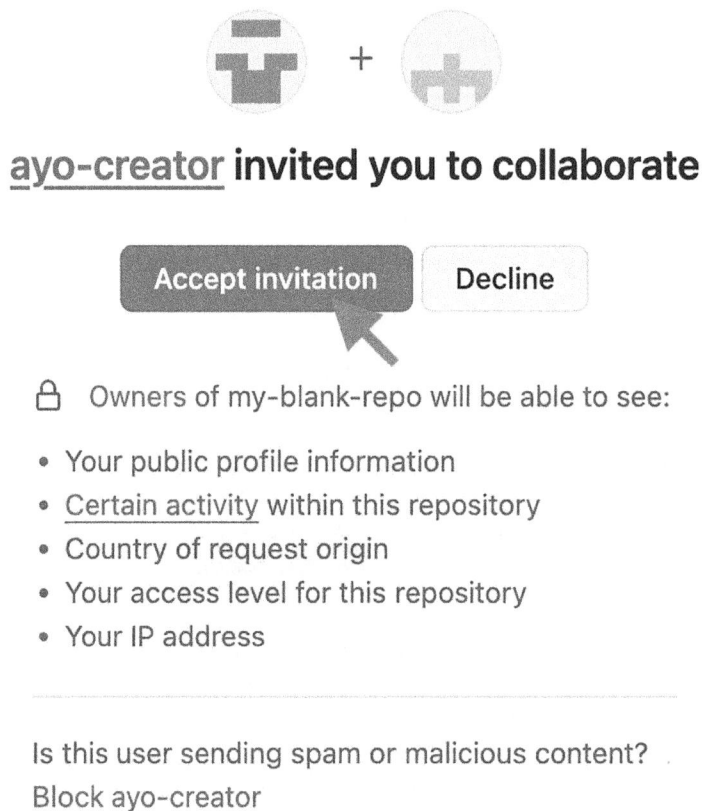

Figure 6.8: Accept the invitation to collaborate

   b. Once accepted, you'll see their username listed under the **Manage access** section for Developer A.

Multi-account support

GitHub supports logging in to multiple accounts in the same browser. You can alternate between different GitHub accounts that you are signed in to using the account switcher. You can find the account switcher in the context menu when you click on your avatar, helping you easily switch between user accounts without re-entering your credentials.

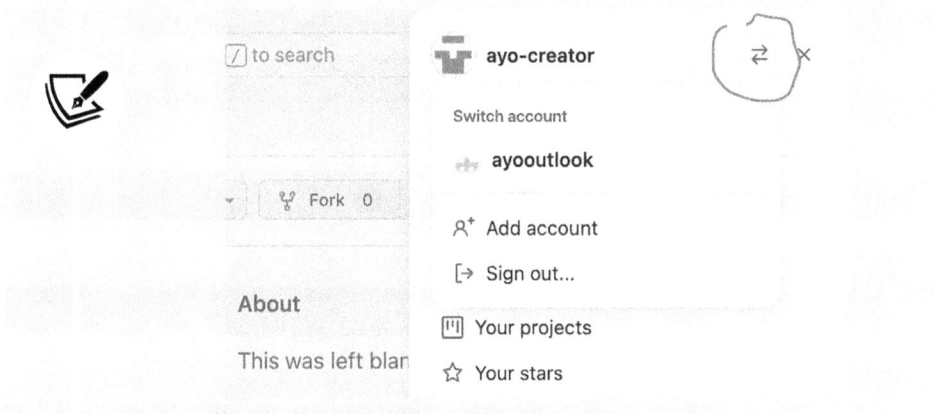

Figure 6.9: GitHub account switcher

Step 3: Clone the repository

Now, let's clone the repo. This *must* be performed by Developer A:

1. Open Terminal or Command Prompt.

2. Clone the `my-blank-repo` repository:

```
git clone https://github.com/<your-username/my-blank-repo.git
```

(Feel free to use any IDE of choice instead of the CLI.)

```
● ● ●                        my-blank-repo — -zsh — 102×35
recordingartist@Ayodejis-MacBook-Pro ~ % cd documents
recordingartist@Ayodejis-MacBook-Pro documents % cd my-repos-home
recordingartist@Ayodejis-MacBook-Pro my-repos-home % git clone https://github.com/ayo-creator/my-blank
-repo.git
Cloning into 'my-blank-repo'...
remote: Enumerating objects: 6, done.
remote: Counting objects: 100% (6/6), done.
remote: Compressing objects: 100% (4/4), done.
remote: Total 6 (delta 0), reused 0 (delta 0), pack-reused 0 (from 0)
Receiving objects: 100% (6/6), done.
recordingartist@Ayodejis-MacBook-Pro my-repos-home %
```

Figure 6.10: A local clone of my-blank-repo

3. Navigate to the repository:

```
cd my-blank-repo
```

Step 4: Make code changes

1. Create a new branch:

```
git checkout -b add-simple-file
```

2. Create a new file – for example, create a file named `hello_world.py`:

```
echo 'print("Hello, World!")' > hello_world.py
```

3. Stage the file:

```
git add hello_world.py
```

4. Commit the changes:

```
git commit -m "Add hello_world.py"
```

5. Push the new branch:

```
git push origin add-simple-file
```

```
● ● ●                          🗂 my-blank-repo — -zsh — 102×35

remote: Total 6 (delta 0), reused 0 (delta 0), pack-reused 0 (from 0)
Receiving objects: 100% (6/6), done.
recordingartist@Ayodejis-MacBook-Pro my-repos-home % cd my-blank-repo
recordingartist@Ayodejis-MacBook-Pro my-blank-repo % git checkout -b add-simple-file
Switched to a new branch 'add-simple-file'
recordingartist@Ayodejis-MacBook-Pro my-blank-repo % echo 'print("Hello, World!")'> hello_world.py
recordingartist@Ayodejis-MacBook-Pro my-blank-repo % git add hello_world.py
recordingartist@Ayodejis-MacBook-Pro my-blank-repo % git commit -m "Add hello world python file hello_
world.py"
[add-simple-file a2930ce] Add hello world python file hello_world.py
 1 file changed, 1 insertion(+)
 create mode 100644 hello_world.py
recordingartist@Ayodejis-MacBook-Pro my-blank-repo % git push origin add-simple-file
Enumerating objects: 4, done.
Counting objects: 100% (4/4), done.
Delta compression using up to 10 threads
Compressing objects: 100% (2/2), done.
Writing objects: 100% (3/3), 324 bytes | 324.00 KiB/s, done.
Total 3 (delta 0), reused 0 (delta 0), pack-reused 0 (from 0)
remote:
remote: Create a pull request for 'add-simple-file' on GitHub by visiting:
remote:      https://github.com/ayo-creator/my-blank-repo/pull/new/add-simple-file
remote:
To https://github.com/ayo-creator/my-blank-repo.git
 * [new branch]      add-simple-file -> add-simple-file
recordingartist@Ayodejis-MacBook-Pro my-blank-repo % 
```

Figure 6.11: Push code changes to remote origin

Step 5: Create a pull request

1. While signed in as Developer A, go to your repository on GitHub. You will notice a yellow banner at the top showing that some changes to a branch have just been discovered. GitHub auto-detects recent changes to a branch and suggests a pull request to you:

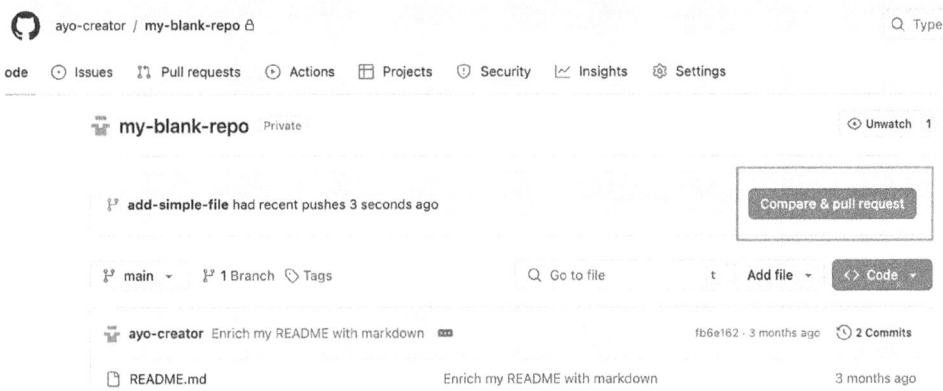

Figure 6.12: Compare & pull request shows in a yellow banner

2. Click on **Compare & pull request**.

3. Ensure that you have the **main** branch selected in the dropdown on the left-hand side (destination) and the **add-simple-file** branch on the right (source). The branch you are merging from should be on the right:

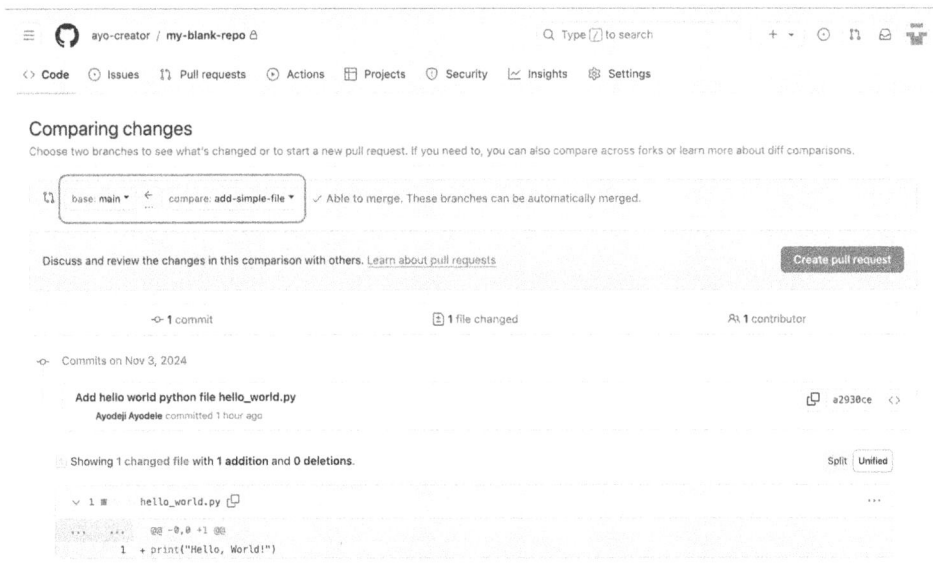

Figure 6.13: Compare branch and the base branch in a pull request

4. GitHub will make a quick assessment, displaying a diff between the compare branch (source) and the base branch (destination) and then adding a green tick at the top if you are "*able to merge*". This means there are no conflicts with the changes you're introducing, were they to be merged.

5. **Add a title and description**: Provide a brief description of the changes under the **Add a title** and **Add a description** fields.

6. On the right-hand side, click on the gear icon (⚙) next to **Reviewers**. A dropdown of users should open. Search for and select Reviewer B's handle.

7. Click on **Create pull request**. Reviewer B should get an email notification that Developer A requested their review.

Step 6: Conduct a code review

1. Switch to the reviewer account (**Reviewer B**) by using the account switcher or log in with the new GitHub user you created if not already signed in.

2. You may notice the information in a yellow banner at the top saying Developer A requested your review. You can take a shortcut by clicking **Add your review**, but we will take the longer process here, just in case you don't:

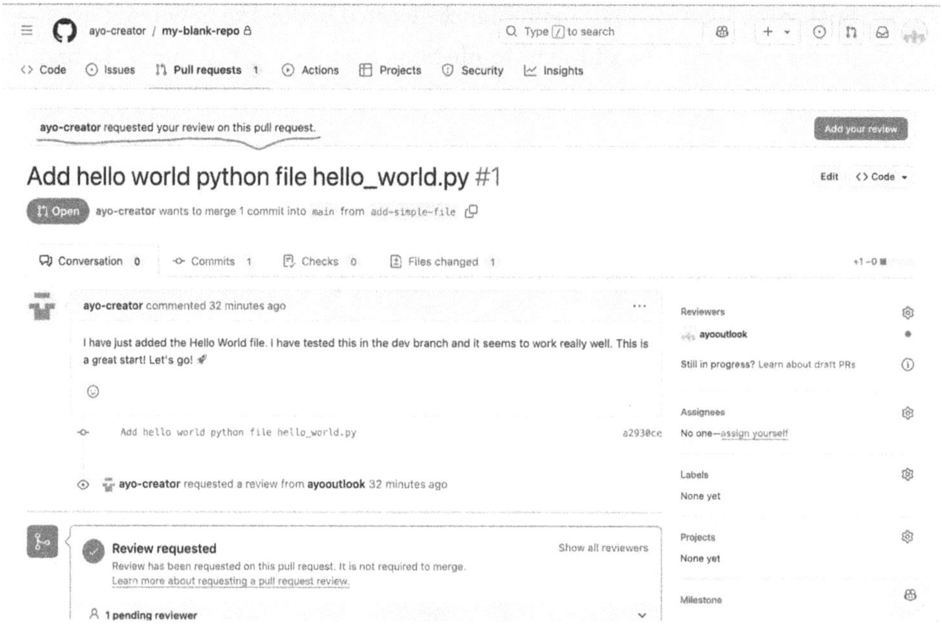

Figure 6.14: Pull Request review suggested to reviewer in a yellow banner

3. Navigate to the **Pull requests** tab in **my-blank-repo** and select the pull request that matches the title you created.

4. In the **Conversation** tab, examine the description and the timeline trail below it.

5. Now navigate to the **Commits** tab and examine the list. This will display all the commits that were proposed to be merged in chronological order.

6. Navigate to the **Files changed** tab.

7. **Review the code**: Check the changes made in `hello_world.py`.

8. **Leave comments**: If you have suggestions or questions, use the comment feature. Every line of code is numbered. To make a comment on a particular line of code, hover over the line number (a plus sign (+) should appear):

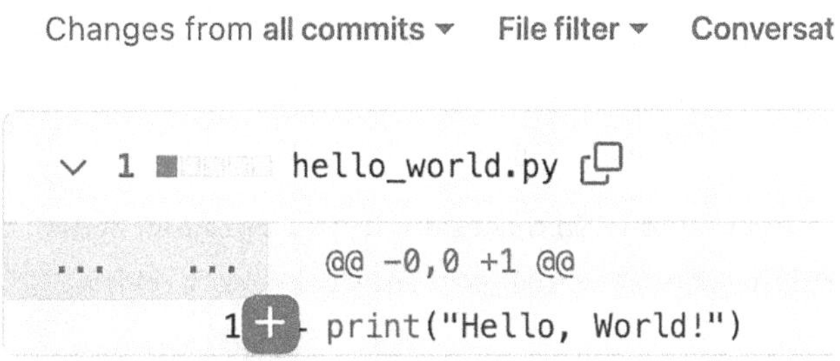

Figure 6.15: Click + to leave comments

When you click on the plus sign next to a line or after selecting multiple lines, the following popup opens:

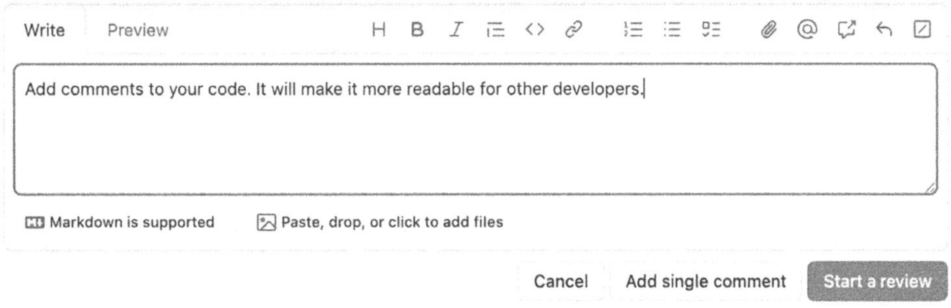

Figure 6.16: Add a review comment

You can add a single comment. You can also do this for multiple lines. Adding a single comment is for just adding comments; it may not require actions from the developer. **Starting a review**, on the other hand, is a new review cycle, which may require back and forth between the developer and reviewer.

Propose your code changes as a reviewer

Furthermore, you can propose your own actual code changes directly from the comment dialog box that shows up. This way, you are suggesting actual code that will be merged with the code that Developer A proposed while within the PR. To do this, click on **Add a suggestion**:

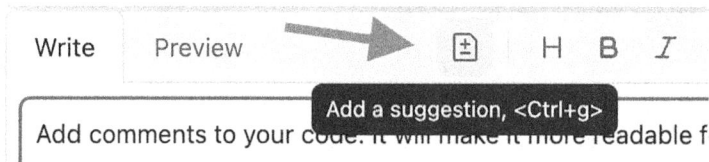

Figure 6.17: You can propose a code suggestion besides just explaining your review

This will append markdown text to the comment box. Write your suggested code within the ``` `suggestion` markdown block. All the code written within that will replace the line number(s) you added the suggestion to (*step 6*).

9. Type in the actual code. In this example, you can add a Python comment, `# This will print Hello, World to the screen`. Click **Start a review**.

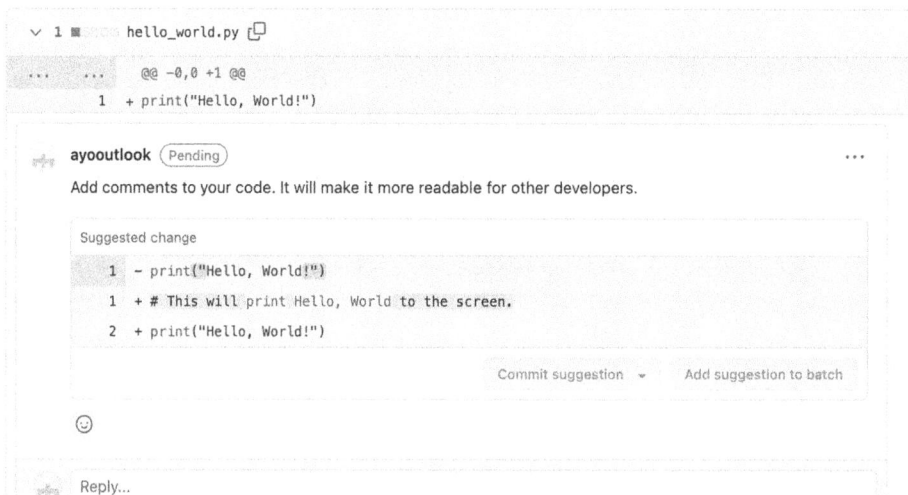

Figure 6.18: Code suggestions by Reviewer B

Now finish your first review by clicking on **Finish your review** on the right.

10. Type your final comments in the box and select **Request changes**. This means Developer A must make those changes before the code can be merged (there are other options available too).

11. Click **Submit review**.

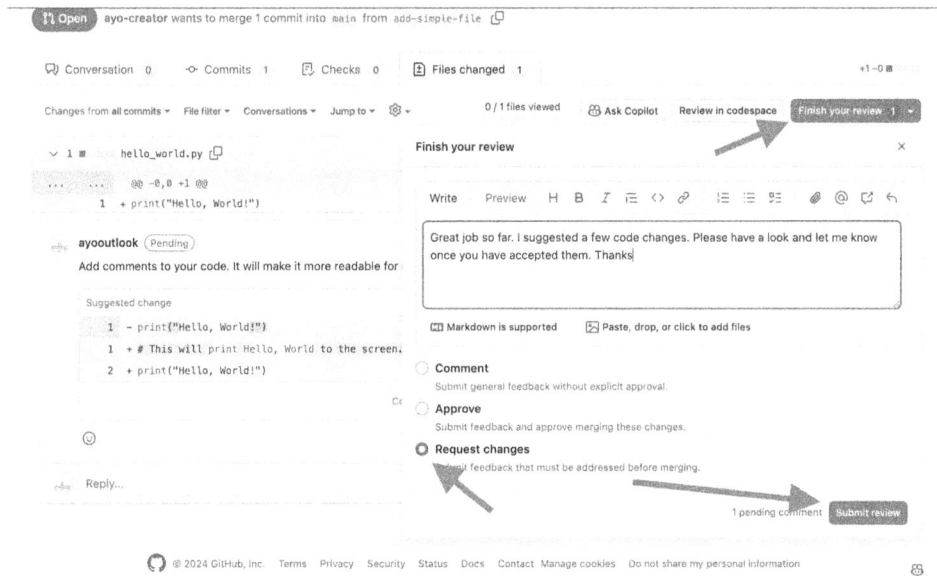

Figure 6.19: Reviewer B submits first review

12. Switch back to Developer A and go to the **Conversation** tab for Developer A to examine the review comments and code change suggestions.

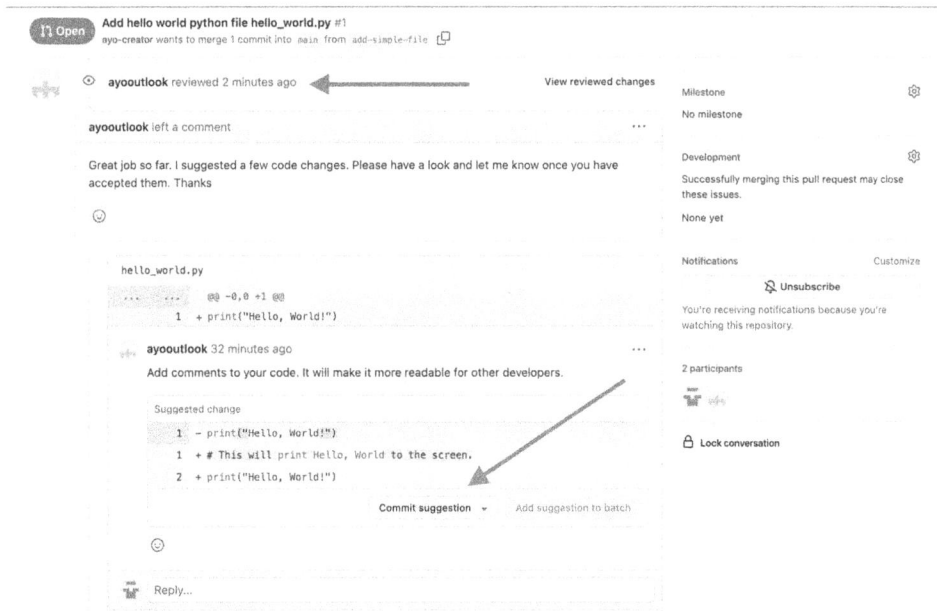

Figure 6.20: Developer A accepts and commits code suggestions

13. To accept the suggestion, select **Commit suggestion** and type a commit message in the ensuing boxes.

14. Click on **Commit changes**.

15. Next to the reviewer at the top right, click the recycle icon to re-request a review. This will prompt Reviewer B that you're ready for a second review.

Step 7: Approve the pull request

1. Switch to Reviewer B for a final review of the work. You will notice some changes have occurred since the last review.

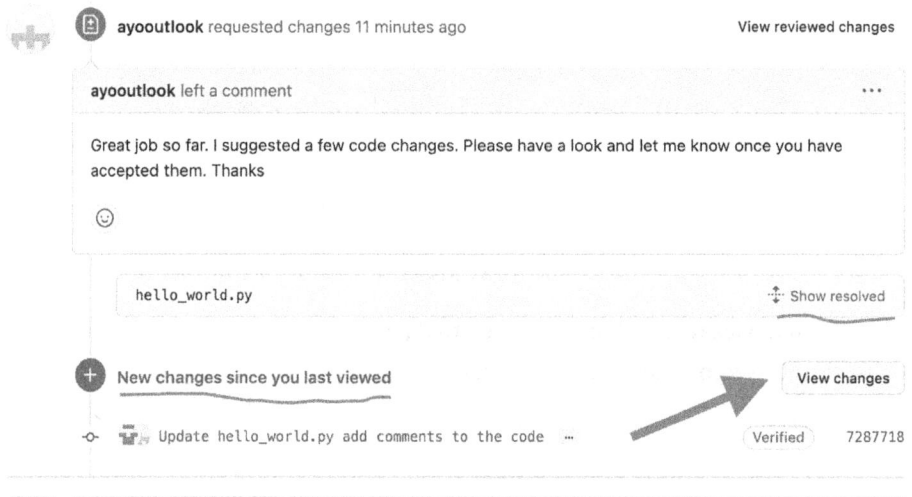

Figure 6.21: Reviewer B reviews additional commits

2. Click **View changes**.

3. **Approve the pull request**: If everything looks good, click on **Review changes** and select **Approve**. Then click **Submit review**.

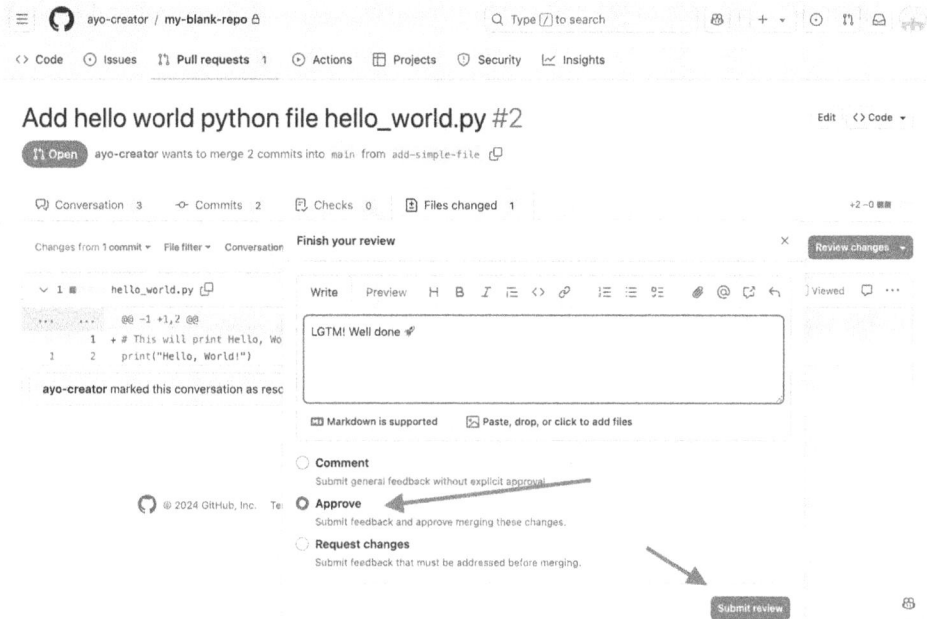

Figure 6.22: Reviewer B approved the pull request

Step 8: Merge the pull request

1. Switch back to your original Developer A account. At the bottom of the **Conversation** tab, you will notice Reviewer B has approved your PR.

2. Click on **Merge pull request** and confirm the merge.

3. Click **Delete the Branch** to optionally remove the add-simple-file branch after merging.

4. Scroll through the conversation timeline and examine the trail. Everything is captured.

> **Certification tip**
>
> You may be given multiple-answer questions to choose two or three answers – for example, which three steps do you need to carry out if you need to make code changes? Clone a repo, make code changes, raise a PR, merge a PR

Congratulations! 🎉 You've successfully created a pull request, conducted a code review, and merged changes into the main branch. Phew! That took a while. Thanks for being patient.

Let us take a deep dive into the code review that you have just practiced and explore how to conduct effective code reviews, a critical component of this lifecycle.

Conducting effective code reviews

Conducting effective code reviews is crucial for maintaining high software development standards. This process ensures code quality and promotes collaboration among team members. Here's a brief overview of how to conduct meaningful code reviews.

Code reviews generally serve two main goals:

- **Ensuring code quality**: The main goal is to verify that the code meets quality standards, checking for correctness and adherence to conventions to catch bugs early
- **Enhancing collaboration**: Code reviews allow team members to learn from each other, sharing insights and best practices

Review techniques

When reading code changes, reviewers should:

- **Understand context**: Familiarize yourself with the purpose of the changes by reading the pull request description
- **Focus on key areas**: Pay attention to critical sections such as algorithms and security

When identifying issues, reviewers should look for:

- **Bugs**: Look for logical errors and unexpected behavior
- **Performance**: Assess code efficiency regarding time complexity and resource usage
- **Security**: Identify vulnerabilities, such as improper input validation

Providing constructive feedback

When delivering feedback, reviewers should:

- **Be specific**: Offer clear, actionable suggestions instead of vague comments
- **Use a respectful tone**: Encourage discussion with phrases such as "Have you considered...?"

When balancing praise and critique, reviewers should:

- **Highlight strengths**: Acknowledge what the author did well to boost morale
- **Constructive criticism**: Focus critiques on the code, not the individual

Using GitHub tools for reviews

GitHub provides several built-in features and AI-powered options that streamline the review process and make collaboration more effective:

- **Comments**: Use inline comments for specific lines to clarify feedback
- **Suggestions**: Propose changes directly in the code to demonstrate feedback
- **Approvals**: Use the approval feature to indicate when the code is ready to merge
- **GitHub Copilot**: Use the AI-powered feature to reduce the review cycle in many ways:
    - Use GitHub Copilot to draft the description of the pull request and an outline of the changes in the commits
    - Invite GitHub Copilot as a reviewer, in addition to humans, to provide suggestions and improvements to code
    - With GitHub Advanced Security, you can use Copilot's AI capabilities to detect vulnerabilities in your code and use Autofix to suggest actual code to fix them

Effective code reviews are vital for developers. By understanding review goals, employing systematic techniques, providing constructive feedback, and utilizing GitHub tools, you can foster a culture of quality and collaboration within your team.

In the next section, we will summarize how you can integrate your code with confidence.

Integrating changes with confidence

Integrating changes into the main codebase is a critical step in the development process. It requires careful consideration to ensure that the integration is smooth and does not introduce issues. We already discussed at length, in previous chapters, some of the topics we will mention, but this section will summarize and guide you through the essential steps for merging changes confidently.

Final checks before merging:

Before merging a pull request, it's vital to perform thorough checks to ensure everything is in order:

- **Tests**: Run all relevant tests to verify that the new code does not break existing functionality. This includes unit tests, integration tests, and any automated tests set up in your CI/CD pipeline.

- **Approvals**: Ensure that the pull request has received the necessary approvals from team members. This not only confirms that the code has been reviewed but also that it meets the project's quality standards.

Understanding merge conflicts and resolutions

When conflicts arise, GitHub provides tools to help you resolve them. You'll need to manually edit the conflicting files, choose which changes to keep, and then commit the resolved files. It's essential to communicate with your team during this process to ensure that everyone is aligned.

Merging strategies

In the previous chapter, *Chapter 5, Branching and Merging Strategies*, we discussed merging strategies such as Merge, Squash, and Rebase. Choosing the right merging strategy is crucial for maintaining a clean and understandable project history.

Consider your team's workflow and preferences. Some teams prefer a clean, linear history (favoring Rebase or Squash), while others value the detailed history provided by traditional merges. Establishing a consistent strategy helps maintain clarity in the project's commit history.

Post-merge best practices

After merging changes, there are a couple of best practices to follow to ensure ongoing project health.

- **Communicating changes to the team:** Notify your team about the merged changes, especially if they impact ongoing work. This can be done through team meetings, project management tools, or direct communication channels. Clear communication helps everyone stay informed and aligned.
- **Monitoring the impact of merged changes**: After merging, keep an eye on the application's performance and functionality. Monitor for any issues that may arise from the new changes, and be prepared to address them quickly. This may involve reviewing logs, running additional tests, or gathering feedback from users.

Integrating changes with confidence is essential for maintaining the integrity of your codebase. By preparing thoroughly, choosing the right merging strategy, and following post-merge best practices, you can ensure that your project remains robust and reliable.

Some food for thought

We are now at the end of the chapter. Congratulations!

Looking at what you have learned thus far in the chapter, this might be a time to pause and think about the following questions:

- How is code reviewed in your current workflow?
- What would you do if your PR receives vague feedback?
- Do you have a review/merge strategy process documented and do you regularly communicate this to the team?

Let us summarize what we learned.

Summary

We focused on pull requests as a cornerstone for maintaining code quality and fostering teamwork. We delved into the intricacies of pull requests and code reviews on GitHub, providing the necessary tools and knowledge to navigate this essential workflow effectively.

We explained the concept of a pull request, which was popularized by GitHub in 2008. A pull request facilitates the process of merging code changes, allowing developers to notify team members that their work is ready for review and can be merged after a successful review. It represents a dialogue between developers, where ideas are exchanged, improvements are suggested, and code is refined.

We highlighted the importance of pull requests in collaborative development, promoting transparency and collaboration. Before pull requests existed, code management relied on different practices and tools, such as version control systems, manual code reviews, branching and merging, and documentation and change logs.

We then went through the lifecycle of a pull request, from creating a pull request to conducting a code review, and finally merging the pull request. We provided a step-by-step guide on initiating a pull request, including best practices for writing clear descriptions and the review process overview.

In the lab exercise, we made code changes, submitted them for review by creating a pull request, and went through the review process to have it approved before merging it into the main branch. We also discussed the concept of a diff, which showed the changes between two versions of a file or codebase.

By understanding the pull request lifecycle, we contributed to a culture of quality and teamwork, ensuring that every change enhanced the project. In the next chapter, we will explore advanced topics in GitHub workflows, further enhancing your skills in collaborative development.

Let's test how much you remember.

Test your knowledge

1. What is the primary purpose of a pull request in collaborative software development?

    a. To create a new branch in the repository

    b. To merge code changes from one branch into another

    c. To delete a branch from the repository

    d. To clone a repository

2. Which of the following is NOT a role typically involved in the code review process?

    a. Author

    b. Reviewer

    c. Maintainer

    d. Tester

3. What is a "diff" in the context of version control systems such as Git?

    a. A tool used to create new branches

    b. A format used to show changes between two versions of a file or codebase

    c. A method to delete files from the repository

    d. A command to push changes to the remote repository

Useful links

*   GitHub launched the pull request: `https://github.blog/news-insights/the-library/oh-yeah-there-s-pull-requests-now/`
*   About pull requests: `https://docs.github.com/articles/using-pull-requests`
*   Comparing commits: `https://docs.github.com/en/pull-requests/committing-changes-to-your-project/viewing-and-comparing-commits/comparing-commits`
*   Linking a pull request to an issue: `https://docs.github.com/en/issues/tracking-your-work-with-issues/linking-a-pull-request-to-an-issue`

Unlock this book's exclusive benefits now

Scan this QR code or go to packtpub.com/unlock, then search this book by name.

Note: Keep your purchase invoice ready before you start.

7

Issues, Projects, Labels, and Milestones

Welcome to yet another interesting chapter, learning more about GitHub. This chapter delves into GitHub's project management tools, focusing on issues, labels, and milestones. It aims to teach you how to use these features to track progress and organize work within a team or larger projects in a team of teams. Let's go!

We will cover the following main topics:

- Introduction to issues
- Lab 7.1: Creating and managing issues
- Lab 7.2: Creating an issue template
- Labels
- Milestones
- Projects

Technical requirements

To complete the lab in this chapter, you will need the following:

- A working computer
- Two GitHub individual accounts to switch between two personas
- A GitHub repository (you can use the same one we already used in previous chapters)

Introduction to issues

First, let's talk about issues. Issues are a fundamental part of GitHub's project management tools. They serve as a way to track tasks, enhancements, bugs, and other project-related activities. Each issue can be assigned to team members, labeled for categorization, and linked to pull requests to streamline the development workflow.

What are issues? **Issues** are used to track work within a repository. They can represent tasks, feature requests, bug reports, or any other type of work item and provide a structured way to manage work and facilitate collaboration among team members. Each issue has a unique identifier and can include a title, description, labels, assignees, and comments. GitHub issues are particularly feature-rich. I particularly love the timeline trail below the issue body, which tracks (in chronological order) all interactions with the issue, including comments, modifications, linked actions, status changes, and so on helping you move the conversation forward.

You can also break down an issue into sub-issues and track progress across child items from the parent in a hierarchical format. This is particularly useful when you break down a large body of work into several smaller tasks or items in a project, program, or portfolio.

Let's go into more detail about some of the features of an issue.

Title and description

Each issue starts with a title and a description. The title provides a summary of the issue, while the description offers more detailed information. This can include the context, steps to reproduce a bug, or specific requirements for a task. The description supports Markdown, allowing you to format text and add links, images, and even code snippets to make the information clear and comprehensive. It also supports emojis.

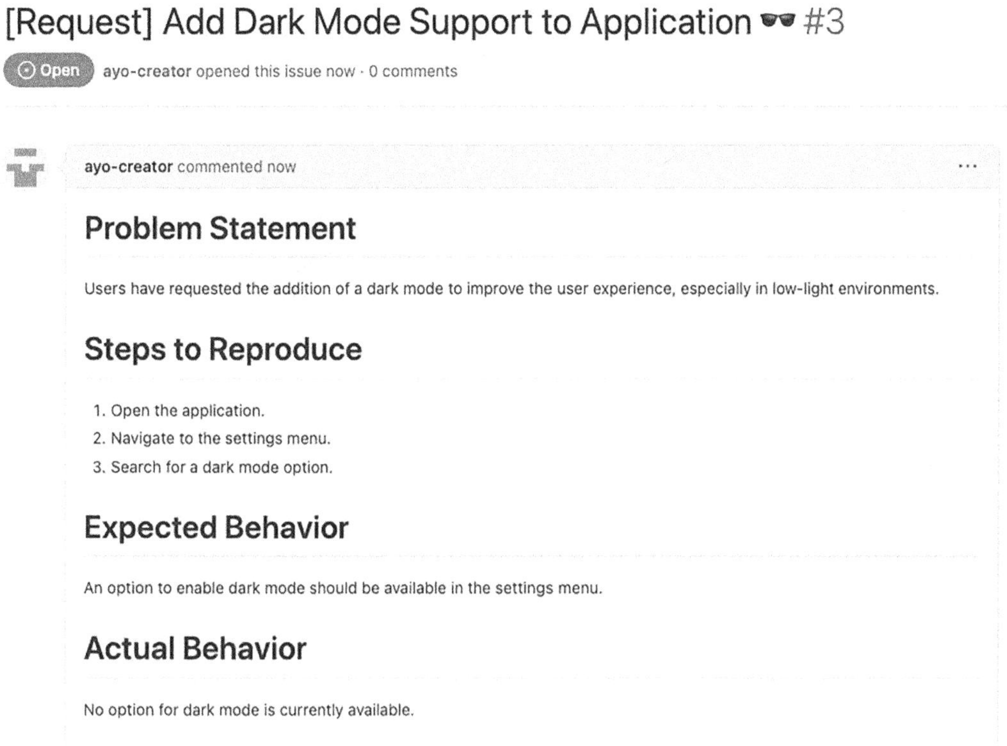

[Request] Add Dark Mode Support to Application 🕶 #3

⊙ Open   **ayo-creator** opened this issue now · 0 comments

---

ayo-creator commented now   ···

Problem Statement

Users have requested the addition of a dark mode to improve the user experience, especially in low-light environments.

Steps to Reproduce

1. Open the application.
2. Navigate to the settings menu.
3. Search for a dark mode option.

Expected Behavior

An option to enable dark mode should be available in the settings menu.

Actual Behavior

No option for dark mode is currently available.

Figure 7.1: An issue of a feature request displaying its title and description

Labels

Labels are used to categorize and prioritize issues. They help in quickly identifying the type of issue (e.g., bug or enhancement), its priority (e.g., high or low), or its status (e.g., in progress or completed). You can create custom labels and apply multiple labels to a single issue, making it easier to filter and search for specific types of work.

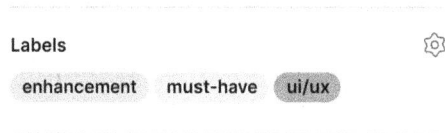

Labels

enhancement   must-have   ui/ux

Figure 7.2: A label helps to categorize an issue

Types

Just like labels, issue types are classifications used to categorize and manage different kinds of issues within a repository or organization. The default issue types include **bug**, **feature**, and **task**, but organizations can create custom types to better suit their workflows. Each issue type can have a specific name and description, helping team members understand its purpose at a glance. This system enhances organization and prioritization, allowing users to filter and search for issues effectively, making project management more streamlined and efficient.

Issue types

Customize the issue types for this organization. Issue types can be used to classify and manage issues in repositories across the organization.

Create new type

3 types (max 10)

Task	A specific piece of work	...
Bug	An unexpected problem or behavior	...
Feature	A request, idea, or new functionality	...

Figure 7.3: List of default issue types in an organization

Assignees

Issues can be assigned to one or more team members. This helps in distributing the workload and ensuring that each task has a clear owner. Assignees can be added or changed at any time, providing flexibility in managing responsibilities.

Assignees

ayo-creator

ayooutlook

Figure 7.4: Issue assignees

Milestones

Milestones are used to group issues that share a common goal or deadline. They help in planning and tracking the progress of larger projects. Each milestone can have a due date and a description, and you can view the percentage of completed issues to gauge progress.

Comments

The comments section allows team members to discuss the issue, ask questions, and provide updates. Comments support Markdown, enabling rich text formatting, and can include mentions to notify specific users. This feature fosters collaboration and ensures that all relevant information is captured in one place. You can also use emojis in comments, similar to the issue description, or write a Markdown file in a repo. Most emojis that come built-in with macOS or Windows are supported. For a list of the supported emojis, visit the emoji cheat sheet (`https://github.com/ikatyang/emoji-cheat-sheet/blob/master/README.md`).

Reactions

Reactions allow users to express their feedback on an issue or comment using emojis. This can be useful for quickly gauging the sentiment of the team or community without adding additional comments. Common reactions include thumbs up, thumbs down, and smiley faces.

Linking issues and pull requests

Issues can be linked to pull requests, which helps in tracking the progress of work and ensuring that issues are automatically closed when the associated pull request is merged. This integration streamlines the workflow and keeps everything connected.

Templates

Issue templates help standardize the information collected for different types of issues. They ensure consistency and make it easier for contributors to provide the necessary details. Templates can be created by adding Markdown files to the `.github/ISSUE_TEMPLATE` directory in your repository.

> **Certification tip**
>
> You may be given a question about issue templates to choose which location to store them. The answer list may contain one correct answer; other answers may be incorrectly spelled. Be sure to study the exact spelling of the location of the issue template.

Notifications

Users can subscribe to issues to receive notifications about updates. This ensures that everyone stays informed about the progress and any changes related to the issue. Notifications can be customized to suit individual preferences.

Search and filtering

GitHub provides robust search and filtering capabilities for issues. You can filter issues by labels, assignees, milestones, and other criteria. This makes it easy to find specific issues and manage large repositories with many open tasks.

Cross-repository issues

For organizations with multiple repositories, GitHub allows you to link issues across repositories. This is useful for tracking dependencies and ensuring that related work in different repositories is coordinated.

By leveraging these features, GitHub issues provide a comprehensive and flexible way to manage work, facilitate collaboration, and keep projects on track. They are an essential tool for any development team using GitHub. Now, let's create an issue to see what this is like.

Lab 7.1: Creating and managing issues

In this lab, we will create an issue and add a few properties to it.

To create an issue, we'll use the following steps:

1. Navigate to the **Issues** tab in your repository:

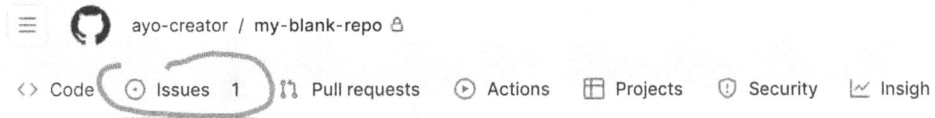

Figure 7.5: The Issues tab in the GitHub repository

2. Click on **New issue**.

3. In the **Add a title** field, enter a brief summary of the issue – for example, `Bug: Application crashes on login`.

4. In the **Add a description** field, provide a detailed description of the issue. Include any relevant information such as steps to reproduce the bug, expected behavior, and actual behavior, as in this example:

```
**Description:**
The application crashes when a user tries to log in with valid
credentials.

**Steps to reproduce:**
1. Open the application.
2. Enter a valid username and password.
3. Click on the "Login" button.

**Expected behavior:**
The user should be logged in successfully.

**Actual behavior:**
The application crashes and displays an error message.
```

5. On the right side of the page, under the **Labels** section, click on the **Labels** title or gear icon (⚙).

6.   Select the default labels that come out of the box, such as **bug, enhancement**, and **help wanted**. This will apply these labels to the issue. For the purpose of this lab, let's select **bug**.

7.   Under the **Assignees** section on the right side of the page, click on the **Assignees** title or gear icon (⚙).

8.   Select your GitHub username to assign the issue to yourself (there's also an **Assign yourself** option that skips adding your own username manually).

9.   Let's assign it to one more person. Select a second GitHub account username that you have access to sign in as. We'll call this `Developer 2`.

10. Once you have filled in all the necessary information, click on the green **Create** button at the bottom of the page.

And that's it! You've successfully created a GitHub issue with a title, description, and labels, and assigned it to yourself. Examine the page and the properties you have set. Now, let us sign in as Developer 2 and add some comments to the same issue.

1.   Switch to Developer 2's profile using the account switcher (log in to GitHub using Developer 2's credentials if not logged in already).

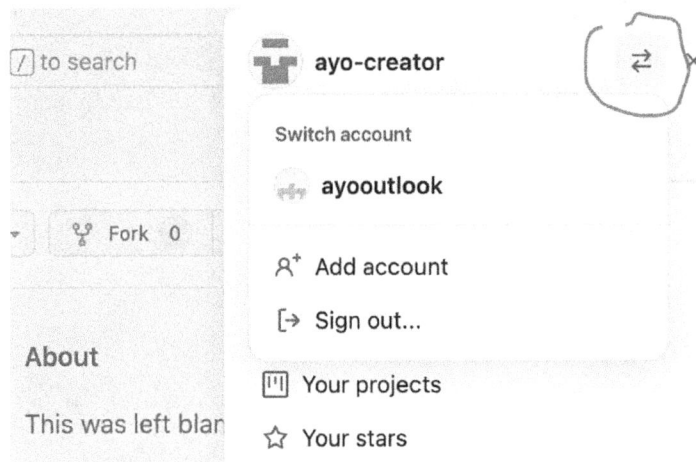

Figure 7.6: GitHub account switcher

2.   Navigate to the repository where the issue is located.

3.   Click on the **Issues** tab to view all issues in the repository.

4.   Locate the issue that has been assigned to Developer 2. You can use the search bar or filter by assignee to find it quickly.

5.   Click on the issue to open it.

6. Scroll down to the **Add a comment** section.

7. In the comment box, write your comment using Markdown for formatting and include an emoji, as in this example:

```
**Update:**
- The issue has been reviewed and the initial analysis is complete.
- Next steps include debugging the login function and testing the
fix.


:smiley: Looking forward to resolving this soon!
```

8. Once you have written your comment, click on the green **Comment** button to submit it:

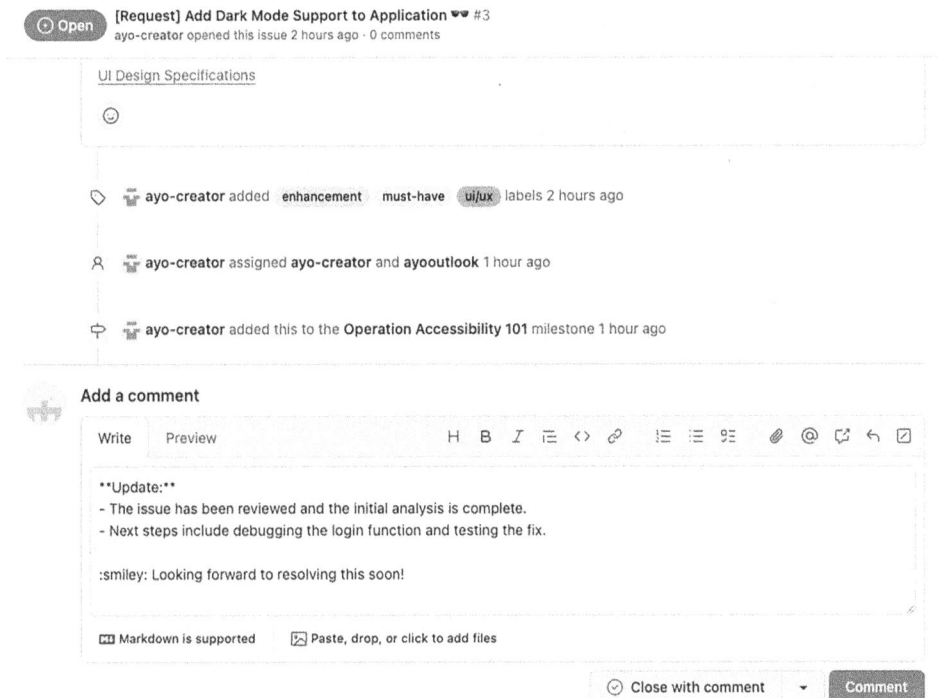

Figure 7.7: Adding comments to issues with timeline trail visible

Well done! You've successfully switched to Developer 2's profile and added a comment with Markdown styles and an emoji to the issue. This helps in keeping the team updated and ensures that all relevant information is documented.

Issues can be managed by updating their status, adding comments, and closing them when the work is completed. This helps in keeping track of the progress and ensuring that all tasks are addressed.

Using issue templates

Issue templates help standardize the information collected for different types of issues. Just like Google Forms or Microsoft Forms, issue templates let you create a form-like view for collecting information for an issue in a more structured manner. They ensure consistency and make it easier for contributors to provide the necessary details. Instead of having just the title and description fields, with issue templates, you can have data-specific fields, such as a drop-down list of categories, a single-line text field for the address, a checkbox for the environment, and so on.

Here are a few real-life use cases where they can be particularly beneficial:

- **Bug reporting**: For software projects, having a bug report template ensures that all necessary information is provided when a bug is reported. This can include steps to reproduce the bug, expected behavior, actual behavior, and any relevant screenshots or logs. This helps developers quickly understand and address the issue.

- **Feature requests**: When users or team members want to suggest new features, a feature request template can guide them to provide detailed information about the feature, its benefits, and any potential impact on existing functionality. This helps in evaluating and prioritizing feature requests effectively.

- **Documentation improvements**: For projects with extensive documentation, a template for documentation improvement requests can help standardize the information needed to update or enhance the documentation. This can include the specific section of the documentation, the proposed changes, and any supporting information.

- **Support requests**: For open source projects or products with a large user base, a support request template can help users provide all necessary details when seeking help. This can include the version of the software, the environment in which it is running, and a detailed description of the issue they are facing.

- **Security vulnerabilities**: For projects that need to handle security vulnerabilities, a security issue template can ensure that sensitive information is reported in a structured and secure manner. This can include details about the vulnerability, steps to reproduce it, and any potential impact.

- **Task management**: For teams using GitHub to manage their projects, task templates can help standardize the way tasks are created and tracked. This can include the task description, assignees, labels, and any relevant deadlines or milestones.

Templates can be created by adding Markdown files to the `.github/ISSUE_TEMPLATE` directory in your repository. This is particularly useful for large projects with multiple contributors, as it helps maintain a uniform format for all issues. Issue templates also support the YAML format if you're looking to build a more robust or complex form.

It will be great to see this in action. Let's do another lab exercise on issue templates.

Lab 7.2: Creating an issue template

Let's create step-by-step instructions on how to create a *bug report* issue template (remember to switch back to the Developer A account). This will help standardize the way bugs are reported in your repository.

Here is a step-by-step guide to creating a bug report issue template:

1. **Navigate to your repository**: Go to your repository on GitHub.

2. **Access the settings:** Click on the **Settings** tab located at the top of the repository page.

3. **Go to issue templates:**

   a. In the left sidebar, click on the **General** section.

   b. Scroll down to the **Features** section and click on the **Set up templates** button under **Issues** in the **Features** section.

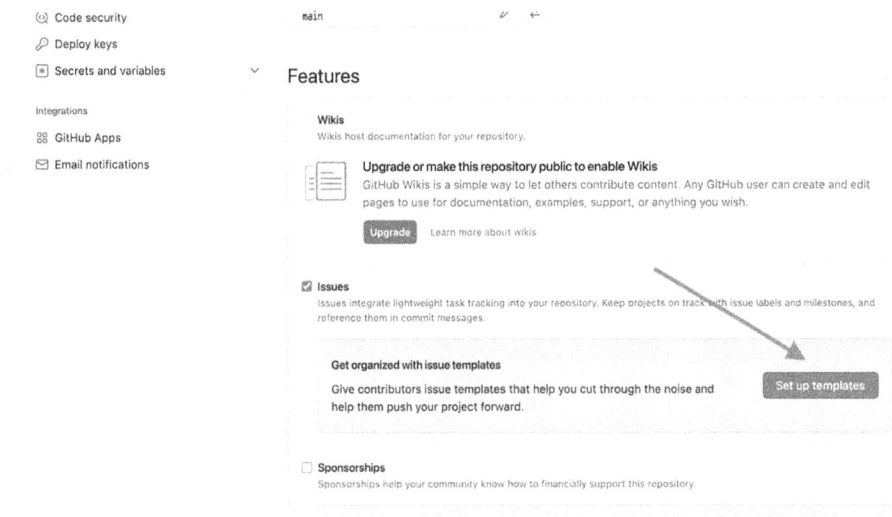

Figure 7.8: Setting up issue templates from repository settings

4. **Select a starting template:**

    a. In the **Add template: select** dropdown, select **Bug report**. This will select the **Bug report** template:

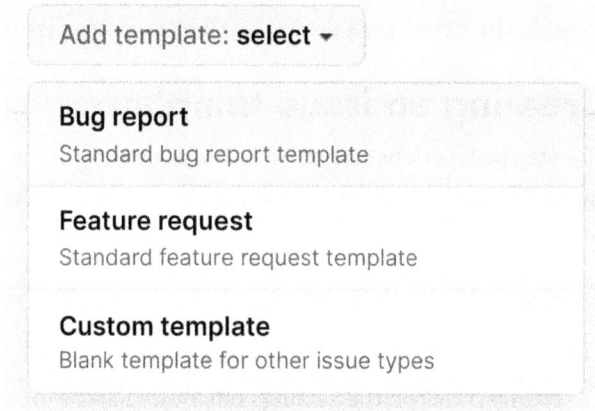

Figure 7.9: List of available starter issue templates

    b. Click on **Preview and edit**. This will display a preview of the template and give you the chance to customize the starter template.

5. **Customize your template:**

    a. Next to the **Issue: Bug report** title, click on the pencil icon ($\mathscr{O}$) to edit.

    b. In the **Template content** field, replace the content for your bug report template with the following Markdown example:

```
**Description**
A clear and concise description of what the bug is.

**Steps to reproduce**
Steps to reproduce the behavior:
1. Go to '...'
2. Click on '...'
3. Scroll down to '...'
4. See error

**Expected behavior**
A clear and concise description of what you expected to happen.
```

```
**Screenshots**
If applicable, add screenshots to help explain your problem.

**Additional context**
Add any other context about the problem here.
```

c. In the **Optional additional items** section, click the **Labels** field or the gear icon next to it and select **bug**. This will ensure that a bug label is automatically applied when anyone submits a bug form (issue).

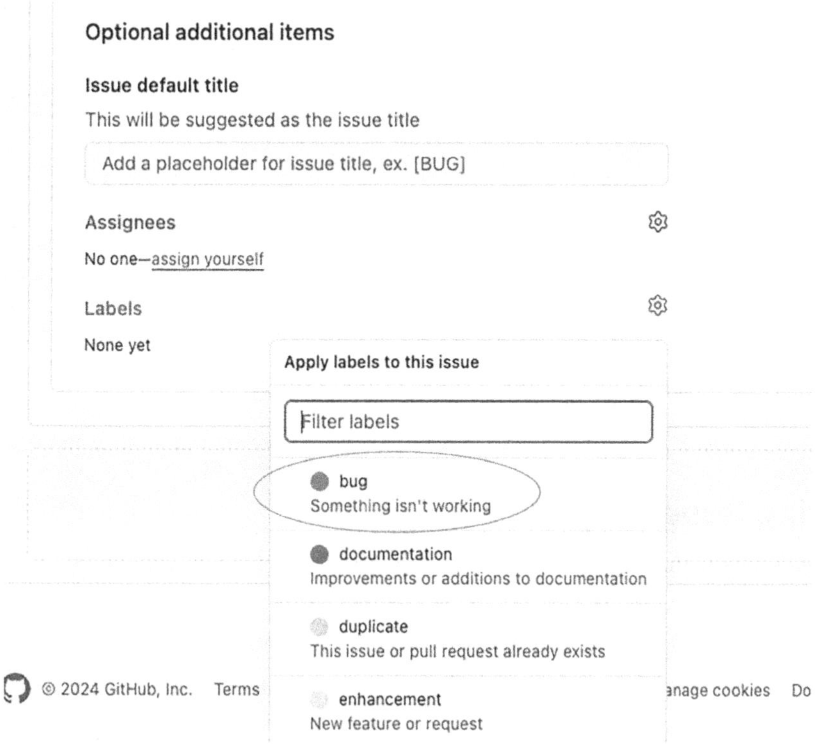

Figure 7.10: You can preselect the labels that issues created through the template will have

6. **Save the template:**

a. Once you have added the content, click on **Propose changes** at the top right of the page.

b. Review your changes, leave the **main** branch selected, and click on **Commit changes** to submit the new template.

And that's it! You've successfully created a bug report issue template. This template will now be available for users to fill out when they create a new issue, ensuring that all necessary information is provided and standardized. You have committed this template file into the repo alongside your code, ensuring that it is managed by the same version control principles guiding your main application/software code.

Let's examine this file and see!

1. Visit the **Code** tab and navigate to the `.github/ISSUE_TEMPLATE` directory in your repository.

2. Click on `bug_report.md` file and examine the contents.

Test the behavior by creating a new issue by visiting the **Issues** tab of the repo. Click **New issue**. You will see the issue template available to use.

Figure 7.11: Issue templates are consumable when you try to create a new issue

Linking issues to pull requests

Linking issues to pull requests helps track the progress of work and ensures that issues are automatically closed when the associated pull request is merged. This can be done by including a prefix such as `closes` followed by `#issue_number` in the pull request description. This integration streamlines the workflow and ensures that all related tasks are linked and tracked together.

Here is a list of possible prefixes you can use. The pull request *must be* on the default branch:

- `close`
- `closes`
- `closed`
- `fix`
- `fixes`
- `fixed`

- resolve
- resolves
- resolved

Throughout GitHub, particularly in places where Markdown is supported, typing the single # sign is a precursor for selecting an issue. Typically, a small box will pop up and you can search for and select the issue. You can also directly type the issue number and GitHub will understand this as a shorthand to link the issue. It behaves just like a hyperlink.

What is a GitHub issue number?

An issue number on GitHub is a unique identifier assigned to each issue created in a repository. It helps in tracking and referencing specific issues. You can find the issue number in several ways:

- **On the issue page**: When you open an issue in a GitHub repository, the issue number is displayed at the top of the page, usually next to the issue title. It looks something like #123.

- **In the URL**: The issue number is also part of the URL when you view an issue. For example, if the URL is `https://github.com/username/repository/issues/123`, the issue number is 123.

- **In the list of issues**: When you browse the list of issues in a repository, each issue will have its number displayed next to the title.

Let's dive deeper into the specifics of labels and milestones in GitHub.

Managing and creating labels

Now that you're familiar with what labels are and how they help categorize and prioritize issues, let's take a closer look at how to create and manage them effectively within a repository. This section will guide you through customizing labels to suit your project's workflow and improving team collaboration through consistent labeling practices:

- **Creating and managing labels**: To create a label, navigate to the **Issues** tab of your repository. Then, click on **Labels** on the right-hand side, next to the filter search box:

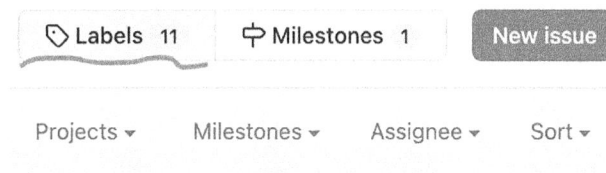

Figure 7.12: Navigation link for labels

Here, you can create new labels by specifying a name, description, and color. This helps in visually distinguishing between different types of labels:

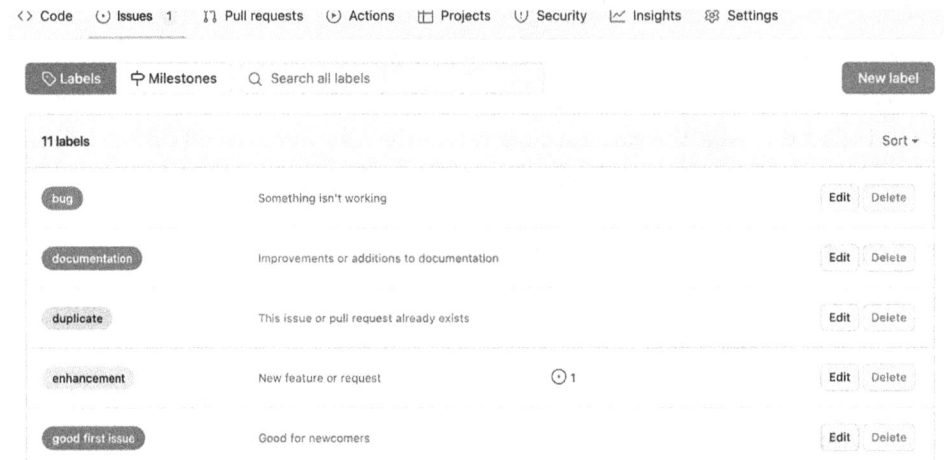

Figure 7.13: List of some of the labels available in a repository

Managing labels involves editing existing labels to update their names, descriptions, or colors, and deleting labels that are no longer needed. This ensures that your labeling system remains relevant and useful.

- **Using labels effectively**: Apply labels to issues and pull requests to provide context and help team members quickly understand their purpose and priority. For example, you might use labels such as bug, enhancement, urgent, or help wanted. Use labels to filter and search for issues. This makes it easier to manage and track work, especially in large projects with many issues and pull requests. For instance, you can filter issues by label to see all bugs that need fixing or all enhancements that are in progress.

Setting and tracking milestones

Milestones are used to group issues and pull requests that share a common goal or deadline. They help you plan and track the progress of your project. Here are some detailed aspects to consider:

- **Setting and tracking milestones**: To create a label, navigate to the **Issues** tab of your repository. Then, click on **Milestones** on the right-hand side, next to the filter search box (next to **Labels**). Here, you can set a title, description, and due date, and associate issues and pull requests with the milestone. This helps in organizing work around specific goals or deadlines.

Track the progress of a milestone by viewing the percentage of completed issues and pull requests. This gives you a clear picture of how close you are to achieving your goal and helps in identifying any bottlenecks or delays:

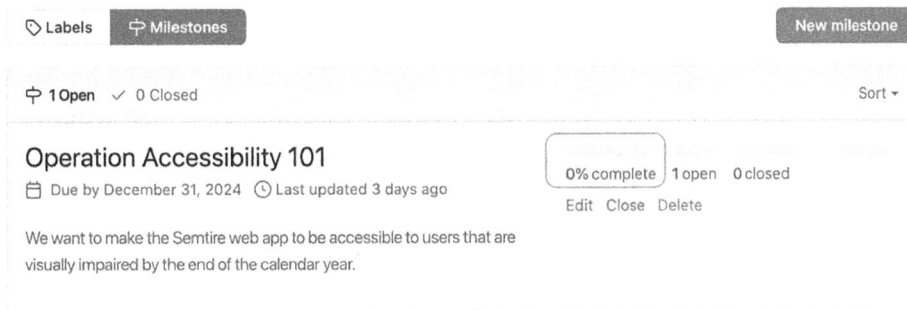

○ Labels   ⇥ Milestones   New milestone

⇥ **1 Open**   ✓ 0 Closed   Sort ▾

Operation Accessibility 101
📅 Due by December 31, 2024   🕐 Last updated 3 days ago

0% complete | 1 open   0 closed

Edit   Close   Delete

We want to make the Semtire web app to be accessible to users that are
visually impaired by the end of the calendar year.

Figure 7.14: You can track the progress of a milestone

- **Best practices for milestones:** Break down large projects into smaller, manageable milestones. This makes it easier to track progress and stay on schedule. For example, you might create milestones for each major feature or release.

  Regularly review and update milestones to reflect changes in project scope or priorities. This ensures that your milestones remain relevant and aligned with your project goals.

By effectively using labels and milestones, you can organize your work, prioritize tasks, and track progress toward your project goals. This not only improves team collaboration but also ensures that everyone is aligned and working toward the same objectives.

Certification tip

Learn a bit more about searching and filtering issues at the end of this lab. Go to the **Issues** tab in your repo and attempt different filtering combinations in the search box to see the result. Questions may come up on searching or filtering issues.

Up next, projects! Before we go into GitHub Projects, bear in mind that Projects is a new powerful tool, built to complement GitHub issues. While it stands on its own, it cannot exist on its own without GitHub issues. We will still talk about GitHub Projects in its own dedicated chapter later on in the book, but let's touch on this entirely related topic briefly.

Projects

We will explore GitHub Projects more deeply in *Chapter 13, Project Management with GitHub Projects*, but let's take a quick look here first as Projects relies deeply on issues and their complementary features.

GitHub Projects is another fantastic feature that aids team collaboration and improves productivity. It is integrated within GitHub, designed to help teams plan, track, and manage their work. It provides a flexible and visual way to organize tasks, issues, and pull requests, making it easier to collaborate and stay on top of project progress.

There are two versions of GitHub Projects: Projects Classic and Projects 2.0. Ultimately, Projects Classic is being deprecated, but it is still in use as at the time of writing this book.

GitHub Projects Classic

GitHub Projects Classic is the original version of GitHub's project management tool. It offers a Kanban-style board where you can create and manage tasks using cards. Each card represents an issue or pull request, and you can move cards between columns to reflect their status. Key features of GitHub Projects Classic include the following:

- **Kanban boards**: Visualize your workflow with customizable columns, such as To do, In progress, and Done
- **Issue and pull request integration**: Link issues and pull requests to project cards, allowing you to track progress and manage work in one place
- **Milestones**: Group related issues and pull requests into milestones to track progress toward specific goals or deadlines
- **Labels**: Categorize and prioritize tasks using labels, making it easier to filter and search for specific work items

- **Assignees**: Assign tasks to team members to distribute workload and ensure accountability

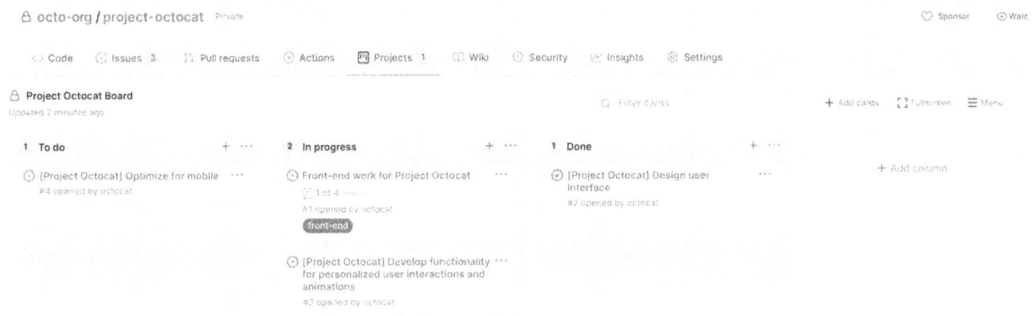

Figure 7.15: Board view of Projects Classic

GitHub Projects Classic is still prevalent in some self-hosted versions of the GitHub Enterprise Server today, though not so common in the GitHub Enterprise Cloud anymore. Projects Classic was removed in version 3.17 on June 3, 2025.

Now, let's discuss Projects 2.0.

GitHub Projects 2.0

GitHub Projects 2.0 is the next generation of GitHub's project management tool, offering enhanced features and improved flexibility. It builds on the foundation of GitHub Projects Classic while introducing new capabilities to better support modern workflows. Key features of GitHub Projects 2.0 include the following:

- **Customizable views**: Create multiple views of your project, such as boards, tables, and timelines, to suit different needs and preferences
- **Advanced filtering and sorting**: Use advanced filters and sorting options to quickly find and organize tasks based on various criteria, such as labels, assignees, and due dates
- **Automations**: Automate repetitive tasks and workflows using built-in automation rules, such as moving cards between columns based on specific triggers
- **Custom fields**: Add custom fields to project cards to capture additional information, such as priority, estimated time, or dependencies

- **Improved collaboration:** Collaborate more effectively with real-time updates, comments, and mentions directly on project cards

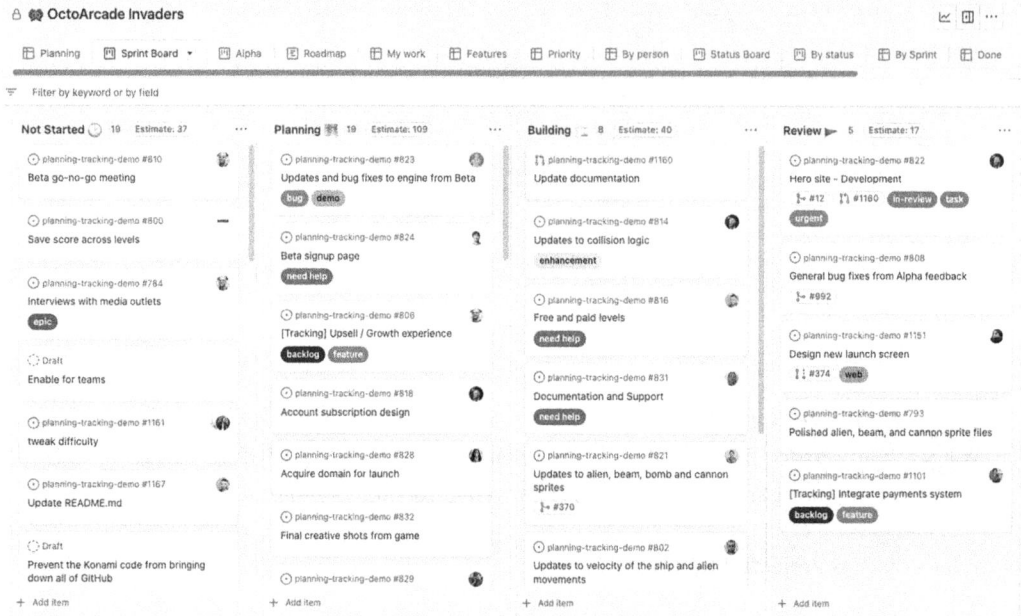

Figure 7.16: Board layout of Projects 2.0

Differences between GitHub Projects Classic and GitHub Projects 2.0

While both versions of GitHub Projects offer powerful project management capabilities, there are several key differences between them:

- **Flexibility:** GitHub Projects 2.0 provides more flexibility with customizable views, advanced filtering, and custom fields, allowing teams to tailor their project management experience to their specific needs
- **Automation:** GitHub Projects 2.0 introduces automation rules, enabling teams to streamline workflows and reduce manual effort
- **Collaboration:** GitHub Projects 2.0 enhances collaboration with real-time updates and improved commenting features, making it easier for teams to stay aligned and communicate effectively
- **User experience:** GitHub Projects 2.0 offers a more modern and intuitive user interface, making it easier to navigate and use the tool

In summary, GitHub Projects Classic provides a solid foundation for project management with its Kanban-style boards and integration with issues and pull requests. GitHub Projects 2.0 builds on this foundation with enhanced flexibility, automation, and collaboration features, making it a more powerful and versatile tool for modern project management.

Congratulations! We have dealt a fair bit with issues and Projects. Let's summarize what we've learned.

Summary

In this chapter, we delved into GitHub's project management tools, focusing on issues, labels, and milestones. We started by discussing the importance of issues, which are fundamental for tracking tasks, enhancements, bugs, and other project-related activities. Each issue can be assigned to team members, labeled for categorization, and linked to pull requests to streamline our development workflow.

We then provided a detailed introduction to issues, explaining their role in tracking work within a repository and facilitating collaboration among team members.

Next, we broke down the features of an issue, such as the title and description, labels, types, assignees, milestones, comments, reactions, linking issues and pull requests, templates, notifications, search and filtering, and cross-repository issues. Each feature was explained in detail, highlighting its importance and how it contributes to effective project management.

We also included practical lab exercises, such as creating and managing issues, adding comments, and creating issue templates. These exercises helped us understand how to apply the concepts discussed and improve our issue management skills on GitHub.

By leveraging these features, we can manage work more comprehensively, facilitate collaboration, and keep our projects on track. GitHub issues are an essential tool for any development team using GitHub, and this chapter provided us with the knowledge and skills to use them effectively.

I recommend you read more about issues and Projects. You will find useful links to resources at the end of this chapter.

Test your knowledge

1. What is the primary purpose of using labels in GitHub issues?

    a. To assign tasks to team members

    b. To categorize and prioritize issues

    c. To provide a summary of the issue

    d. To track the chronological order of interactions

2. Which of the following is NOT a default issue type in GitHub?

    a. Bug

    b. Feature

    c. Task

    d. Enhancement

3. How can issues be linked to pull requests in GitHub to ensure they are automatically closed when the associated pull request is merged?

    a. By including the issue number in the pull request title

    b. By adding the issue number in the pull request description with a specific prefix

    c. By assigning the same label to both the issue and the pull request

    d. By mentioning the issue number in the comments section of the pull request

Useful links

*   *Emoji-cheat-sheet*: `https://github.com/ikatyang/emoji-cheat-sheet/blob/master/README.md`

*   *Linking a pull request to an issue*: `https://docs.github.com/en/issues/tracking-your-work-with-issues/using-issues/linking-a-pull-request-to-an-issue`

*   *Managing issue types in an organization*: `https://docs.github.com/en/issues/tracking-your-work-with-issues/configuring-issues/managing-issue-types-in-an-organization`

*   *Automating your project*: `https://docs.github.com/en/issues/planning-and-tracking-with-projects/automating-your-project`

Unlock this book's exclusive benefits now

Scan this QR code or go to packtpub.com/unlock, then search this book by name.

Note: Keep your purchase invoice ready before you start.

8

GitHub Actions and Automation

Welcome to automation with GitHub Actions! This is my second most-loved GitHub feature (second to GitHub Copilot 😊). I've always been a proponent of DevOps and the practices of continuous integration and continuous delivery. It felt magical that I could automate the testing and deployment of my apps, and even the provisioning of infrastructure in the cloud. I fell in love with the "everything as code" concept (we will explore this in more detail in this chapter).

However, a more magical feature, GitHub Copilot, blew me away completely less than 3 years ago. GitHub Copilot and **Generative AI (GenAI)** have fundamentally revolutionized the way we build software today. We will discuss GitHub Copilot in *Chapter 12, Enhancing Development with GitHub Copilot*, but let's focus on GitHub Actions for now.

In this chapter, we will discuss GitHub's approach to continuous integration, continuous delivery, and automation. We will examine what really makes GitHub Actions a unique automation tool. Let's get right into it.

We will cover the following main topics:

- Introduction to GitHub Actions
- Creating custom workflows
- CI/CD with GitHub Actions

Technical requirements

To conduct the labs in this chapter, you will need the following:

- A working computer
- An individual GitHub account

You will find the corresponding code files in this folder of the book repository: `https://github.com/PacktPublishing/GitHub-Foundations-Certification-Guide`

Introduction to GitHub Actions

When you write software, you want to test its functionality to be sure it meets the intended goal and returns the expected results. In addition, you want to scan the software for potential vulnerabilities that could be exploited by bad actors. Finally, you want to deploy it to production safely and securely into the hands of the end users. GitHub Actions aids the automation of code builds, unit tests, code quality checks, vulnerability and static application security tests, deployment to various environments (e.g., dev, staging, production, etc.,), packaging, and the distribution of your software in a seamless, fully integrated manner.

GitHub Actions is a powerful automation tool integrated into GitHub, designed to help developers automate their workflows directly within their repositories. It enables **continuous integration and continuous deployment (CI/CD)**, automating tasks such as testing, building, and deploying code. Unlike many other CI/CD automation tools, GitHub Actions does not require building automation pipelines with the user interface but rather through text-based instructions using YAML, a popular form of markup language used for writing configuration files and similar scripts. This concept of using text-based scripts to instruct a CI or CD automation pipeline is called **pipeline-as-code** (more about it in the next section).

GitHub Actions has key benefits, some of which include the following:

- **Integration with GitHub**: Seamlessly integrates with GitHub repositories, making it easy to trigger workflows based on repository events
- **Customizability**: Highly customizable workflows using YAML syntax
- **Scalability**: Supports complex workflows with multiple jobs and steps
- **Community and Marketplace**: Access to a vast library of pre-built actions in the GitHub Marketplace

How Pipeline as Code supports GitHub Actions

Pipeline as Code is a practice in software development where the entire CI/CD pipeline is defined and managed using code. This approach treats the pipeline configuration as part of the application's source code, allowing it to be version-controlled, reviewed, and audited just like any other code.

Continuous Delivery versus Continuous Deployment

You will notice, as I have written in this chapter thus far, the CD in CI/CD can both mean Continuous Deployment and Continuous Delivery. They are slightly different but used in the same acronym. Continuous delivery and continuous deployment are both practices in the CI/CD pipeline, but they differ in their approach to releasing software.

Continuous delivery ensures that code changes are automatically tested and prepared for a release to production, but the actual deployment requires manual approval. This allows teams to deploy updates at their discretion. In contrast, continuous deployment takes automation a step further by automatically deploying every change that passes all stages of the production pipeline, including testing, directly to production without any manual intervention. This means that new features, bug fixes, and improvements are delivered to users as soon as they are ready, providing a faster feedback loop and more frequent updates.

Pipeline as code brings several benefits. Let's consider some of them:

1. **Version control**: Changes to the pipeline can be tracked, reviewed, and rolled back if necessary

2. **Consistency**: Ensures that the same pipeline is used across different environments, reducing the risk of discrepancies

3. **Automation**: Automates the build, test, and deployment processes, leading to faster and more reliable software delivery

4. **Collaboration**: Facilitates collaboration among team members, as pipeline changes can be reviewed and approved through pull requests

So, how does GitHub Actions support pipeline as code? With GitHub Actions, you can define your CI/CD pipelines using YAML files, which are stored in your repository under the `.github/workflows` directory of the repo. These YAML files describe the steps and conditions for your workflows, allowing you to version control your pipeline configurations just like any other code. This approach integrates seamlessly with GitHub, making it easy to automate your build, test, and deployment processes directly from your repository.

Let's take a quick look at some key components and terminologies of GitHub Actions.

Key components of GitHub Actions

- **Workflows**: A workflow is a configurable automated process made up of one or more jobs. Workflows are defined using YAML syntax and are stored in the `.github/workflows` directory of your repository. They can be triggered by events, manually, or on a schedule.

- **Events**: These are specific activities in your repository that **trigger** workflows. All workflows must be triggered by an event if automated or can be manually triggered. Examples include pushing code, opening a pull request, or creating an issue.

- **Jobs**: A job is a set of steps in a workflow that execute on the same runner (*see* **Runners** *for definition*). Jobs can run sequentially or in parallel and can have dependencies on other jobs.

- **Steps**: Steps are individual tasks within a job. Each step can run a script or an action. Steps are executed in order and can share data with each other.

- **Actions**: Actions are reusable units of code that perform specific tasks. They can be created by you or used from the GitHub Marketplace. Actions help reduce repetitive code in your workflows.

- **Runners**: Runners are servers that execute your workflows (*other CI/CD platforms may call these agents*). These runners can be either **virtual machines** (**VMs**) or containers. GitHub provides hosted runners (mostly VMs) with Linux, Windows, and macOS environments, or you can use self-hosted runners.

In the following section, we will delve into the inner workings of a workflow.

Events that trigger a workflow

As stated previously, workflows are defined by YAML files in your repository. They consist of one or more jobs that run in response to specific events. The YAML syntax is a pre-defined structure the file must follow. The basic structure includes name, on (events), jobs, and steps.

What are the possible values for an event trigger? Let's look at the most widely used ones:

Event Name	Description
push	Triggered on a push to a branch.
pull_request	Triggered on events related to pull requests.
Issues	Triggered on issue-related events.
issue_comment	Triggered when a comment is created or edited on issues or pull requests.

release	Triggered when a release is published, edited, or deleted.
schedule	Triggered on a scheduled time using cron syntax.
workflow_dispatch	Manually triggered via the GitHub UI.
repository_dispatch	Triggered by a repository dispatch event.
check_run	Triggered on check run events.
check_suite	Triggered on check suite events.
deployment	Triggered on deployment events.
deployment_status	Triggered on deployment status changes.
fork	Triggered when a repository is forked.
create	Triggered when a branch or tag is created.
delete	Triggered when a branch or tag is deleted.
public	Triggered when a repository is made public.
status	Triggered on status changes of a commit.
watch	Triggered when someone stars a repository.
workflow_run	Triggered when a workflow run is requested or completed.

Table 8.1: List of some commonly used events that trigger a workflow

For more information on events that trigger a workflow, visit: `https://docs.github.com/en/actions/writing-workflows/choosing-when-your-workflow-runs/events-that-trigger-workflows`

Certification tip

Focus on how to interpret the events that trigger a workflow. The keyword will usually tell you. Get familiar with the most common ones.

Let's discuss the contents of jobs that are executed as soon as the events are triggered and where they run.

Jobs, steps, and runners

As soon as the event is triggered, the jobs in the workflow will begin execution. A job is a parent of one or more steps and a step is the smallest indivisible executable task in a workflow. The following diagram illustrates the relationship between all these components:

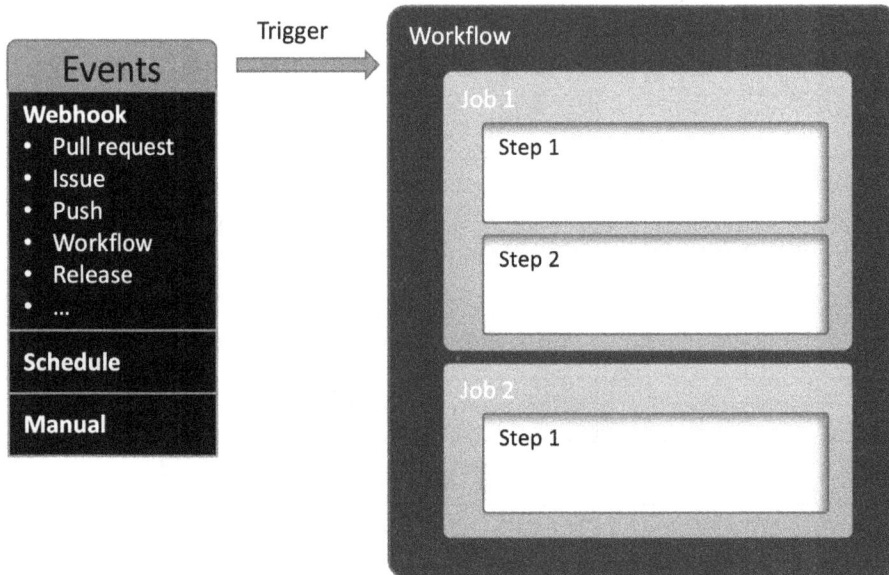

Figure 8.1: Relationship between workflow components

Each step can run commands or use actions, that is, other GitHub Actions workflows defined elsewhere by you, by GitHub, or any other third party that have been made accessible to the current one.

Each job in the workflow is then executed by a runner. When there are multiple jobs to be executed, they are queued up until the runner picks them. A runner can be Linux, Windows, or MacOS, running on a VM or container. Runners can belong to a runner group, which are logical groupings that allow you to categorize multiple runners that have the same specifications and behavior. The benefit of using a runner group is that it aids scaling such that any idle runner in the group can immediately pick any waiting job to execute rather than all jobs being queued up waiting for one single runner.

The following image illustrates how the jobs in a workflow are picked up by runners to be executed. The specification of the runner can be pre-specified.

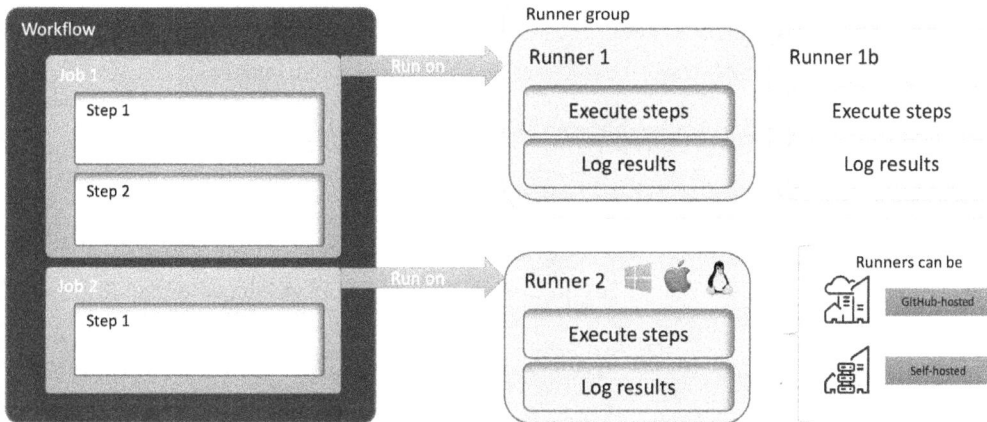

Figure 8.2: How runners pick up jobs

A runner can be perpetual (always-on) or ephemeral. Ephemeral runners are a type of runner that is designed to run a single job and then automatically unregister themselves. This ensures that each job runs in a clean environment, which is particularly useful for maintaining security and consistency. Ephemeral runners are more widely used and recommended as good practice because they ensure a clean, secure environment for each job, reducing the risk of contamination and improving consistency. A runner can be GitHub-hosted or self-hosted.

GitHub-hosted versus self-hosted runners

A GitHub-hosted runner is a virtual machine managed by GitHub that comes pre-configured with commonly used software, tools, and packages, providing a quick and easy setup for running workflows. In contrast, a self-hosted runner is managed by you, offering greater customization and control over the hardware, operating system, and software environment used to run your jobs.

GitHub-Hosted runners are autoscaling by default – meaning multiple runners (VMs) are provisioned to run and execute jobs concurrently, as many as are ready to be executed, increasing (scaling out) and decreasing/deprovisioning (scaling in) the number of available runners as the need dictates, automatically, without manual intervention. This means virtual machines don't have to be powered on perpetually, consuming energy, network, and data resources.

On the other hand, self-hosted runners don't autoscale by default. You will need to leave them powered on or use a third-party or community-backed autoscaling technology such as GitHub Actions Runner Controller or the Philips Labs autoscalers. For more information about autoscaling self-hosted runners, visit https://docs.github.com/en/actions/hosting-your-own-runners/managing-self-hosted-runners/autoscaling-with-self-hosted-runners.

In the next section, we will examine the workflow syntax in a YAML file.

Workflow syntax and file structure

A workflow is triggered by an event denoted by a corresponding event name (keyword) following an on prefix. Afterwards, the instructions on the jobs to execute as well as on which runners to execute them follow.

Here is a sample workflow YAML file.

```
.github/workflows/triage-an-issue.yml

1   name: Label issues
    on:
2     issues:
3       types:
4           - reopened
          - opened
5   jobs:
      label_issues:
6       runs-on: ubuntu-latest
7       permissions:
          issues: write
8       steps:
9         - run: echo "Hello World"
          - uses: actions/github-script@v6
10          with:
11            script: |
12              github.rest.issues.addLabels({
13                issue_number: context.issue.number,
                  owner: context.repo.owner,
14                repo: context.repo.repo,
                  labels: ["triage"]
15              })
16
```

Figure 8.3: Sample GitHub Actions workflow written in YAML

Here is a file named triage-an-issue.yml stored in the workflows directory inside the .github directory of the repository. Also, all workflow files must be stored in the same manner in the .github directory.

Note

The first line showing the filename is not part of the YAML file but is only included in this case to show you the file path of this example workflow file.

The first line of the workflow file is the title. This is preceded by the keyword name: followed by the title.

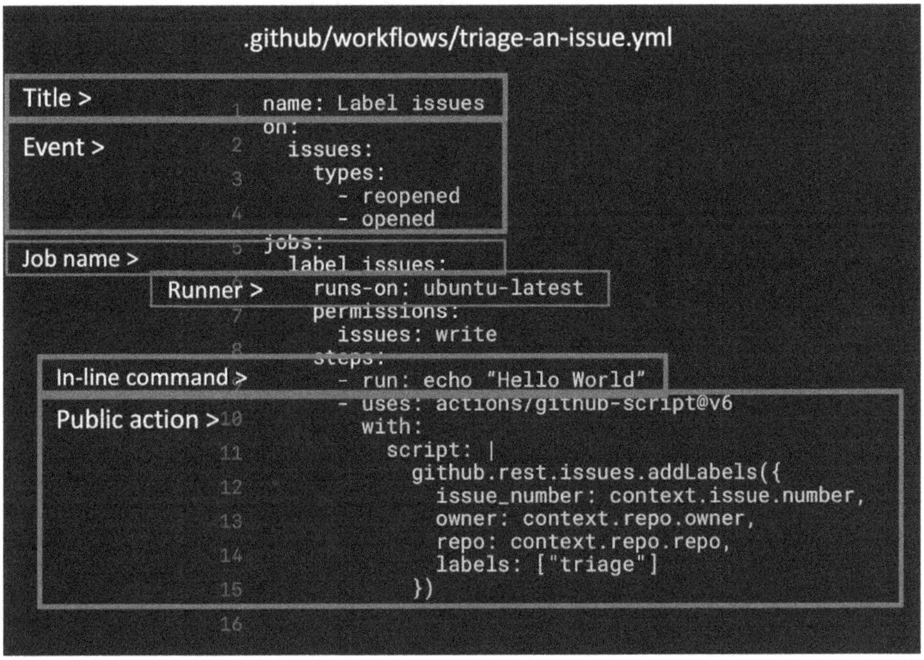

```
.github/workflows/triage-an-issue.yml

Title >               1   name: Label issues
                          on:
Event >               2     issues:
                      3       types:
                                - reopened
                      4         - opened
                      5   jobs:
Job name >                  label_issues:
          Runner >            runs-on: ubuntu-latest
                      7       permissions:
                                issues: write
                      8       steps:
In-line command >             - run: echo "Hello World"
    Public action > 10        - uses: actions/github-script@v6
                     11          with:
                     12            script: |
                     13              github.rest.issues.addLabels({
                     14                issue_number: context.issue.number,
                                      owner: context.repo.owner,
                                      repo: context.repo.repo,
                     15               labels: ["triage"]
                                    })
                     16
```

Figure 8.4: Some common lines in a workflow's YAML file and their descriptions

Up next is the event, which is preceded by the keyword on: followed by the event type (one of the event types we discussed earlier). Afterwards, the jobs are defined. All jobs must come indented under the parent keyword, jobs:. It is under this that all jobs are defined. In this example, the first job is named label_issues, and its steps are defined indented under it. You will see the steps to be executed under the job prefixed with a hyphen (-). Every hyphen denotes a separate step.

This example shows a workflow that is triggered whenever a GitHub issue is *opened* or *reopened* in the GitHub repository. It has one job named label_issues and this job runs on GitHub's latest Linux Ubuntu runners. Let's explain some of the lines in this configuration.

Lab 8.1: Getting started with GitHub Actions

Let's do some lab exercises to see how this works.

Setting up your first workflow

Create a new workflow file in the .github/workflows directory:

1. Navigate to your repository on GitHub.

2. Create a new directory named .github in the root of your repository if it doesn't already exist.

3. Within the .github directory, create another directory named workflows.

4. Inside the workflows directory, create a new file named first-workflow.yml.

Defining a simple workflow that runs a basic command, such as printing "Hello, World!"

Apply the following steps:

1. Open the first-workflow.yml file in a text editor.

2. Add the following YAML code to define a simple workflow:

```yaml
name: First Workflow

on: [push]

jobs:
  hello_world_job:
    runs-on: ubuntu-latest

    steps:
    - name: Print Hello, World!
      run: echo "Hello, World!"
```

3. Save the file and commit it to your repository.

4. Push the changes to GitHub. This will trigger the workflow to run whenever you push changes to the repository.

> **Certification tip**
>
> You may be given the content of a simple workflow YAML file and asked to choose from the options in what cases the workflow will run.

Exploring the GitHub Actions Marketplace

Browse the GitHub Marketplace to find pre-built actions that can be integrated into your workflows:

1. Go to the GitHub Actions Marketplace by navigating to GitHub Marketplace (`https://github.com/marketplace`).

2. Use the search bar to find actions that suit your needs. For example, you can search for "linting" or "testing" actions.

3. Explore the available actions by reading their descriptions, usage instructions, and reviews.

Incorporating these actions into your workflow

Learning how to incorporate these actions into your workflow files helps to extend functionality:

1. Select an action from the marketplace that you want to use – for example, choose a popular action such as `actions/checkout`.

2. Read the usage instructions provided on the action's page. This typically includes how to reference the action in your workflow file.

3. Modify your workflow file to include the action. For example, to use the `actions/checkout` action, update your `first-workflow.yml` file as follows:

```yaml
name: First Workflow

on: [push]

jobs:
  hello_world_job:
    runs-on: ubuntu-latest

    steps:
    - name: Checkout repository
      uses: actions/checkout@v2

    - name: Print Hello, World!
      run: echo "Hello, World!"
```

4. Save the changes and push them to GitHub. The workflow will now include the pre-built action.

5. We discussed earlier how a step in a job can either run commands or use other actions from GitHub or third parties. These other actions created by third parties are hosted in the GitHub Actions marketplace.

> **Certification tip**
>
> Expect to encounter some questions about the GitHub Marketplace. Spend some time understanding its purpose, what various components are available on it (e.g., actions, apps, GenAI models, etc.), and who can host/publish on it.

The GitHub Actions Marketplace

The GitHub Actions Marketplace is a repository of pre-built actions created by the community and GitHub itself. These actions can perform a wide range of tasks, from code linting and testing to deployment and notifications. By leveraging these actions, you can save time and avoid reinventing the wheel.

To integrate an action from the marketplace into your workflow, you need to reference it in your workflow file using the **uses** keyword. Each action typically comes with detailed documentation on how to configure and use it. This might include specifying input parameters, setting environment variables, or combining multiple actions to create a more complex workflow.

Many pre-built actions are highly configurable. You can customize them by providing input parameters that tailor the action to your specific needs. For example, a testing action might allow you to specify the version of a testing framework or the directory containing your tests.

You can also combine multiple actions in a single workflow.

Combining actions

One of the powerful features of GitHub Actions is the ability to combine multiple actions within a single workflow. This allows you to create sophisticated workflows that can handle complex CI/CD pipelines. For instance, you might use one action to check out your code, another to set up your programming environment, and a third to run tests or deploy your application.

By exploring and utilizing the GitHub Actions Marketplace, you can significantly enhance the capabilities of your workflows, making your development process more efficient and streamlined.

Up next, we will look at best practices considerations when creating a workflow.

Best practices in creating workflows

Designing workflows involves several key steps. First, it's essential to plan and structure your workflows by identifying your goals. These goals could include automated testing, deployment, or code quality checks. Next, define the triggers for your workflow, such as a push, pull request, or scheduled event. Once the triggers are set, outline the workflow steps, breaking them down into individual jobs and ensuring each step logically follows the previous one.

When designing workflows, it's important to follow best practices. Create modular workflows that are reusable and easy to maintain. Write clear and concise workflow files, adding comments to explain complex steps. Additionally, optimize your workflows to minimize execution time and resource usage.

Writing workflow files requires an understanding of YAML syntax and conventions. Start with the basic structure of a YAML file, including proper indentation and key-value pairs. Define jobs and steps within the workflow file, specifying the actions to be performed. Each job can run on specific runners, such as `ubuntu-latest`, and include multiple steps. These steps might involve running commands, using actions, or setting environment variables.

Using pre-built actions from the GitHub Actions Marketplace can save time and effort. Explore the marketplace to find actions that suit your needs and learn how to integrate them into your workflow files by referencing them in your steps. Customize these actions by configuring input parameters and combining multiple actions to create complex workflows.

Creating custom actions can be done using JavaScript or Docker. For JavaScript actions, set up the action metadata and write the necessary code. For Docker actions, define the Dockerfile and action metadata. Once your custom actions are ready, you can publish them to the GitHub Marketplace for others to use. Remember to version your actions and maintain them over time.

Debugging and testing workflows is crucial to ensure they function correctly. Learn to identify and understand errors in your workflow runs and explore common troubleshooting techniques to resolve issues. Use tools such as `act` to test your workflows locally before pushing them to GitHub, and simulate workflow runs to verify they work as expected in different scenarios.

In an SDLC, the main use cases for GitHub Actions are in the CI and CD processes and stages. In the next section, we will discuss a few things about implementing CI/CD practices with GitHub Actions.

CI/CD with GitHub Actions

Continuous Integration (CI) is the practice of automatically integrating code changes from multiple contributors into a shared repository several times a day. This process includes automated testing to ensure new code changes do not break the existing codebase. **Continuous Deployment (CD)**, on the other hand, is the practice of automatically deploying every change that passes the CI process to production. This ensures that the software is always in a deployable state.

CI/CD offers several benefits in software development. Improved code quality is one of the primary advantages, as automated tests catch bugs early in the development process. Faster delivery is another benefit, as automated deployments speed up the release cycle. Additionally, automation reduces the need for manual testing and deployment, freeing up developer time for other tasks.

Setting up Continuous Integration (CI)

Here are some CI practices.

- **Automating tests and builds**: To set up continuous integration, start by automating tests and builds. Define test jobs in your workflow to run automated tests using frameworks such as Jest, Mocha, or JUnit. Build automation involves setting up jobs to build your application, ensuring that it compiles correctly before deployment.

- **Integrating with testing frameworks**: Integrate your CI process with various testing frameworks. Run unit tests to verify individual components of your application. Execute integration tests to ensure different parts of your application work together as expected. Measure code coverage to ensure that your tests cover a significant portion of your codebase.

Implementing Continuous Deployment (CD)

CD practices include the following:

- **Automating deployment processes**: Automate your deployment processes by defining jobs in your workflow to deploy your application to various environments, such as staging or production. Implement deployment strategies such as blue-green deployments or canary releases to minimize downtime and risk.

- **Deploying to various environments**: Deploy your application to a staging environment for final testing before production. Automate the deployment to the production environment to ensure a smooth and reliable release process.

Advanced CI/CD techniques

There are also some advanced techniques. The most commonly used ones are as follows:

- **Managing secrets and environment variables**: Use GitHub secrets to securely store and manage sensitive information such as API keys and passwords. Define environment variables in your workflows to configure different environments.

- **Using matrix builds for multiple configurations**: Set up matrix builds to run your tests and builds across multiple configurations, such as different operating systems or versions of a programming language. Run jobs in parallel to speed up the CI/CD process.

- **Monitoring and maintaining CI/CD pipelines**: Access detailed logs of your workflow runs to diagnose and fix issues. Set up alerts and notifications to stay informed about the status of your workflows.

- **Maintaining and updating CI/CD pipelines**: Regularly review and update your CI/CD pipelines to incorporate new best practices and tools. Continuously improve your CI/CD processes based on feedback and performance metrics.

That's it! We have just covered the fundamentals of GitHub Actions. If you are interested in learning about more advanced concepts and use cases for CI/CD, access the resources in the *Useful links* section.

Summary

In this chapter, we delved into the world of GitHub Actions and automation, a feature I absolutely love. We explored GitHub's approach to continuous integration, continuous delivery, and automation, highlighting what makes GitHub Actions a unique tool. We discussed how GitHub Actions aids in automating code builds, unit tests, code quality checks, vulnerability scans, and deployments to various environments, all in a seamless and integrated manner.

We explained the concept of Pipeline as Code, where the entire CI/CD pipeline is defined and managed using code, allowing it to be version-controlled, reviewed, and audited just like any other code. We also differentiated between continuous delivery and continuous deployment, emphasizing their roles in the CI/CD pipeline.

The chapter outlined the key benefits of Pipeline as Code, such as version control, consistency, automation, and collaboration. We described how GitHub Actions supports this approach by allowing us to define our CI/CD pipelines using YAML files stored in our repository. We also highlighted integration with GitHub, customizability, scalability, and access to a vast library of pre-built actions in the GitHub Marketplace.

We then moved on to the key components and terminologies of GitHub Actions, including workflows, events, jobs, steps, actions, and runners. We provided a detailed explanation of how workflows are defined by YAML files and how they consist of jobs that run in response to specific events. We also listed the possible events that can trigger a workflow.

The chapter further explained the differences between GitHub-hosted and self-hosted runners, their benefits, and how they can be used to execute jobs in a workflow. We also discussed the importance of using ephemeral runners for maintaining security and consistency.

Finally, we provided practical lab exercises to help us get started with GitHub Actions, including setting up our first workflow and exploring the GitHub Actions Marketplace. We emphasized the importance of best practices in creating workflows, such as planning and structuring workflows, writing clear and concise workflow files, and optimizing workflows to minimize execution time and resource usage.

By the end of this chapter, we had gained a comprehensive understanding of GitHub Actions and how to leverage it for automating our software development processes.

In the next chapter, we will discuss yet another great feature of GitHub that aids collaboration and social coding – GitHub Discussions.

Test your knowledge

1. Which of the following is NOT listed as a key benefit of Pipeline as Code?

    a. Version control

    b. Consistency

    c. Integrity

    d. Automation

2. In the context of GitHub Actions, what is the purpose of an ephemeral runner?

    a. To run multiple jobs concurrently on a single runner.

    b. To ensure each job runs in a clean environment by unregistering itself after a single job.

    c. To provide a perpetual environment for continuous integration.

    d. To allow manual intervention during job execution.

3. Which of the following is not an event that triggers a workflow pipeline?

    a. schedule

    b. pull

    c. push

    d. release

Useful links

-   Training for GitHub on MS Learn: `https://learn.microsoft.com/en-us/training/github/#:~:text=GitHub%20Actions,-Gain%20the%20skills`

-   Events that trigger workflows: `https://docs.github.com/en/actions/writing-workflows/choosing-when-your-workflow-runs/events-that-trigger-workflows`

-   Autoscaling with self-hosted runners: `https://docs.github.com/en/actions/hosting-your-own-runners/managing-self-hosted-runners/autoscaling-with-self-hosted-runners`

Unlock this book's exclusive benefits now

Scan this QR code or go to packtpub.com/unlock, then search this book by name.

Note: Keep your purchase invoice ready before you start.

9

Engaging with the Community through GitHub Discussions

Welcome to the social chapter! GitHub thrives on and embodies collaboration. It's known for making software development feel more social, encouraging teams to work together, build together, and remove silos. In this chapter, we will be discussing another fantastic feature of GitHub – GitHub Discussions – a collaborative and social tool for fostering developer communities.

We will cover the following main topics:

- Introduction to GitHub Discussions
- Starting a GitHub discussion
- Best practices for community engagement
- Leveraging discussions for project feedback

Technical requirements

For the lab in this chapter, you will need the following:

- A GitHub Individual account
- A repository where you have administrative access

Introduction to GitHub Discussions

GitHub Discussions is a powerful feature designed to foster community engagement within a GitHub repository or organization. It provides a dedicated space for conversations, reducing the burden of managing active work in issues and pull requests.

It allows developers to create and participate in conversations without needing third-party tools. Discussions can be used to ask and answer questions, share information, make announcements, and conduct conversations about a project.

GitHub Discussions can either be at the repo level or the organization level.

> By default, Discussions is not activated in a GitHub repo. You must activate it first. We will examine how to do this in the practical section following this introduction.

Let's examine some of its key features.

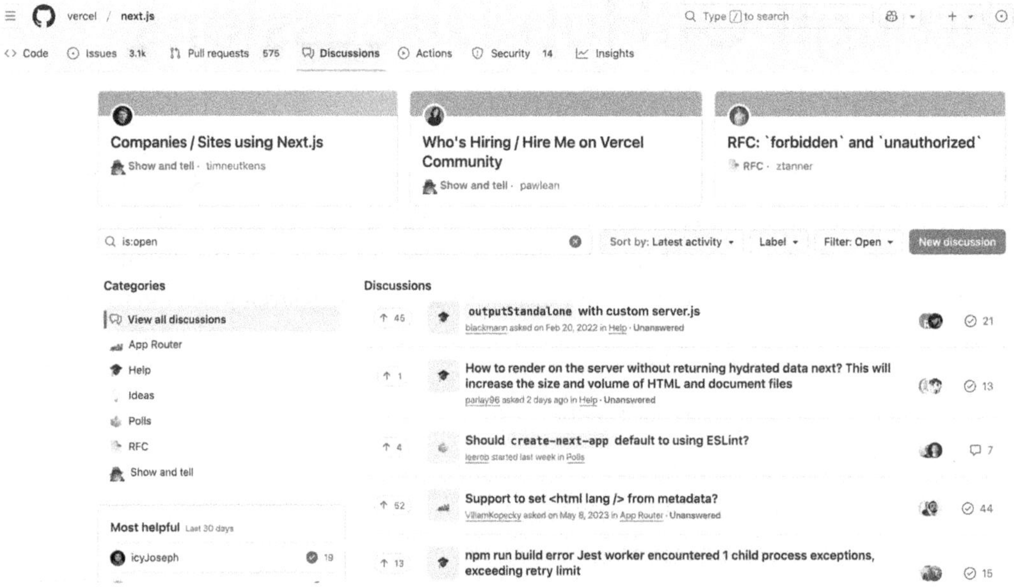

Figure 9.1: Cross-section of next.js Discussion forum

Threaded conversations

Threaded conversations are a feature designed to keep context intact and conversations on track. This functionality allows users to create and participate in nested discussions, making it easier to follow and manage complex conversations. They help maintain the flow of dialogue by grouping related comments together. This structure ensures that responses are directly connected to the original comment, making it easier to follow the conversation and understand the context. Threaded conversations provide a dedicated space for open-ended topics, brainstorming, and community support. Unlike GitHub issues, which focus on task tracking, discussions are designed for more general conversations.

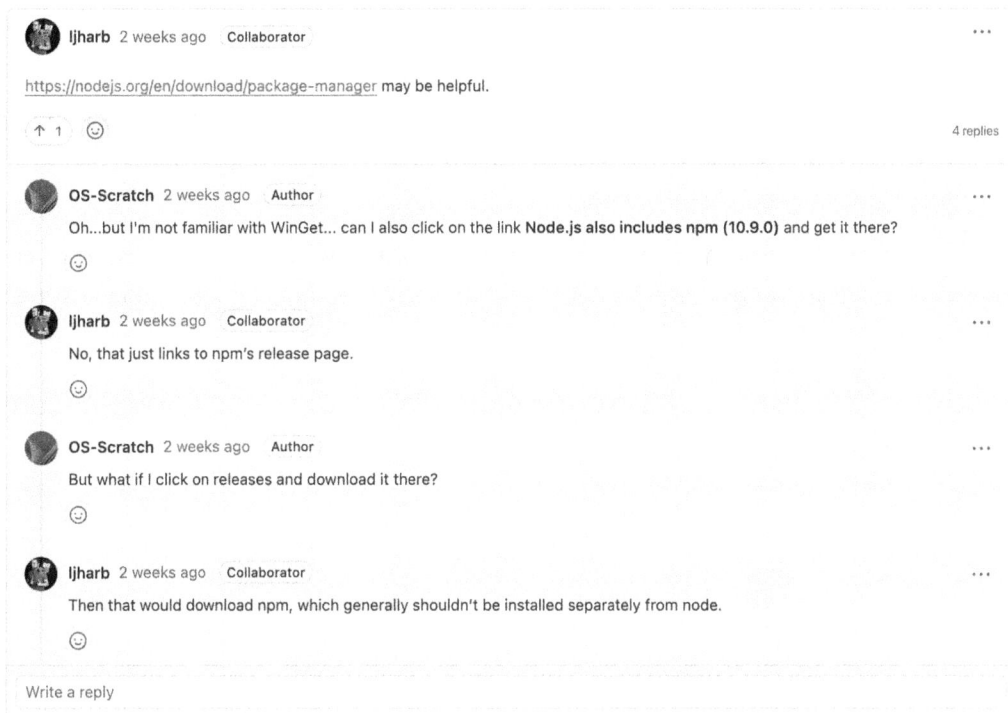

ljharb 2 weeks ago   Collaborator   ...

https://nodejs.org/en/download/package-manager may be helpful.

↑ 1   ☺   4 replies

OS-Scratch 2 weeks ago   Author   ...

Oh...but I'm not familiar with WinGet... can I also click on the link **Node.js also includes npm (10.9.0)** and get it there?

☺

ljharb 2 weeks ago   Collaborator   ...

No, that just links to npm's release page.

☺

OS-Scratch 2 weeks ago   Author   ...

But what if I click on releases and download it there?

☺

ljharb 2 weeks ago   Collaborator   ...

Then that would download npm, which generally shouldn't be installed separately from node.

☺

Write a reply

Figure 9.2: Threaded conversations show a timeline of various comments and replies

Categories and custom categories

Categories help teams organize conversations for their community members. All discussions must be created in a category. Here is a list of the default categories that come in a discussion:

Category	Description
📣 Announcements	Updates from maintainers
💬 General	Chat about anything and everything here
💡 Ideas	Share ideas for new features
🗳 Polls	Take a vote from the community
🙏 Q&A	Ask the community for help
🙌 Show and tell	Show off something you've made

Table 9.1: List of default categories in a GitHub discussion

Repository admins and people with write access can create custom categories to better organize discussions. Custom categories can have unique names, emojis, and descriptions to clearly state their purpose.

Polls

Polls on GitHub Discussions are a great way to engage with your community and gather opinions on various topics. They allow members of the developer community to vote and interact on an idea without having to comment. This feature is particularly useful for gathering feedback on new ideas, features, or project directions.

Repo admins can create polls for the community to vote on, as well as locking polls to prevent further voting when required. Participating in polls from anywhere is also possible via the GitHub Mobile app.

Changing the license of the code examples in the docs to public dom universal" #53740

Isam-Lakehal started this conversation in **Polls**

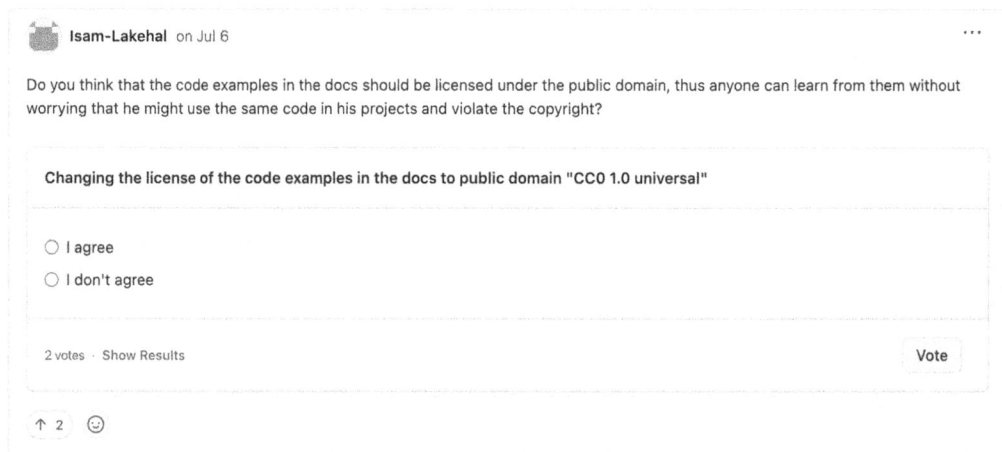

Isam-Lakehal on Jul 6   ...

Do you think that the code examples in the docs should be licensed under the public domain, thus anyone can learn from them without worrying that he might use the same code in his projects and violate the copyright?

> **Changing the license of the code examples in the docs to public domain "CC0 1.0 universal"**
>
> ○ I agree
>
> ○ I don't agree
>
> 2 votes · Show Results   Vote

↑ 2   ☺

Figure 9.3: Polls help to gather feedback

Understanding how Discussions improves collaboration is key to answering certification questions about GitHub's community features. For example, they might ask something like the following:

"Which of the following is a primary use case for GitHub Discussions?"

- Submitting a pull request
- Tracking bugs in a repository
- Gathering feedback and conducting community discussions ☑
- Assigning tasks to team members

You might be wondering how Discussions posts, issues, and pull requests are so similar in their formatting. This is because they all use the markdown format and, quite frankly, I wouldn't be surprised if they were built from the same codebase or base class. Now let us look at the main differences and in what scenarios to use them.

Here are some ways in which discussions differ from issues and pull requests.

Feature	GitHub Discussions	GitHub Issues	GitHub Pull requests
Purpose	Community engagement, brainstorming, Q&A	Bug tracking, feature requests, task management	Code changes, collaboration, review
Format	Threaded discussions	Task-based with assignees, labels, and milestones	Code diffs, inline comments, approvals
Voting/Polls?	✅ Yes	✖ No	✖ No
Best For	Open-ended discussions, feedback, engagement	Reporting and tracking issues, planning work	Reviewing and merging code

Table 9.2: GitHub Discussions versus issues versus pull requests

In the next section, we will examine practical steps for starting a discussion – time for some hands-on practice.

Starting a GitHub discussion

Engaging with the community is a crucial aspect of any successful open source project. GitHub Discussions provides a platform for project maintainers and contributors to communicate, share ideas, and solve problems collaboratively. In this section, we will explore how to initiate a discussion on GitHub, including setting up discussion categories, creating discussion threads, and best practices for framing your questions or topics to encourage meaningful participation.

GitHub Discussions is available both at the organization level and at the repository level.

Enabling GitHub Discussions

Let's first activate GitHub Discussions at the repo level.

1. **Navigate to your repository**

    a. Once logged in, navigate to the repository where you want to enable Discussions.

    b.   You can find your repositories by clicking on your profile icon in the top-right corner and selecting **Your repositories**.

2.   **Access repository settings**

    a.   In your repository, click on the **Settings** tab located at the top of the page, next to the **Insights** tab.

3.   **Enable Discussions**

    a.   In the **Settings** menu, scroll down to the **Features** section.

    b.   Look for the **Discussions** option. It should be listed along with other features such as **Issues**, **Wikis**, and **Projects**.

    c.   Check the box next to **Discussions** to enable this feature for your repository.

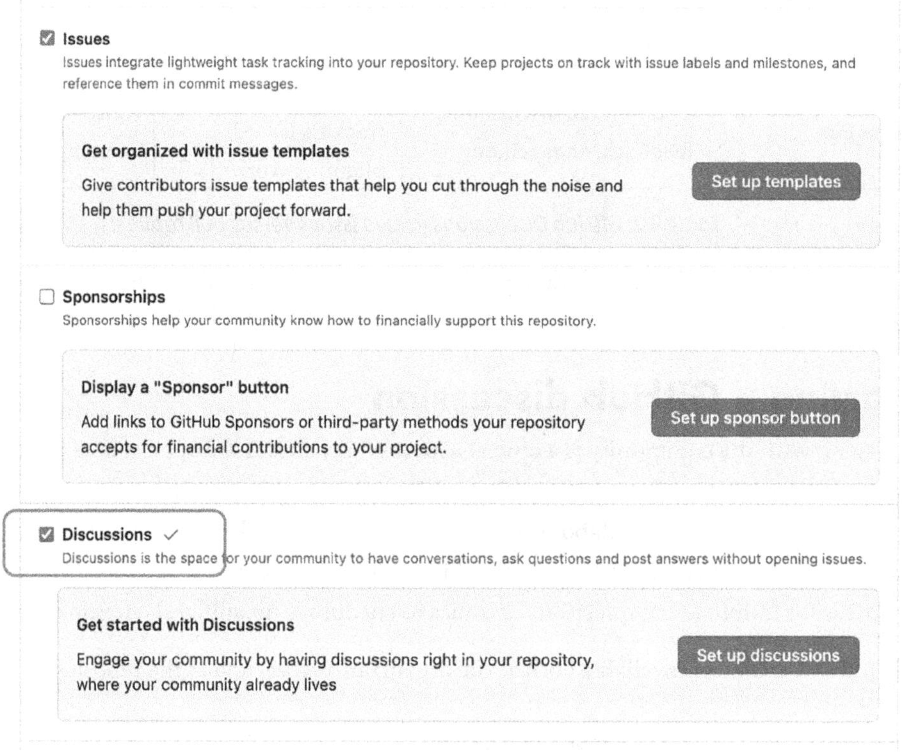

☑ Issues

Issues integrate lightweight task tracking into your repository. Keep projects on track with issue labels and milestones, and reference them in commit messages.

Get organized with issue templates

Give contributors issue templates that help you cut through the noise and help them push your project forward.

`Set up templates`

☐ Sponsorships

Sponsorships help your community know how to financially support this repository.

Display a "Sponsor" button

Add links to GitHub Sponsors or third-party methods your repository accepts for financial contributions to your project.

`Set up sponsor button`

☑ Discussions ✓

Discussions is the space for your community to have conversations, ask questions and post answers without opening issues.

Get started with Discussions

Engage your community by having discussions right in your repository, where your community already lives

`Set up discussions`

Figure 9.4: The Discussions feature must be enabled in the settings of the repo

When you enable the checkbox in the settings, you can see the **Discussions** tab in the repository.

That's it! You have successfully enabled GitHub Discussions for your repository. This feature will help you engage with your community, gather feedback, and foster collaboration.

Next, we will look at creating categories, then beginning a thread, and consider a few tips for fostering engagement.

Setting up discussion categories

After enabling Discussions, you can configure categories to organize your discussions:

1. Click on the **Discussions** tab that now appears at the top of your repository page.

2. Click on the pencil icon (✎) at the top of the left navigation of **Categories** to edit, create, and customize categories such as **General**, **Q&A**, **Ideas**, and so on.

3. Click **New category** to create a new one, or the edit icon (✎) next to an existing one to modify. Add a name and description for each category and save your changes.

4. You can consider creating sections to group two or more categories together. To do this, click on **New section**, give the section a name (for example, "Community Topics" or "Technical Help"), and then assign relevant categories to it. This helps users navigate discussions more easily by topic or purpose.

Creating a new discussion thread

Let us now start a new discussion.

1. **Start a new discussion**

   a. **Navigate to the Discussions tab**: Click on the **Discussions** tab in your repository.

   b. **Click on New discussion**: This button is usually located at the top right of the **Discussions** page.

   c. **Select a category**: Choose the **Ideas** category by clicking on **Get started** next to it, to indicate that this discussion is about new feature ideas.

   d. **Enter a title**: For example, `Feedback Needed: New Dark Mode Feature`.

e. **Write the body**: Provide a detailed description of the feature – here's an example:

```
# We need your feedback :speech_balloon:


Hi everyone :wave: ,


We're considering adding a new dark mode feature to our
project and would love to get your feedback. The dark mode
will provide an alternative color scheme that is easier on
the eyes, especially in low-light environments.


Here are some specific questions we'd like your input on:
- Do you think a dark mode would be beneficial for our users?
- Are there any specific color schemes or design elements you
would like to see in the dark mode?
- Do you have any concerns or suggestions regarding the
implementation of this feature?


Your feedback is invaluable to us, and we appreciate your
time and input!


Thanks.
```

f. **Publish the discussion**: Click **Start discussion** to make your post live.

2. **Formatting your post**: Use Markdown to format your discussion posts. This includes headings, lists, code blocks, and links to make your post clear and engaging.

3. **Tagging and labels:** Apply relevant categories and labels to your discussion to help categorize and prioritize it. Labels can indicate the topic area of discussion (e.g., "repos," "actions") or its status (e.g., "open," "resolved").

Feedback Needed: New Dark Mode Feature #1

ayo-creator started this conversation in **Ideas**

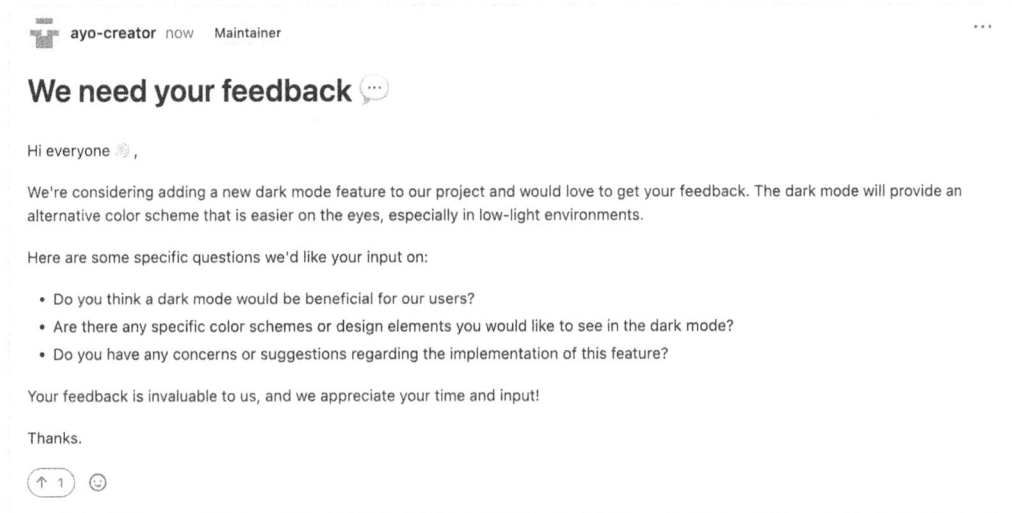

---

ayo-creator now   Maintainer   ...

We need your feedback 💬

Hi everyone 👋 ,

We're considering adding a new dark mode feature to our project and would love to get your feedback. The dark mode will provide an alternative color scheme that is easier on the eyes, especially in low-light environments.

Here are some specific questions we'd like your input on:

- Do you think a dark mode would be beneficial for our users?
- Are there any specific color schemes or design elements you would like to see in the dark mode?
- Do you have any concerns or suggestions regarding the implementation of this feature?

Your feedback is invaluable to us, and we appreciate your time and input!

Thanks.

(↑ 1) ☺

Figure 9.5: Preview of a newly published discussion

Verification

Before moving on, it's important to verify that Discussions has been enabled and is functioning correctly:

- Verify that the **Discussions** tab is visible and accessible in your repository
- Ensure that you can create new discussions and that they appear under the appropriate categories
- Also, examine the properties and action links on the right-hand pane of the discussion

Framing questions and topics

Here are some tips for framing questions and topics in a way to get good engagement:

- **Clear and concise titles**: Craft titles that are specific and descriptive. This helps attract the right audience and sets clear expectations for the discussion.

- **Detailed descriptions**: Provide sufficient context in your initial post. Include background information, specific questions, and any relevant links or resources.

- **Open-ended questions**: Use open-ended questions to encourage a broader range of responses and foster deeper discussions. For example, instead of asking "Is this feature useful?", ask "How do you think this feature could be improved?"

Encouraging participation and engagement

It is good to encourage participation in a discussion:

- **Inviting contributions**: Directly invite community members to join the discussion by mentioning them or sharing the discussion link in relevant channels.

- **Responding promptly**: Maintain active participation by responding to comments and questions in a timely manner. This keeps the discussion lively and shows that you value community input.

- **Acknowledging contributions**: Recognize and appreciate valuable contributions. This can be as simple as thanking participants or highlighting insightful comments.

By following these steps, you can effectively start and manage discussions on GitHub, fostering a collaborative and engaged community around your project.

Up next, we will examine some other good practices in managing a developer community.

Examples of public GitHub discussions

Some popular public repositories that have good examples of GitHub Discussions usage include the following:

- `nodejs/node`: The Node.js project has active discussions on various topics, including feature requests, questions, and **Requests for Comments (RFCs)**

- `kubernetes-sigs/cluster-api`: The repository is a subproject of `sig-cluster-lifecycle` that provides a Kubernetes-style declarative API and tooling to manage clusters

- `vercel/next.js`: The Next.js repository has discussions for sharing ideas, feature requests, and community questions

- `microsoft/vscode`: The Visual Studio Code repository uses discussions for feature requests, questions, and general conversations about the project

You can visit these repositories and explore their **Discussions** tab to see how they utilize this feature for community engagement and project management. And of course, you can also visit the ever-popular GitHub Community at `https://github.com/orgs/community/discussions` and explore how we use it on GitHub.

> I'm not sure whether you have noticed in the book thus far, but sometimes repos are written in the format `owner/repo` where owner can be the individual account names or the organization account slug and repo is the name of the repository. These two together uniquely identify any repository on GitHub. It is a shorthand for representing the URL to the GitHub repo. For example,
>
> `owner/repo` ≡ `https://github.com/owner/repo`, where the "≡" symbol indicates that the shorthand format is equivalent to the full repository URL.

Best practices for community engagement

Building a vibrant and engaged community around your project requires more than just starting discussions. It involves fostering a welcoming environment, actively participating in conversations, and recognizing valuable contributions. This section will cover the best practices for community engagement.

Fostering a welcoming environment

Creating an inclusive and welcoming environment is the foundation of a successful community.

Using **inclusive language** is crucial. This means using respectful terms, avoiding jargon or slang that might exclude or alienate members, and being generally mindful of the community's uniqueness. Regularly reviewing and updating your communication guidelines can help ensure they promote inclusivity.

Establish **clear community guidelines** and a code of conduct that outline acceptable behavior, contribution standards, and conflict resolution processes. Include these guidelines in your repository's `README` or a dedicated `CONTRIBUTING.md` file. Implement a code of conduct and outline consequences for violations. GitHub provides a template that you can customize for your project. Ensuring that these guidelines are visible and consistently enforced helps maintain a positive community atmosphere.

Onboarding new members effectively can make a significant difference in their engagement. Sending **welcome messages** to new members, introducing them to the community, and providing useful resources can help them feel comfortable. Creating **starter guides or FAQs** can assist new members in understanding how to participate and contribute. Additionally, implementing **mentorship programs** where experienced members guide newcomers can foster a supportive environment.

Active participation and moderation

You can show engagement and leadership through regular interaction with the community, such as scheduled check-ins or office hours, where maintainers are available to answer questions and engage with members. This can significantly enhance community involvement.

Effective moderation techniques are necessary to keep discussions on-topic and respectful. Proactive moderation involves actively monitoring discussions and using GitHub's moderation tools to manage them, such as locking threads or hiding inappropriate comments. Appointing trusted community members as moderators can help manage discussions and enforce guidelines.

Handling spam and inappropriate content swiftly is crucial to maintaining a healthy community environment. Using automated spam filters can reduce the amount of spam in discussions. Providing clear mechanisms for community members to report spam or inappropriate content ensures that issues are addressed promptly. Taking swift and decisive action against spam and inappropriate content helps maintain the integrity of the community.

Handling conflicts and disagreements

Conflicts and disagreements are inevitable in any community. Addressing conflicts early and constructively is essential for maintaining a positive atmosphere. Acting as a mediator to facilitate discussions between conflicting parties and finding common ground can help resolve issues. Documenting conflict resolution processes and outcomes provides transparency and learning opportunities.

Encouraging respectful debate is important for promoting diverse viewpoints. Setting clear guidelines for discussions and debates helps ensure that all voices are heard and respected. Encouraging constructive feedback and discouraging personal attacks or inflammatory language fosters a healthy environment for debate.

Defining clear criteria for when issues should be escalated to maintainers or GitHub support is part of effective conflict management. Outlining the steps for escalating issues, including who to contact and what information to provide, ensures that conflicts are handled appropriately. Following up on escalated issues provides resolution and maintains community trust.

Recognizing and rewarding contributions

Recognizing and rewarding valuable contributions is key to maintaining an engaged community. Regularly highlighting and showcasing valuable contributions from community members in newsletters, blog posts, or social media can motivate others to contribute. Featuring contributors in spotlight posts or interviews recognizes their efforts and achievements.

Implementing a system of badges or other forms of recognition for active and valuable contributors can encourage participation. Creating leaderboards or other visual representations of top contributors fosters friendly competition and recognition.

Organizing community events, such as **Ask Me Anything** (**AMAs**) or live discussions, where community members can interact directly with maintainers and ask questions, can enhance engagement. Hosting hackathons, sprints, or other collaborative events encourages contributions and strengthens community bonds. Celebrating milestones and achievements with the community, such as project anniversaries or major releases, acknowledges the collective effort and fosters a sense of accomplishment.

By implementing these best practices, you can build a vibrant and engaged community around your project, fostering collaboration and continuous improvement. Now that we know the guidelines, let's see how you can leverage the power of feedback from the community in your software projects.

Leveraging Discussions for project feedback

Engaging with your community through GitHub Discussions is a powerful way to gather valuable feedback and insights. This section will guide you on how to effectively solicit, analyze, and incorporate community feedback into your project development process.

Soliciting feedback from the community

To gather meaningful feedback, it's essential to create dedicated threads specifically for this purpose. Setting up these threads with clear instructions on the type of feedback you are seeking can significantly enhance the quality of responses. For instance, you might have separate threads for feedback on features, usability, and documentation. Pinning these threads to the top of the **Discussions** page ensures they remain visible and accessible to all community members.

Surveys and polls are also effective tools for collecting structured feedback. By creating surveys using tools such as Google Forms or SurveyMonkey, and sharing the links in your discussions, you can gather detailed insights on specific topics. Additionally, GitHub's built-in poll feature allows you to quickly gauge community opinions on particular questions or decisions. Regularly reviewing and analyzing the results of these surveys and polls will help you identify trends and actionable insights.

Take, for example, GitHub's request for feedback on **Refreshed Pull Requests Commit Page** (`https://github.com/orgs/community/discussions/137725`). A dedicated discussion post was created soliciting feedback. You will notice the word *"feedback"* clearly stated in the title. In addition, labels such as *"Feedback Wanted,"* *"Product Feedback,"* and that of the related product were applied. This garnered great engagement with over a hundred responses and multiple threaded conversations.

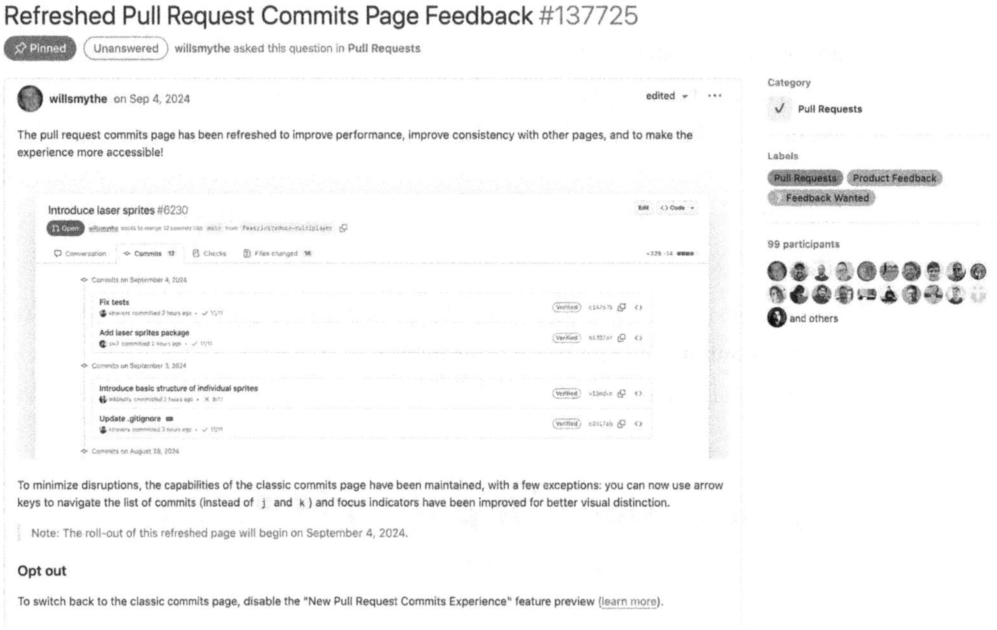

Figure 9.6: Example of a product feedback discussion

Encouraging honest feedback is crucial for the continuous improvement of your project. Foster an environment where community members feel comfortable sharing their thoughts without fear of negative repercussions. Offering options for anonymous feedback can further encourage candid responses. Always acknowledge and thank contributors for their feedback, emphasizing its value to the project's development.

Analyzing and interpreting community input

Once you have collected feedback, the next step is to analyze and interpret it. Look for common themes and patterns to identify recurring issues or popular feature requests. Categorizing feedback into different areas, such as bugs, feature requests, and usability issues, can make this process more manageable. Visualization tools such as charts and graphs can help you interpret and present feedback data effectively.

Prioritizing feedback is essential to ensure that the most impactful and feasible suggestions are addressed first. Evaluate feedback based on its potential impact on the project and the feasibility of implementation. Allowing the community to vote on feedback items can also help prioritize what is most important to them. Integrating high-priority feedback into your project roadmap and communicating these priorities to the community will keep everyone aligned and informed.

Utilizing data analysis tools and software can help manage and analyze large volumes of feedback. Setting up automated reports to regularly summarize and highlight key feedback trends can save time and ensure that important insights are not overlooked. Creating dashboards to provide a real-time overview of community feedback and its status can also be beneficial.

Incorporating feedback into project development

Incorporating community feedback into your project development process is crucial for continuous improvement. Establish a regular schedule for reviewing feedback and discussing it with your development team. Develop action plans for addressing feedback, including timelines and responsible team members. Maintaining transparency by regularly updating the community on how their feedback is being addressed fosters trust and engagement.

Sharing your project roadmap publicly shows how community feedback is influencing development priorities. Providing regular updates on the progress of roadmap items, highlighting completed tasks and upcoming milestones, keeps the community informed and involved. Involving the community in roadmap discussions ensures alignment with their needs and expectations.

Adopting agile methodologies allows for iterative development and continuous improvement based on feedback. Conducting beta testing with community members can gather early feedback on new features and improvements. Continuously integrating feedback into the development process helps refine and enhance the project.

Continuous improvement and iteration

Continuous improvement is a key aspect of successful project development. Maintain a detailed changelog to document all changes and updates made to the project. Publish comprehensive release notes for each new version, highlighting new features, bug fixes, and improvements. Use GitHub Discussions, newsletters, or social media to announce updates and keep the community informed.

Celebrating significant project milestones, such as major releases or anniversaries, with the community is important. Recognize and thank community members who have made significant contributions to reaching these milestones. Hosting events or activities to celebrate milestones and engage with the community can further strengthen the bond between maintainers and contributors.

Finally, be open to changing project direction based on evolving community needs and feedback. Encourage a culture of continuous learning and improvement within the project team. Establish regular feedback cycles to ensure ongoing alignment with community expectations and project goals.

By leveraging GitHub Discussions for project feedback, you can create a dynamic and responsive development process that continuously evolves to meet the needs of your community.

Let's summarise what we've learned.

Summary

In this chapter, we discussed how GitHub fosters collaboration and community engagement through GitHub Discussions. We explored how this feature provides a dedicated space for conversations, reducing the burden of managing active work in issues and pull requests. We highlighted the importance of threaded conversations, which allow us to maintain the flow of dialogue by grouping related comments together. This structure ensures that responses are directly connected to the original comment, making it easier to follow the conversation and understand the context.

We also examined the use of polls to engage with our community and gather opinions on various topics. This feature allows members to vote and interact on ideas without having to comment, which is particularly useful for gathering feedback on new ideas, features, or project directions. Additionally, we discussed the importance of categories and custom categories in organizing conversations for our community members.

Furthermore, we looked at practical steps to start a discussion on GitHub, including setting up discussion categories, creating discussion threads, and best practices for framing questions or topics to encourage meaningful participation. We emphasized the importance of fostering a welcoming environment, actively participating in conversations, and recognizing valuable contributions to build a vibrant and engaged community.

Finally, we explored how to leverage GitHub Discussions for project feedback, including soliciting, analyzing, and incorporating community feedback into our project development process. By following these steps, we aimed to create a dynamic and responsive development process that continuously evolved to meet the needs of our community.

Test your knowledge

1. Which feature of GitHub Discussions helps maintain the flow of dialogue by grouping related comments together?

    a. Polls

    b. Threaded conversations

    c. Categories

    d. Custom categories

2. What is the primary purpose of creating custom categories in GitHub Discussions?

    a. To lock polls and prevent further voting

    b. To organize conversations for community members

    c. To create nested discussions

    d. To enable discussions at the organization level

3. Which of the following is *not* a recommended best practice for fostering community engagement in GitHub Discussions?

    a. Using inclusive language

    b. Establishing clear community guidelines

    c. Ignoring spam and inappropriate content

    d. Recognizing and rewarding valuable contributions

Useful links

- GitHub Discussions: `https://github.com/features/discussions`
- Create a home for your community with GitHub Discussions: `https://github.blog/open-source/maintainers/create-a-home-for-your-community-with-github-discussions/`
- GitHub Topics – Forums: `https://github.com/topics/forums`

Unlock this book's exclusive benefits now

Scan this QR code or go to `packtpub.com/unlock`, then search this book by name.

Note: Keep your purchase invoice ready before you start.

Part 3

Leveraging GitHub for Career Advancement

This section equips you with strategies to use GitHub for networking, showcasing your work, and advancing your career in the tech industry. By the end of this part, you will have the knowledge to build a strong GitHub presence, contribute to open source projects, and utilize GitHub's features to enhance your professional development.

This part of the book includes the following chapters:

- *Chapter 10, Building and Showcasing Your GitHub Presence*
- *Chapter 11, Contributing to Open Source Projects*
- *Chapter 12, Enhancing Development with GitHub Copilot*
- *Chapter 13, Funding Your Projects with GitHub Sponsors*

10

Building and Showcasing Your GitHub Presence

A strong GitHub presence can give you an edge when applying for technical roles, especially when employers want to see real examples of your work. This chapter will guide you through the essential steps to create a professional and compelling GitHub profile that stands out to recruiters and collaborators. You'll learn how to effectively showcase your projects and contributions, making your work easily accessible and impressive to potential employers. Additionally, we'll explore how to leverage GitHub Pages to build a personal portfolio that enhances your personal brand. By the end of this chapter, you'll have the tools and knowledge to optimize your GitHub presence to help advance your career in the tech industry. While a polished GitHub profile isn't a direct test item, you will still come across questions regarding an advanced profile README in personal repos or components of items that may be found on a profile page.

We will cover the following main topics:

- Crafting a professional GitHub profile
- Showcasing projects and contributions
- Utilizing GitHub Pages for personal branding
- Lab 10.1: Creating a GitHub page to showcase your profile and skills

Technical requirements

- A GitHub Individual account
- A good-looking photo suitable for a profile photo

Crafting a professional GitHub profile

Your GitHub profile is often the first impression you make on potential employers, collaborators, and the broader tech community. A well-crafted profile not only presents your technical skills but also reflects your professionalism and attention to detail. In this section, we will explore the key elements of creating a standout GitHub profile, from selecting the right username to optimizing your activity overview.

Profile basics

The foundation of a professional GitHub profile starts with the basics: your username, display name, and profile picture. Your username should be professional and memorable, ideally incorporating your real name or a recognizable variation of it. This helps others easily identify you and associate your contributions with your personal brand. Alongside your username, your display name should be your full name, ensuring consistency across all professional platforms.

Your profile picture is another crucial element. Choose a high-resolution headshot where your face is clearly visible (around *500 x 500 pixels and not more than 1 MB*). The photo should be taken in a professional or neutral setting, avoiding overly casual or distracting backgrounds.

A friendly and approachable expression can make a positive impact, making you appear more accessible to potential collaborators and employers.

Figure 10.1: Sample GitHub profile showing basic details

Contact information

Including your contact information on your GitHub profile is essential for networking and professional opportunities. Add a professional email address, preferably one that includes your name, to make it easy for others to reach out to you. Additionally, link to your other professional profiles, such as LinkedIn or your personal website. This not only provides multiple ways for people to connect with you but also reinforces your professional presence across different platforms.

Pinned repositories

Pinned repositories are a powerful feature on GitHub that allows you to highlight your best work. Select a few high-quality projects that present your skills and align with your career goals. Quality is more important than quantity here; it's better to pin a few standout projects than many mediocre ones. For each **pinned** repository, write a clear and informative description that highlights the purpose and key features of the project. Use relevant tags to make your projects more discoverable. For example, you can **pin** your prioritized repositories on your profile page. To do this, visit your profile page. At the top of the **Popular repositories** or **Pinned** section, click **Customize your pins** and select which repository to pin. Then click **Save pins**.

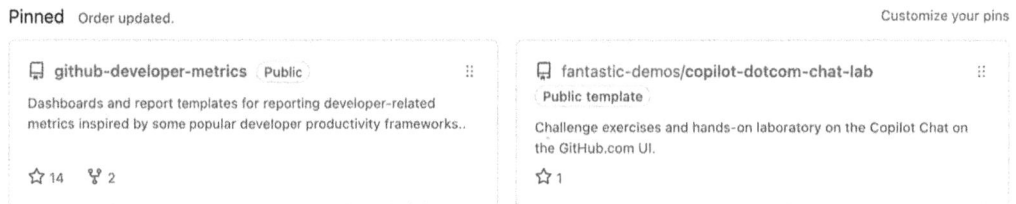

Figure 10.2: Pinned repositories on a profile page

Activity overview

Your activity overview, including your contribution graph and recent activity feed, provides a snapshot of your engagement on GitHub. A consistent and active contribution graph can demonstrate your commitment to coding and open source projects. Focus on making meaningful contributions rather than just increasing the number of commits. Regularly contribute to projects, whether through code, documentation, or issue tracking, to keep your activity feed updated and relevant.

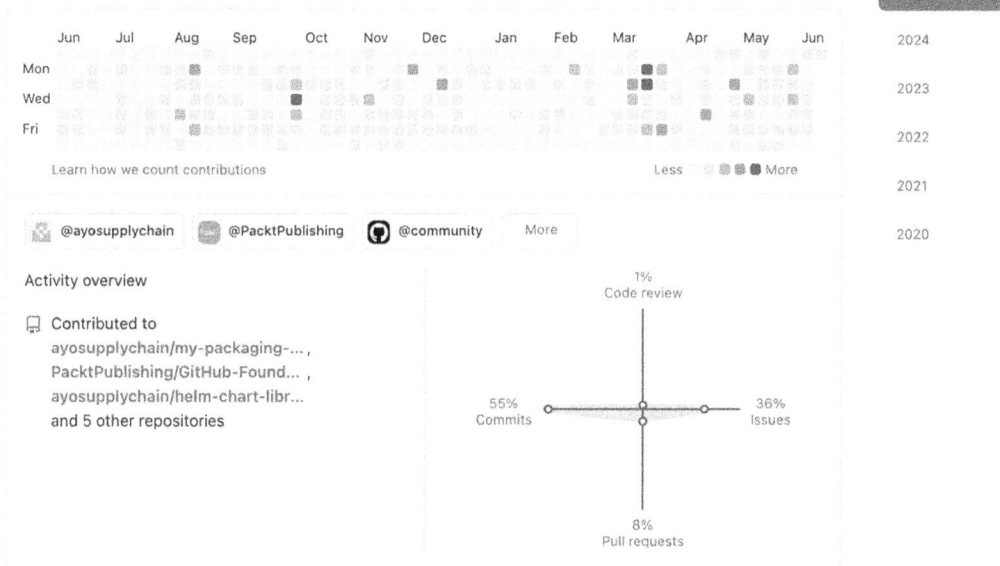

Figure 10.3: Sample contribution graph and activity overview

By paying attention to these details, you can craft a GitHub profile that not only promotes your technical abilities but also presents you as a professional and dedicated member of the tech community. This foundation will set the stage for effectively showcasing your projects and contributions, which we will explore in the next section.

Showcasing projects and contributions

Effectively showcasing your projects and contributions on GitHub is crucial for demonstrating your skills and experience to potential employers and collaborators. This section will guide you through selecting the right projects, documenting them comprehensively, and highlighting your contributions in a way that stands out.

Project selection

Focus on projects that align with your career goals and the skills you want to highlight. For instance, if you are aiming for a role in web development, prioritize projects that demonstrate your proficiency in relevant technologies such as HTML, CSS, JavaScript, and frameworks such as React or Angular. Additionally, showcasing a variety of projects (not GitHub projects) can demonstrate your versatility and ability to tackle different types of challenges. Highlight projects that have made a significant impact or received recognition, as these can add credibility to your profile.

Documentation

Comprehensive documentation is key to making your projects accessible and understandable to others. Start with a well-written README file for each project.

> If you need help creating a repository or writing a README, revisit *Chapter 3, Repository Creation and Management.*

A good README should include an introduction that explains the project's purpose, installation instructions, usage examples, and contribution guidelines. Use a consistent structure for all your README files to make them easy to navigate. Beyond the README, consider using wikis and project boards to provide additional context and organization. Wikis can be used to document more detailed aspects of your project, while project boards can help visualize the project's progress and workflow.

Contribution guidelines

Highlighting your contributions to open source projects can significantly enhance your GitHub profile. Open source contributions demonstrate your ability to collaborate with others and contribute to the broader tech community. When showcasing these contributions, focus on meaningful interactions such as pull requests, issue tracking, and code reviews. Write clear and concise commit messages that explain the changes you made and why they were necessary. This not only shows your technical skills but also your ability to communicate effectively with other developers.

Visuals and media

Adding visuals and media to your projects can make them more engaging and easier to understand. Use high-quality screenshots and GIFs to highlight key features and functionalities of your projects. Visuals can provide a quick overview of what your project does and how it works, which can be particularly useful for complex projects. Additionally, consider creating video demonstrations that walk viewers through your project. Videos can be a powerful way to exhibit your work, as they allow you to explain your thought process and highlight specific aspects of your project in detail.

By carefully selecting and documenting your projects, highlighting your contributions, and using visuals and media effectively, you can create a compelling GitHub portfolio that showcases your skills and experience. This will not only make your profile more attractive to potential employers and collaborators but also help you stand out in the competitive tech industry.

Advanced profile setup

Did you know that in addition to setting your basic profile details, you can create a more comprehensive profile of yourself using a profile README.md file? Using a profile README.md file helps you to share more information about yourself with the community. As the file extension implies, you write your information in markdown syntax, giving you the flexibility to use rich text and add multimedia and hyperlinks to your other portfolios of work.

By default, GitHub automatically displays the contents of your profile README.md directly on your profile page. All you have to do is ensure you carry out and meet the following pre-requisites:

- A repository with a name that *exactly matches* your GitHub handle (username)
- Set the repository's visibility to **Public**
- Add the README.md file to the root of this repo with the contents you desire for your profile

> **Certification tip**
>
> You may be asked to select from a list of options where a profile README.md is stored.

So, what kind of information can you add to your profile README.md? You can include sections such as a summary of your bio to describe your work, your social media profile and blog links, your most important work or contributions, and how developers can best reach you to collaborate.

> **Important**
>
> This advanced profile README setup only works if you created this repo with the same name as your handle after July 2020.

Badges

Badges are dynamic images that display real-time information about your project. They're often used to show build status, test coverage, license type, version, and more. Let's look at some common types of badges.

Badge Type	Purpose
Build Status	Shows if the latest build is passing or failing (e.g., GitHub Actions, Travis CI)
Test Coverage	Displays code coverage percentage (e.g., Codecov, Coveralls)
License	Indicates the type of license (e.g., MIT, GPL)
Version	Shows the current version of the project
Last Commit	Displays the date of the last commit
Open Issues/PRs	Shows the number of open issues or pull requests
Downloads	Indicates how many times the project has been downloaded (e.g., via npm, PyPI)
Dependencies	Shows if dependencies are up to date (e.g., David, Snyk)
Social	Stars, forks, watchers, or GitHub followers

Table 10.1: List of common badge types and their purposes

How can you add badges to your profile? You can do this in three easy steps:

1. **Find a Badge Provider:**

   - Shields.io – the most popular and customizable badge generator
   - CI/CD tools such as GitHub Actions, Travis CI, and CircleCI often provide their own badges
   - Coverage tools such as Codecov or Coveralls

2. **Copy the Markdown or HTML:** Shields.io provides both Markdown and HTML snippets, for example.

3. **Paste into Your README:** Place badges at the top of your README.md for maximum visibility

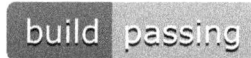

Figure 10.4: Sample build badge showing the status of your build pipeline

Stars

GitHub stars are a way for users to show appreciation for a repository they find useful, interesting, or well-made. Think of them as similar to "likes" on social media. A high star count signals to others that your project is valuable or popular, which can attract more users and contributors. Starred repositories are more likely to appear in GitHub search results and trending lists, increasing exposure. When potential employers, collaborators, or clients view your GitHub profile, starred projects can demonstrate your skills and impact. Stars can also help you gauge interest in your project and prioritize features or improvements based on user feedback.

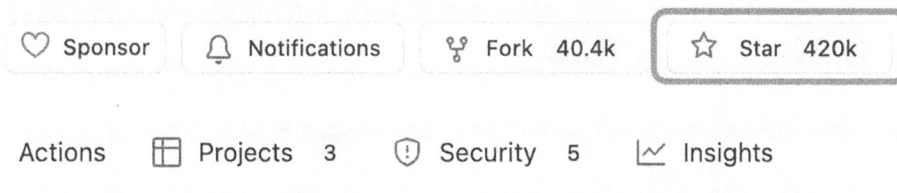

Figure 10.5: Stars on your repos is also an indicator of its popularity

Utilizing GitHub Pages for personal branding

GitHub Pages is a powerful tool that allows you to create a personal website directly from a GitHub repository. This section will guide you through setting up GitHub Pages, creating content that exhibits your skills and projects, and optimizing your site for personal branding.

Setting up GitHub Pages

Creating a GitHub Pages site is a straightforward process that begins with setting up a repository. Start by creating a new repository named <username>.github.io, where <username> is your GitHub username. This repository will serve as the source for your GitHub Pages site. Once the repository is created, you can choose a theme from the GitHub Pages theme chooser or customize your own. Selecting a theme that aligns with your personal brand is important, as it sets the tone for your site. Customize the theme to reflect your style and preferences, ensuring it is both visually appealing and professional.

Content creation

The content you create for your GitHub Pages site should highlight your skills, projects, and experiences. Start by building a portfolio section that highlights your key projects. Each project should include a brief description, key features, and links to the repository and live demo if available. Use high-quality images and media to make your portfolio visually engaging. In addition to your portfolio, consider adding a blog section where you can share your knowledge and experiences. Writing blog posts on topics related to your field can demonstrate your expertise and keep your site updated with fresh content. This not only enhances your personal brand but also provides value to your audience.

SEO and analytics

Optimizing your GitHub Pages site for search engines is crucial for increasing its visibility. Use relevant keywords throughout your site, especially in titles, headings, and meta descriptions. This helps search engines understand the content of your site and rank it higher in search results. Additionally, setting up analytics is essential for tracking the performance of your site. Tools such as Google Analytics can provide insights into visitor behavior, helping you understand which content is most engaging and where improvements can be made. For more practical steps in integrating Google Analytics, visit *Use Analytics with your site* (`https://support.google.com/sites/answer/97459`). Regularly review your analytics data to make informed decisions about your site's content and structure.

Continuous improvement

Maintaining and improving your GitHub Pages site is an ongoing process. Regularly update your site with new projects, blog posts, and other content to keep it fresh and relevant. Seek feedback from peers and mentors to identify areas for improvement. This feedback can provide valuable insights into how others perceive your site and what changes could enhance its effectiveness. Additionally, stay informed about new features and best practices for GitHub Pages to ensure your site remains up to date with the latest trends and technologies.

By effectively utilizing GitHub Pages, you can create a personal website that showcases your skills and projects, enhances your personal brand, and helps you stand out in the tech industry. This not only provides a platform for sharing your work but also demonstrates your ability to leverage modern tools and technologies for personal and professional growth.

Let's put this into practice in a lab exercise through step-by-step instructions on how to create a GitHub Page to promote your profile and skills.

Lab 10.1: Creating a GitHub page to showcase your profile and skills

By the end of this exercise, you will have created a personal GitHub Pages site to promote your profile, projects, and skills.

Step 1: Create a new repository

1. **Log in to GitHub**: Go to GitHub and log in to your account.

2. **Create a repository**:

    a. Click on the + icon in the top-right corner and select **New repository**.

    b. Name the repository `<username>.github.io`, where `<username>` is your GitHub username.

    c. Optionally, add a description.

    d. Set the repository to **Public**.

    e. Click **Create repository**. (*Copy the HTTPS URL of the repo for use in Step 2.*)

> You need a paid plan or a public repo to use GitHub Pages.

Step 2: Clone the repository

1. **Open terminal or command prompt**: Open your terminal (Mac/Linux) or command prompt (Windows).

2. **Clone the repository**:

    a. Run the following command to clone the repository to your local machine:

    ```
    git clone https://github.com/<username>/<username>.github.
    io.git
    ```

    b. Replace `<username>` with your GitHub username.

Step 3: Create your website

1. **Navigate to the repository:**

    a. Change directory to your repository:

    ```
    cd <username>.github.io
    ```

2. **Create an index file:**

    a. Create an index.html file:

    ```
    touch index.html
    ```

    b. Open index.html in your preferred text editor and add the following basic HTML structure:

    ```html
    <!DOCTYPE html>
    <html lang="en">
    <head>
        <meta charset="UTF-8">
        <meta name="viewport" content="width=device-width,
            initial-scale=1.0">
        <title>My GitHub Page</title>
    </head>
    <body>
        <h1>Welcome to My GitHub Page</h1>
        <p>This is my personal website where I highlight my
            projects and skills.</p>
    </body>
    </html>
    ```

Step 4: Customize your site (optional)

1. **Add content:**

    a. Customize the index.html file to include sections such as About Me, Projects, and Contact.

    b. Use Markdown or HTML to format your content.

2. **Add styles:**

    a. Create a styles.css file to add custom styles to your site.

b. Link the CSS file in your `index.html`:

```
<link rel="stylesheet" href="styles.css">
```

Step 5: Commit and push changes

1. **Add changes:**

   a. Stage your changes:

   ```
   git add .
   ```

2. **Commit changes:**

   a. Commit your changes with a message:

   ```
   git commit -m "Initial commit"
   ```

3. **Push changes:**

   a. Push your changes to GitHub:

   ```
   git push origin main
   ```

Step 6: Enable GitHub Pages

1. **Go to Repository Settings:**

   a. Navigate to your repository on GitHub.

   b. Click on **Settings**.

2. **Enable GitHub Pages:**

   a. Select **Pages** from the left navigation.

   b. Under **Source**, select **Deploy from a branch**.

   c. Under **Branch**, select the branch you wish to deploy from (usually *main* or *master*).

   d. Click **Save**.

Step 7: View your site

1. **Access your site:**

   a. Your site should now be live at `https://<username>.github.io`.

   b. Open this URL in your web browser to view your site.

Step 8: Continuous improvement

1. **Update regularly:**

    a. Regularly update your site with new projects, blog posts, and other content.

2. **Seek feedback:**

    a. Ask peers and mentors for feedback to continuously improve your site.

Congratulations! You have successfully created a GitHub Pages site, a straightforward way to promote yourself online. Keep refining and updating your site to reflect your latest work and achievements.

Let's summarize what we learned in this chapter.

Summary

In this chapter, we explored how to build and promote our GitHub presence to enhance our careers in the tech industry. We learned the importance of crafting a professional GitHub profile, starting with the basics, such as choosing a professional username, display name, and profile picture. We also emphasized the significance of including contact information and utilizing pinned repositories to highlight our best work.

We delved into the activity overview, understanding how a consistent and active contribution graph can demonstrate our commitment to coding and open source projects. By focusing on meaningful contributions, we aimed to keep our activity feed updated and relevant.

Next, we discussed how to effectively exhibit our projects and contributions. We learned to select projects that align with our career goals, document them comprehensively, and highlight our contributions in a way that stands out. We also explored the use of visuals and media to make our projects more engaging. Metrics such as GitHub stars, forks, or contributor counts can reinforce a project's credibility.

Additionally, we covered advanced profile setup using a profile README.md file to share more information about ourselves with the community. We also learned how to utilize GitHub Pages to create a personal website that displays our skills and projects, enhances our personal brand, and helps us stand out in the tech industry.

Finally, we put our knowledge into practice through a lab exercise, creating a GitHub Pages site as an example way to promote one's profile online. By the end of this chapter, we had the tools and knowledge to optimize our GitHub presence and advance our careers in the tech industry.

That's it for now about showcasing your presence. In the next chapter, we will discuss in detail how you might contribute to open source projects. Read along with me.

Test your knowledge

1. What is a prerequisite for setting up a profile README.md file on GitHub?

    a. The repository must be private.

    b. The repository name must match your GitHub handle (username).

    c. The repository must contain at least three projects.

    d. The repository must be created before July 2020.

2. Which of the following is *not* a recommended section to include in your profile README.md file?

    a. A summary of your bio.

    b. Your social media profile and blog links.

    c. Your favorite recipes.

    d. Your most important work or contributions.

3. What is the first step in creating a GitHub Pages site?

    a. Selecting a theme from the GitHub Pages theme chooser.

    b. Creating a new repository named <username>.github.io.

    c. Writing a blog post.

    d. Adding a README.md file to the repository.

Useful links

- Examples of awesome GitHub profiles: https://github.com/coderjojo/creative-profile-readme

- Setting up your profile: https://docs.github.com/en/get-started/start-your-journey/setting-up-your-profile

- What is GitHub Pages: https://docs.github.com/en/pages/getting-started-with-github-pages/what-is-github-pages

- Use Analytics with your site: https://support.google.com/sites/answer/97459

Unlock this book's exclusive benefits now

Scan this QR code or go to packtpub.com/unlock, then search this book by name.

Note: Keep your purchase invoice ready before you start.

11

Contributing to Open Source Projects

In this chapter, you'll learn how to navigate the open source landscape, identify projects that align with your interests and skills, and understand the significance of open source licensing. By the end of this chapter, you'll be equipped with the knowledge and confidence to make meaningful contributions to open source projects, enhancing your skills and visibility in the tech community.

We will cover the following main topics:

- Navigating the open source landscape
- Lab 11.1: Making your first contribution
- Understanding open source licensing

Technical requirements

This lab exercise in this chapter requires the following:

- A GitHub account
- Git installed on your computer (Windows, Linux, or macOS)
- A code editor or IDE of your choice
- Access to a terminal/command-line interface

Exploring the world of open source

Diving into the open source ecosystem can be both thrilling and a bit daunting. With a vast array of projects available, it's important to know how to pinpoint those that align with your goals and abilities. This chapter will walk you through the process of identifying and assessing open source initiatives, helping you contribute in ways that are both impactful and fulfilling. You'll discover how to leverage tools such as GitHub's **Explore** page and refine your search by language or technology stack. We'll also touch on the value of community involvement and how to become an engaged participant in open source circles, enriching both your experience and your career.

Introduction to open source

We dealt a little bit with the open source concept in *Chapter 2, Navigating the GitHub Interface*, but we will go in-depth in this chapter. We will provide a comprehensive introduction to the concept and discuss the significance of open source, as well as the personal and professional benefits of contributing to open source projects.

What is open source and why does it matter?

Open source software is built on the principle of transparency and collaboration. Its source code is publicly accessible, allowing anyone to use, modify, and share it. This openness encourages a collaborative development model where contributors from around the world can improve software by fixing bugs, adding features, and enhancing performance.

The open source model plays a crucial role in making technology more accessible. By removing financial and licensing barriers, it empowers individuals and organizations of all sizes to leverage powerful tools and platforms. This inclusivity fuels innovation and ensures that technological progress is shared more broadly. Clearly, there is much to learn from open source projects, but what are the benefits of contributing to them?

Why you should contribute

Getting involved in open source offers a wealth of advantages. For developers, it's a hands-on way to sharpen technical skills and gain experience with real-world codebases. It's also a great way to learn new tools and frameworks while receiving constructive feedback from seasoned contributors.

Beyond skill-building, your contributions can serve as a living portfolio. Hiring managers often look favorably on candidates who actively participate in open source, as it reflects initiative, teamwork, and a passion for learning. This visibility can open doors to new job opportunities and collaborations.

There's also a strong social component. Open source communities are vibrant spaces where developers connect, share knowledge, and support one another. Being part of such a community can be both motivating and rewarding.

Finally, your work can have a lasting impact. By contributing to widely used projects, you help shape the tools and technologies that others rely on, making software more robust, inclusive, and innovative.

Up next, we will talk about how best to find the right open source projects to contribute to.

How to discover the right projects

Here are a number of ways to effectively find and evaluate open source projects on GitHub, setting the stage for successful contributions.

Using GitHub's Explore feature

GitHub's **Explore** feature is a powerful tool for discovering open source projects. By navigating to the **Explore** page, you can browse trending repositories, curated collections, and recommended projects based on your interests and activity. The **Explore** page also highlights popular topics and showcases projects that are gaining traction within the community. This feature is especially helpful for uncovering active, well-maintained repositories that align with your areas of interest.

Searching for projects by language, topic, or technology

To find open source projects that match your specific interests, you can use GitHub's search functionality to filter repositories by programming language, topic, or technology. For example, if you're proficient in Python, you can search for repositories tagged with **Python** to find projects written in that language. Similarly, you can search for projects related to specific technologies tagged accordingly. This targeted approach helps you quickly find projects where your contributions will be most relevant and appreciated.

Evaluating project activity and community engagement

Once you've identified potential projects, it's important to evaluate their activity and community engagement to ensure they are suitable for contribution. Start by examining the repository's commit history and recent activity. Active projects typically have frequent commits, open issues, and ongoing discussions. Additionally, review the number of contributors and the responsiveness of maintainers to pull requests and issues. A healthy open source project will have an engaged community where contributors collaborate, provide feedback, and support each other.

Criteria	Project A	Project B
Last commit	2 days ago	6 months ago
Number of maintainers	3	1
Contribution guide	Yes	No
Good first issue present	Yes	No
→ *"Choose Project A — more active and beginner-friendly."*		

By choosing projects with active and welcoming communities, you increase the likelihood of having a positive and productive contribution experience.

Joining open source communities

Let's talk about the importance of engaging with open source communities and providing practical steps to becoming active and valued members.

Engaging with project maintainers and contributors

Building relationships with project maintainers and other contributors is a key part of becoming an active participant in any open source initiative. A good first step is to introduce yourself through the project's communication channels—this might be an issue thread, a discussion forum, or a dedicated chat space. Let them know that you're interested in contributing and ask where your help might be most valuable. Maintainers and seasoned contributors can often point you toward beginner-friendly tasks or areas that need attention.

As you begin contributing, keep the lines of communication open. Share updates on your progress, ask for input when needed, and be open to suggestions. This kind of collaboration not only accelerates your learning but also helps you build credibility and trust within the community. Always aim to be courteous and constructive—open source communities thrive on respectful and supportive interactions.

Participating in forums, chat rooms, and mailing lists

Most open source projects maintain active spaces for discussion and collaboration, such as forums, chat platforms, or mailing lists. These are great places to stay informed, ask questions, and engage with others who share your interests.

Look for the project's official communication platforms—these might include Slack, Discord, Gitter, or Discourse forums. Once you've joined, don't hesitate to participate. Whether you're asking for help, offering advice, or simply sharing your thoughts, your involvement helps strengthen the community. Mailing lists can also be a valuable source of updates and a venue for deeper conversations about the project's direction and goals.

By actively participating in these spaces, you'll gain a better understanding of the project's culture and priorities. You'll also have the chance to connect with other contributors, expand your professional network, and learn from a diverse group of developers. This kind of engagement can make your open source journey more rewarding and impactful.

Lab 11.1: Forking a repository — a complete contribution workflow

Embarking on your first contribution? This section will guide you through the essential steps to get started, from setting up your development environment to understanding the contribution workflow. You'll learn how to fork and clone repositories, create new branches for your changes, and effectively communicate with project maintainers and contributors. By following these steps, you'll be well prepared to make meaningful contributions and become an active member of the open source community.

Let's do a quick lab exercise.

Setting up your environment

Let us begin by forking the repo.

Forking the repository

Forking creates a complete copy of the repository under your GitHub account, allowing you to make changes without affecting the original repository.

Following are the steps to fork:

1. **Navigate to the repository**: Go to `https://github.com/PacktPublishing/GitHub-Foundations-Certification-Guide`.

2. **Fork the repository**:

   a. Click the **Fork** button (`⑂ Fork 1.3k ▾`) in the top-right corner of the repository page.

   b. Select your GitHub account as the destination.

   c. Keep the default repository name or customize it if desired.

   d. Ensure **Copy the main branch only** is checked (default).

   e. Click **Create fork**.

3. **Verify your fork:**

   a. You should now see the repository under your account: **https://github.com/YOUR_ USERNAME/GitHub-Foundations-Certification-Guide**, where YOUR_USERNAME is your GitHub handle.

   b. Notice the **forked from PacktPublishing/GitHub-Foundations-Certifica-tion-Guide** indicator below the repository name.

Cloning your fork

Cloning downloads your fork to your local machine for development.

Following are the steps to clone:

1. **Get the clone URL:**

   a. On your fork's GitHub page, click the green **Code** button.

   b. Copy the HTTPS URL (e.g., `https://github.com/YOUR_USERNAME/GitHub-Foundations-Certification-Guide.git`).

2. **Choose your local directory:**

   a. Open your terminal.

   b. Navigate to where you want to store the project:

   ```
   cd ~/Documents/github-projects  # or your preferred location
   ```

3. **Clone the repository:**

   ```
   git clone https://github.com/YOUR_USERNAME/GitHub-Foundations-
   Certification-Guide.git
   cd GitHub-Foundations-Certification-Guide
   ```

4. **Verify the clone:**

   ```
   git remote -v
   ```

You should see your fork as the `origin` remote.

Configuring the upstream remote

To keep your fork synchronized with the original repository, add it as an upstream remote:

```
git remote add upstream https://github.com/PacktPublishing/GitHub-
Foundations-Certification-Guide.git
git remote -v
```

💡 **Quick tip:** Enhance your coding experience with the **AI Code Explainer** and **Quick Copy** features. Open this book in the next-gen Packt Reader. Click the **Copy** button (**1**) to quickly copy code into your coding environment, or click the **Explain** button (**2**) to get the AI assistant to explain a block of code to you.

```
                                              Copy      Explain
function calculate(a, b) {
    return {sum: a + b};                        1           2
};
```

📱 **The next-gen Packt Reader** is included for free with the purchase of this book. Scan the QR code OR go to packtpub.com/unlock, then use the search bar to find this book by name. Double-check the edition shown to make sure you get the right one.

You should now see both origin (your fork) and upstream (the original repository).

Understanding the contribution flow

Now, let's see how we contribute.

Understanding the workflow

The typical contribution workflow follows this pattern:

1. **Sync:** Keep your fork updated with the upstream repository.
2. **Branch:** Create a feature branch for your changes.
3. **Develop:** Make your changes and commit them.
4. **Push:** Push your branch to your fork.
5. **Pull request:** Submit your changes for review.
6. **Iterate:** Address feedback and make revisions.
7. **Merge:** Once approved, your changes are merged.

Keeping your fork updated

Before starting any new work, sync your fork:

```
# Switch to main branch
git checkout main

# Fetch upstream changes
git fetch upstream

# Merge upstream changes
git merge upstream/main

# Push updates to your fork
git push origin main
```

💡 **Quick tip:** Enhance your coding experience with the **AI Code Explainer** and **Quick Copy** features. Open this book in the next-gen Packt Reader. Click the **Copy** button (1) to quickly copy code into your coding environment, or click the **Explain** button (2) to get the AI assistant to explain a block of code to you.

```
                                                    Copy        Explain

function calculate(a, b) {
    return {sum: a + b};                             1            2
};
```

📖 **The next-gen Packt Reader** is included for free with the purchase of this book. Scan the QR code OR go to packtpub.com/unlock, then use the search bar to find this book by name. Double-check the edition shown to make sure you get the right one.

Following is the branch-based workflow, which helps keep your development organized, isolated, and easier to review - by creating focused feature branches instead of working directly on main:

- Never work directly on the main branch
- Create feature branches for all changes
- Use descriptive branch names (e.g., `add-contributor-name` or `fix-documentation-typo`)
- Keep branches focused on a single feature or fix

Creating a new branch for your changes

For this exercise, we'll add your name to the contributors list.

Following are the steps for creating and switching to a new branch:

```
# Create and switch to a new branch
git checkout -b add-my-name-to-contributors

# Verify you're on the new branch
git branch
```

The branch name should be descriptive and follow common conventions:

- Use lowercase letters and hyphens
- Be specific about what the branch does
- Keep it concise but clear

Making and committing changes

Your task is to add your name to the contributors table.

Now, you'll make your contribution by adding your name to the contributors table:

1. **Open the contributors file:**

    a. Navigate to `CONTRIBUTORS.md` in your code editor.

    b. If the file doesn't exist, create it with the following content:

    ```
    # Contributors

    Thank you to all the contributors who have helped make this project
    better!

    | Name | GitHub Username | Contribution Date |
    |------|-----------------|-------------------|
    | Ayo | @github | 2025-06-01 |
    ```

2. **Add your information**: Add a new row to the table with your information:

```
| Your Name | @your-github-username | 2024-MM-DD |
```

(Replace the placeholders with your actual name, your GitHub handle, and the date of contribution.)

3. **Save your changes**: Save the file in your editor.

Commit your changes

1. **Check the status**:

```
git status
```

You should see CONTRIBUTORS.md as modified or untracked.

2. **Stage your changes**:

```
git add CONTRIBUTORS.md
```

3. **Commit your changes**:

```
git commit -m "Add [Your Name] to contributors list

- Add contributor information to CONTRIBUTORS.md
- Include name, GitHub username, and contribution date"
```

Best practices for commits

- Use present tense (*"Add feature"* not *"Added feature"*)
- Keep the first line under 50 characters
- Include a blank line before additional details
- Be descriptive about what and why, not just what

Submitting a pull request

Now that the work is done, we need to submit our contribution with a pull request.

Pushing changes to your fork

Push your branch to your fork on GitHub:

```
git push origin add-my-name-to-contributors
```

Then, verify your push, as follows:

1. Go to your fork on GitHub.

2. You should see a banner suggesting to create a pull request.

3. Your new branch should be visible in the branch dropdown.

Submitting your contribution

1. **Navigate to your fork**: Go to your fork on GitHub.

2. **Create pull request**:

   a. Click **Compare & pull request** (if the banner appears).

   b. Or, click **Contribute | Open pull request**.

3. **Fill out the pull request details**:

   a. **Title**: Use a descriptive title (e.g., Add [Your Name] to contributors list).

   b. **Description**: Explain your changes:

```
## Description
Adding my name to the contributors list as part of Lab 11.1
exercise.

## Changes Made
- Added my information to CONTRIBUTORS.md
- Included name, GitHub username, and contribution date

## Testing
- Verified markdown formatting is correct
- Confirmed table structure is maintained
```

4. **Review your changes**: Check the **Files changed** tab to verify your modifications.

5. **Submit**: Click **Create pull request**.

Handling feedback and revisions

This section will help you understand how to handle feedback and revisions, ensuring your contributions are successfully merged into open source projects.

After submitting your pull request, maintainers may do the following:

- Approve and merge your changes

- Request modifications
- Ask questions or provide feedback
- Suggest improvements

Following are some common types of feedback:

- **Code style**: Formatting, naming conventions, or structure
- **Documentation**: Clarity, completeness, or accuracy
- **Functionality**: Logic, edge cases, or performance
- **Testing**: Coverage, test cases, or validation

Receiving feedback from maintainers is a crucial part of the open source contribution process. When maintainers review your pull request, they may suggest changes, ask questions, or provide constructive criticism. It's important to respond to this feedback promptly and professionally. Acknowledge the feedback by thanking the maintainers for their time and insights. Address each comment individually, providing explanations or clarifications where necessary. If you need more information or have questions about the feedback, don't hesitate to ask for further clarification.

So, when you receive feedback, do the following:

1. **Read it carefully**: Understand all comments and suggestions.
2. **Ask questions**: If something is unclear, ask for clarification.
3. **Be responsive**: Acknowledge feedback and provide timelines for changes.
4. **Stay professional**: Keep discussions focused and constructive.

For example, you might respond with the following:

Thank you for the feedback! I've addressed the comments and made the necessary changes. Please let me know if there's anything else that needs to be adjusted.

This approach shows that you value the maintainers' input and are committed to improving your contribution.

Based on the feedback you received, make the necessary revisions and updates to your code. This may involve fixing bugs, improving code quality, adding tests, or updating documentation. Ensure that your changes align with the project's guidelines and standards. After making the revisions, commit the changes to your branch with a clear commit message that indicates the updates made in response to the feedback.

The steps for updating your pull request are as follows:

1. **Switch to your branch:**

```
git checkout add-my-name-to-contributors
```

2. **Make the requested changes:** Edit the files based on feedback.

3. **Commit the changes:**

```
git add .
git commit -m "Address review feedback

- Fix table formatting in CONTRIBUTORS.md
- Update date format to YYYY-MM-DD
- Add brief contribution description"
```

> 💡 **Quick tip:** Enhance your coding experience with the **AI Code Explainer** and **Quick Copy** features. Open this book in the next-gen Packt Reader. Click the **Copy** button
>
> **(1)** to quickly copy code into your coding environment, or click the **Explain** button
>
> **(2)** to get the AI assistant to explain a block of code to you.

```
                                            Copy      Explain
function calculate(a, b) {
  return {sum: a + b};                       1          2
};
```

> 🔒 **The next-gen Packt Reader** is included for free with the purchase of this book. Scan the QR code OR go to packtpub.com/unlock, then use the search bar to find this book by name. Double-check the edition shown to make sure you get the right one.

4. **Push the updates:**

```
git push origin add-my-name-to-contributors
```

5. **Monitor and respond to updates:**

    a. Your pull request will automatically update with new commits.

    b. Reviewers will be notified of changes.

    c. Continue this process until approval.

Merging your contribution once approved

Once the maintainers are satisfied with your changes and approve your pull request, the final step is to merge your contribution into the main codebase. In many projects, maintainers will handle the merging process. However, in some cases, you may be asked to perform the merge yourself.

If you are responsible for merging, ensure that your branch is up to date with the main branch.

These are the final steps:

1. **Approval:** Wait for the maintainer's approval.

2. **Merge:** The maintainer will merge your pull request

3. **Cleanup:** Delete your feature branch (optional but recommended):

```
# Switch back to main
git checkout main

# Delete local branch
git branch -d add-my-name-to-contributors

# Delete remote branch (optional)
git push origin --delete add-my-name-to-contributors
```

4. **Sync your fork:** Update your fork with the merged changes:

```
git fetch upstream
git merge upstream/main
git push origin main
```

Best practices summary

Some tips for successful contributions:

- **Start small**: Begin with small, focused contributions
- **Follow conventions**: Adhere to the project's coding and contribution standards
- **Communicate clearly**: Write good commit messages and PR descriptions
- **Be patient**: Review processes take time; maintainers are often volunteers
- **Stay engaged**: Respond to feedback promptly and professionally
- **Test thoroughly**: Ensure your changes work as expected
- **Document well**: Update documentation for any new features

Some common pitfalls to avoid:

- Working directly on the main branch
- Making large, unfocused changes
- Ignoring project contribution guidelines
- Poor commit messages
- Not testing changes locally
- Being unresponsive to feedback

Congratulations! Your contribution is now part of the project. Take a moment to celebrate your achievement and thank the maintainers for their support throughout the process.

Perfect! We now know how to contribute to open source projects.

Following are some suggested next steps:

- Explore other open source projects to contribute to
- Practice with more complex contributions
- Learn about advanced Git workflows (rebasing, squashing, etc.)
- Participate in project discussions and community activities

How about licensing intellectual property, and navigating the limits of reusing someone else's work? It's true some projects are open source, but there might be restrictions on which part of the code you can use or how you are allowed to use it. Up next, we will discuss open source licensing. Remember: Open source contribution is about more than just code—it's about collaboration, learning, and building something meaningful together with the community!

Understanding open source licensing

Understanding open source licensing is crucial for anyone involved in open source projects. Licensing not only defines how software can be used, modified, and distributed but also protects the rights of both the original authors and the users. This section will guide you through the importance of licensing in open source projects, introduce you to some of the most common open source licenses, and help you choose the right license for your contributions.

Introduction to open source licenses

Let's do some intros. We will discuss the importance of licensing in open source projects and introduce you to some of the most common open source licenses.

Importance of licensing in open source projects

Licensing is a fundamental aspect of open source projects, as it defines the terms under which the software can be used, modified, and distributed. An open source license grants users the freedom to use the software for any purpose, access the source code, make modifications, and share the software with others. Without a proper license, the legal status of the software is unclear, which can lead to potential legal issues and restrict the software's use and distribution.

Licenses ensure that contributors and users understand their rights and obligations, fostering a collaborative and transparent environment. They protect the intellectual property of the original authors while promoting innovation and sharing within the community. By clearly outlining the permissions and restrictions, licenses help maintain the integrity and sustainability of open source projects.

Common open source licenses

There are several widely used open source licenses, each with its own set of terms and conditions. Here are three of the most common licenses:

- **MIT License:** The MIT License is one of the most permissive open source licenses. It allows users to do almost anything with the software, including using, copying, modifying, merging, publishing, distributing, and sublicensing it. The only requirement is that the original copyright notice and permission notice must be included in all copies or substantial portions of the software. This license is popular because it imposes minimal restrictions, making it easy for developers to integrate MIT-licensed code into their projects.

- **GNU General Public License (GPL):** The GPL is a copyleft license, which means that any derivative work must also be distributed under the same license. This ensures that the software and any modifications remain free and open. The GPL requires that the source code be made available to users, and any changes or additions must be released under the GPL. This license is ideal for projects that aim to ensure that all derivative works remain open source and that users have the freedom to modify and share the software.

- **Apache License:** The Apache License is a permissive license similar to the MIT License but with additional provisions. It allows users to use, modify, and distribute the software, but it also includes explicit terms regarding patent rights. The license grants users a perpetual, worldwide, non-exclusive, no-charge, royalty-free, irrevocable patent license to use the software. This helps protect users from patent litigation. The Apache License also requires that any modifications to the original code be documented, ensuring transparency and traceability.

Certification tip

You may be asked to identify or compare open source licenses—focus on their key differences, such as permissiveness and obligations.

Now that we know some of the most common open source licenses, let's explore the implications of each of them.

Choosing the right license for your contributions

This section will help you understand the implications of different licenses and how to apply a license to your own projects.

Understanding the implications of different licenses

Choosing the right license for your contributions is crucial, as it determines how others can use, modify, and distribute your work. Different licenses come with varying levels of permissions and restrictions, and understanding these implications helps you make an informed decision:

- **Permissive licenses (e.g., MIT, Apache):** Permissive licenses, such as the MIT and Apache licenses, allow users to freely use, modify, and distribute your code with minimal restrictions. These licenses are ideal if you want to maximize the adoption and integration of your code into other projects. However, permissive licenses do not require derivative works to be open source, meaning others can use your code in proprietary software without sharing their modifications.

- **Copyleft licenses (e.g., GPL):** Copyleft licenses, such as the GNU GPL, require that any derivative works be distributed under the same license. This ensures that the software and any modifications remain free and open. If you want to ensure that your contributions and any derived works stay open source, a copyleft license is a good choice. However, this can limit the use of your code in proprietary projects, as companies may be reluctant to comply with the copyleft requirements.

- **Weak copyleft licenses (e.g., LGPL):** Weak copyleft licenses, such as the **Lesser General Public License (LGPL)**, strike a balance between permissive and copyleft licenses. They allow your code to be used in proprietary software, provided that any modifications to the LGPL-licensed components are shared under the same license. This can be a good option if you want to encourage both open source and proprietary use while ensuring that improvements to your code remain open.

Understanding these implications helps you align your licensing choice with your goals for your contributions and the broader open source community.

How to apply a license to your own projects

Applying a license to your own projects is a straightforward process, but it's important to do it correctly to ensure your intentions are clear. Here are the steps to apply a license to your project:

1. **Choose a license:** Decide which license best fits your goals and the nature of your project. Consider the implications of each license type and how you want others to use your work.

2. **Add a license file:** Create a file named `LICENSE` or `LICENSE.txt` in the root directory of your project. This file should contain the full text of the license you have chosen. You can find the text of common open source licenses on websites such as choosealicense.com or the **Open Source Initiative (OSI)**.

3. **Include a license header in your source files:** It's a good practice to include a short license header at the top of each source file in your project. This header typically includes the name of the license, the copyright holder, and the year. For example, for the MIT License, you might include the following:

```
MIT License
Copyright (c) [Year] [Your Name]

Permission is hereby granted, free of charge, to any person
obtaining a copy of this software and associated documentation files
(the "Software"), to deal in the Software without restriction,
including without limitation the rights to use, copy, modify, merge,
publish, distribute, sublicense, and/or sell copies of the Software,
and to permit persons to whom the Software is furnished to do so,
subject to the following conditions:...
```

4. **Update Your documentation**: Mention the chosen license in your project's README file or other documentation. This ensures that users and contributors are aware of the licensing terms from the outset.

By following these steps, you can clearly communicate the licensing terms of your project, ensuring that others understand how they can use, modify, and distribute your work.

License compliance

Let's talk about the importance of license compliance and the legal and ethical considerations involved in contributing to open source projects.

Ensuring your contributions comply with the project's license

When contributing to an open source project, it's essential to ensure that your contributions comply with the project's license. This compliance helps maintain the legal integrity of the project and protects both you and the project's maintainers. Here are some steps to ensure compliance:

*   **Read and understand the license**: Before contributing, thoroughly read and understand the project's license. Pay attention to any specific requirements or restrictions, such as attribution, distribution terms, or modification guidelines. If you have any questions or uncertainties, don't hesitate to ask the maintainers for clarification.

*   **Follow contribution guidelines**: Many projects have a CONTRIBUTING.md file that outlines the contribution process and any specific requirements related to licensing. Follow these guidelines closely to ensure your contributions align with the project's expectations.

*   **Respect attribution requirements**: Some licenses, such as the MIT License, require that you include the original copyright notice and permission notice in any copies or substantial portions of the software. Make sure to include these notices in your contributions where applicable.

- **Avoid infringing on third-party rights**: Ensure that your contributions do not include code, libraries, or other content that infringes on the intellectual property rights of third parties. If you use third-party code, make sure it is compatible with the project's license and properly attributed.

- **Document your changes**: Clearly document your changes and contributions, including any modifications to existing code. This transparency helps maintainers understand the scope of your contributions and ensures that the project's licensing terms are upheld.

Understanding the legal and ethical considerations

Understanding the legal and ethical considerations of open source licensing is crucial for responsible contribution. Here are some key points to consider:

- **Respect for original authors**: Open source licenses are designed to protect the rights of the original authors while promoting collaboration and sharing. Always respect the terms set by the original authors and give proper credit for their work.

- **Ethical use of open source software**: Use open source software ethically and in accordance with the license terms. Avoid using open source code in ways that violate the license or the intentions of the original authors. This includes respecting any restrictions on commercial use, distribution, or modification.

- **Legal implications of license violations**: Violating the terms of an open source license can have legal consequences. License violations can lead to legal disputes, loss of rights to use the software, and damage to your reputation within the open source community. Always ensure that your contributions and use of open source software comply with the relevant licenses.

- **Contributing back to the community**: Open source is built on the principles of collaboration and reciprocity. When you benefit from using open source software, consider contributing back to the community by sharing your improvements, reporting bugs, or helping with documentation. This fosters a healthy and sustainable open source ecosystem.

By understanding and adhering to these legal and ethical considerations, you can contribute to open source projects responsibly and help maintain the integrity and sustainability of the open source community.

Case studies and examples

Here are some practical examples and best practices for maintaining compliance with open source licenses.

Real-world examples of licensing issues and resolutions

Understanding real-world examples of licensing issues can provide valuable insights into the complexities and importance of open source licensing. Here are a few notable cases:

- **The BusyBox case**: BusyBox, a software suite providing Unix utilities, is licensed under the GPL. In several instances, companies used BusyBox in their products without complying with the GPL's requirements to provide the source code. The BusyBox maintainers took legal action, resulting in settlements where the companies agreed to comply with the GPL and release the source code. This case highlights the importance of adhering to copyleft licenses and the potential legal consequences of non-compliance.

- **The React license controversy**: In 2017, Facebook's React library was initially licensed under the BSD license with an additional patent grant. However, the patent grant included a clause that many in the open source community found problematic, as it could potentially revoke the license if the user engaged in patent litigation against Facebook. This led to significant backlash, and several major projects, including WordPress, decided to move away from React. In response, Facebook relicensed React under the MIT License, resolving the controversy and addressing the community's concerns. This example underscores the importance of community feedback and the impact of licensing terms on project adoption.

- **The MongoDB Server Side Public License (SSPL)**: MongoDB originally used the AGPL license but switched to the SSPL to address concerns about cloud providers offering MongoDB as a service without contributing back to the community. The SSPL requires that anyone offering the software as a service must open source their entire service stack. This change sparked debate within the open source community, and the SSPL has not been approved by the OSI. This case illustrates the challenges and considerations involved in choosing and modifying licenses to protect project interests.

Best practices for maintaining compliance

Maintaining compliance with open source licenses is essential for both contributors and users. Here are some best practices to ensure compliance:

- **Understand the license terms**: Before using or contributing to an open source project, thoroughly read and understand the license terms. Ensure you are aware of any specific requirements, such as attribution, distribution, or modification guidelines.

- **Keep documentation up to date**: Maintain clear and accurate documentation for your project, including the license file and any relevant notices. Ensure that contributors and users can easily find and understand the licensing terms.

- **Respect attribution and notices**: Always include the original copyright and license notices in your contributions and distributions. This is especially important for permissive licenses such as MIT and Apache, which require attribution.

- **Conduct regular license audits**: Periodically review your project's dependencies and contributions to ensure compliance with all applicable licenses. Use tools such as FOSSA, Black Duck, or OpenChain to automate license compliance checks and identify potential issues.

- **Engage with the community**: Stay informed about licensing trends and best practices by engaging with the open source community. Participate in discussions, attend conferences, and follow relevant blogs and forums to keep up to date with the latest developments.

- **Seek legal advice when necessary**: If you encounter complex licensing issues or are unsure about compliance, seek legal advice from professionals with expertise in open source licensing. This can help you navigate potential pitfalls and ensure your project remains compliant.

By understanding the implications of different licenses and how to apply them to your projects, you can ensure that your work is legally sound and aligned with the collaborative spirit of the open source community. You will be able to follow these best practices and help maintain the legal integrity of your open source projects and contribute responsibly to the open source community.

Great! We have reached the end of this chapter. Let's summarize what we have learned.

Summary

In this chapter, we explored how to navigate the open source landscape and identify projects that matched our interests and expertise. We learned strategies to discover opportunities aligned with our goals and emphasized the importance of community engagement to enhance our contributions and professional growth.

Contributing to open source projects offered significant benefits, such as advancing technical skills, building professional networks, and improving career prospects. These efforts not only help us grow individually but also foster innovation and accessibility within the tech industry, highlighting the value of collaboration and shared progress.

We also understood the importance of licensing in open source, which defines how software can be used, modified, and distributed. By protecting the rights of creators and users, licensing ensures transparency and sustainability. By the end of this chapter, we were equipped with the knowledge and confidence to make meaningful contributions to open source projects, driving both personal and community-wide progress.

Test your knowledge

1. What is the primary benefit of contributing to open source projects?

    a. Financial gain

    b. Gaining practical experience and improving coding skills

    c. Reducing workload

    d. Avoiding collaboration

2. Which feature page on GitHub helps in discovering open source projects that align with your interests and skills?

    a. GitHub Pages

    b. GitHub Actions

    c. GitHub Explore

    d. GitHub Issues

3. What is the first step in contributing to an open source project on GitHub?

    a. Cloning the repository

    b. Forking the repository

    c. Creating a new branch

    d. Submitting a pull request

Useful links

*   Explore open source projects on GitHub: `https://github.com/explore`
*   Trending projects on GitHub: `https://github.com/trending`
*   GitHub Docs: *Fork a repository*: `https://docs.github.com/en/get-started/quickstart/fork-a-repo`
*   Git Handbook: `https://guides.github.com/introduction/git-handbook`
*   *How to Contribute to Open Source*: `https://opensource.guide/how-to-contribute`
*   First contributions guide: `https://github.com/firstcontributions/first-contributions`

Unlock this book's exclusive benefits now

Scan this QR code or go to packtpub.com/unlock, then search this book by name.

Note: Keep your purchase invoice ready before you start.

12

Enhancing Development with GitHub Copilot

The advent of **generative AI (GenAI)** has revolutionized the way we approach software development, bringing unprecedented efficiency and creativity to coding practices. GitHub Copilot, a prime example of GenAI, leverages advanced machine learning models to assist developers by suggesting code snippets and entire functions, thereby streamlining the coding process. This chapter delves into the capabilities of GitHub Copilot, guiding you through its setup, usage, and best practices to enhance your development workflow and elevate your coding experience.

We will cover the following main topics:

- Introduction to GitHub Copilot
- Setting up GitHub Copilot
- Using GitHub Copilot effectively

Technical requirements

You will need the following to follow this chapter:

- A GitHub individual account
- Access to a GitHub Copilot plan (you can start with a free plan to explore the limited features first)
- A compatible IDE/editor (preferably VS Code):
    - **Visual Studio**: Version 2022 17.8 or later (for Windows) is needed, with 17.10 or later recommended for the unified extension

- **Visual Studio Code (VS Code):** Requires the GitHub Copilot extension for Visual Studio Code
- **For JetBrains IDEs, Eclipse IDE, Xcode, Azure Data Studio, and Windows Terminal:** Specific version compatibility may apply; consult the respective documentation

- Hardware and network requirements:
  - **RAM:** A minimum of 4 GB
- A stable internet connection

What is GitHub Copilot?

GitHub Copilot is an integrated AI assistant that supports developers through code completion, conversational coding (Copilot Chat), autonomous coding agents, and smart code reviews. It enhances productivity by understanding context, generating code, editing across files, and integrating with external tools—all within your IDE, terminal, or the GitHub platform. It is a cutting-edge AI tool designed to assist software developers throughout the coding lifecycle. Developed by GitHub in collaboration with OpenAI originally, Copilot integrates directly into popular development environments such as VS Code, Visual Studio, JetBrains IDEs, Xcode, Neovim, Eclipse, and the **command-line interface (CLI)**, offering real-time support and automation.

GitHub Copilot is available on your favorite platforms:

Figure 12.1: GitHub Copilot is available in these IDEs and environments

At its core, GitHub Copilot functions as an intelligent coding companion. It provides context-aware code suggestions, generates entire functions or modules, and even assists with debugging and documentation. Through its conversational interface (Copilot Chat), developers can interact with the AI to ask questions, refine code, and receive explanations, all within their workflow.

Beyond simple code completion, GitHub Copilot includes advanced features such as the following:

- **Autonomous coding agents** that can make multi-file edits and resolve GitHub issues
- **Pull request summarization** and **code review suggestions** to streamline collaboration
- **Custom instructions and extensions** that tailor the assistant to individual or organizational needs

- **Enterprise-grade controls**, including policy management, audit logs, and content exclusions

GitHub Copilot represents a *significant shift* in how software is developed, moving from manual coding to a more collaborative, AI-augmented process. It empowers developers to focus on problem-solving and creativity while automating repetitive or boilerplate tasks.

Figure 12.2: The GitHub Copilot logo can be found in IDEs and on the GitHub platform

Historical context

The emergence of GitHub Copilot in 2021 marked a pivotal moment in the evolution of software development. Prior to Copilot, code completion tools were largely limited to syntax-based suggestions, intellisense, and static analysis. GitHub Copilot introduced a new model of interaction—leveraging **large language models** (**LLMs**) trained on billions of lines of public code to provide context-aware, dynamic code generation.

This innovation was built on the foundation of OpenAI's Codex model, itself a descendant of GPT-3, and later evolved with more advanced models such as GPT-4. The tool was initially released in preview and quickly gained traction among developers for its ability to reduce boilerplate coding and accelerate prototyping.

> GitHub Copilot should not be confused with other Copilot products owned by Microsoft, such as M365 Copilot. GitHub Copilot helps developers write and understand code within their development environments, while Microsoft 365 Copilot is an AI productivity assistant that enhances tools such as Word, Excel, Edge, and Outlook by generating content, analyzing data, and automating tasks across the Microsoft 365 suite.

Support for multiple LLMs

Initially starting with OpenAI's GPT models, GitHub Copilot now supports multiple LLMs to choose from, including the following (as of the time of writing this book):

- **OpenAI models**:
    - GPT-4.1
    - GPT-4o

- o3
  - o3-mini
  - o4-mini
- **Anthropic models:**
  - Claude Opus 4
  - Claude Sonnet 3.5
  - Claude Sonnet 3.7
  - Claude Sonnet 3.7 Thinking
  - Claude Sonnet 4
- **Google models:**
  - Gemini 2.5 Pro
  - Gemini 2.0 Flash

These models have varying strengths and suitability for different use cases. When do you use which model?

Choosing the right AI model for your work

The following table highlights the available models and their recommended use cases as listed by GitHub:

Model	Task area	Excels at (primary use case)
GPT-4.1	General-purpose coding and writing	Fast, accurate code completions and explanations
GPT-4o	General-purpose coding and writing	Fast completions and visual input understanding
o3	Deep reasoning and debugging	Multi-step problem solving and architecture-level code analysis
o3-mini	Fast help with simple or repetitive tasks	Quick responses for code snippets, explanations, and prototyping
o4-mini	Fast help with simple or repetitive tasks	Fast, reliable answers to lightweight coding questions
Claude Opus 4	Deep reasoning and debugging	Complex problem-solving challenges and sophisticated reasoning

Claude Sonnet 3.5	Fast help with simple or repetitive tasks	Quick responses for code, syntax, and documentation
Claude Sonnet 3.7	Deep reasoning and debugging	Structured reasoning across large, complex codebases
Claude Sonnet 4	Deep reasoning and debugging	Performance and practicality, perfectly balanced for coding workflows
Gemini 2.5 Pro	Deep reasoning and debugging	Complex code generation, debugging, and research workflows
Gemini 2.0 Flash	Working with visuals (diagrams, screenshots, etc.)	Real-time responses and visual reasoning for UI and diagram-based tasks

Table 12.1: Available LLMs on GitHub Copilot

The model you are able to use with Copilot depends on which IDE client you are using, which Copilot feature you are interacting with, or which Copilot plan you're subscribed to.

Let's discuss the available plans.

Available Copilot plans

Let's look at the latest subscription options for GitHub Copilot as of the time of writing this book.

Here are the individual plans, as shown in *Figure 12.3*:

- **Copilot Free:**
    - **Price:** $0/month
    - **Who it's for:** Individual GitHub users who don't have access through an organization or enterprise
    - **Features:**
        - Limited access to Copilot Chat and code completion
        - Up to 50 premium requests per month
        - Basic model access (e.g., GPT-4.1)
- **Copilot Pro:**
    - **Price:** $10/month or $100/year
    - **Who it's for:** Individual developers seeking full access

- Features:

  - Unlimited completions and chat interactions

  - Access to premium models (e.g., GPT-4.1, Claude, and Gemini)

  - 300 premium requests/month

  - Includes Copilot coding agent and extensions

  - Free for verified students, teachers, and open source maintainers

- **Copilot Pro+:**

  - **Price:** $39/month or $390/year

  - **Who it's for:** Power users needing maximum flexibility

  - **Features:** Everything in Pro, plus the following:

    - 1,500 premium requests/month

    - Full access to all available models

    - Ideal for advanced AI workflows and multi-file editing

Here are the plans for businesses, as shown in *Figure 12.4*:

- **Copilot Business:**

  - **Price:** $19/user/month

  - **Who it's for:** Teams using GitHub Free or Team plans

  - **Features:**

    - Centralized management and policy control

    - 300 premium requests/user/month

    - Access to Copilot coding agent, chat, and extensions

    - Organization-wide customization and content exclusions

- **Copilot Enterprise:**

  - **Price:** $39/user/month

  - **Who it's for:** Enterprises using GitHub Enterprise Cloud

  - **Features:** All Business features, plus the following:

    - 1,000 premium requests/user/month

    - Enterprise-grade security, audit logs, and knowledge bases

    - SAML SSO authentication and advanced policy controls

Certification tip

You may be given scenarios where you are presented with a use case and asked to select which Copilot plan will meet those needs. Spend some time understanding how to describe the plans and the differences in what they offer.

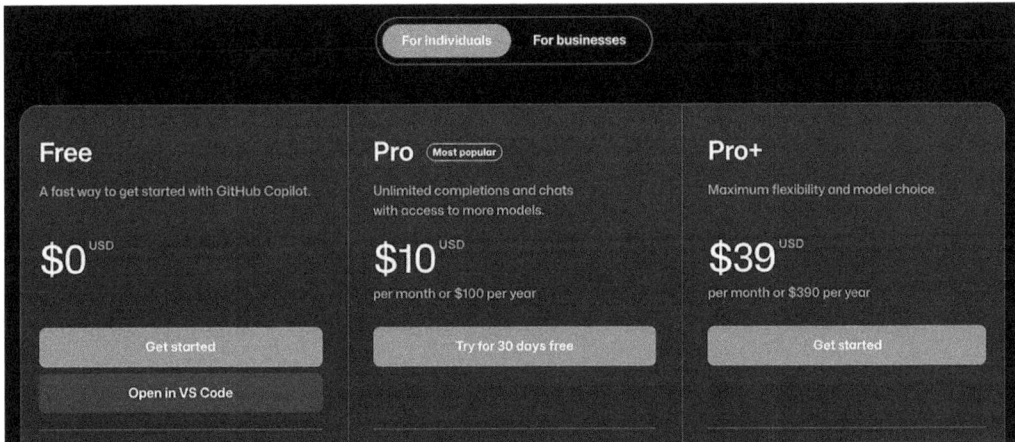

Figure 12.3: Copilot plans available for individuals

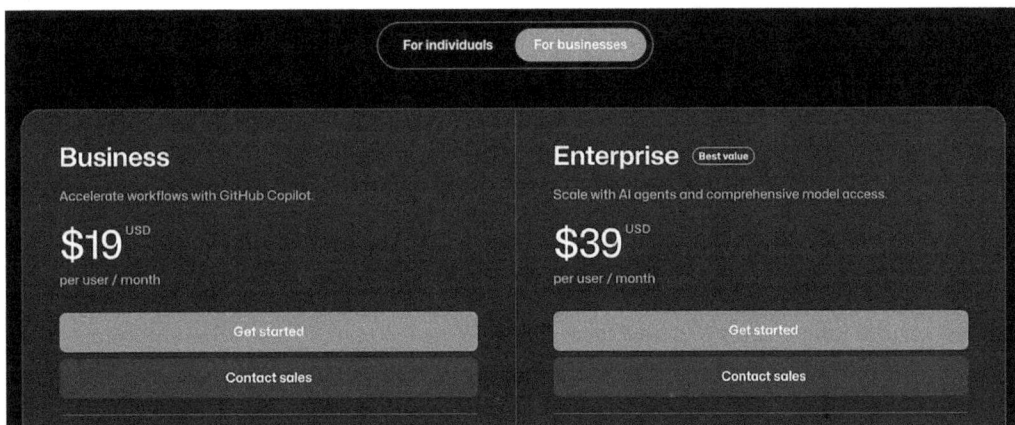

Figure 12.4: Copilot plans available for businesses

These subscription plans cater to different user needs, from individual developers to large enterprises, ensuring that everyone can benefit from GitHub Copilot's AI-powered coding assistance.

> **Changes to Copilot subscriptions**
>
> **Disclaimer:** These prices and titles are accurate at the time of writing this book and may be subject to change.
>
> **Premium requests**
>
> Premium requests are used for advanced features such as Copilot Chat, agent mode, code review, and extensions. Additional requests can be purchased at $0.04/request.

How does it work?

Copilot leverages a deep learning model trained on a vast dataset of public code repositories. As you type, it analyzes the code and provides suggestions that are relevant to the current context. These suggestions can range from simple **code completions** to more complex functions and algorithms. Developers can accept, reject, or modify these suggestions, making Copilot a flexible and adaptive tool.

Some benefits of using Copilot are as follows:

- **Increased productivity**: By providing instant code suggestions, Copilot helps developers write code faster and reduces the time spent on repetitive tasks
- **Improved code quality**: Copilot's suggestions are based on best practices and common patterns, helping developers write cleaner and more efficient code
- **Learning and skill development**: Copilot can serve as a learning tool, offering insights into new coding techniques and best practices
- **Enhanced collaboration**: By reducing the cognitive load on developers, Copilot allows them to focus more on higher-level design and problem-solving tasks

GitHub Copilot is beyond just code completion and suggestions; you can also interact with it through various integrations and interfaces. Let's examine some of these other interfaces.

Copilot Chat

Copilot Chat is an extension of GitHub Copilot that provides conversational AI assistance directly within your development environment. It allows developers to interact with the AI in a more natural, dialogue-based manner, asking questions, seeking explanations, and getting real-time help with coding tasks. This feature enhances the traditional code completion capabilities of Copilot by offering a more interactive and intuitive way to receive assistance.

What is its relationship with ChatGPT?

Copilot Chat is also a conversational bot, just like ChatGPT, which is developed by OpenAI. Both tools leverage LLMs to understand and generate human-like text based on the input they receive. While ChatGPT is a general-purpose conversational AI that can be used across various domains and applications, GitHub Copilot Chat is specifically tailored for software development. It integrates seamlessly with development environments, providing context-aware assistance that is directly relevant to the code and tasks at hand.

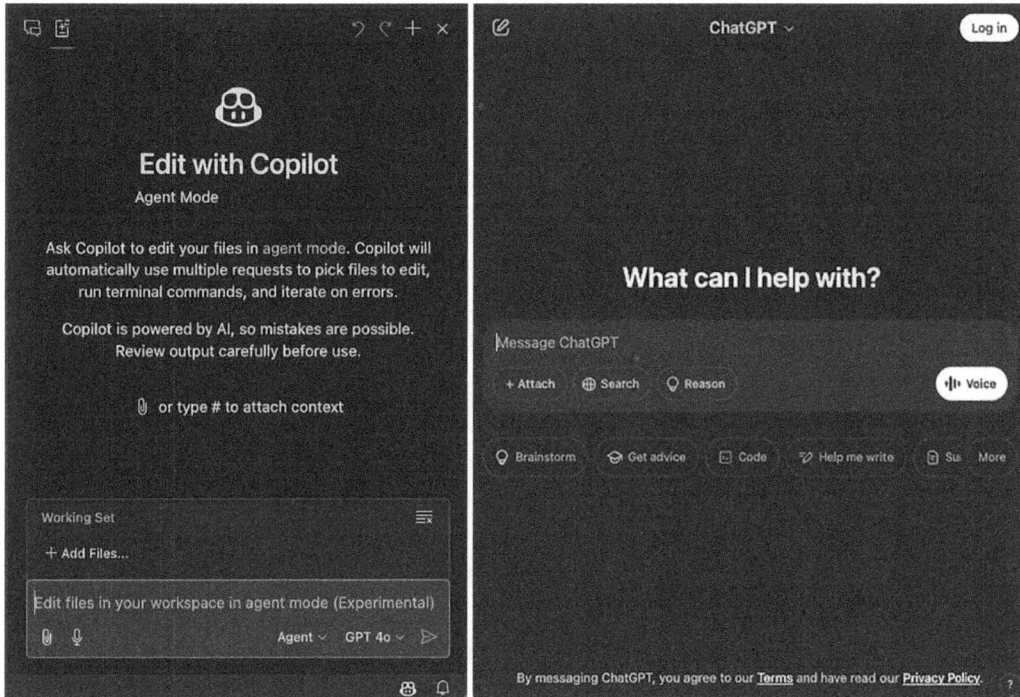

Figure 12.5: GitHub Copilot Chat interface vs. ChatGPT interface

Copilot Chat can be used in three modes:

- **Ask**: Use this mode to pose questions or request explanations about your code, frameworks, or concepts without making changes to the code itself. For example, you can ask, "What does this function do?" or "How can I improve the performance of this loop?" Copilot responds with explanations, best practices, or relevant examples, acting as an on-demand coding assistant.

- **Edit:** In this mode, Copilot takes your instructions and makes direct changes to your code. You can highlight a code block and say, "Refactor this to use async/await" or "Add error handling here", and Copilot will apply the edits in place. This is ideal for quick improvements, bug fixes, or stylistic updates without writing the changes manually.

- **Agent mode:** This mode allows Copilot to make autonomous edits locally. It analyzes code, proposes changes, runs tests, and validates results across multiple files. You can also extend the capabilities with **Model Context Protocol (MCP)** servers, which extend the reach of Copilot to platforms and tools outside the IDE. For example, with a Figma MCP server, Copilot can fetch mockup screens from your UI designers and translate them to a working app.

By combining the widely adopted conversational style of ChatGPT with the code-specific knowledge of GitHub Copilot, Copilot Chat offers a powerful tool for developers to enhance their productivity and coding experience..

Copilot CLI

The GitHub Copilot CLI is an extension of GitHub Copilot designed to assist developers directly within the CLI. This tool provides a chat-like interface in the terminal, allowing developers to ask for command suggestions and explanations, making it easier to navigate and utilize the command line effectively.

Some key features of the Copilot CLI are as follows :

- **Command suggestions:** Developers can use the gh copilot suggest command to get suggestions for various command-line tasks. For example, if you're unsure how to undo the last commit, you can ask the Copilot CLI for a suggestion, and it will provide the appropriate command.

- **Command explanations:** With the gh copilot explain command, you can ask the Copilot CLI to explain what a specific command does. This is particularly useful for understanding complex or unfamiliar commands.

- **Interactive sessions:** The Copilot CLI can start interactive sessions to gather more information about what you need, ensuring that the suggestions are tailored to your specific requirements.

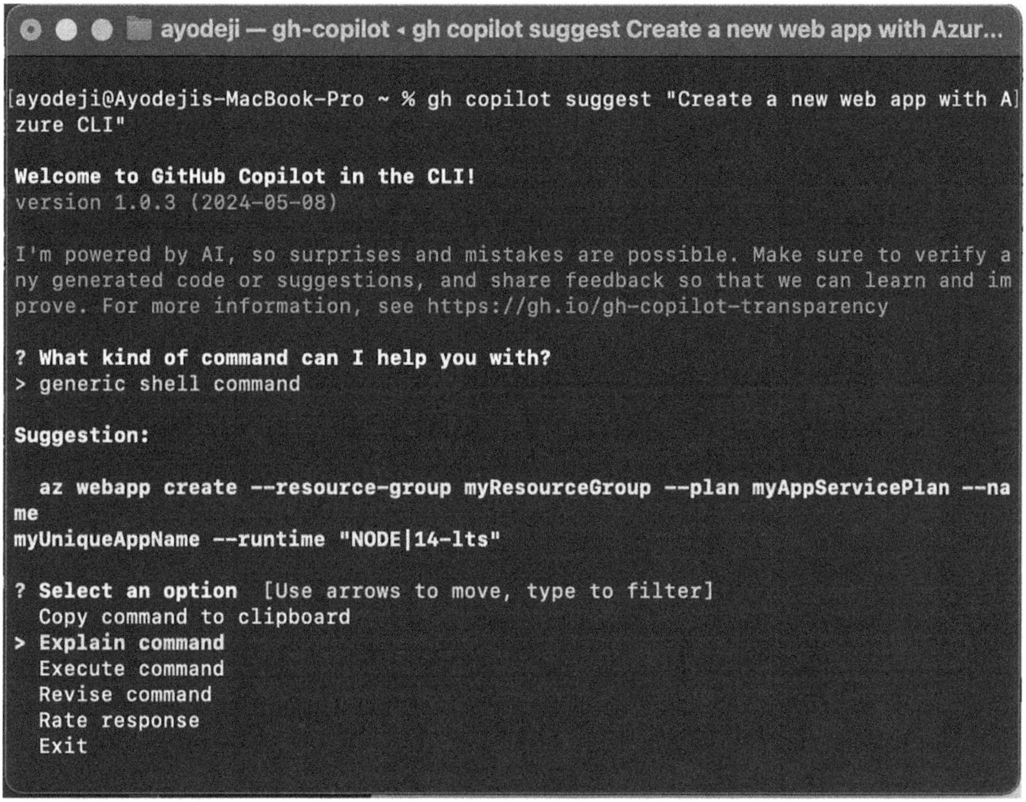
ayodeji — gh-copilot ◂ gh copilot suggest Create a new web app with Azur...
[ayodeji@Ayodejis-MacBook-Pro ~ % gh copilot suggest "Create a new web app with A]
zure CLI"
Welcome to GitHub Copilot in the CLI!
version 1.0.3 (2024-05-08)
I'm powered by AI, so surprises and mistakes are possible. Make sure to verify a
ny generated code or suggestions, and share feedback so that we can learn and im
prove. For more information, see https://gh.io/gh-copilot-transparency
? What kind of command can I help you with?
> generic shell command
Suggestion:
az webapp create --resource-group myResourceGroup --plan myAppServicePlan --na
me
myUniqueAppName --runtime "NODE|14-lts"
? Select an option [Use arrows to move, type to filter]
Copy command to clipboard
> Explain command
Execute command
Revise command
Rate response
Exit

Figure 12.6: The Copilot CLI

Getting started with the Copilot CLI

To use the GitHub Copilot CLI, you need to have an active GitHub Copilot subscription and the GitHub CLI installed. Here are the basic steps to get started:

1. **Install the GitHub CLI:** Follow the installation instructions for the GitHub CLI from the official GitHub repository.
2. **Authenticate:** Authenticate using the GitHub CLI OAuth app with the `gh auth login --web` command.

3. **Install the Copilot CLI extension**: Use the `gh extension install github/gh-copilot` command to install the Copilot CLI extension.

4. **Start using the Copilot CLI**: Begin using the Copilot CLI with commands.

Here are some examples of ways to use it:

- **Suggest a command**: `gh copilot suggest "Create a new web app with Azure CLI"`
- **Explain a command**: `gh copilot explain "git lfs migrate import --everything --include=\"*.gz,*.png,*.jar\""`

By integrating the Copilot CLI into your workflow, you can enhance your productivity and gain a deeper understanding of command-line operations, making it a valuable tool for both novice and experienced developers.

Copilot within the github.com UI

GitHub Copilot is not just limited to IDEs and the command line; it also integrates seamlessly within the github.com **user interface** (**UI**), enhancing the overall development experience directly on the platform.

Some key features of Copilot within github.com are as follows:

- **Pull request assistance**: Copilot can help you create and review pull requests by suggesting descriptions, summarizing changes, and even generating code snippets to address feedback. This streamlines the code review process and ensures that pull requests are well documented and easy to understand.

- **Issue management**: When creating or managing issues, Copilot can suggest relevant tags, titles, and descriptions based on the context of the repository and the issue content. This helps in organizing and prioritizing tasks more effectively.

- **Code suggestions in the browser**: While browsing code on github.com, Copilot can provide inline code suggestions and completions, making it easier to understand and navigate large codebases. This feature is particularly useful for quick edits and code reviews directly in the browser.

- **Documentation generation**: Copilot can assist in generating documentation for your code by suggesting comments, docstrings, and README content. This ensures that your code is well documented and easier for others to understand and contribute to.

- **Chat:** Chat is also available within the github.com UI, just as you have it embedded in your IDE. Starting a conversation with Chat on github.com is sometimes referred to as the *immersive mode*.

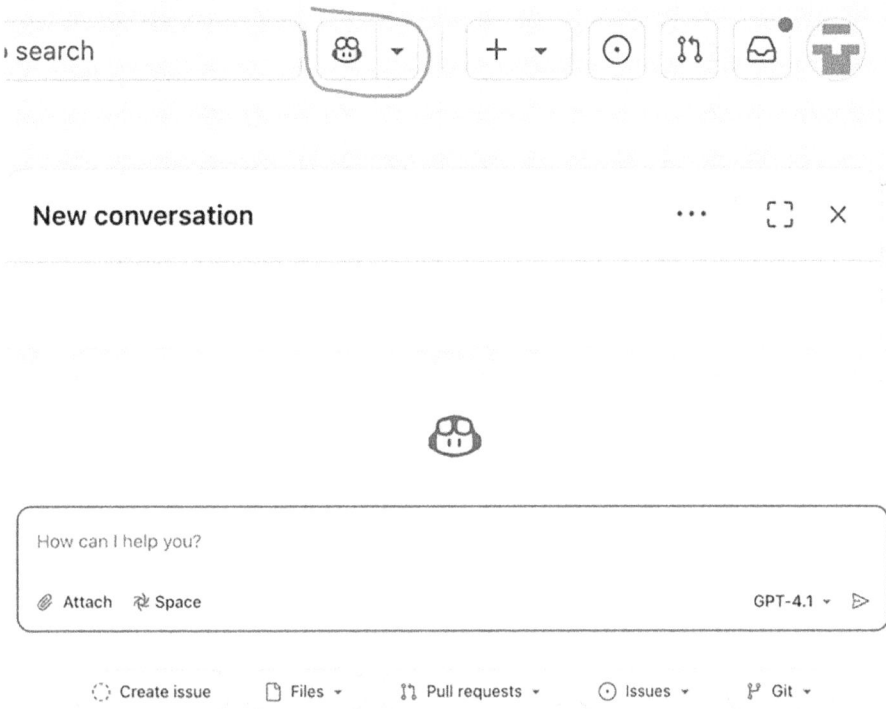

Figure 12.7: Copilot Chat can be invoked within the GitHub.com UI to get an immersive experience

Getting started with Copilot on github.com

To start using GitHub Copilot within the github.com UI, you need to have an active GitHub Copilot subscription. Here are the basic steps:

1. **Enable Copilot:** Go to your GitHub settings and enable GitHub Copilot for your account. You can do this by directly navigating to `https://github.com/settings/copilot/features`.

2. **Integrate with repositories:** Ensure that Copilot is enabled for the repositories you want to use it with. This can be done through the repository settings.

3. **Start using Copilot**: Begin using Copilot features while creating pull requests, managing issues, and browsing code on github.com.

By integrating Copilot within the github.com UI, developers can leverage AI-powered assistance throughout the entire development lifecycle, from code writing and review to issue management and documentation.

Copilot Spaces

GitHub Copilot Spaces provides contextual environments that enhance Copilot's ability to generate relevant and accurate responses by providing it with curated, task-specific information. Each space acts as a scoped container where users can aggregate content relevant to a particular project or domain.

Supported content types include the following:

- Source code from repositories
- Pull requests and issues
- Uploaded files (e.g., PDFs, images, and spreadsheets)
- Free-form notes and documentation
- Custom instructions for Copilot

By referencing only the materials within a space, Copilot delivers responses that are more precise and context-aware. This is particularly useful for complex projects, onboarding workflows, and support scenarios where domain-specific knowledge is essential.

Spaces can be created under personal or organizational accounts. Organizational spaces support access controls, allowing for private or read-only sharing across teams.

Copilot Spaces is available to all GitHub Copilot users. Free-tier users are limited to 50 chat messages per month, while premium users benefit from expanded usage based on their plan.

In essence, Copilot Spaces transforms Copilot from a general-purpose assistant into a focused collaborator, tailored to the specific needs of your development context.

Getting started with GitHub Copilot Spaces

To begin using Copilot Spaces, follow these steps:

1. **Access Copilot Spaces**: Navigate to `github.com/copilot/spaces`.
2. **Create a new space**: From the Copilot Chat interface, click on the **Spaces** tab. Select **New Space** to initiate a workspace.

3. **Name and describe the space**: Provide a clear name and optional description. This helps define the scope and purpose of the space (e.g., `Customer Onboarding Automation` or `Q3 Support Playbooks`).

4. **Add contextual content**: Populate the space with relevant materials:

    - Link GitHub repositories or specific files

    - Upload documents (PDFs, images, and spreadsheets)

    - Add notes or Markdown files (these may be documentation files)

    - Include custom instructions for Copilot (e.g., `Always adhere to tailwind.css styling`)

5. **Use the space in Chat**: Once the space is active, Copilot will use its contents to inform responses. You can ask questions, request code, or generate documentation—all within the context of the space.

6. **Share (optional)**: For organizational accounts, you can share the space with teammates. Choose between private or read-only access.

7. **Manage and iterate**: Continuously refine the space by updating content as your project evolves. This ensures that Copilot remains aligned with your current needs.

Copilot on GitHub Mobile

GitHub Copilot in the GitHub mobile app brings the power of AI-assisted coding to developers on the go. With the integration of GitHub Copilot Chat, developers can ask coding questions, get code suggestions, and gain insights into both public and private repositories directly from their mobile devices. This feature supports all GitHub Copilot plans, making it accessible to a wide range of users. This mobile integration aims to democratize access to coding assistance, making it easier for developers to work efficiently from anywhere.

Copilot agents

We have saved the best till last! This is the most exciting innovation that has come so far. GitHub Copilot agents are autonomous AI-powered tools designed to perform software development tasks directly within your GitHub workflow. They extend Copilot's capabilities beyond code suggestions in the IDE, enabling it to act as a background contributor that can plan, write, test, and submit code changes via pull requests.

There are two main types.

Copilot coding agent

This agent works autonomously in a secure, GitHub Actions-powered environment. It can fix bugs, implement features, improve test coverage, update documentation, or even address technical debt. You assign tasks by assigning GitHub issues to Copilot as an **assignee**. GitHub Copilot then performs the following:

1. Creates a branch
2. Writes and commits code
3. Opens a pull request
4. Awaits your review and feedback

In terms of **security** and **governance**, Copilot only pushes to branches prefixed with `copilot/`. It cannot merge pull requests or approve its own work. It operates in a sandboxed environment with limited internet access, and only users with write access can assign tasks to it.

Copilot code review

Code review is a feature within GitHub Copilot that enhances the code review process by providing AI-generated suggestions and insights directly within pull requests. It analyzes the changes made in a pull request and offers contextual feedback, such as identifying potential bugs, suggesting improvements, and highlighting areas that may benefit from refactoring. This helps reviewers focus on higher-level design and logic decisions rather than getting bogged down in syntax or style issues.

In addition to automated suggestions, Copilot code review can generate summaries of pull requests, making it easier for team members to understand the scope and intent of the changes. This is especially useful in large or fast-moving projects where manual review can be time-consuming. By integrating seamlessly into GitHub workflows, Copilot code review streamlines collaboration, improves code quality, and accelerates the development cycle.

In the next section, we'll talk about how to set it up in your development environment.

Lab 12.1: Getting started with GitHub Copilot

GitHub Copilot is available free, albeit with some limitations or missing features that you can get in the paid versions. To get started with GitHub Copilot Free, visit `https://github.com/settings/copilot/features`. Alternatively, you can go to **Settings** | **Copilot** | **Features**.

You will find three tasks to help you get started:

- **Install Copilot in your editor**
- **Chat with Copilot anywhere**
- **Start building with Copilot**

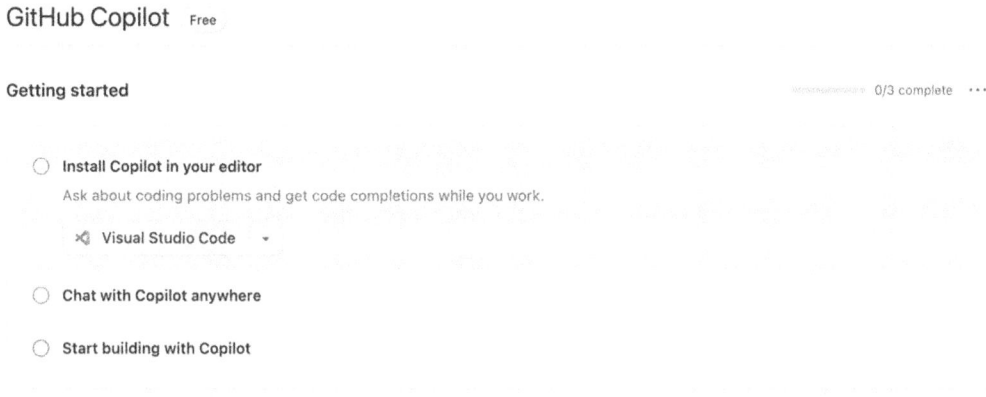

GitHub Copilot Free

Getting started   0/3 complete ···

○ Install Copilot in your editor
    Ask about coding problems and get code completions while you work.

    ✕ Visual Studio Code   ▾

○ Chat with Copilot anywhere

○ Start building with Copilot

Figure 12.8: Getting started with GitHub Copilot; you can complete three tasks

Let's start with the first task, installing Copilot in your editor.

Installing Copilot in your editor

We will start with installation and configuration. To start using GitHub Copilot, you need to install and configure it within your development environment.

Here are the steps to get you started:

1. **System requirements**: Ensure your system meets the minimum requirements for running GitHub Copilot. This typically includes having a compatible operating system and the latest version of your preferred IDE.

2. **Installing Copilot in popular IDEs:**

    - **Visual Studio Code:**

        a. Open Visual Studio Code.

        b. Go to the **Extensions** view by clicking on the **Extensions** icon in the activity bar on the side of the window, or press *Ctrl + Shift + X*.

        c. Search for GitHub Copilot and click **Install**.

- **JetBrains IDEs (e.g., IntelliJ IDEA and PyCharm):**

  a. Open your JetBrains IDE.

  b. Go to **File | Settings | Plugins** (or **Preferences** on macOS).

  c. Search for GitHub Copilot and click **Install**.

3. **Integrating Copilot with your development environment:**

    - **Initial setup and configuration:** After installation, you may need to sign in to your GitHub account from within the IDE to activate Copilot:

      a. Click on the **Accounts icon** (bottom-left corner).

      b. Select **Sign in with GitHub** and follow the prompts.

      c. Follow the on-screen instructions to complete the setup process.

    - **Customizing settings for optimal performance:** Access the Copilot settings within your IDE to customize its behavior. This will vary from IDE to IDE. You can also adjust settings such as suggestion frequency, language preferences, and more to suit your workflow.

Getting started with Copilot Chat in the IDE

Follow these steps:

1. Install the GitHub Copilot Chat extension (*Some newer versions of VS Code come with GitHub Copilot pre-instaled*):

    a. In the **Extensions** view, search for GitHub Copilot Chat.

    b. Install the extension.

2. Open the **Copilot Chat** panel:

    a. First, open an existing Git repository that you have cloned locally to your system.

    b. Click the **Copilot** icon (😳) in the top bar.

    c. This opens the **Copilot Chat** panel.

3. Start chatting:

    a. Type a question or prompt, such as the following:

        - Explain this function
        - Write a unit test for this code
        - Refactor this into a class

      b.   Copilot will respond with suggestions or explanations based on the open file and cursor context.

Autocompletion in the IDE

Once you have installed and configured GitHub Copilot, you can start using it to enhance your coding experience. Here are some tips to get you started:

- **Using the autocompletion feature**: Using GitHub Copilot starts simply by beginning to type your code as usual. Copilot will analyze the context and provide suggestions in real time, showing *ghost text* to help you autocomplete the next lines of code you are about to write. Use the *Tab* key to accept a suggestion, or continue typing to refine it.

  This behavior is a feature of Copilot called **autocompletion**. There are several other ways to interact with GitHub Copilot, but I have limited it to autocompletion for the scope of this book. This is the behavior common to all IDEs, whereas some other features may be absent depending on which IDE you use.

- **Understanding and accepting suggestions**: Copilot's suggestions are based on the context of your code. Review the suggestions carefully and accept those that fit your needs. You can also modify the suggested code to better align with your coding style and requirements.

- **Editing and refining Copilot-generated code**: After accepting a suggestion, you can edit and refine the code as needed. Use Copilot's suggestions as a starting point and build upon them to create more complex and customized solutions.

By following these steps, you can effectively set up and start using GitHub Copilot to enhance your development workflow.

The next section will cover how to use Copilot effectively, including tips and best practices for maximizing its potential.

Using GitHub Copilot effectively

To get the most out of GitHub Copilot, it's important to customize its behavior to match your coding preferences:

- **Tailoring Copilot to your coding style**: Access the Copilot settings within your IDE to adjust its behavior. You can specify the types of suggestions you prefer and how frequently they appear. Customize language preferences to ensure that Copilot provides suggestions that are relevant to the programming languages you use most often. You can make use of **custom instructions** and **prompt files** that can be stored in the repository to further guide Copilot's responses and tasks.

- **Managing and filtering suggestions:** Use the settings to filter out suggestions that don't align with your coding standards or project requirements. You can also provide feedback on suggestions to help improve Copilot's accuracy and relevance over time.

Best practices and tips

To maximize the benefits of GitHub Copilot, consider the following best practices and tips:

- **Maximizing productivity with Copilot:** Use Copilot to handle repetitive coding tasks, such as generating boilerplate code, so you can focus on more complex and creative aspects of development. Leverage Copilot's ability to suggest entire functions and algorithms to speed up your workflow.

- **Avoiding common pitfalls:** Always review Copilot's suggestions carefully to ensure they meet your project's requirements and coding standards. Be mindful of potential security implications when accepting code suggestions, especially for sensitive or critical applications. Copilot's suggestions are sometimes syntactically correct but logically flawed; always double-check logic!

That's it on GitHub Copilot. We barely scratched the surface, but it was important to discuss the basics to pass the certification exam. Let's summarize what we learned.

Summary

In this chapter, we explored how GitHub Copilot enhances modern software development by integrating AI-powered assistance directly into our workflows. We learned that Copilot supports developers through intelligent code completion, conversational coding via Copilot Chat, autonomous agents, and smart code reviews. We walked through how to install and configure Copilot in popular IDEs such as Visual Studio Code, and how to use features such as autocompletion and Copilot Chat to streamline our coding tasks. We also examined how Copilot integrates into the GitHub.com UI, the command line, and even mobile devices, offering a consistent and powerful experience across platforms.

We gained insight into the different subscription plans available—ranging from the Free tier to Pro, Pro+, Business, and Enterprise—each offering varying levels of access to premium models and features. Additionally, we explored Copilot Spaces, a contextual environment that enhances Copilot's relevance by scoping its responses to specific projects. By understanding how to tailor Copilot to our coding style, manage suggestions, and integrate it into team workflows, we are now equipped to use GitHub Copilot not just as a tool but as a collaborative partner in our development journey.

Quiz time! Yay!!

Test your knowledge

Focus your revision on Copilot's IDE integration, CLI commands, and configuration steps. These are most likely to appear in the GitHub Foundations exam:

1. What is the primary function of GitHub Copilot Chat, and how does it differ from ChatGPT?

    a. GitHub Copilot Chat provides code suggestions, while ChatGPT offers general conversational AI assistance

    b. GitHub Copilot Chat is tailored for software development, providing context-aware assistance within development environments, whereas ChatGPT is a general-purpose conversational AI

    c. GitHub Copilot Chat is used for CLI assistance, while ChatGPT is used for code completion

    d. GitHub Copilot Chat is a standalone application, while ChatGPT is integrated within GitHub Copilot

2. Which of the following is NOT a feature of GitHub Copilot within the GitHub.com UI?

    a. Pull request assistance

    b. Issue management and analysis

    c. Code suggestions in the browser

    d. Real-time collaboration with other developers

3. What is the key difference between GitHub Copilot Pro and GitHub Copilot Business subscriptions?

    a. GitHub Copilot Pro offers team collaboration tools, while GitHub Copilot Business does not

    b. GitHub Copilot Pro is available for individual users, while GitHub Copilot Business is designed for organizations and enterprises

    c. GitHub Copilot Pro includes enhanced security features, while GitHub Copilot Business does not

    d. GitHub Copilot Pro is free for all users, while GitHub Copilot Business requires a subscription

Useful links

- *What is GitHub Copilot?*: https://docs.github.com/en/copilot/about-github-copilot/what-is-github-copilot

- *GitHub Copilot* blog: https://github.blog/ai-and-ml/github-copilot/

- *Copilot Chat Cookbook*: https://docs.github.com/en/copilot/copilot-chat-cookbook

Unlock this book's exclusive benefits now

Scan this QR code or go to packtpub.com/unlock, then search this book by name.

Note: Keep your purchase invoice ready before you start.

13

Funding Your Projects with GitHub Sponsors

Securing financial support can make it easier to maintain and grow your open source projects, especially when you're contributing regularly or managing popular repositories. GitHub Sponsors offers a unique platform that enables developers to receive funding directly from the community that benefits from their work. This chapter will guide you through the essentials of setting up and managing sponsorship for your projects. From creating an appealing sponsorship profile to engaging with your sponsors effectively, you'll learn how to leverage GitHub Sponsors to not only sustain your projects but also build meaningful relationships with your supporters.

We will cover the following main topics:

- Introduction to GitHub Sponsors
- Setting up sponsorship for your projects
- Engaging with your sponsors

Introduction to GitHub Sponsors

The **GitHub Sponsors** feature allows developers and maintainers to receive financial backing directly from individuals and organizations who benefit from their work. By providing a platform for sponsorship, GitHub enables creators to focus more on their projects without the constant worry of funding.

Sponsors can contribute on a recurring basis or make one-time donations, offering flexibility and ongoing support. This financial assistance can be used for various purposes, such as covering development costs, funding new features, or even supporting the developer's livelihood. What are the benefits?

Benefits of using GitHub Sponsors

The benefits of GitHub Sponsors extend beyond just financial support. Here are some key advantages:

- **Sustainability**: Regular sponsorships provide a steady stream of income, allowing developers to plan and execute long-term projects

- **Recognition**: Being sponsored is a form of recognition and validation from the community, highlighting the importance and impact of your work

- **Community engagement**: Sponsors often become more engaged with the projects they support, leading to a more active and involved community

- **Motivation**: Financial backing can boost morale and motivation, encouraging developers to continue their contributions to the open source world

> **Certification tip**
>
> You might be asked to choose from a list of options what GitHub Sponsors offer, its benefits, or who is eligible to be sponsored.

There are some eligibility criteria to consider.

Eligibility and requirements

To become a sponsored developer on GitHub, there are certain eligibility criteria and requirements that need to be met:

- **GitHub account**: You must have an active GitHub account.

- **Open source contributions**: Your projects should be open source and publicly accessible.

- **Supported region**: Your projects can be sponsored if you are in a location where GitHub does business. GitHub Sponsors is available in a wide range of regions globally. For a list of supported regions, visit `https://docs.github.com/en/sponsors/getting-started-with-github-sponsors/about-github-sponsors#supported-regions-for-github-sponsors`.

- **Compliance with GitHub policies**: You must adhere to GitHub's community guidelines and terms of service. Also, you must adhere to additional terms for GitHub Sponsors. You can find more information here: `https://docs.github.com/en/site-policy/github-terms/github-sponsors-additional-terms`
- **Application process**: Developers need to apply for the GitHub Sponsors program and provide necessary details about their projects and contributions.

Once approved, you can set up your sponsorship profile and start receiving support from the community.

Success stories

Many developers and projects have successfully leveraged GitHub Sponsors to achieve remarkable milestones. For instance, the popular JavaScript library **Lodash** has received significant sponsorship, enabling its maintainers to dedicate more time to its development and maintenance. Similarly, the **Homebrew** package manager for macOS has benefited from community sponsorship, ensuring its continued growth and improvement.

These success stories demonstrate the potential of GitHub Sponsors to transform the open source landscape, providing developers with the resources they need to innovate and excel.

> To find a developer to sponsor, visit `https://github.com/sponsors/explore`. GitHub will even suggest developers to sponsor based on the dependencies in your repos.

Say your application has been approved, what's next? In the next section, we will discuss how you may set up your GitHub Sponsors profile.

Setting up sponsorship for your projects

The first step to receiving financial support through GitHub Sponsors is to create an appealing **sponsorship profile**. This profile serves as your public face on the platform, showcasing your projects and explaining why they deserve support.

> **Certification tip**
>
> This section covers navigating the settings and account linking – concepts that connect to other GitHub UI and profile customization questions.

Here's how to get started:

1. **Accessing GitHub Sponsors**: Navigate to the **GitHub Sponsors** section in your account settings. If you're eligible, you'll find an option to join the program.

2. **Profile information**: Fill out your profile with relevant information about yourself and your projects. Highlight your contributions, goals, and the impact of your work.

3. **Visual appeal**: Use a professional profile pictures and banner image. Add graphics and colorful elements. Visual elements can make your profile more attractive and engaging. Read more about crafting a professional GitHub profile and showcasing projects and contributions in *Chapter 10, Building and Showcasing Your GitHub Presence*.

4. **Personal story**: Share your journey as a developer. Personal stories resonate with potential sponsors and can motivate them to support your work.

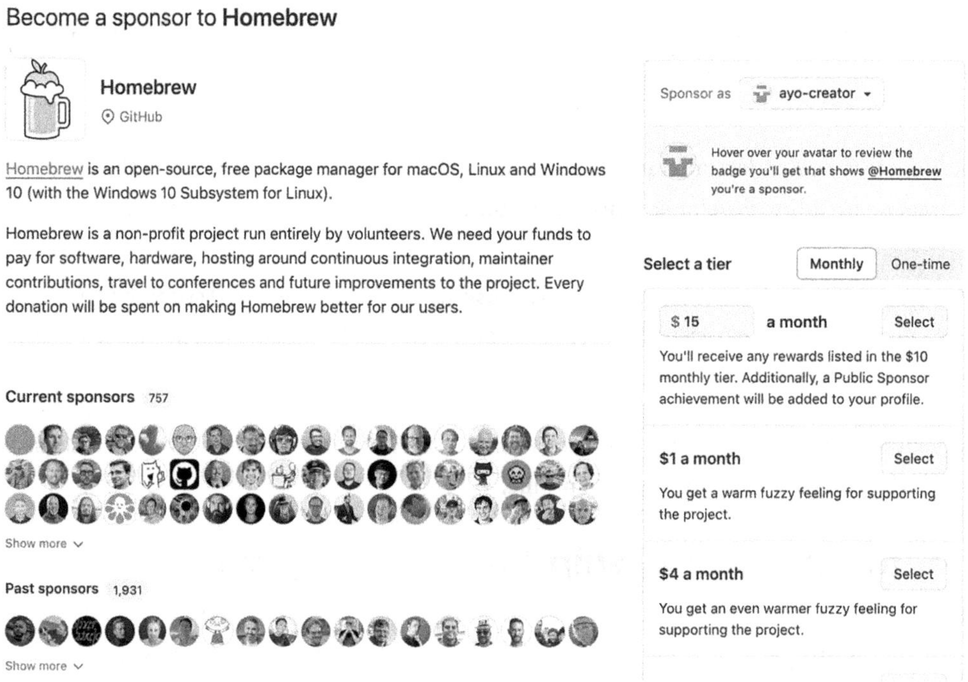

Become a sponsor to **Homebrew**

Homebrew
⊙ GitHub

Homebrew is an open-source, free package manager for macOS, Linux and Windows 10 (with the Windows 10 Subsystem for Linux).

Homebrew is a non-profit project run entirely by volunteers. We need your funds to pay for software, hardware, hosting around continuous integration, maintainer contributions, travel to conferences and future improvements to the project. Every donation will be spent on making Homebrew better for our users.

Sponsor as   ayo-creator ▾

Hover over your avatar to review the badge you'll get that shows @Homebrew you're a sponsor.

Select a tier   Monthly   One-time

$ 15   a month   Select

You'll receive any rewards listed in the $10 monthly tier. Additionally, a Public Sponsor achievement will be added to your profile.

Current sponsors 757

Show more ⌄

$1 a month   Select

You get a warm fuzzy feeling for supporting the project.

Past sponsors 1,931

Show more ⌄

$4 a month   Select

You get an even warmer fuzzy feeling for supporting the project.

Figure 13.1: Sponsorship profile page of Homebrew

You can set up sponsorship for an individual account or your entire organization. In the case of the latter, you will need to set up your organization profile. What are the main differences between setting up sponsorship as an individual or for the entire organization? Let's examine this side by side.

Feature	Individual profile	Organization account
Who can use it?	Solo developers and maintainers	Teams, companies, and open source collectives
Sponsorship target	The individual personally	The organization as a whole
Payment destination	Personal account	Organization's account
Tier management	Personal tiers and benefits	Organization-wide tiers and benefits
Visibility	Appears on personal GitHub profile	Appears on the organization's GitHub page
Use case	Supporting personal contributions to open source	Supporting collaborative or company-managed projects
Setup	Apply to GitHub Sponsors as an individual	Apply to GitHub Sponsors as an organization

Sponsorship buttons

The **Sponsor** button appears on a developer's or organization's GitHub profile or repository page. It enables members of the community to contribute money to support you or your project. You will typically find this on your profile page (next to the **Follow** button) or on the repository page, if the repository owner has enabled sponsorship. When members click on the **Sponsor** button, it will take them to the sponsorship page, displaying the sponsorship tiers (read about tiers in the next section), each with different monthly contribution amounts and potential benefits. It will also allow you to choose a one-time or recurring donation and then process the payment through GitHub's integrated system.

To enable the **Sponsor** button, you need to do the following:

- Join the GitHub Sponsors program
- Set up a `.github/FUNDING.yml` file in your repository to configure the button and link to external funding platforms (such as Patreon, OpenCollective, Ko-fi, etc.)

There are sponsorship tiers you can create with attached benefits. Let's look at these.

Defining sponsorship tiers

Sponsorship tiers allow you to offer different levels of support with corresponding benefits. Here's how to set them up:

1. **Tier creation**: Decide on the number of tiers you want to offer. Common tiers include Bronze, Silver, and Gold, but you can customize them to fit your needs.

2. **Benefits and rewards**: Define the benefits for each tier. These could include early access to new features, exclusive content, or personalized thank-you notes.

3. **Pricing**: Set a monthly or one-time price for each tier. Ensure the pricing reflects the value of the benefits offered.

4. **Descriptions**: Write clear and compelling descriptions for each tier. Explain what sponsors will receive and how their support will make a difference.

Tier	Price	Benefit
Bronze	$5/month	Thank-you mention
Silver	$15/month	Early access to releases
Gold	$50/month	Feature request priority

Now that you have defined the various tiers, let us define the payment options next.

Setting up payment methods

To receive funds from your sponsors, you need to set up payment methods. GitHub Sponsors supports various payment options:

- **Payment options**: Choose from available payment methods such as bank transfers, PayPal, or other supported services.

- **Payout schedule**: Understand the payout schedule and how often you'll receive funds. GitHub typically processes payouts on a monthly basis.

- **Financial management**: Keep track of your earnings and manage your finances effectively. Consider using accounting software to streamline this process.

> There might be tax implications for the money you receive through GitHub Sponsors, varying based on your region or country. You will need to submit your tax information during this setup.

Promoting your sponsorship profile

Once your profile is set up, it's time to promote it and attract sponsors. Here are some strategies:

- **GitHub community**: Engage with the GitHub community by participating in discussions (`https://github.com/orgs/community/discussions`), contributing to other projects, and sharing your work.

- **Social media**: Use platforms such as X/Twitter, LinkedIn, and Facebook to promote your sponsorship profile. Share updates, achievements, and milestones to keep your audience engaged.

- **Display a Sponsor button by using FUNDING.yml**: Add a `.github/FUNDING.yml` file to your repository to display a **Sponsor** button directly on your project page. This makes it easy for visitors to find and support your GitHub Sponsors profile or through other external funding platforms.

- **Blogging and content creation**: Write blog posts, create videos, or host webinars about your projects. Providing valuable content can attract potential sponsors.

- **Networking**: Attend conferences, meetups, and other events to network with fellow developers and potential sponsors. Personal connections can lead to sponsorship opportunities.

A good engagement can build strong connections with sponsors and help improve your ability to secure funding. In the next section, I'll speak briefly about engaging sponsors.

Certification tip

Understand how GitHub tracks contributions and repository activity. This knowledge supports questions related to public engagement and profile visibility.

Engaging with your sponsors

Effective communication is essential for building and maintaining strong relationships with your sponsors. Regular updates about your project's progress, including new features, bug fixes, and upcoming plans, keep sponsors informed and engaged. Here are some good practices.

Transparency

Transparency about how sponsorship funds are being used builds trust and demonstrates that their contributions are making a tangible difference. Personalized thank-you messages can further strengthen your relationship by acknowledging their support on a personal level. Additionally, encouraging sponsors to provide feedback and suggestions not only makes them feel valued but also offers valuable insights for your projects.

Providing value to sponsors

Sponsors support your projects because they believe in your work, and providing additional value can enhance their experience and encourage continued support. Offering exclusive content, such as early access to new features, behind-the-scenes updates, or special tutorials, can make sponsors feel appreciated. Depending on the sponsorship tier, you can provide perks such as merchandise, personalized thank-you notes, or access to private repositories. Public recognition of your sponsors in project documentation, release notes, or on social media not only shows appreciation but also gives them visibility, further incentivizing their support.

Building long-term relationships

Long-term relationships with sponsors can provide sustained support for your projects. Consistent engagement through regular communication and updates helps build a strong rapport. Celebrating project milestones with your sponsors, whether through special updates, thank-you messages, or small virtual events, can foster a sense of community and shared achievement. Hosting exclusive events, such as webinars, Q&A sessions, or live coding sessions, provides sponsors with a unique experience and strengthens their connection to your project. Listening to your sponsors' feedback and adapting your approach based on their suggestions shows that you value their input and are committed to continuous improvement.

Handling sponsorship challenges

While sponsorship can be incredibly beneficial, it may also come with challenges. Managing expectations by clearly communicating what sponsors can expect from their support helps avoid misunderstandings. If conflicts arise, addressing them promptly and professionally through open communication and a willingness to find a solution can resolve most issues. Balancing your commitments to sponsors with your project goals is crucial; managing your time and resources effectively ensures that you can meet both ends without compromising on either.

Let's summarize what we discussed.

Summary

Reflecting on our journey with GitHub Sponsors, we explored the transformative potential of GitHub Sponsors for our open source projects. We delved into the essentials of setting up and managing sponsorships, from creating an appealing profile to engaging effectively with our sponsors. By leveraging GitHub Sponsors, you are able to secure financial support, build meaningful relationships with the GitHub community, and sustain your projects. Through GitHub Sponsors, you can turn your passion for open source into a sustainable endeavor, ensuring the continued growth and success of your project. Up next, we will look at GitHub Projects, a relatively new feature on GitHub. We will cover a comprehensive guide on using GitHub Projects for effective project management, covering topics such as setting up project boards, automating workflows, and integrating with issues and milestones.

Test your knowledge

While some GitHub Sponsors functionality may not appear directly on the exam, questions about profile setup, repo visibility, and collaboration tools are fair game. Review those as you answer the following:

1. What is one of the primary goals of GitHub Sponsors?

    a. To provide developers with free software tools

    b. To create a sustainable ecosystem where open source projects can thrive

    c. To offer developers a platform for social networking

    d. To promote proprietary software development

2. Which of the following is NOT a benefit of using GitHub Sponsors?

    a. Sustainability through regular sponsorships

    b. Recognition and validation from the community

    c. Guaranteed project success

    d. Increased community engagement

3. What is a key requirement for becoming a sponsored developer on GitHub?

    a. Having a private GitHub account

    b. Contributing to proprietary software

    c. Adhering to GitHub's community guidelines and terms of service

    d. Being located in a region where GitHub does not do business

Useful links

- GitHub Sponsors: `https://github.com/sponsors`
- *Supported regions for GitHub Sponsors*: `https://docs.github.com/en/sponsors/getting-started-with-github-sponsors/about-github-sponsors#supported-regions-for-github-sponsors`
- *Receiving sponsorships through GitHub Sponsors:* `https://docs.github.com/en/sponsors/receiving-sponsorships-through-github-sponsors`

Unlock this book's exclusive benefits now

Scan this QR code or go to `packtpub.com/unlock`, then search this book by name.

Note: Keep your purchase invoice ready before you start.

Part 4

Advanced GitHub and Exam Preparation

This part is designed to equip you with advanced GitHub skills and prepare you for the Certification exam. By the end of this section, you will have a deep understanding of project management with GitHub Projects, security practices, and user management. Additionally, you will be well prepared for the Certification exam after going through mock exams and effective study strategies.

This part of the book includes the following chapters:

- *Chapter 14, Project Management with GitHub Projects*
- *Chapter 15, Security Practices and User Management*
- *Chapter 16, Mock Exams and Study Strategies*

14

Project Management with GitHub Projects

We dealt briefly with GitHub Projects in *Chapter 7, Issues, Projects, Labels, and Milestones*. In this chapter, I will go into more detail in a few more areas that will help you prepare well for the certification exam. Get ready to organize your tasks, track your progress, and automate your workflows with more efficiency. Whether you're managing a solo project or leading a team, GitHub Projects will help you stay on top of your game. Bear in mind that we will be discussing Projects 2.0 solely in this chapter. So, let's get started by exploring how GitHub Projects can help you manage work more efficiently for your certification exam.

We will cover the following main topics:

- Introduction to GitHub Projects
- Lab 14.1: Setting up project boards
- Automating project workflows

Technical requirements

To complete the lab in this chapter, you will need the following:

- A GitHub individual account
- A GitHub repository with at least one issue in it

Introduction to GitHub projects

GitHub Projects is a versatile tool designed to enhance project management within the GitHub ecosystem. It allows teams to organize their work visually, making it easier to track progress and collaborate effectively. By providing a centralized space for managing tasks, GitHub Projects helps streamline workflows, ensuring that all team members are aligned on project goals and timelines. This integration with GitHub's core functionalities, such as issues and pull requests, means that developers can manage their code and project tasks in one place, reducing the friction often associated with switching between different tools.

The significance of GitHub Projects extends beyond mere task management; it fosters a culture of transparency and accountability within teams. By visualizing tasks and their statuses, team members can quickly identify bottlenecks, prioritize work, and allocate resources more effectively. This visibility not only enhances individual productivity but also promotes collaboration, as team members can easily see what others are working on and how their contributions fit into the larger project. Overall, GitHub Projects empowers teams to work more efficiently and cohesively, ultimately leading to better project outcomes.

Getting started with GitHub Projects

To kick off your journey with GitHub Projects, start by creating a new project within your repository. Navigate to the **Projects** tab, which you can find in the main menu of your repository. Click on the **New project** button, and you'll be prompted to choose a project template. Options such as Kanban boards or basic tables are available, allowing you to select a layout that best suits your workflow. After selecting a template, you can click on **Create project**.

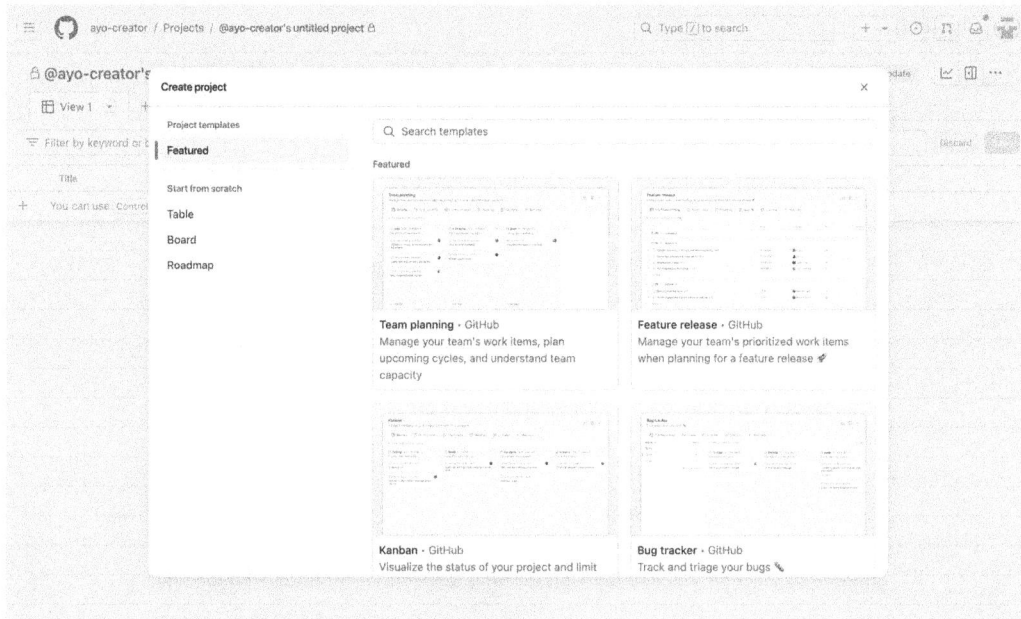

Figure 14.1: Creating a new project using a template

Creating and customizing board columns

When setting up your project board, you can create and customize columns to reflect your specific workflow. For instance, you might start with basic columns such as **To Do, In Progress**, and **Done**, but you can also add more specific stages, such as **Review** or **Testing**, based on your team's needs. Customizing these columns allows you to tailor the board to your project's requirements, ensuring that it accurately represents the flow of work. You can easily rename columns, change their order, or even add new ones as your project evolves, providing a dynamic and adaptable workspace.

Now, let us consider some vital features of a project.

Project layout

GitHub Projects offers three main layouts to help teams visualize and manage their work effectively: **Board**, **Table**, and **Roadmap**.

The **board layout** is designed for a Kanban-style approach, allowing users to organize tasks into customizable columns that represent different stages of progress, such as "To Do," "In Progress," and "Done." This layout is ideal for teams looking to track work visually and manage tasks dynamically. It is commonly used by agile teams. You may, for example, add a "Backlog" column for backlog grooming, or a "Awaiting Review" column to highlight tasks that are waiting on external input before they can be picked up. This simple addition improves visibility and coordination during standups or reviews.

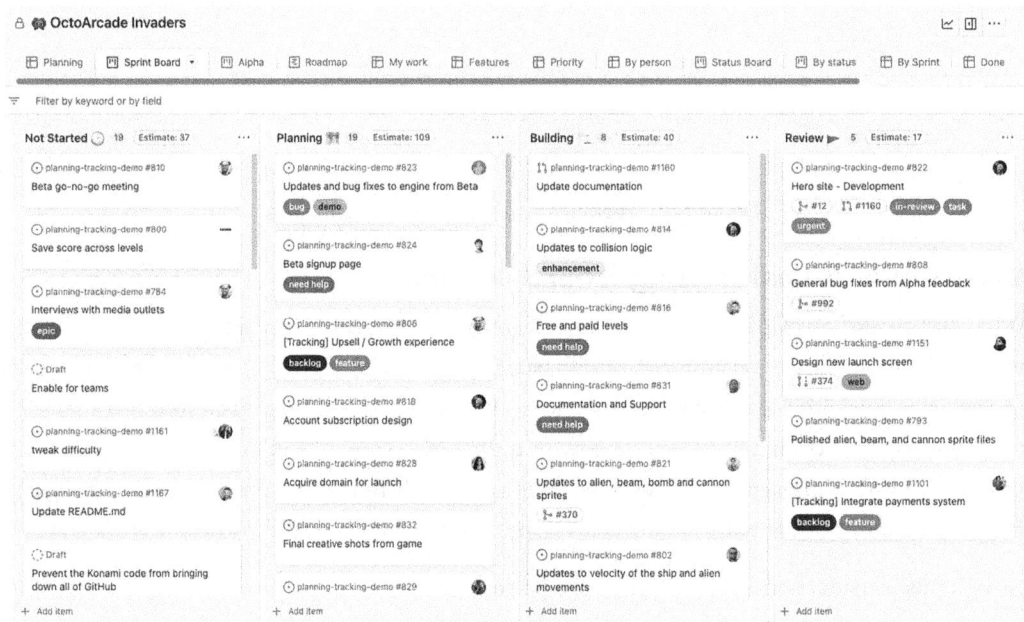

Figure 14.2: Board layout

🔍 **Quick tip:** Need to see a high-resolution version of this image? Open this book in the next-gen Packt Reader or view it in the PDF/ePub copy.

📖 **The next-gen Packt Reader** and a **free PDF/ePub copy** of this book are included with your purchase. Scan the QR code OR visit `packtpub.com/unlock`, then use the search bar to find this book by name. Double-check the edition shown to make sure you get the right one.

The **table layout** provides a high-density spreadsheet view, where users can see issues, pull requests, and custom fields in a structured format. This layout is particularly useful for teams that need to sort, filter, and group tasks based on various criteria. It's also the best for bulk-editing multiple items. Imagine if you need to update a new target date for all issues in the backlog, or assign eight items to the same team member during sprint planning.

Figure 14.3: Table layout

Lastly, the **roadmap layout** offers a timeline-style view, enabling teams to visualize their project over time. This layout allows users to set start and target dates for tasks, making it easier to track progress against deadlines and milestones.

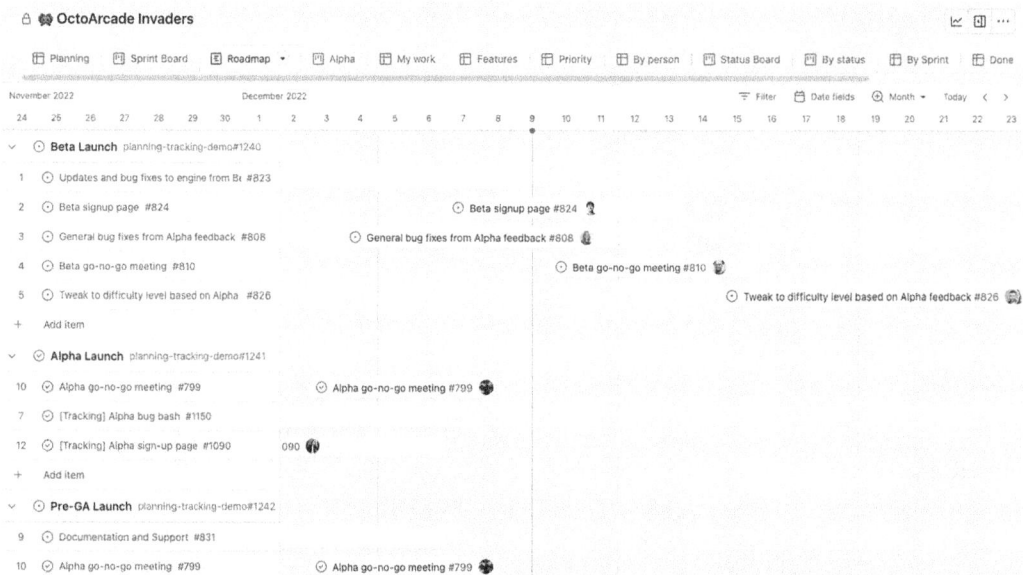

Figure 14.4: Roadmap layout

Each layout can be customized to fit the specific needs of the project, ensuring that teams can work in the way that suits them best.

> **Certification tip**
>
> Expect a few questions on board layouts and when to use them effectively. Know the different features of **Board** versus **Table** versus **Roadmap**.

Views

There is a variety of views that allow teams to tailor their project management experience to their specific needs. Each view is displayed on a separate tab within the project, enabling users to focus on different aspects of their work. For instance, you can create a view that filters for all items not yet started, helping to identify tasks that need attention. Another useful view might group tasks by team workload, allowing for better resource allocation and visibility into who is handling what. Additionally, you can sort items by various criteria, such as due dates or priority levels, to ensure that the most critical tasks are highlighted.

These customizable views enhance collaboration and efficiency by allowing team members to quickly access the information they need. Users can save their views for easy access later, making it simple to return to specific filters or groupings as projects evolve. This flexibility not only helps in managing ongoing tasks but also supports strategic planning by providing insights into project timelines and team capacities. By leveraging these project views, teams can maintain clarity and focus, ultimately driving better project outcomes.

> **Certification tip**
>
> Expect a few questions on managing views. Get familiar with terms such as *group by*, *slice by*, and other view properties that help you customize and add flexibility. The lab in this chapter will help you learn more about view options.

Custom fields

Custom fields in GitHub Projects allow teams to enrich their project management experience by adding specific metadata to issues, pull requests, and notes. You can create various types of custom fields, such as text fields for notes, number fields for metrics, and date fields for deadlines. This flexibility enables teams to capture essential information that goes beyond the default attributes, such as assignees and labels. By tailoring these fields to your project's needs, you can enhance visibility and organization, making it easier to filter and sort tasks based on specific criteria.

Adding and editing items

Adding and editing items in GitHub Projects is straightforward. You can add issues, pull requests, or draft issues individually or in bulk. To add an item, simply paste the URL of an existing issue or pull request into the project board, or use the command palette for quick access. You can also create new issues directly from the project interface, ensuring that all relevant tasks are captured without navigating away from your project. Editing items is equally efficient; you can update multiple items at once using bulk editing features, allowing for quick adjustments to assignees, labels, or custom fields.

Archiving items

Archiving items is a useful feature for maintaining a clean project board while preserving context. When you archive an item, it is removed from the active project view but remains accessible for future reference. This is particularly helpful for managing the maximum item limits in a project, which is capped at 1,200 active items and 10,000 archived items.

Some improvements are coming to GitHub Projects, to eliminate item restrictions, thereby removing the cap on active items. This is currently in public preview as of the time of writing this book. Refer to GitHub's official roadmap for current limits.

You can manually archive items or set up automated workflows to archive items that meet specific criteria, ensuring that your project board stays organized without losing important historical data. This capability allows teams to focus on current tasks while keeping past items available for review or restoration if needed.

There are some nuances, advanced features, and good practices to note if you want to get the most out of GitHub Projects. Let's discuss some of them.

Understanding project visibility (public versus private)

An important aspect of GitHub Projects is understanding project visibility. When creating a project, you can choose between making it public or private. A public project is accessible to anyone on GitHub, which is ideal for open source projects where collaboration and transparency are key. On the other hand, a private project restricts access to only those you invite, making it suitable for sensitive or proprietary work. This choice is crucial for managing who can view and contribute to your project, ensuring that your team can work securely and efficiently.

Project scope (organization versus user)

Furthermore, a project can be created at either the organization level or at the individual (user) level. The distinction between **organization projects** and **user projects** lies primarily in **ownership**, **access control**, and **collaboration scope**. Here's a breakdown of the key differences:

	Organization	User
Ownership	GitHub organization	GitHub individual user
Access control	Managed via organization-level permissions. You can assign roles such as admin, write, or read to members or teams.	Only the owner has full control. Others can collaborate if the project is public, but with limited permissions.
Collaboration	Ideal for teams working across multiple repositories. Members of the organization can collaborate easily.	More limited compared to organization projects. You can't assign roles or use teams.

Visibility	Can be public or private.	Can be public or private.
Use case	Best for managing work across a company, open source community, or any group with multiple contributors.	Best for personal projects, solo developers, or small-scale planning.

Table 14.1: Key differences between GitHub Organizations and Individual User Accounts

Integrating projects with issues and milestones

One of the strengths of GitHub Projects is its integration with issues and milestones. You can link issues and pull requests to cards on your project board, making it easy to track the status of work and ensure that everything is aligned with your project goals. Milestones can be used to group related issues and track progress toward larger objectives.

For example, you can create a milestone for a major release and link all related issues and pull requests to that milestone. This helps in tracking the progress of the release and ensuring that all tasks are completed before the release date. You can also use labels to categorize issues and pull requests, making it easier to filter and search for specific tasks.

Let's test this out in a lab exercise!

Lab 14.1: Setting up project boards

By the end of this section, you'll have a fully customized project board that helps you manage your tasks and track progress efficiently.

Creating a project board

Ready to set up your board? Let's get started!

1. **Navigate to your repository**: Open your GitHub repository where you want to create the project board.
2. **Access the Projects tab**: Click on the **Projects** tab located at the top of the repository page.
3. **Create a new project**: Click the **New project** button.
4. **Choose a template**: In the **Featured** list, select a template that fits your needs. Let's select **Kanban** in this lab.

> GitHub provides several templates to help you get started quickly. Choose a template that matches your project type and customize it as needed.

5. **Name your project:** Enter a name for your project (e.g., Feature Development).

6. **Create project:** Click the **Create project** button to finalize.

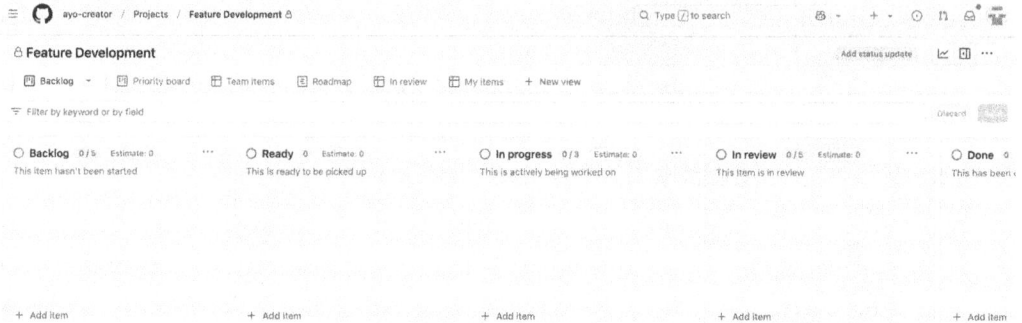

Figure 14.5: Newly created project using a Kanban template

Customizing columns

Let's customize the columns and see. First, we will delete the **Ready** column and then rename another one:

1. **Delete columns:** Click the ellipses (**…**) next to the **Ready** column. This will show a drop-down menu. Then, click **Delete** to delete the column.

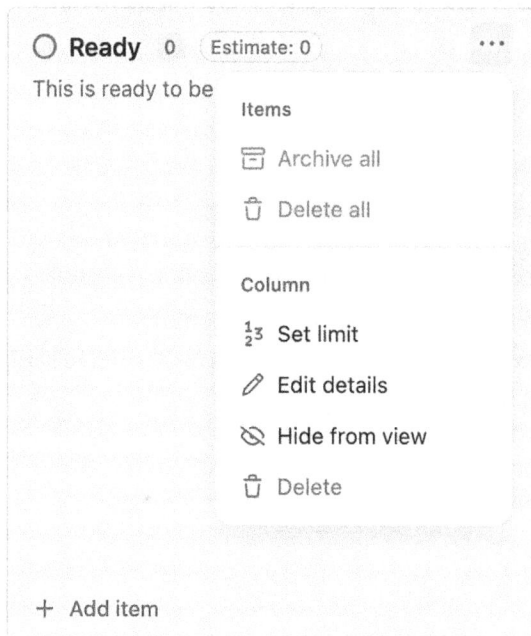

Figure 14.6: Context menu of a Kanban column

2. **Rename columns**: On the **In review** column, click on the ellipses to reveal the context menu and click **Edit details**. Rename the column `Awaiting approval`. Optionally, you can select a different *color*. Colors help to visually distinguish items and cards on the board.

3. **Reorder columns**: Drag and drop columns to reorder them according to your workflow. You can do this by merely dragging the column name to the right or to the left of other columns on the board.

Adding and managing cards

Once your project board is set up, you can start populating it with cards to track tasks and ideas across columns.

1. **Create new cards**: Click the **+ Add item** button at the bottom of a column to add new cards. This should open a text box at the bottom. Type the title of the card in the box, say, `Improve usability of the login page`. As you begin typing, a context menu appears at the top. Select **Create a draft** or just press the *Return* key.

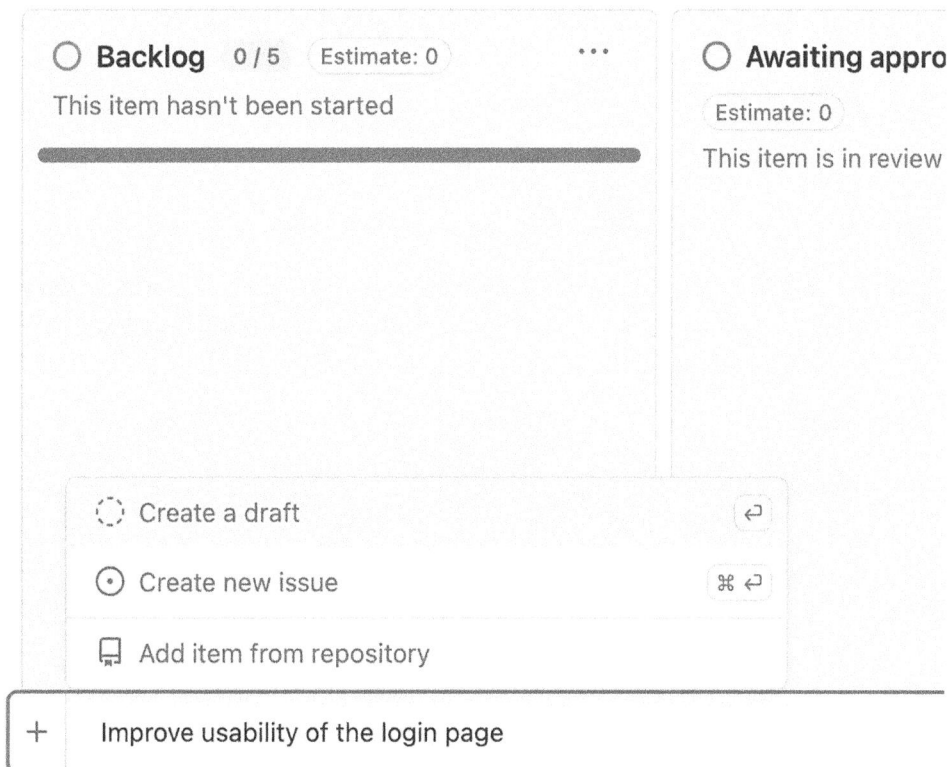

Figure 14.7: Creating a card has three options

You have now created a draft issue. Let's add an existing issue and see.

2. **Add issues and pull requests**: Click the **+ Add item** button at the bottom of the **Backlog** column, and this time, click the + button to the left of the text box. Then, select **Add item from repository**. This will open a dialog box of a form for selecting an existing issue. Select one of the issues you have created in the past. Then, click the **Add selected items** button.

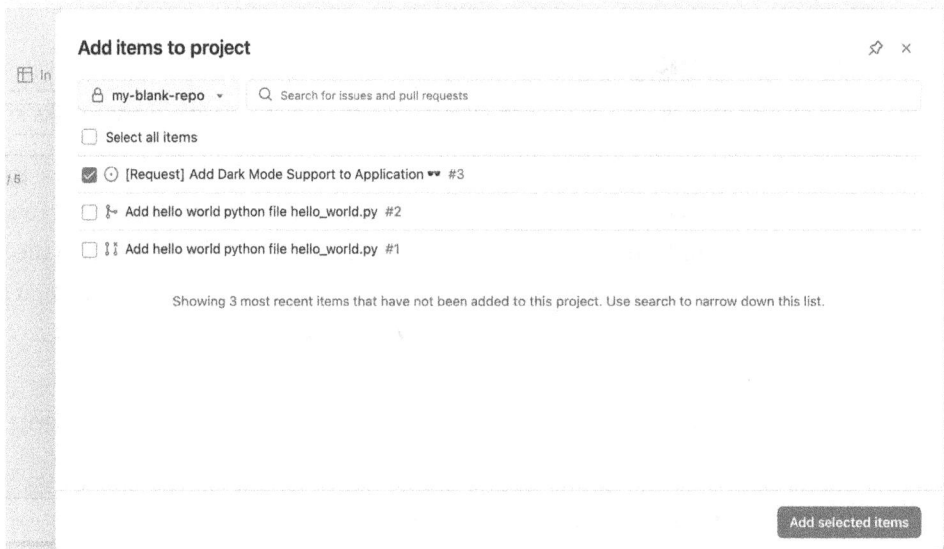

Figure 14.8: You can add existing issues to a project board

3. **Move cards**: Drag and drop cards between columns to update their status. When you drag and drop an issue between columns, this change is captured in the timeline of that issue. You can see the timeline by just scrolling through the issue.

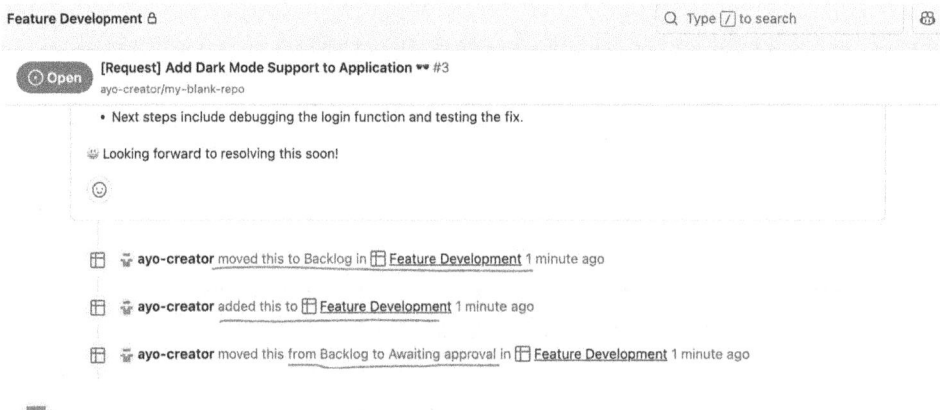

Figure 14.9: The issue timeline captures project changes made to an issue

Certification tip

You may be asked which types of items can be converted into cards, or how to associate cards with issues across repos.

Modifying visible fields

You can customize which information appears on your project board by modifying the visible fields in each view.

1. **View options**: Open up the view options of your current view by clicking on the chevron icon (⏷) next to the name of the view (**Backlog**) and select **Fields** from the ensuing menu. This will display all the available fields to choose from.

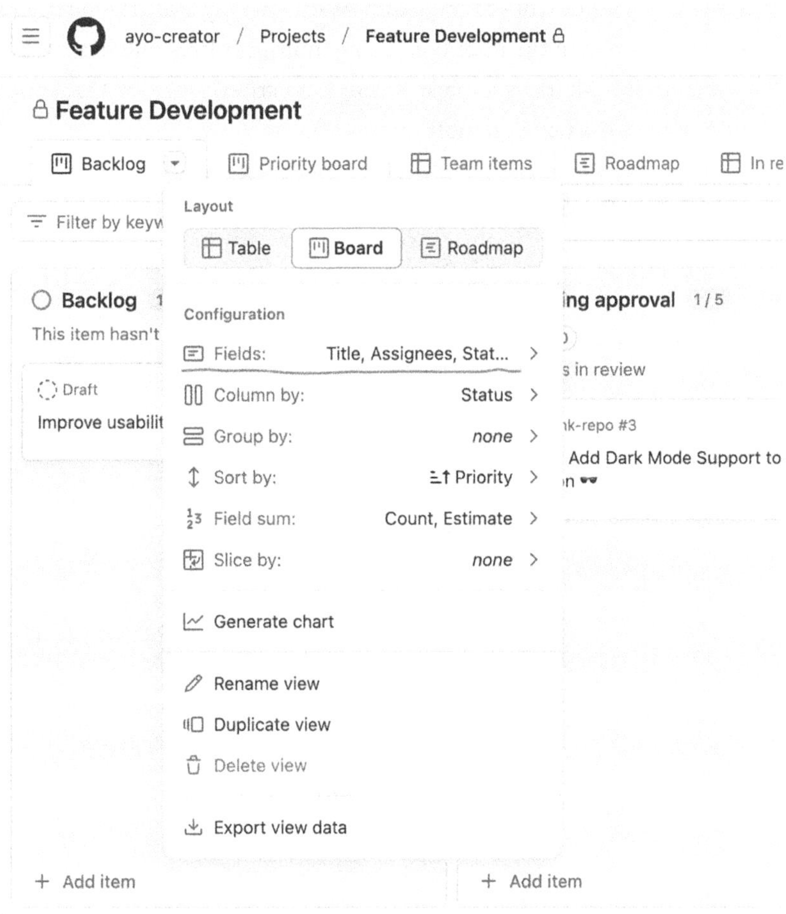

Figure 14.10: You can customize the visible fields on a card

2. Select the fields you desire and click **Save** on the right-hand side of the project board (*keep this in mind whenever you make changes to your project's views*).

3. Spend some time studying these view options. Other activities you can carry out on the **Board layout** include selecting which field you want to use as the Kanban lanes, grouping cards by a field, slicing by, and applying aggregates. For example, you can sort cards by different criteria (e.g., due date or priority).

Filtering and sorting

To focus on specific tasks, you can filter and sort cards on your project board using various criteria like labels, assignees, or milestones:

1. **Filter cards**: Use the filter bar at the top of the project board to filter cards by labels, assignees, milestones, or other custom fields you may add. The filter you specify will be interpreted as text in the filter box. Using multiple filters will behave like a logical AND. You can separate filters by a space. If your filter criteria is a text that contains spaces, you should enclose the text in double quotes (").

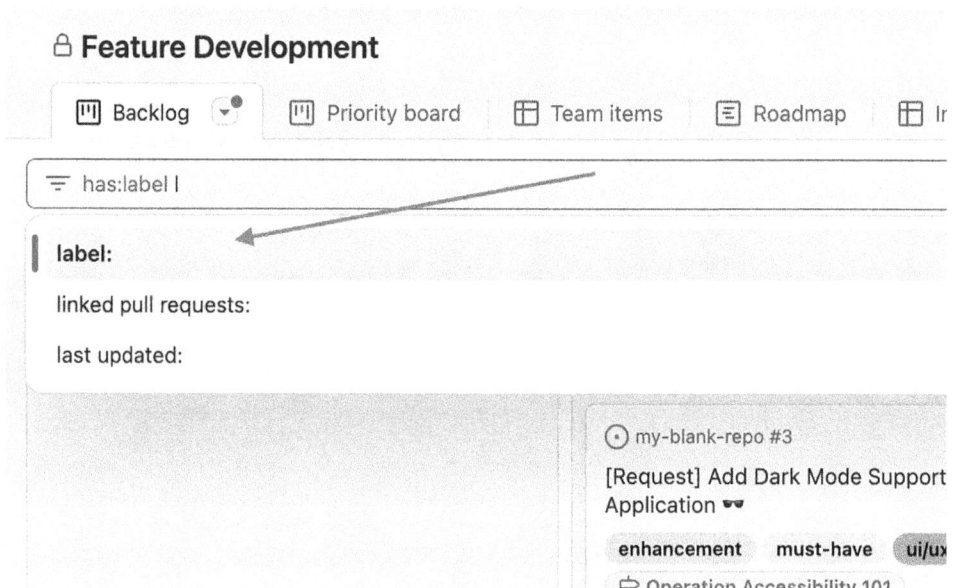

Figure 14.11: Filtering cards using the filter box

This marks the end of our lab exercise. Spend some extra time tweaking your view and switching to different layouts to discover the nuances and differences.

Up next, we will see how we can automate our project flows using rules.

> **Certification tip**
>
> Expect questions that test your ability to organize project views using filters and labels to manage large sets of issues.

Automating project workflows

GitHub Projects offers a range of built-in workflows that can help you automate repetitive tasks and streamline your project management. These workflows are designed to save you time and ensure that your project board stays up to date with minimal manual effort. In this section, we'll explore the various automation options available and how you can leverage them to enhance your workflow.

Automation in GitHub Projects allows you to set up rules that trigger specific actions based on certain events. For example, you can automatically move an issue to the "In progress" column when it's assigned to someone, or close an issue when it's marked as "Done." These automations help keep your project board organized and reduce the need for manual updates.

Some of the ways you can automate your projects include the following:

- Using built-in automations
- Using GitHub Actions
- Using the REST API

We will examine these one by one.

Using built-in automations

GitHub Projects provides built-in workflows that can automatically add items from repositories that match a filter, move items to different columns based on specific criteria, and archive items that meet certain conditions. These built-in automations help keep the project board organized and reduce the need for manual updates.

To use built-in automations, visit your project board, click the ellipses (**...**) on the right-hand side, and select **Workflows**.

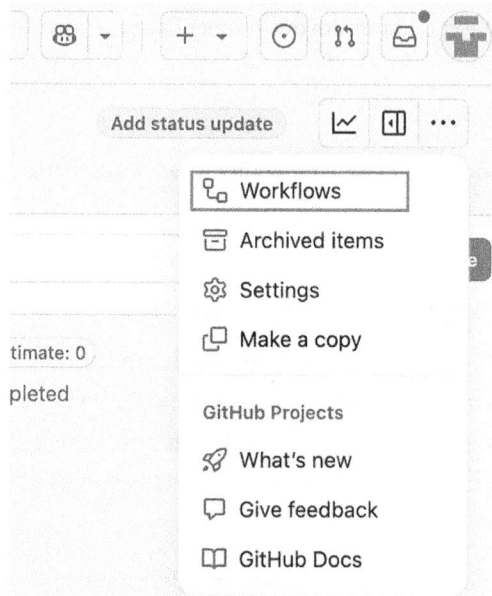

Figure 14.12: Built-in workflows are accessible from the project's menu

This will display a list of available built-in workflows.

To modify a workflow, select it and click **Edit**. This will switch to edit mode. Make the changes and click **Save and turn on workflow**. The example in the following figure will automatically mark a card as **Done** if the corresponding issue or pull request is closed.

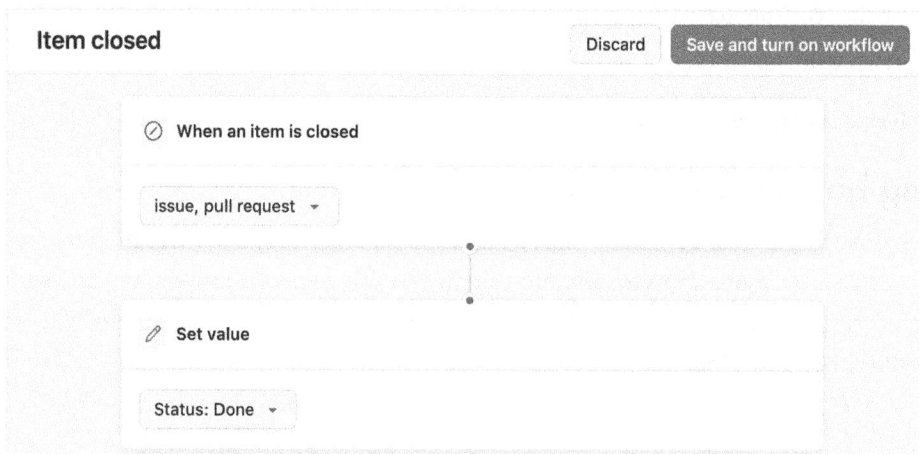

Figure 14.13: Workflow to mark items as "Done" when closed

Here is a list of built-in workflows available on GitHub Projects as of the time of writing this book:

Workflow	Description
Item added to project	Set the value of a card's Kanban lane as soon as its issue or pull request is added to the project.
Item reopened	Set the value of a card's Kanban lane as soon as its issue or pull request is reopened.
Item closed	Set the value of a card's Kanban lane as soon as its issue or pull request is closed.
Code changes requested	Set the value of a card's Kanban lane as soon as its pull request has a change request review.
Code review approved	Set the value of a card's Kanban lane as soon as its pull request is approved.
Pull request merged	Set the value of a card's Kanban lane as soon as its pull request is merged to the destination branch.
Auto-archive items	Archive cards that meet defined criteria.
Auto-add to project	Automatically add items from a repo that meet a defined criteria to the project.
Auto-close issue	Automatically close a corresponding issue when the card is set to a predefined Kanban status.
Auto-add sub-issues to project	When an item in the project has sub-issues, add sub-issues to the project.

Table 14.2: List of built-in workflows on GitHub Projects

If automation doesn't trigger as expected, ensure your issue has the correct label applied.

Built-in automations are limited to predefined triggers. If you need more customized behavior—such as updating labels based on review status or auto-assigning reviewers—you'll need to use GitHub Actions or webhooks.

Using GitHub Actions

GitHub Actions allows you to create custom workflows that automate various project management tasks. For example, you can create a workflow that runs every time an issue is created to add a label and leave a comment. GitHub Actions can also be used to automate tasks such as adding pull requests to a project and updating the status of issues. I won't go into details of creating a GitHub Actions workflow here due to the advanced level of understanding required. For more information on how to do this, visit the GitHub documentation to learn more: `https://docs.` `github.com/en/issues/planning-and-tracking-with-projects/automating-your-project/` `automating-projects-using-actions`.

Using the REST API

The GitHub REST API enables you to programmatically manage your projects. You can use the API to create, update, and delete project boards, columns, and cards. This allows for more advanced and customized automation, such as integrating with other tools and services to enhance your project management workflows. This is beyond the scope of this book, but you can learn more by reading the GitHub documentation: `https://docs.github.com/en/issues/planning-and-` `tracking-with-projects/automating-your-project/using-the-api-to-manage-projects`.

By effectively using project boards and implementing subtle automations, you can improve team collaboration, visualize work, and ensure that everyone is aligned and working toward the same goals. This not only enhances productivity but also helps in managing complex projects more efficiently.

Awesome! What a chapter packed with a lot of learning! Let's summarize what we have learned.

Summary

As we reach the end of this chapter, we reflect on our journey through the intricacies of GitHub Projects. We delved into the various features and functionalities and explored how to effectively manage tasks, track progress, and enhance collaboration within a project team.

We learned how to create and customize project boards, add and manage cards, and utilize built-in automations to keep our projects organized. You can now automate tasks using built-in workflows and GitHub Actions. We also practiced integrating Projects with issues, milestones, and cards.

The knowledge and skills you have acquired would undoubtedly empower you to work more efficiently and cohesively, ultimately leading to better project outcomes.

Up next, we'll explore GitHub's built-in security tools and permission settings to help you protect your repositories and manage user access — a key area tested in the certification exam.

Let's do a short quiz.

Test your knowledge

Remember the steps for creating a board, managing columns and cards, and using built-in automation. These are core objectives in the Foundations exam blueprint.

1. Which of the following automation options in GitHub Projects allows you to automatically add items from repositories that match a filter?

    a. GitHub Actions

    b. Built-in automations

    c. REST API

    d. Manual updates

2. In GitHub Projects, which layout is particularly useful for teams that need to track work visually and manage tasks dynamically?

    a. Board layout

    b. Table layout

    c. Roadmap layout

    d. Kanban layout

3. What is the maximum number of active items allowed in a GitHub project before archiving is required?

    a. 1,000 active items

    b. 1,200 active items

    c. 10,000 active items

    d. 12,000 active items

Useful links

-   *Planning and tracking with Projects*: https://docs.github.com/en/issues/planning-and-tracking-with-projects

-   *Automating your project*: https://docs.github.com/en/issues/planning-and-tracking-with-projects/automating-your-project

Unlock this book's exclusive benefits now

Scan this QR code or go to packtpub.com/unlock, then search this book by name.

Note: Keep your purchase invoice ready before you start.

15

Security Practices and User Management

Welcome to *Chapter 15*, where we explore the essentials of GitHub security and user management! By now, you're familiar with the essentials, you have collaborated effectively, and you've started leveraging GitHub for your career. Now, it's time to focus on protecting your work. In this chapter, we'll explore GitHub's built-in security features – such as setting up two-factor authentication, managing user permissions, and securing your CI/CD pipelines. These practices are critical for maintaining repository integrity and will also help you prepare for the certification exam.

We will cover the following main topics:

- GitHub security features
- Managing access and permissions
- Best practices for repository security

Technical requirements

- A GitHub individual account
- The organization you created in *Chapter 2*, *Navigating the GitHub Interface*

GitHub security features

In this section, we'll explore the various security features GitHub offers to help you protect your repositories and manage user access effectively.

Two-Factor Authentication (2FA)

Two-factor authentication adds an extra layer of security to your GitHub account beyond just your password. By requiring a second form of verification, it ensures that even if someone gets hold of your password, they won't be able to access your account without the second factor.

2FA is crucial for securing your account for enhanced security, mitigating against credential theft, protecting against phishing, and complying with security standards in many organizations and projects. Which 2FA methods are configurable on GitHub?

Available 2FA methods

GitHub offers several methods for enabling **Two-Factor Authentication (2FA)** to enhance the security of your account. Here are the available 2FA methods:

- **Time-Based One-Time Password (TOTP) authenticator apps**:
  - Use apps such as Google Authenticator, Authy, or Microsoft Authenticator to generate a time-based code
  - Recommended for its reliability and security

- **Short Message Service (SMS)**:
  - Receive a verification code via text message
  - Less secure compared to TOTP apps, but still an option

- **Physical security keys**:
  - Use hardware devices such as **YubiKeys** that support FIDO U2F or WebAuthn standards
  - Provide a high level of security by requiring physical possession of the key

- **Virtual security keys**:
  - Utilize built-in security features of personal devices, such as Windows Hello, Face ID, or Touch ID
  - Convenient and secure, leveraging device-specific authentication

- **GitHub Mobile:**

  - Use the GitHub Mobile app to authenticate using public-key cryptography
  - Does not rely on TOTP and provides a seamless experience

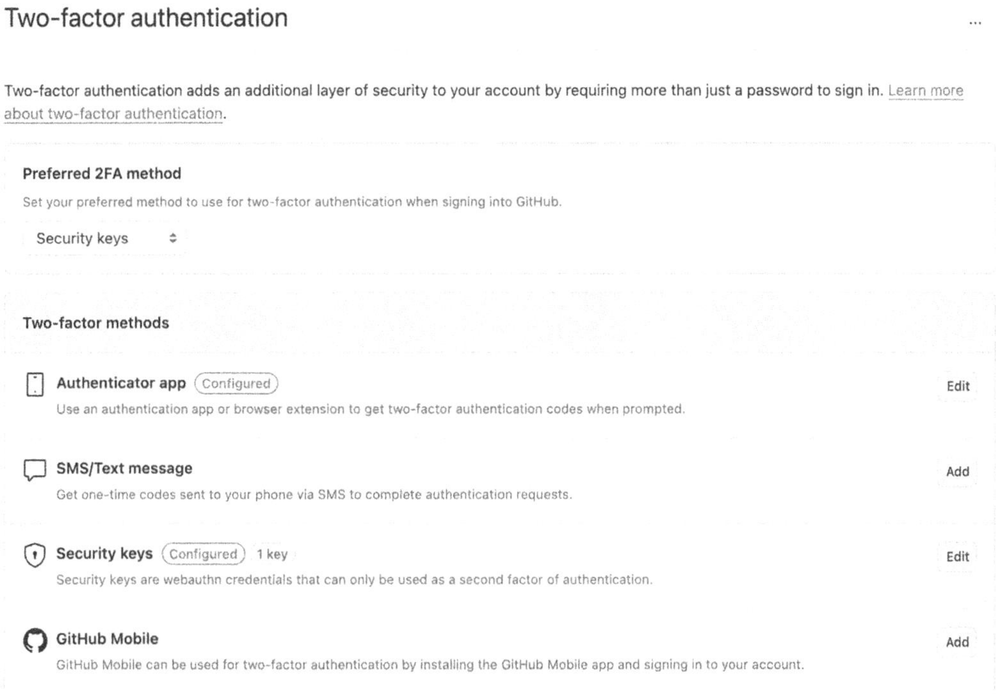

Two-factor authentication   ...

Two-factor authentication adds an additional layer of security to your account by requiring more than just a password to sign in. Learn more about two-factor authentication.

Preferred 2FA method

Set your preferred method to use for two-factor authentication when signing into GitHub.

Security keys   ⇕

Two-factor methods

⬚ **Authenticator app** (Configured)   Edit
   Use an authentication app or browser extension to get two-factor authentication codes when prompted.

💬 **SMS/Text message**   Add
   Get one-time codes sent to your phone via SMS to complete authentication requests.

⊙ **Security keys** (Configured) 1 key   Edit
   Security keys are webauthn credentials that can only be used as a second factor of authentication.

○ **GitHub Mobile**   Add
   GitHub Mobile can be used for two-factor authentication by installing the GitHub Mobile app and signing in to your account.

Figure 15.1: Available 2FA methods on GitHub

These methods offer flexibility and varying levels of security, allowing you to choose the one that best fits your needs. For the highest security, it's recommended to use TOTP apps or physical security keys. Let's take a look at how to set this up.

Certification tip

The GitHub Foundations exam often includes questions on 2FA setup and best practices. Make sure you understand both how to enable 2FA and how to use recovery methods.

Setting up 2FA on GitHub

To add an extra layer of security to your GitHub account, enable two-factor authentication (2FA) by following these steps:

1. Go to your GitHub individual account settings by clicking on your *avatar* in the top-right-hand corner and clicking on **Settings**.

2. In the left sidebar, under **Access**, click on **Password and authentication**.

3. If not enabled yet, select **Enable two-factor authentication**.

4. Under **Two-factor authentication**, click **Add** next to the 2FA method of choice.

5. Follow the prompts to set up 2FA using the method selected.

Optionally, you could set your preferred 2FA method if you enrolled in more than one.

That's it! You're all set up.

You will also notice **Recovery codes** under the **Recovery options** section (this section will appear only if the 2FA method is set).

Recovery codes are essential for regaining access to your GitHub account if you lose access to your 2FA credentials. These codes act as a backup method, allowing you to log in even if you can't use your primary 2FA method, such as an authentication app or SMS. When you enable 2FA, GitHub provides a set of recovery codes that you should store securely, such as in a password manager or a safe place. If you ever lose access to your 2FA device, you can use one of these recovery codes to regain entry to your account, ensuring you are not permanently locked out.

> GitHub gives you 8 recovery codes. Store them securely. You can regenerate these if needed, but old ones will be invalidated.

Branch protection rules

> We discussed branch protection rules extensively in *Chapter 5, Branching and Merging Strategies*. Be sure to read this in preparation for your exam.

Branch protection rules help you enforce certain workflows and requirements before changes can be merged into your protected branches. This ensures that your codebase remains stable and secure. You can configure branch protection rules and, among many other measures, enforce code reviews, ensuring that all changes are reviewed and approved before they are merged.

> **Certification tip**
>
> You'll need to know how to configure branch protection rules and enable Dependabot alerts for the exam.

Security configurations

GitHub provides various security settings as a collection that you can configure to enhance the security of the repositories in your organization. You can create a customized security configuration from scratch or choose the GitHub-recommended configuration that already comes preset with its settings.

GitHub-recommended security configurations are predefined settings that follow best practices to enhance security, such as enabling Dependabot alerts and secret scanning by default. Custom configurations, on the other hand, allow you to tailor security settings to meet specific needs or requirements of your project or organization, providing flexibility to adjust features such as branch protection rules and access controls.

To manage security settings at the **organization level**:

1. Go to your organization's main page on GitHub (remember that this is an organization, not a repo). *For more information on how to create an organization, review Lab 2.1 in Chapter 2, Navigating the GitHub Interface.*
2. Click on **Settings**.
3. In the left sidebar, under **Security**, click **Advanced Security** to expand.
4. Then click on **Configurations**.
5. Choose to edit the GitHub-recommended security configuration by clicking on the edit (⌀) icon. Alternatively, you can click on **New configuration** to customize a new one.
6. Configure the security settings as needed.

To manage **repository-specific** security settings:

1. Navigate to the repository's main page on GitHub.

2. Click on **Settings**.

3. In the left sidebar, under **Security**, click **Advanced Security**.

4. Enable or configure security features such as **Dependabot alerts,** secret scanning, and code scanning. The latter two may be missing from your view if the repository is private or internal.

> Secret scanning and code scanning are GitHub Advanced Security features and are only available as a paid subscription for private or internal repositories, or free if your repository is open source, that is, visibility is **Public**.

5. Optionally, if you wish to configure secret scanning or code scanning, click on **General** from the left sidebar and scroll down to **Danger Zone**. Next to **Change repository visibility**, click on **Change visibility** and select **Change to public**. Be sure to follow the instructions.

> **Certification tip**
>
> Questions may come up regarding changing the visibility of a repository from public to private, or vice versa. Be sure to understand the implications of making a repo public. Read more about public repositories in *Chapter 2, Navigating the GitHub Interface* and *Chapter 11, Contributing to Open Source Projects*.

Dependabot, secret scanning, and code scanning are all examples of security features that GitHub offers. Some of these features require a paid subscription, some are free only for public repositories, while others are completely free out of the box.

What is Dependabot?

Dependabot is a feature on GitHub that helps keep your project's dependencies up to date automatically. It works by regularly checking your project's dependency files (such as package.json, requirements.txt, etc.) for outdated packages and then creating pull requests to update them to the latest versions.

Key features of Dependabot include the following:

- **Automated dependency updates**: It scans your project and creates pull requests to update dependencies

- **Security alerts**: It integrates with GitHub's security features to alert you about vulnerabilities in your dependencies and can automatically fix them

- **Customizable configuration**: You can configure how often it checks for updates, which dependencies to ignore, and more, using a `dependabot.yml` file

- **Supports multiple languages**: Works with JavaScript, Python, Ruby, Java, PHP, and more

Here is an example flow:

1. You enable Dependabot in your GitHub repository.

2. It checks for outdated or vulnerable dependencies.

3. It creates a pull request with the updated version.

4. You review and merge the pull request.

Now let's talk about managing alerts and vulnerabilities.

Security alerts and vulnerability management

GitHub helps you stay on top of potential security issues with automated alerts and tools to manage vulnerabilities. Let's examine some of these:

- **Dependabot alerts and security updates:**

  - **Dependabot alerts**: Automatically scans your dependencies for known vulnerabilities and notifies you if any are found

  - **Dependabot security updates**: Automatically generates pull requests to update vulnerable dependencies to secure versions

  How can you enable and manage Dependabot alerts?

  a. Go to the repository's main page on GitHub.

  b. Click on **Settings**.

  c. In the left sidebar, under **Security**, click **Advanced Security**.

  d. Under **Dependabot alerts**, click **Enable** if not already enabled.

  e. Afterward, you can review and manage alerts from the **Security** tab of the repository.

- **Code scanning:**

    - **CodeQL**: A powerful code analysis engine that scans your code for security vulnerabilities and coding errors. It integrates with GitHub Actions to run scans on every push or pull request.

    - **Autofix**: Uses AI to suggest fixes for detected vulnerabilities, streamlining the remediation process.

- **Secret scanning**: Detects and alerts you if sensitive information, such as API keys or passwords, is accidentally committed to your repository. This helps prevent unauthorized access and potential security breaches.

- **Security overview dashboard**: Provides a centralized view of your security alerts and vulnerabilities across all repositories. This dashboard helps you prioritize and manage security issues more effectively.

- **Vulnerability management integrations**: Integrates with third-party vulnerability management tools to consolidate and prioritize vulnerabilities, automate risk mitigation, and visualize alerts within your existing security posture.

Talking about third-party integrations, GitHub supports receiving **Static Analysis Results Interchange Format (SARIF)** reports from various third-party security tools. Some of the commonly used tools include the following:

- **ESLint**: A popular tool for identifying and reporting on patterns found in ECMAScript/ JavaScript code

- **Bandit**: A tool designed to find common security issues in Python code

- **Brakeman**: A static analysis tool that checks Ruby on Rails applications for security vulnerabilities

- **Checkmarx**: A comprehensive **Static Application Security Testing (SAST)** tool

- **Fortify**: A suite of tools for static and dynamic application security testing

- **SonarQube**: An open source platform for continuous inspection of code quality

- **Veracode**: A cloud-based service for static and dynamic application security testing

These tools generate SARIF files that can be uploaded to GitHub, allowing you to view and manage security alerts directly within your repository.

To handle security advisories and alerts, navigate to the **Security** tab of the repository (*you will find this tab on both the organization and the repository levels*). Examine the difference between the **Security** tabs of both levels. You will notice a stark difference in what you see. This is because the security overview at the organization level rolls up all the security advisories across all its repos, whereas the scope of the repo level is limited to only vulnerability findings of that repo.

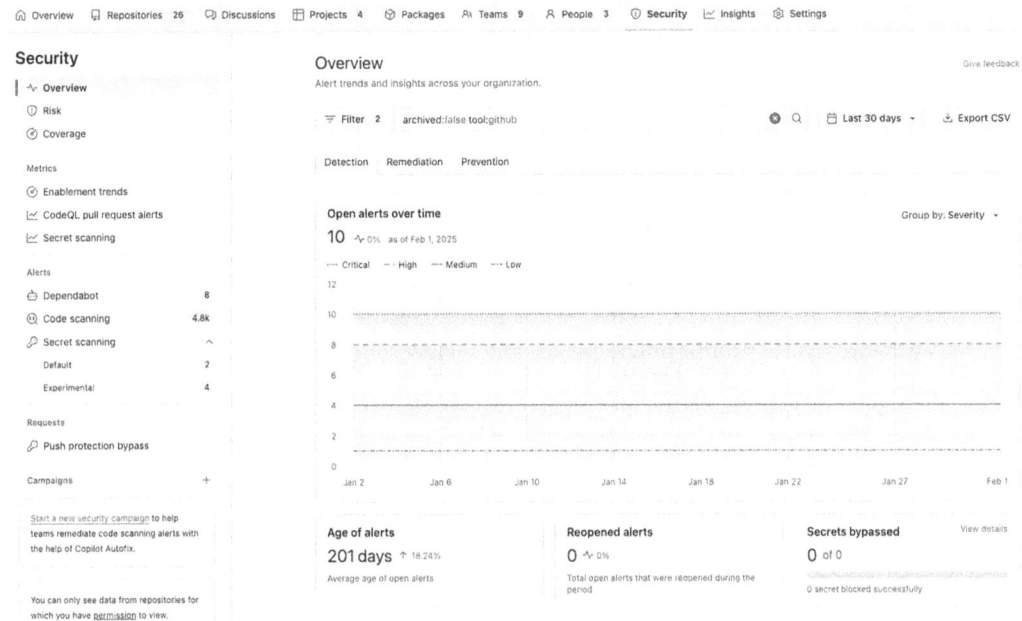

Figure 15.2: Security Overview at the organization level

These tools and features help you maintain a robust security posture by automating the detection and management of vulnerabilities, ensuring your codebase remains secure.

In the next section, we will talk about how permissions and authorization can help in securing your code.

Managing access and permissions

Effective management of access and permissions is crucial for maintaining the security and integrity of your GitHub repositories. This section delves into the various methods GitHub provides to control who has access to your repositories and what they can do.

User roles and permissions

GitHub offers a range of user roles to help you manage access and permissions effectively. Understanding these roles is key to maintaining a secure and organized workflow.

Overview of different user roles

User roles on GitHub come in three tiers: roles at the Enterprise level, Organization level, and Repository level. Here are the default roles at the Enterprise and Organization levels:

- **Owner:** The owner has full administrative access to the organization and its repositories. This role can manage settings, users, and billing.

- **Member:** Members have basic access to repositories, typically for contributing code. They can create issues, submit pull requests, and review code.

- **Billing manager:** Billing managers can manage billing settings such as changing billing plans, managing payment methods, downloading and receiving receipts, or managing sponsorships.

When inviting new collaborators to your organization for the first time, you choose one of these three.

> **Certification tip**
>
> Be prepared to identify role-based use cases. The exam may ask you to match specific user scenarios with appropriate GitHub roles.

Assigning roles to users

To manage access within your organization, you can assign specific roles to members by following these steps:

1. Navigate to your organization's main page on GitHub.

2. Click on the **People** tab in the organization's navigation bar.

3. If the user doesn't already exist in the organization, you can invite them by clicking on **Invite member**.

4. Supply the user's GitHub handle and click on **Invite**.

5. For an existing member, locate the user you want to assign a role to and click on the ellipsis dropdown next to their name and select **Change role...**.

6. Select the appropriate role and click on **Send invitation** (for new invitations) or **Change role** (existing members).

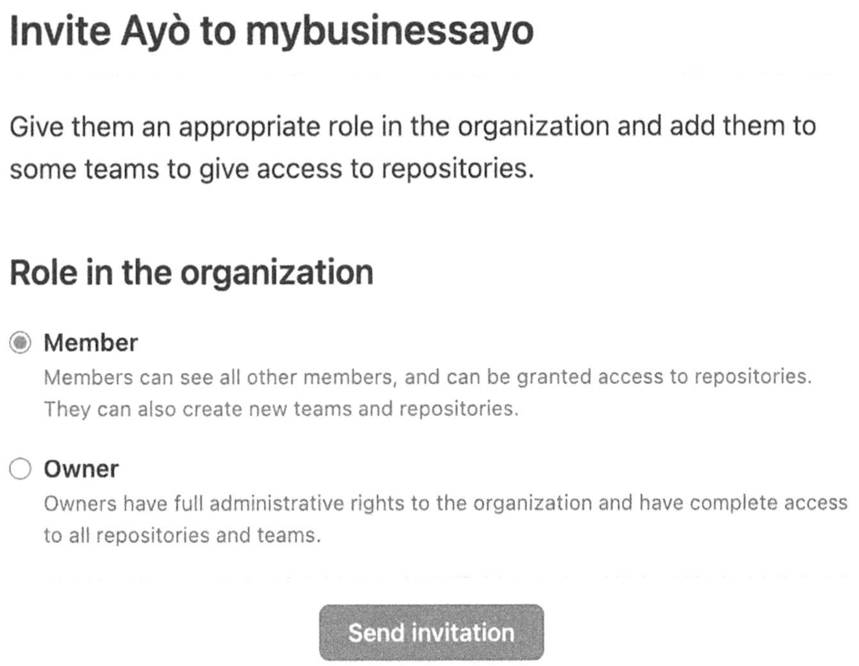

Invite Ayò to mybusinessayo

Give them an appropriate role in the organization and add them to some teams to give access to repositories.

Role in the organization

◉ **Member**
   Members can see all other members, and can be granted access to repositories.
   They can also create new teams and repositories.

○ **Owner**
   Owners have full administrative rights to the organization and have complete access
   to all repositories and teams.

Send invitation

Figure 15.3: Example invitation showing the default available roles

7. Click on **Change role...**

8. Select the appropriate role (**Owner** or **Member**) from the list displayed.

9. Click on **Change role**.

10. Alternatively, if the user only needs to be a billing manager, click on the **Invite a billing manager** link at the bottom of the user invitation screen (Step 3), or go to the organization's settings and select **Billing and licensing** from the left navigation bar and invite them.

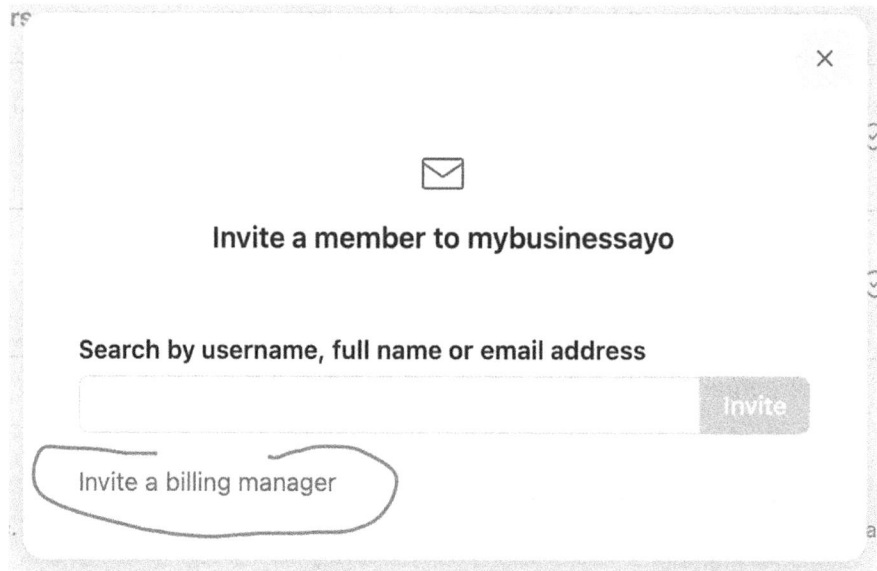

Fig.15.4: Inviting a billing manager to GitHub

In addition to these three, GitHub provides some more granular roles that help you define granular permissions to what a member can or cannot do at the different levels.

Here is a table of additional pre-defined roles that can be used:

Organization Roles	Repository Roles
All-repository read	Read
Grants read access to all repositories in the organization.	Read and clone repositories. Open and comment on issues and pull requests.
All-repository write	Write
Grants write access to all repositories in the organization.	Triage permissions plus read, clone, and push to repositories.
All-repository triage	Triage
Grants triage access to all repositories in the organization.	Read permissions plus manage issues and pull requests.

All-repository maintain	Maintain
Grants maintenance access to all repositories in the organization.	Write permissions plus manage issues, pull requests, and some repository settings.
All-repository admin	Admin
Grants admin access to all repositories in the organization.	Full access to repositories, including sensitive and destructive actions.
CI/CD admin	
Grants admin access to manage Actions policies, runners, runner groups, network configurations, secrets, variables, and usage metrics for an organization.	
Security manager	
Grants the ability to manage security policies, security alerts, and security configurations for an organization and all its repositories.	

Table 15.1: List of predefined roles at can be used at the Organization and Repository levels

In addition to these predefined roles, you can create custom roles with a select combination of permissions if one of these predefined roles doesn't exactly fit your needs. This can be done at the Enterprise, Organization, and Repository levels.

> The custom role feature is only available on GitHub Enterprise. In addition, the custom role at the Enterprise level is only available for preview as of early 2025. Refer to GitHub Docs for the latest availability.

Now let's move on to using teams for access control.

Team management

Teams allow you to group users and manage their access to repositories more efficiently. This is particularly useful for larger organizations with multiple projects. A team can either be **visible** or **secret**.

Visible teams can be seen and @mentioned by members of the organization, while secret teams can only be seen by their members. This will be specified during team creation. Teams can also be nested, with one team being the parent of another team.

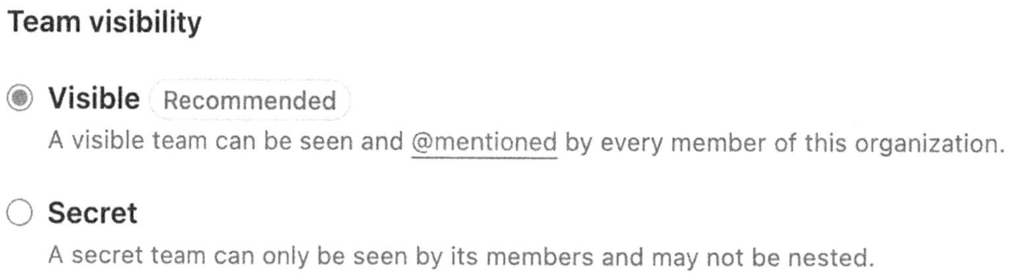

Team visibility

⦿ **Visible** (Recommended)

    A visible team can be seen and @mentioned by every member of this organization.

◯ **Secret**

    A secret team can only be seen by its members and may not be nested.

Figure 15.5: A GitHub Team can be visible or secret

Let's see how we create teams.

Creating and managing teams

Here's how to create a team:

1. Go to your organization's main page on GitHub.
2. Click on **Teams** in the organization's navigation bar.
3. Click **New team** to create a new team.
4. Enter the team name and description, then click **Create team**.
5. Add members to the team by clicking **Add a member** and selecting users from the list.

Here are some important use cases for team visibility and notifications:

Feature	Description	Common Use Cases
Visibility	Controls who can see the team in the organization (e.g., visible, secret).	Publicly list teams for collaboration. Hide sensitive teams (e.g., security) from general org members.
Notification	Determines how team members receive notifications (e.g., mentions, discussions).	Ensure relevant members are notified about issues/PRs. Avoid notification fatigue for non-critical teams.

Assigning repository access to teams

To assign access to repositories to teams, do the following:

1. Navigate to the team's page on GitHub.

2. Click on the **Repositories** tab in the team's navigation bar.

3. Click **Add a repository** and select the repository you want to grant access to.

4. Set the desired permission level (**Read**, **Triage**, **Write**, or others) for the team. *More roles and the ability to create custom roles are available if you have a paid GitHub Enterprise subscription.*

Collaborator access control

Collaborators are individuals who are granted access to specific repositories. This is useful for managing external contributors or contractors.

Adding collaborators to repositories:

To give others access to a specific repository without adding them to the entire organization, you can add them as collaborators:

1. Navigate to the repository's main page on GitHub.

2. Click on **Settings** in the repository's navigation bar.

3. In the left sidebar, click **Collaborators and teams** (org-owned repos) or **Collaborators** (user-owned repos).

4. Click **Add people** and start typing the username of the person you want to add.

5. Select their name and set the appropriate permission level (**Read**, **Triage**, **Write**, **Maintain**, **Admin**) for the collaborator.

Setting permissions for collaborators:

Once collaborators are added, you can adjust their access levels using the following steps:

1. In the **Collaborators and teams** section, find the collaborator you want to manage.

2. Click on their permission dropdown and select the desired permission level.

One common pitfall is **misconfigured roles or permissions**, which can inadvertently expose sensitive code. For example, imagine a scenario where a developer creates a private repository for an internal tool but mistakenly assigns a **Read** role to an external contractor at the organization level. Because the repository inherits permissions from the organization, the contractor now has unintended access to the private repository. This kind of oversight can lead to accidental data leaks or unauthorized code access.

To prevent such incidents, always follow the principle of least privilege, regularly audit repository access, and use fine-grained personal access tokens for automation and integrations.

Another great feature to manage access and permissions is tokens. Two examples of tokens on GitHub are OAuth and **Personal Access Tokens (PAT)**.

OAuth and personal access tokens

OAuth and personal access tokens provide secure ways to authenticate and authorize access to your GitHub account and repositories. These methods are essential for integrating third-party applications and services, that is, when you are not using an interactive login of a person. Here's where you'll find each of these on GitHub:

Managing OAuth applications

To review and manage third-party applications connected to your GitHub account, follow these steps:

1. Go to your GitHub account settings.

2. In the left sidebar, click **Developer settings**.

3. Click **OAuth Apps** to view and manage your OAuth applications.

4. Review the list of authorized applications and revoke access if necessary.

Creating and using personal access tokens

To authenticate non-interactive scripts or services, you can generate a personal access token as shown below:

1. Go to your GitHub account settings.

2. In the left sidebar, click **Developer settings**.

3. Click **Personal access tokens**.

4. Select either **Fine-grained tokens** or **Tokens (classic)** in the submenu.

5. Click **Generate new token** (for fine-grained tokens) or select **Token (classic)** again for the classic token option.

6. Select the scopes or permissions you want to grant this token, such as repo, admin:org, or user.

7. Click **Generate token** and copy the token for use in your applications. Store it securely, as it will not be displayed again.

You would notice by now that there are two types of personal access tokens on GitHub: **classic** and **fine-grained**.

Both types co-exist, with classic being the older. It is expected that GitHub will deprecate classic PAT in favour of fine-grained PAT in the future, but both of them can be used interchangeably today. Let's quickly enumerate the differences between the two.

Feature	Fine-grained PAT	Classic PAT
Granularity of Permissions	Highly specific – can grant access to individual repositories and specific actions (e.g., read-only for issues)	Broad – grants access to all repositories the user has access to, with less control over specific actions
Repository Scope	Can be limited to specific repositories	Applies to all repositories the user has access to
Token Expiration	Supports setting expiration dates	Optional expiration (can be set or left indefinite)
Security	More secure due to the least-privilege principle and fine-grained control	Less secure due to broader access scope
Use Case	Ideal for automation, CI/CD, and integrations requiring limited access	Suitable for legacy systems or tools that don't yet support fine-grained tokens
Revocation	Can revoke access to individual repositories without revoking the entire token	Must revoke the entire token to remove access
Availability	Recommended for new integrations	Still supported but being phased out in favor of fine-grained tokens
Token Visibility	Token permissions are visible and auditable in detail	Less visibility into specific permissions granted
Scopes	Uses granular repository and permission settings	Uses broad OAuth-like scopes (e.g., `repo`, `admin:org`)

In summary, GitHub offers a range of measures to manage access and grant permissions to users and third-party applications and services. It is important to know which ones to combine to ensure the security of your code. Up next, let's consider some good security practices for repo security.

Best practices for repository security

Ensuring the security of your repositories is paramount to protecting your code and maintaining the integrity of your projects. In this section, we'll cover best practices for securing your repositories on GitHub.

Code scanning with Static Application Security Testing (SAST) tools

Static Application Security Testing (SAST) tools help identify security vulnerabilities in your codebase before they become issues in production. GitHub has a code scanning product. It is sold separately but can be integrated natively into your repos and organizations. It's labelled **GitHub Advanced Security (GHAS)**. GHAS is a *paid* subscription product, an add-on that you can purchase in addition to your GitHub subscription. If your codebase is open source, most of GHAS's security features are **free** for use.

Here's how to integrate and use these tools. You have to do this on a public repo if you haven't purchased GHAS:

- **Integrating SAST tools in your workflow**: Here's how to set up code scanning with SAST tools:

  a. Navigate to the repository's main page on GitHub.

  b. Click on **Security** in the repository's navigation bar.

  c. Click **Set up code scanning**.

  d. Choose a code scanning tool, such as CodeQL, and follow the prompts to configure it.

  Examples of SAST tools include the following:

  - **CodeQL**: A powerful code analysis engine that scans your code for security vulnerabilities and coding errors

  - **Dependabot Alerts**: Automatically scans your dependencies for known vulnerabilities and notifies you if any are found

- **Interpreting scan results**: To review and act on scan results, take the following steps:

    a. Go to the **Security** tab of the repository.

    b. Click on **Code scanning alerts** to view the results.

    c. Review the alerts and take appropriate action to fix the identified issues.

CI/CD pipeline security measures

Securing your **Continuous Integration/Continuous Deployment (CI/CD)** pipelines is crucial to ensure that your code remains secure throughout the development lifecycle. Follow these steps to secure your pipelines:

- **Securing CI/CD Pipelines Using GitHub Actions**: To secure your CI/CD pipelines, take these steps:

    a. Navigate to the repository's main page on GitHub.

    b. Click on **Actions** in the repository's navigation bar.

    c. Set up workflows to include security checks, such as running SAST tools or dependency checks.

Mini-case example

A development team noticed that their CI/CD pipeline was deploying code with outdated dependencies that had known vulnerabilities. The issue stemmed from a missing dependency scanning step in their GitHub Actions workflow. To mitigate this, they integrated Dependabot and added a step in their workflow to run `npm audit` during each build. This change helped catch vulnerable packages early and prevented insecure code from reaching production.

- **Implementing secrets management in workflows**: To manage secrets securely in your workflows, take these steps:

    a. Go to the repository's main page on GitHub.

    b. Click on **Settings**.

    c. In the left sidebar, click **Secrets and variables**.

    d. Then, select **Actions** from the submenu.

    e. Click **New repository secret** to add secrets, such as API keys or tokens, securely.

    f. Reference these secrets in your GitHub Actions workflows to avoid exposing sensitive information.

Monitoring and auditing activities

Regular monitoring and auditing of repository activities help you detect and respond to suspicious actions promptly. Here's how to monitor and audit activities:

- **Using audit logs to monitor repository activities**: To monitor repository activities, take these steps:

  a.   Go to your organization's main page on GitHub.

  b.   Click on **Settings**.

  c.   In the left sidebar, under the **Archive** section, click **Logs,**

  d.   Then, select **Audit log** from the submenu.

  e.   Review the audit log entries to monitor activities such as user logins, repository changes, and permission updates.

- **Setting up alerts for suspicious activities**: To set up alerts for suspicious activities, take these steps:

  a.   Use GitHub's built-in security alerts to notify you of potential security issues.

  b.   Integrate with third-party monitoring tools to receive real-time alerts for suspicious activities.

Incident response and recovery

Being prepared for security incidents and having a plan for recovery is essential for minimizing the impact of security breaches. Follow these steps for incident response and recovery:

- **Preparing for security incidents**: To prepare for security incidents, take these steps:

  a.   Develop an incident response plan that outlines the steps to take in case of a security breach.

  b.   Ensure that all team members are aware of the plan and their roles in the response process.

- **Steps for incident response and recovery**: To respond to and recover from security incidents, take these steps:

  a.   Identify and contain the breach to prevent further damage.

  b.   Investigate the cause of the breach and assess the impact.

  c.   Remediate the vulnerabilities that led to the breach.

    d.   Communicate with stakeholders and provide updates on the incident and recovery efforts.

    e.   Review and update security policies and practices to prevent future incidents.

Et voila! This concludes the basics when it comes to security on GitHub. Let's summarize what we learned.

Summary

In this chapter, we delved into the intricacies of security practices and user management on GitHub. We had already mastered the essentials of effective collaboration, but we know that with great code comes great responsibility. We explored the robust security features GitHub offers, such as two-factor authentication, which added an extra layer of security to our accounts. We learned about the various methods available for 2FA, including authenticator apps, SMS, physical security keys, and GitHub Mobile.

We also discussed branch protection rules, which ensured our codebase remained stable and secure by enforcing workflows and requirements before changes could be merged. Additionally, we examined security configurations, both GitHub-recommended and custom, to enhance the security of our repositories. We looked at the management of security alerts and vulnerabilities through tools such as Dependabot, CodeQL, and secret scanning, which helped us stay on top of potential security issues.

Managing access and permissions was another crucial aspect we covered. We understood the importance of user roles and permissions at different levels, from enterprise to repository, and how to assign these roles effectively. We also explored the use of teams for access control, creating and managing teams to streamline our workflow. Finally, we looked at OAuth and personal access tokens, which provided secure ways to authenticate and authorize access to our GitHub account and repositories.

Overall, this chapter equipped us with the knowledge and tools to maintain a robust security posture and manage user access effectively on GitHub.

Let's do a short quiz.

Test your knowledge

Review all GitHub security and user management features, especially permission models, 2FA, and CI/CD hardening techniques – they appear frequently on the certification.

1. Which of the following methods is considered the most secure for enabling **Two-Factor Authentication (2FA)** on GitHub?

    a. **Short Message Service (SMS)**

    b. **Time-Based One-Time Password (TOTP)** authenticator apps

    c. Virtual security keys

    d. Physical security keys

2. What is the primary purpose of **Dependabot Security Updates** in GitHub?

    a. To scan your code for security vulnerabilities and coding errors

    b. To automatically generate pull requests to update vulnerable dependencies to secure versions

    c. To detect and alert you if sensitive information is accidentally committed to your repository

    d. To provide a centralized view of your security alerts and vulnerabilities across all repositories

3. Which role in GitHub is best suited to managing security policies, security alerts, and security configurations for an organization and all its repositories?

    a. Owner

    b. Security manager

    c. Admin

    d. CI/CD admin

Useful links

- Authentication documentation: `https://docs.github.com/en/enterprise-cloud@latest/authentication`

- About GitHub security features: `https://docs.github.com/en/enterprise-cloud@latest/code-security/getting-started/github-security-features#about-githubs-security-features`

- About GitHub Advanced Security: `https://docs.github.com/en/enterprise-cloud@latest/get-started/learning-about-github/about-github-advanced-security`

16

Mock Exams and Study Strategies

Welcome to the final chapter of your *GitHub Foundations Certification* journey! As you prepare to demonstrate your newfound knowledge, this chapter will guide you through a series of mock exam questions designed to simulate the actual certification experience. These practice tests will help you gauge your readiness, identify areas for improvement, and build the confidence needed to excel.

We will cover the following topics:

- Areas of concentration – what to expect
- Mock exam questions

Let's start with some tips.

Areas of concentration

Back in my uni days, the last class of the semester always had the highest attendance. Not many students attend the classes early in the semester – some are just settling in from a different university, or switching subjects or courses. Throughout the rest of the semester, attendance usually fluctuates even if the lecturer attracts students with engaging lectures, assignments, or the lack thereof ☺.

However, as a student, there's one class you don't want to miss: the final class of the semester. This is because it is in the last class that the lecturer will share insights into what to expect in the exam and discuss the **areas of concentration** – that is, topic areas and domains of the subject to focus your reading on to be well prepared for the exam.

I hereby present to you your areas of concentration.

What to expect

As mentioned in *Sprint 0, Preparing for the Certification*, you should get familiar with the proctor-led exam process, where you want to take the exam (virtual or test center), identification requirements, system requirements for the device you want to use if virtual, and the format of the exam questions. Please read the chapter again and visit the exam registration website to know the latest changes (if any) in the process and exam preparation guide.

Introduction to Git and GitHub questions — big deal

According to the exam preparation guide, questions on the basics of Git and GitHub, along with questions on the collaborative features on GitHub, together cover about half of the exam score. Therefore, I would strongly recommend spending more time understanding the concept of Git in general, including some of the basic commands and interpreting what they do. You may be asked to choose which Git command is correct from the options. Many of the options will have incorrect syntax or semantics. Watch out for such tricky questions. Pay attention to the flags, parameters, and where to use quotes.

Furthermore, you should understand the collaborative and social features that make GitHub great. Perform activities such as creating issues/labels, commenting on issues, raising pull requests, writing Markdown documents, and searching for issues using the search box and filter criteria. GitHub has enhanced the search and filter functionality a lot.

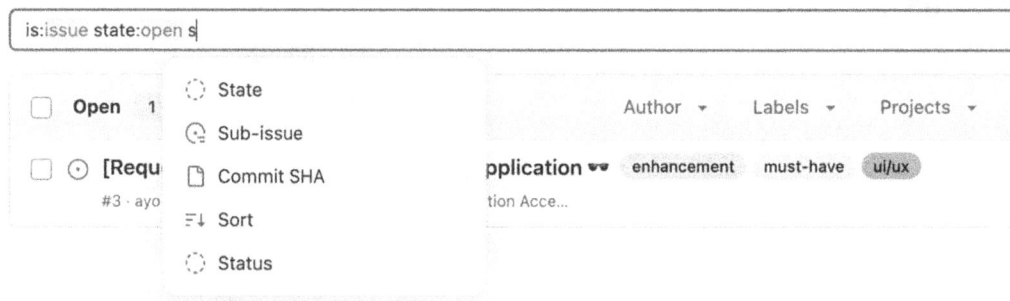

Figure 16.1: The GitHub search functionality has a syntax

Play around with this and examine the behavior. For more information, go to `https://docs.`
`github.com/en/issues/tracking-your-work-with-issues/using-issues/filtering-and-`
`searching-issues-and-pull-requests`.

Nuances of buttons and icons

You may be asked questions about the use of icon buttons on the different toolbars available on
GitHub. For example, on issue creation/commenting, they may ask what the purpose of the **Task
list** ( ) button is. Be sure to test out these buttons and examine their behaviors.

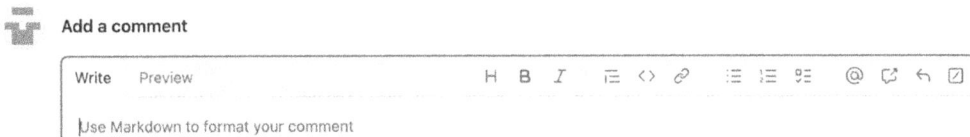

Figure 16.2: Toolbar buttons

The GenAI evolution

GenAI-assisted coding is now becoming commonplace for software developers, and GitHub Copilot is not an exception. Today, GitHub Copilot is a big part of the GitHub platform, so you will come across a few questions about it.

Multiple-answer questions

Some questions will require you to select multiple answers from the choices provided. In such cases, the question will typically tell you exactly how many answers to select. Therefore, even if you feel there are more answers that match the question, do **not** select more than the number of answers specified. Here's an example:

You have just completed development work for all the new features in the current iteration of your project, and you have just drafted a pull request. You are required to link the corresponding issues and tasks for the features developed to the pull request to ensure they are closed as soon as the merge is successful. Which of the following statements do you need to add to the pull request? (Select three.)

- *Closes #45*
- *close #45*
- *fix #45*
- *complete #45*
- *Completes #45*

In this question, any of the first three options can satisfy the question, but you have to select all three correct answers, not fewer and not more.

GitHub gists and wikis

We didn't spend much time talking about GitHub gists or wikis, but they are also product features you may encounter as a developer. A **wiki** is a section that helps you host documentation in a structured format and outline (think of Wikipedia pages).

On the other hand, **gists** provide quick ways to save and share code snippets (think of the Jupyter Notebook interface). Both are quick ways to create documentation, and they also support the Markdown format, among others. Spend some time reading about them, though I don't expect that you will encounter them in more than 5% of the exam questions. Visit *About wikis* (https://docs.github.com/en/communities/documenting-your-project-with-wikis/about-wikis) and *Creating gists* (https://docs.github.com/en/get-started/writing-on-github/editing-and-sharing-content-with-gists/creating-gists) to learn more.

The amazing GHCertified!

Some wonderful members of the GitHub community have contributed heaps of practice questions with which you can test your knowledge. These questions are not from the original GitHub exams. In fact, the code of conduct for contributing questions warns that they do not support the inclusion of questions copied from the exams. However, they will no doubt help you in your preparations. Visit ghcertified.com and attempt the over 130 questions available.

GitHub Docs is your friend

Read the official documentation on docs.github.com, particularly the **Get started** section, as well as the landing "overview" pages of each of the subcategories. In addition, there is now an AI-powered search box at the top of every page where you can get relevant answers to any questions. In the following figure, I have highlighted the areas and topics you should focus on for this exam:

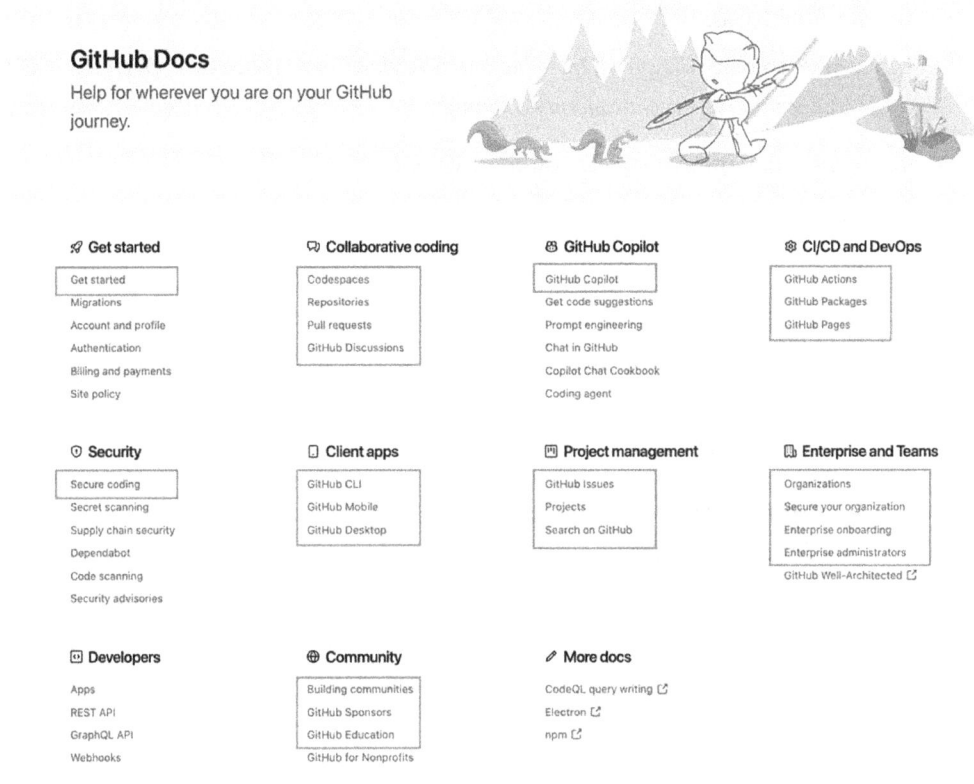

GitHub Docs
Help for wherever you are on your GitHub journey.

⚗ **Get started**	⚲ **Collaborative coding**	ⓑ **GitHub Copilot**	⚙ **CI/CD and DevOps**
Get started	Codespaces	GitHub Copilot	GitHub Actions
Migrations	Repositories	Get code suggestions	GitHub Packages
Account and profile	Pull requests	Prompt engineering	GitHub Pages
Authentication	GitHub Discussions	Chat in GitHub	
Biling and payments		Copilot Chat Cookbook	
Site policy		Coding agent	

⊙ **Security**	▢ **Client apps**	▦ **Project management**	▣ **Enterprise and Teams**
Secure coding	GitHub CLI	GitHub Issues	Organizations
Secret scanning	GitHub Mobile	Projects	Secure your organization
Supply chain security	GitHub Desktop	Search on GitHub	Enterprise onboarding
Dependabot			Enterprise administrators
Code scanning			GitHub Well-Architected ⤢
Security advisories			

⟨⟩ **Developers**	⊕ **Community**	✎ **More docs**
Apps	Building communities	CodeQL query writing ⤢
REST API	GitHub Sponsors	Electron ⤢
GraphQL API	GitHub Education	npm ⤢
Webhooks	GitHub for Nonprofits	

Figure 16.3: GitHub Docs is very resourceful

Now, let's improve our muscle memory by practicing some mock questions.

Mock exam questions

Let's first answer the knowledge questions in each of the previous chapters.

Answers to chapter quizzes

1. Git and GitHub can be used interchangeably.

    - **Answer:** False
    - **Where to read:** *Chapter 1, Introduction to Version Control with Git – Overview of Git – Understanding the Git concept – Cloning*

2. Which of the following is not a version control system?

    - **Answer:** GitHub
    - **Where to read:** *Chapter 1, Introduction to Version Control with Git – Examples of version control systems*

3. You made some changes to the Python code in your repository. You need to ensure that these changes have been added to version control. Which two commands do you need to run to ensure your changes have been recorded?

    - **Answer:** `git add` and `git commit`
    - **Where to read:** *Chapter 1, Introduction to Version Control with Git – Overview of Git – Interacting with Git Repos – Git jargon and commands*

4. A Git repository contains which of the following? (Select one.)

    - **Answer:** `.gitignore`
    - **Where to read:**

        - *Chapter 2, Navigating the GitHub Interface – Introduction to GitHub product features*
        - *Chapter 1, Introduction to Version Control with Git – Overview of Git – Git configuration files*

5. Which of the following can own a repository on GitHub? (Select two.)

    - **Answer:** Individual and organization
    - **Where to read:** *Chapter 2, Navigating the GitHub Interface – GitHub account types*

6. You have just joined an online fashion store company as a web developer, and your new manager has asked you to run `gh issue create -t "New Employee" -a "@onboarding-bot"` to begin your onboarding process. On which of the following tools/products will you run this?

   - **Answer**: GitHub CLI. GitHub CLI commands start with the gh keyword. You can only run commands in a terminal (i.e., CLI).

   - **Where to read**: *Chapter 2, Navigating the GitHub Interface – Other GitHub tools and features – GitHub CLI*

7. A developer on your team created a log file temporarily in their local repo. This log file is still important for local development, but they don't want to commit it to the repo. What can they do to keep the file saved without adding it to version control?

   - **Answer**: Add the log file's name to `.gitignore`

   - **Where to read**: *Chapter 3, Repository Creation and Management – Creating a new repository – Initializing with README and .gitignore*

8. Which of the following Markdown statements will produce this output: The **Universe** is vast, *reach for the stars*.

   - **Answer**: `The **Universe** is vast, _reach for the stars._`

   - **Where to read**: *Chapter 3, Repository Creation and Management – The Markdown language and the GitHub Markdown*

9. When setting up a new repo, which of the following Git commands do you need to run to make the directory Git-aware?

   - **Answer**: `git init`

   - **Where to read**: *Chapter 4, Basic Git Commands and Workflows – Common Git commands – Setting up a repository*

10. Which of the following branching models does not support short-lived branches?

    - **Answer**: Git Flow

    - **Where to read**: *Chapter 4, Basic Git Commands and Workflows – Git workflows*

11. What is the primary benefit of using branches in Git for collaborative development?

  - **Answer**: It allows developers to work on different features simultaneously without interfering with each other's work.
  - **Where to read**: *Chapter 5, Branching and Merging Strategies – Understanding branches in Git – Introduction to branches – Benefits of using branches*

12. Which command is used to create and switch to a new branch simultaneously in Git?

  - **Answer**: `git checkout -b <branch-name>`
  - **Where to read**: *Chapter 5, Branching and Merging Strategies – Understanding branches in Git – Creating branches – Using the git command*

13. What is a squash merge in Git?

  - **Answer**: A merge strategy that combines all the commits from a feature branch into a single commit before merging it into the main branch
  - **Where to read**: *Chapter 5, Branching and Merging Strategies – Merging and conflict resolution – Types of merges.*

14. What is the primary purpose of a pull request in collaborative software development?

  - **Answer**: To merge code changes from one branch into another
  - **Where to read**: *Chapter 6, Pull Requests and Code Reviews – What is a pull request?*

15. Which of the following is NOT a role typically involved in the code review process?

  - **Answer**: Tester
  - **Where to read**: *Chapter 6, Pull Requests and Code Reviews – The pull request lifecycle – Review process overview*

16. What is a "diff" in the context of version control systems such as Git?

  - **Answer**: A format used to show changes between two versions of a file or codebase
  - **Where to read**: *Chapter 6, Pull Requests and Code Reviews – Lab 6.1.*

17. What is the primary purpose of using labels in GitHub Issues?

  - **Answer**: To categorize and prioritize issues
  - **Where to read**: *Chapter 7, Issues, Projects, Labels, and Milestones – Introduction to Issues – Labels*

18. Which of the following is NOT a default issue type in GitHub?

    - **Answer:** Enhancement
    - **Where to read:** *Chapter 7, Issues, Projects, Labels, and Milestones – Introduction to Issues – Types*

19. How can issues be linked to pull requests in GitHub to ensure they are automatically closed when the associated pull request is merged?

    - **Answer:** By adding the issue number in the pull request description with a specific prefix
    - **Where to read:** *Chapter 7, Issues, Projects, Labels, and Milestones – Introduction to Issues – Linking issues to pull requests*

20. Which of the following is NOT listed as a key benefit of pipeline as code?

    - **Answer:** Integrity
    - **Where to read:** *Chapter 8, GitHub Actions and Automation – Introduction to GitHub Actions – How pipeline as code supports GitHub Actions*

21. In the context of GitHub Actions, what is the purpose of an ephemeral runner?

    - **Answer:** To ensure each job runs in a clean environment by unregistering itself after a single job
    - **Where to read:** *Chapter 8, GitHub Actions and Automation – Introduction to GitHub Actions – Key components of GitHub Actions – Jobs, steps, and runners*

22. Which of the following is not an event that triggers a workflow pipeline?

    - **Answer:** Pull
    - **Where to read:** *Chapter 8, GitHub Actions and Automation – Introduction to GitHub Actions – Key components of GitHub Actions – Events that trigger a workflow*

23. Which feature of GitHub Discussions helps maintain the flow of dialogue by grouping related comments together?

    - **Answer:** Threaded conversations
    - **Where to read:** *Chapter 9, Engaging with the Community Through GitHub Discussions – Introduction to GitHub Discussions*

24. What is the primary purpose of creating custom categories in GitHub Discussions?

    • **Answer**: To organize conversations for community members
    • **Where to read**: *Chapter 9, Engaging with the Community Through GitHub Discussions – Introduction to GitHub Discussions – Categories and custom categories*

25. Which of the following is NOT a recommended best practice for fostering community engagement in GitHub Discussions?

    • **Answer**: Ignoring spam and inappropriate content
    • **Where to read**: *Chapter 9, Engaging with the Community Through GitHub Discussions – Best practices for community engagement*

26. What is a prerequisite for setting up a profile README.md file on GitHub?

    • **Answer**: The repository name must match your GitHub handle (username).
    • **Where to read**: *Chapter 10, Building and Showcasing Your GitHub Presence – Showcasing projects and contributions – Advanced profile setup*

27. Which of the following is NOT a recommended section to include in your profile README.md file?

    • **Answer**: Your favorite recipes
    • **Where to read**: *Chapter 10, Building and Showcasing Your GitHub Presence – Showcasing projects and contributions – Advanced profile setup*

28. What is the first step in creating a GitHub Pages site?

    • **Answer**: Creating a new repository named <username>.github.io
    • **Where to read**: *Chapter 10, Building and Showcasing Your GitHub Presence – Utilizing GitHub Pages for personal branding – Setting up GitHub Pages*

29. What is the primary benefit of contributing to open source projects?

    • **Answer**: Gaining practical experience and improving coding skills
    • **Where to read**: *Chapter 11, Contributing to Open Source Projects – Navigating the open source landscape – Introduction to open source – Benefits of contributing to open source projects*

30. Which feature page on GitHub helps in discovering open source projects that align with your interests and skills?

   - **Answer**: GitHub Explore
   - **Where to read**: *Chapter 11, Contributing to Open Source Projects – Navigating the open source landscape – Finding open source projects – Using GitHub's Explore feature*

31. What is the first step in contributing to an open source project on GitHub?

   - **Answer**: Forking the repository
   - **Where to read**: *Chapter 11, Contributing to Open Source Projects – Lab 11.1: Making your first contribution*

32. What is the primary function of GitHub Copilot Chat, and how does it differ from ChatGPT?

   - **Answer**: GitHub Copilot Chat is tailored for software development, providing context-aware assistance within development environments, whereas ChatGPT is a general-purpose conversational AI.
   - **Where to read**: *Chapter 12, Enhancing Development with GitHub Copilot – Introduction to GitHub Copilot – Copilot Chat*

33. Which of the following is NOT a feature of GitHub Copilot within the GitHub.com user interface?

   - **Answer**: Real-time collaboration with other developers
   - **Where to read**: *Chapter 12, Enhancing Development with GitHub Copilot – Introduction to GitHub Copilot – Copilot within the GitHub.com UI*

34. What is the key difference between GitHub Copilot Pro and GitHub Copilot Business subscriptions?

   - **Answer**: GitHub Copilot Pro is available for individual users, while GitHub Copilot Business is designed for organizations and enterprises.
   - **Where to read**: *Chapter 12, Enhancing Development with GitHub Copilot – Introduction to GitHub Copilot – Available subscriptions*

35. What is one of the primary goals of GitHub Sponsors?

   - **Answer**: To create a sustainable ecosystem where open source projects can thrive
   - **Where to read**: *Chapter 13, Funding Your Projects with GitHub Sponsors – Introduction to GitHub Sponsors*

36. Which of the following is NOT a benefit of using GitHub Sponsors?

    - **Answer:** Guaranteed project success
    - **Where to read:** *Chapter 13, Funding Your Projects with GitHub Sponsors – Introduction to GitHub Sponsors*

37. What is a key requirement for becoming a sponsored developer on GitHub?

    - **Answer:** Adhering to GitHub's community guidelines and terms of service
    - **Where to read:** *Chapter 13, Funding Your Projects with GitHub Sponsors – Introduction to GitHub Sponsors – Eligibility and requirements*

38. Which of the following automation options in GitHub Projects allows you to automatically add items from repositories that match a filter?

    - **Answer:** Built-in automations
    - **Where to read:** *Chapter 14, Project Management with GitHub Projects – Automating project workflows*

39. In GitHub Projects, which layout is particularly useful for teams that need to track work visually and manage tasks dynamically?

    - **Answer:** Board layout
    - **Where to read:** *Chapter 14, Project Management with GitHub Projects – Introduction to GitHub Projects – Important features – Project layout*

40. What is the maximum number of active items allowed in a GitHub project before archiving is required?

    - **Answer:** 1,200 active items
    - **Where to read:** *Chapter 14, Project Management with GitHub Projects – Introduction to GitHub Projects – Important features – Archiving items*

41. Which of the following methods is considered the most secure for enabling **Two-Factor Authentication (2FA)** on GitHub?

    - **Answer:** Physical security keys
    - **Where to read:** *Chapter 15, Security Practices and User Management – GitHub security features – Two-Factor Authentication (2FA)*

42. What is the primary purpose of Dependabot security updates in GitHub?

- **Answer**: To automatically generate pull requests to update vulnerable dependencies to secure versions
- **Where to read**: *Chapter 15, Security Practices and User Management – GitHub security features – Security alerts and vulnerability management*

43. Which role in GitHub is best suited to manage security policies, security alerts, and security configurations for an organization and all its repositories?

- **Answer**: Security Manager
- **Where to read**: *Chapter 15, Security Practices and User Management – Managing access and permissions – User roles and permissions*

Additional questions

1. Which of the following best describes the concept of "pipeline as code" in GitHub Actions?

    a. A practice where the CI/CD pipeline is defined and managed using a graphical user interface

    b. A method of defining CI/CD pipelines using YAML files stored in the repository, allowing version control and collaboration

    c. A technique for automating code builds and deployments without using any configuration files

    d. A process of manually triggering workflows through the GitHub UI

    Where to read: *Chapter 8, GitHub Actions and Automation – Introduction to GitHub Actions*

2. What is the primary difference between continuous delivery and continuous deployment in the CI/CD pipeline?

    a. Continuous delivery requires manual approval for deployment, while continuous deployment automatically deploys every change that passes all stages of the production pipeline

    b. Continuous delivery automates the build process, while continuous deployment automates the testing process

    c. Continuous delivery is used for testing code, while continuous deployment is used for building code

    d. Continuous delivery and continuous deployment are the same and can be used interchangeably

    Where to read: *Chapter 8, GitHub Actions and Automation – Introduction to GitHub Actions*

3. Which of the following is NOT a key benefit of using GitHub Actions for CI/CD pipelines?

    a. Integration with GitHub repositories, making it easy to trigger workflows based on repository events

    b. Customizability of workflows using YAML syntax

    c. The ability to define and manage pipelines using a graphical user interface

    d. Access to a vast library of prebuilt actions in the GitHub Marketplace

    Where to read: *Chapter 8, GitHub Actions and Automation – Introduction to GitHub Actions – Key benefits of pipeline as code*

4. In GitHub Discussions, what is the primary purpose of using polls?

    a. To create nested discussions

    b. To gather feedback on new ideas, features, or project directions

    c. To organize conversations for community members

    d. To manage active work on issues and pull requests

    Where to read: *Chapter 9, Engaging with the Community Through GitHub Discussions – Introduction to GitHub Discussions*

5. How do you fork a repository on GitHub?

    a. By using the `git fork` command

    b. By clicking the **Fork** button on the repository's GitHub page

    c. By using the `github fork` command

    d. By using the `git --f repo` command

    Where to read: *Chapter 3, Repository Creation and Management – Collaboration and permissions – Forking and pull requests*

6. Which of the following are GitHub Copilot subscription plans? (Select two.)

    a. Copilot Enterprise

    b. Copilot Organization

    c. Copilot Free

    d. Copilot Premium

    Where to read: *Chapter 2, Navigating the GitHub Interface – GitHub overview and offerings – Available plans and offerings*

7. Which of the following is a correct hierarchical relationship on GitHub? (Select two.)

    a. Enterprise à Repository

    b. Organization à Repository

    c. Tenant à Enterprise à Repository

    d. Enterprise à Organization à Repository

    Where to read: *Chapter 2, Navigating the GitHub Interface – GitHub overview and offerings – GitHub account types*

8. How do you add a collaborator to a GitHub repository?

    a. By using the `git add-collaborator` command

    b. By navigating to the repository settings and adding the collaborator

    c. By using the `github add-collaborator` command

    d. By sending them a friend request from the top-right corner

    Where to read: *Chapter 15, Security Practices and User Management – Managing access and permissions – Collaborator access control*

9. What is the primary difference between a branch head and HEAD in Git?

    a. A branch head refers to the latest commit in a branch, while HEAD refers to the current branch or commit being worked on

    b. A branch head refers to the current branch or commit being worked on, while HEAD refers to the latest commit in a branch

    c. Both a branch head and HEAD refer to the latest commit in a branch

    d. Both a branch head and HEAD refer to the current branch or commit being worked on

    Where to read: *Chapter 5, Branching and Merging Strategies – Understanding branches in Git*

10. Which command is used to switch to an existing branch in Git?

    a. `git branch <branch-name>`

    b. `git checkout <branch-name>`

    c. `git checkout -b <branch-name>`

    d. `git switch <branch-name>`

    Where to read: *Chapter 5, Branching and Merging Strategies – Understanding branches in Git – Creating branches*

11. What is the primary purpose of branch protection rules on GitHub?

    a. To prevent direct pushes and accidental deletions

    b. To simplify the commit history by combining all commits into a single commit

    c. To automatically resolve conflicts between different branches

    d. To create and switch to a new branch simultaneously

Where to read: *Chapter 5, Branching and Merging Strategies – Branch management techniques – Branch protection rules on GitHub*

12. How do you protect a branch on GitHub?

    a. By using the `git protect-branch` command

    b. By navigating to the repository settings and configuring branch protection rules

    c. By clicking on the padlock button next to the repo to activate branch protection

    d. By using the `github protect-branch` command

Where to read: *Chapter 5, Branching and Merging Strategies – Branch management techniques – Branch protection rules on GitHub*

13. Which of the following is NOT a feature of GitHub Issues?

    a. Timeline trail

    b. Sub-issues

    c. Custom fields

    d. Reactions

Where to read: *Chapter 7, Issues, Projects, Labels, and Milestones – Introduction to Issues*

14. Imagine you are working on a software project and encounter a bug where the application crashes upon login. Which of the following steps is NOT part of the process to create a GitHub issue for this bug?

    a. Enter a brief summary of the issue in the **Title** field

    b. Provide a detailed description of the issue, including steps to reproduce the bug

    c. Assign the issue to multiple team members

    d. Automatically close the issue by merging a pull request

Where to read: *Chapter 7, Issues, Projects, Labels, and Milestones – Introduction to Issues*

15. How do you enable GitHub Discussions for a repository?

    a. By navigating to the repository settings and enabling **Discussions**

    b. GitHub Discussions is only available in the GitHub Pro subscription

    c. By creating a new organization

    d. By using the `git enable-discussions` command

    Where to read: *Chapter 9, Engaging with the Community Through GitHub Discussions – Lab 9.1: Enabling GitHub Discussions at the repository level*

16. You are managing a large project with multiple tasks and deadlines. Which GitHub feature would you use to group related issues and track progress toward a common goal?

    a. Labels

    b. Milestones

    c. Assignees

    d. Reactions

    Where to read: *Chapter 7, Issues, Projects, Labels, and Milestones*

17. In GitHub Actions, what is the role of a runner group?

    a. To execute workflows manually

    b. To categorize multiple runners with the same specifications and behavior

    c. To trigger workflows based on repository events

    d. To store YAML files in the repository

    Where to read: *Chapter 8, GitHub Actions and Automation – Introduction to GitHub Actions – Understanding workflows*

18. What is a GitHub gist?

    a. A full repository

    b. A snippet of code or text

    c. A branch

    d. A pull request

    Where to read: *Chapter 16, Mock Exams and Study Strategies – Areas of concentration*

19. You are part of a development team that needs to run tests on multiple operating systems and configurations. Which GitHub Actions feature would help you achieve this efficiently?

    a.   Single runner

    b.   Ephemeral runner

    c.   Matrix builds

    d.   GitHub-hosted runner

Where to read: *Chapter 8, GitHub Actions and Automation – CI/CD with GitHub Actions – Advanced CI/CD techniques*

Conclusion

As we reach the end of our journey through the *GitHub Foundations Certification* guide, it's time to reflect on the incredible progress you've made and the exciting opportunities that lie ahead. This book has equipped you with the essential knowledge and skills to navigate the world of Git and GitHub with confidence and proficiency.

From learning about the basics of version control and repository management to understanding the intricacies of collaborative development, you've built a solid foundation that will serve you well in your career. You've learned how to leverage GitHub's powerful features to streamline your workflows, enhance team collaboration, and contribute meaningfully to the open source community.

We also explored how to showcase your GitHub presence and use it as a platform to advance your career. By building a strong profile, engaging with the community, and contributing to open source projects, you've positioned yourself as a valuable asset in the tech industry. The GitHub Foundations Certification is not just a testament to your technical skills but also a reflection of your commitment to continuous learning and professional growth. The skills you've acquired will be your guiding light.

In the final chapters, we delved into advanced topics and exam preparation strategies to ensure you're fully equipped to ace the certification. The mock exams and study tips provided will help you approach the exam with confidence and clarity. Remember, the key to success is not just memorizing facts but understanding concepts and applying them in real-world scenarios.

Thank you for taking the time to read through this guide. Your dedication to improving your GitHub skills is commendable, and I hope you found the information valuable.

What's next after certification?

Once you have achieved this certification, it's time to put your new skills into practice. Continue exploring GitHub's features and stay updated with the latest developments. You will typically find the latest news on `https://github.blog`, and new feature releases and changes on `https://github.blog/changelog`.

Remember, the journey of learning never truly ends. You can consider pushing your boundaries by taking other GitHub certification exams. I would recommend either the GitHub Copilot or the GitHub Administration Certification exam.

Engage with the community, contribute to open-source projects, and keep building your portfolio. Your next big project is just around the corner!

If this book has helped you pass the exam or you learned a thing or two from reading the book, I'd love to hear from you. Please reach out to me on LinkedIn (`https://www.linkedin.com/in/ayodeji-ayodele?originalSubdomain=au`).

Happy coding and good luck in your exams!

Unlock this book's exclusive benefits now

Scan this QR code or go to `packtpub.com/unlock`, then search this book by name.

Note: Keep your purchase invoice ready before you start.

17

Unlock Your Book's Exclusive Benefits

Your copy of this book comes with the following exclusive benefits:

- ❖ Next-gen Packt Reader
- ❖ AI assistant (beta)
- 📖 DRM-free PDF/ePub downloads

Use the following guide to unlock them if you haven't already. The process takes just a few minutes and needs to be done only once.

How to unlock these benefits in three easy steps

Step 1

Have your purchase invoice for this book ready, as you'll need it in *Step 3*. If you received a physical invoice, scan it on your phone and have it ready as either a PDF, JPG, or PNG.

For more help on finding your invoice, visit `https://www.packtpub.com/unlock-benefits/help`.

> **Note:** Did you buy this book directly from Packt? You don't need an invoice. After completing Step 2, you can jump straight to your exclusive content.

Step 2

Scan this QR code or go to `packtpub.com/unlock`.

On the page that opens (which will look similar to Figure X.1 if you're on desktop), search for this book by name. Make sure you select the correct edition.

Figure 17.1: Packt unlock landing page on desktop

Step 3

Once you've selected your book, sign in to your Packt account or create a new one for free. Once you're logged in, upload your invoice. It can be in PDF, PNG, or JPG format and must be no larger than 10 MB. Follow the rest of the instructions on the screen to complete the process.

Need help?

If you get stuck and need help, visit `https://www.packtpub.com/unlock-benefits/help` for a detailed FAQ on how to find your invoices and more. The following QR code will take you to the help page directly:

Note: If you are still facing issues, reach out to `customercare@packt.com`.

‹packt›

Other Books You May Enjoy

If you enjoyed this book, you may be interested in these other books by Packt:

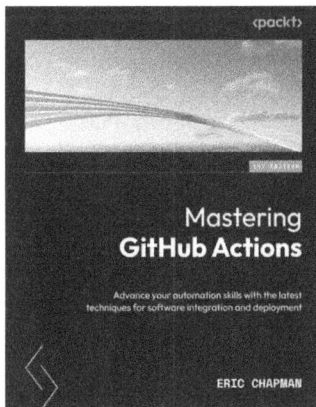

Mastering GitHub Actions

Eric Chapman

ISBN: 978-1-80512-862-5

- Explore GitHub Actions' features for team and business settings
- Create reusable workflows, templates, and standardized processes to reduce overhead
- Get to grips with CI/CD integrations, code quality tools, and communication
- Understand self-hosted runners for greater control of resources and settings
- Discover tools to optimize GitHub Actions and manage resources efficiently
- Work through examples to enhance projects, teamwork, and productivity

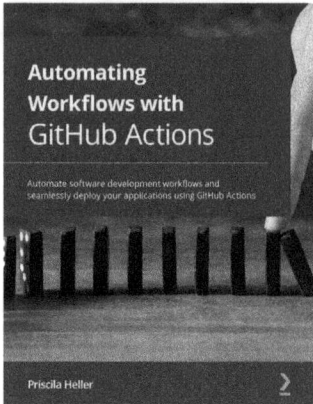

Automating Workflows with GitHub Actions

Priscila Heller

ISBN: 978-1-80056-040-6

- Get to grips with the basics of GitHub and the YAML syntax
- Understand key concepts of GitHub Actions
- Find out how to write actions for JavaScript and Docker environments
- Discover how to create a self-hosted runner
- Migrate from other continuous integration and continuous delivery (CI/CD) platforms to GitHub Actions
- Collaborate with the GitHub Actions community and find technical help to navigate technical difficulties
- Publish your workflows in GitHub Marketplace

Packt is searching for authors like you

If you're interested in becoming an author for Packt, please visit authors.packtpub.com and apply today. We have worked with thousands of developers and tech professionals, just like you, to help them share their insight with the global tech community. You can make a general application, apply for a specific hot topic that we are recruiting an author for, or submit your own idea.

Share your thoughts

Now you've finished *GitHub Foundations Certification Guide*, we'd love to hear your thoughts! Scan the QR code below to go straight to the Amazon review page for this book and share your feedback or leave a review on the site that you purchased it from.

https://packt.link/r/1836206054

Your review is important to us and the tech community and will help us make sure we're delivering excellent quality content.

Index

www.ingramcontent.com/pod-product-compliance
Lightning Source LLC
Chambersburg PA
CBHW061742210326
41599CB00034B/6760